To Gary

Learn as much as you can.

Casey Mabry

Summer 2014

IN MEAT WE TRUST

IN
MEAT
WE
TRUST

AN UNEXPECTED HISTORY
of CARNIVORE AMERICA

Maureen Ogle

HOUGHTON MIFFLIN HARCOURT
Boston | New York   2013

For information about permission to reproduce selections from this book,
write to Permissions, Houghton Mifflin Harcourt Publishing Company,
215 Park Avenue South, New York, New York 10003.

www.hmhbooks.com

Library of Congress Cataloging-in-Publication Data
Ogle, Maureen.
In meat we trust : an unexpected history of carnivore America / Maureen Ogle.
pages cm
ISBN 978-0-15-101340-1 (hardback)
1. Meat — Social aspects — United States. 2. Meat industry and trade — United States.
3. Food preferences — United States. I. Title.
TX371.O39 2013
664'.9 — dc23
2013026083

Book design by Chrissy Kurpeski
Typeset in Miller

Printed in the United States of America
DOC 10 9 8 7 6 5 4 3 2 1

For Bernard and Jen
What they made and shared is so much finer than a book

CONTENTS

INTRODUCTION

"TRULY WE MAY be called a carnivorous people," wrote an anonymous American in 1841, a statement that is as accurate today as it was then. But to that general claim a twenty-first-century observer would likely add a host of caveats and modifiers: Although we Americans eat more meat than almost anyone else in the world, our meat-centric diets are killing us — or not, depending on whose opinion is consulted. Livestock production is bad for the environment — or not. The nation's slaughterhouses churn out tainted meat and contribute to outbreaks of bacteria-related illnesses. Or not.

The only thing commentators might agree on is this: in the early twenty-first century, battles over the production and consumption of meat are nearly as ferocious as those over, say, gun control and gay marriage. Why is that? Why do food activists want to ban the use of antibiotics, gestation stalls, and confinement in livestock production? Why have livestock producers, whether chicken growers, hog farmers, or cattle ranchers, turned to social media, blogs, and public relations campaigns to defend not just meat but their role in putting it on the nation's tables?

This book answers those questions and more by looking at the history of meat in America.

The American system of making meat is now, and has long been, spectacularly successful, producing immense quantities of meat at prices that nearly everyone can afford—in 2011, 92 billion pounds of beef, pork, and poultry (about 15 percent of which was exported to other countries). Moreover, measured by the surest sign of efficiency—seamless invisibility—ours is not just the largest but also the most successful meat-making apparatus in the world, so efficient that until recently, the entire infrastructure was like air: invisible. Out of sight, out of mind.

No more. For the past quarter-century, thoughtful critics have challenged the American way of meat. They've questioned our seemingly insatiable carnivorous appetite and the price we pay to satisfy it, from pollution of water and air to the dangers of high-speed slaughtering operations; from the industry's reliance on pharmaceuticals to the use of land to raise food for animals rather than humans. In response, meat producers have reduced their use of antibiotics and other drugs; have abandoned cost-cutting products like Lean Finely Textured Beef ("pink slime"); have taken chickens out of cages and pregnant sows out of tiny gestation stalls. Men and women around the country have committed themselves to raising livestock and making meat in ways that hark back to the pre-factory era. This book examines how we got from there to here.

In recent years, books about food in general and meat in particular have abounded and in sufficient variety to suit every political palate. Few of them, however, examine the historical underpinnings of our food system. That's particularly true of ones that focus on meat. Most are critical of the American way of meat and assert an explanation of our carnivorous culture and its flaws that goes (briefly) like this:

Back in the old days, farm families raised a mixture of livestock and crops, and their hogs, cattle, and chickens grazed freely, eating natural diets. That Elysian idyll ended in the mid- to late twentieth century when corporations barged in and converted rural America into an industrial handmaiden of agribusiness. The corporate farmers moved livestock off pasture and into what is called confinement: from birth to death, animals are penned in large feedlots or small crates, often spending their entire lives indoors and on concrete, forced to eat diets rich in hormones and antibiotics. Eventually these cattle, hogs, and chickens, diseased and infested with bacteria, end up at the nation's slaughterhouses (also controlled by agribusiness), where poorly paid employees (many of them illegal immigrants) working in dangerous conditions transform live animals into meat products. Agribusiness profits; the losers are family farmers who can't compete with Big Ag's ruthless devotion to profit, and consumers who are doomed to diets of tainted, tasteless beef, pork, and chicken.

I respect the critics and share their desire for change. But I disagree both with their explanation of how we got to where we are and with their reliance on vague assertions as a justification for social change, no matter how well intended — especially when many of those assertions lack substance and accuracy. Consider, for example, this counternarrative, which is rooted in historical fact:

The number of livestock farmers has declined significantly in the last seventy or so years, but many people abandoned livestock production for reasons that had nothing to do with agribusiness. From the 1940s on, agriculture suffered chronic labor shortages as millions of men and women left rural America for the advantages of city life. Those who stayed on the land embraced factorylike, confinement-based livestock production because doing so enabled them to maximize their output and their profits even as labor supplies dwindled. Confinement livestock systems were born on the family farm and only subsequently adopted by corporate producers in the 1970s.

We may not agree with the decisions that led to that state of affairs, and there's good reason to abhor the consequences, but on one point we can surely agree: real people made real choices based on what was best for themselves and their families. Make no mistake: the history of meat in America has been shaped by corporate players like Gustavus Swift, Christian gentleman and meatpacking titan, and good ol' Arkansas boy Don Tyson, a chicken "farmer" who built one of the largest food-making companies in the world. But that history also includes millions of anonymous Americans living in both town and country who, over many generations, shaped a meat-supply system designed to accommodate urban populations, dwindling supplies of farmland, and, most important, consumers who insisted that farmers and meatpackers provide them with high-quality, low-cost meat.

The tale chronicled here ranges from the crucial, formative colonial era to the early twenty-first century, although the bulk of the narrative focuses on the second half of the twentieth century. It answers important questions about meat's role in our society. How did the colonial experience shape American attitudes toward meat? Why did Americans move the business of butchering out of small urban shops into immense, factorylike slaughterhouses? Why do Americans now eat so much chicken, and why, for many decades, did they eat so little? Why a factory model of farming? When and why did manure lagoons, feedlots, and antibiotics become tools for raising livestock? What is integrated livestock production and why should we care? Why *is* ours a "carnivore nation"? My hope is that this historical context will enrich the debate over the future of meat in America.

My many years engrossed in a study of meat's American history led me to a surprising conclusion: meat is the culinary equivalent of gasoline.

Think about what happens whenever gas prices rise above a vaguely defined "acceptable" level: we blame greedy corporations and imagine a future of apocalyptic poverty in which we'll be unable to afford new TV sets or that pair of shoes we crave; instead, we'll be forced to spend every dime (or so it seems) to fill the tank. But we pay up, cursing corporate greed as the pump's ticker clicks away our hard-earned dollars. Then the price drops a few cents;

our routine, half-mile, gas-powered jaunts are once again afford-able; and we rejoice. And because it's so easy to blame corpora-tions, few of us contemplate the morality and wisdom of using a car to travel a half-mile to pick up one item at a grocery store, which is what most of us do when gas prices are low.

So it is with meat. Most of us rarely think about it. After all, grocery store freezer and refrigerator cases are stuffed with it; burger- and chicken-centric restaurants abound; and nearly everyone can afford to eat meat whenever they want to. But when meat's price rises above a (vaguely defined) acceptable level, tem-pers flare and consumers blame rich farmers, richer corporations, or government subsidy programs. We're Americans, after all, and we're entitled to meat. So we either pay up or stretch a pound of burger with rice or pasta (often by using an expensive processed product). Eventually the price of steak and bacon drops, and back to the meat counter we go with nary a thought about changing our diets or, more important, about the true cost of meat, the one that bar-coded price stickers don't show.

That sense of entitlement is a crucial element of the history of meat in America. Price hikes as small as a penny a pound have inspired Americans to riot, trash butcher shops, and launch na-tional meat boycotts. We Americans want what we want, but we rarely ponder the actual price or the irrationality of our desires. We demand cheap hamburger, but we don't want the factory farms that make it possible. We want four-bedroom McMansions out in the semirural suburban fringe, but we raise hell when we sniff the presence of the nearby hog farm that provides afford-able bacon. We want packages of precooked chicken and micro-wavable sausages — and family farms, too. After years of working on this book, I'm convinced that we can't have it all. But I also believe that if we understand that the past is different from the present, the future is ours to shape. My hope is that this book will help all of us understand how we got to where we are so that, if we are willing, we can imagine a different future and write a new history of meat in America.

1

CARNIVORE AMERICA

THE WHITE EUROPEANS who colonized North America in the seventeenth century encountered extraordinary abundance. Immense bird flocks blackened the sky. Rivers and streams ran thick with fish. Shorelines teemed with crab and turtle, and forests with deer, bear, and other game. Above all, there was land, millions of acres, stretching off into a distance that would require several lifetimes to map and measure. Of all the cultural shocks that rattled colonists' psyches, this was perhaps the greatest. Those first settlers emigrated from a world where land was scarce and ownership limited. Not so in North America, where land abundance enabled colonists to develop a meat-centered diet on a scale that the Old World could neither imagine nor provide. By the time Americans celebrated their first centennial, they had built a meat-making infrastructure that spread from East Coast to West.

In the earliest years, settlers trapped, snared, shot, netted, and feasted on venison, squirrel, and lobster; pigeon, pheasant, and possum. But they wanted more. Civilized people ate civilized food: beef, mutton, and pork. Civilized people exercised dominion over not just land but animals, too, especially cattle, sheep, and swine. To the men and women who settled North America, the idea of a world without livestock was as peculiar, and dangerous, as the notion of a world without God. Therein lay the road to savagery. Europeans had not traveled halfway around the world to emulate the natives they encountered in North America, wrote a chronicler of one settlement, for those "savages" "[ran] over the grass" like "foxes and wild beasts," leaving "the land untilled" and "the cattle not settled." Native villages scarcely deserved the name, for they contained neither pen nor barn. That lack of "civilized" markers spelled their doom: because the "savage people" "inclose[d] no ground" and kept no "cattell," Massachusetts leader John Winthrop decreed, they forfeited any claim to the land and its wealth. Instead, white Europeans would rule and use the land to produce meat, thereby demonstrating the superiority of their own culture. Early success affirmed that belief: from the outset, colonists' imported domestic livestock thrived beyond belief or expectation. One South Carolinian boasted that his colony was so "advantageously . . . scituated, that there [was] little or no need of Providing Fodder for Cattle in the Winter." From north to south, hogs snuffled through forest floors carpeted with acorns and other mast, growing fat on nature's bounty and multiplying to the point of nuisance. "Hogs swarm like Vermine upon the Earth," grumbled one man, but the happy result was that colonial Americans never wanted for ham, bacon, and sausage.

But livestock also represented wealth and provided the easiest way to convert land to profit. Not everyone could afford, say, the slave labor on which rice and tobacco farming depended. Nor did every family have the hands needed to contest the forest; removing trees and undergrowth demanded years of backbreaking struggle. But everyone could spare the labor to keep a cow or two, and hogs required almost none at all. Livestock translated into tangible wealth that, with good management, multiplied more readily than silver or gold. In Maryland in the late 1600s, one cow and a calf carried as much monetary value as six or seven hundred pounds of tobacco, a third of a year's crop for one man. Life in North America even transformed the meaning of the word *stock*. Back in England, the term referred to wealth in general, whether money, furniture, or tools. But by the late eighteenth century, Americans defined it as "live stock, or the beasts that are kept upon a farm."

Settlers prized livestock as evidence of civilization and sources of wealth, but of course they also valued meat for its nutritional value. When we bite into a piece of "meat," we're eating muscle, or, more precisely, the tissue from which muscle is constructed, tissue that contains water, protein, and fat. The proportion of each depends on the age, size, and species of the animal, but a general average is 75 percent water, 20 percent protein, and 5 percent fat, all of which humans require for life. Nowadays, fat suffers an undeserved bad reputation, but it's one of the body's most efficient tools for storing energy; stored fat provided the fuel that enabled early hominids to run from danger. But colonists also favored meat because foodstuffs now deemed more healthful — vegetables and fruits — required more labor to produce in the form of planting, hoeing, and harvesting. Not that making meat was labor-free: all flesh, whether cattle, hog, or human, contains water that nurtures mold and bacteria, so it must be eaten immediately or preserved. During warm weather, when flesh putrefied quickly, a household might slaughter a lamb or calf, small animals that yielded relatively little meat that could be eaten before it spoiled. But most meats were preserved. Americans pounded chicken to a paste, stuffed it into ceramic pots, and sealed the container with a layer of fat or oil. They dried beef in the sun and salted and smoked fresh pork. Colonial diets tended to be pork-centric not only because hogs abounded but because pork takes to preservation more readily than beef.

Abundance and desire translated into meat on the table. Statistics are hard to come by for an era that predated census bureaus and questionnaires, but the evidence compiled by historians allows a broad generalization: the average white colonial American ate more and more varied food, and especially more meat, than anyone on the planet (aside from queens, czars, and other exceptionally privileged persons). Across Europe, a non-royal was lucky to see meat once or twice a week. A typical American adult male, in contrast, put away about two hundred pounds a year. (Slaves were chronically underfed and ate less of every kind of food.) Anecdotal evidence supports the estimates. A man who visited Pennsylvania in the 1750s marveled at the abundance of beef cattle. "[E]ven in the humblest or poorest houses, no meals are served without a meat course." Servants accustomed to scraps and scraping by in the Old World assumed and expected hefty meat rations in the New. One visitor to North America encountered an indentured servant who had run away "because he thought he ought to have meat every day" and his master refused to cooperate. Another servant, William Clutton, complained that his master, one Thomas Beale, served only rations of bread and cheese when it was the "Custom of ye Country for servants to have meat 3 times a week." Clutton threatened to strike unless the meat was forthcoming and urged his friends to petition the king to "have [the matter] redressed." He was hauled to court, where officials charged him with mutiny and sedition. But Beale's cheapskatery backfired: several people testified that Clutton was a "very honest civill [*sic*] person." He paid his court costs and walked free, presumably headed back to work and the meat to which he believed he was entitled.

Over time, carnivorous paradise begot lethal legacy. The abundance of meat spawned waste and fostered indifference bordering on cruelty. "The Cattle of *Carolina* are very fat in Summer," charged one critic, but bone bags in winter because their owners refused to protect them from "cold Rains, Frosts, and Snows." Settlers dismissed such criticisms, claiming they could spare neither time nor labor to build animal shelters or fencing, occupied as they were with "too many other Affairs." (That their free-roaming livestock placed them on the same plane as the natives they despised was an irony white settlers chose to ignore.) As a result, cattle and hogs scattered their droppings hither and yon, left uncollected because no one could spare the labor to gather and spread them on corn and tobacco fields. Thus developed a cycle of destructive extravagance that Americans passed from one generation to the next. Abundance of land nurtured an abundance of the livestock that enabled settlers to eat well and to accumulate tangible wealth with a minimal investment of labor. The more livestock a household owned, the more secure its financial future, and the more meat it had to eat. The more meat people ate, the more they assumed and expected a meat-centered diet, and the more land they wanted, especially for cattle; a single adult bovine required anywhere from five to twenty acres for grazing. As the years passed, settlers exhausted their soil and overgrazed their land. Rather than build fences or sell off their livestock, they moved on to fresh ground. And why not? In America, millions of acres lay just over the horizon.

The cycle of extravagance spawned conflict, violence, and war. Grazing generated endless court cases and squabbling among neighbors as livestock owners tried to determine who owned which animals. Laws aimed at quelling disputes proliferated, and colonial legislators established mechanisms for ownership — branding was the most common — and penalties for theft, which of course could be applied only if a litigant proved he or she owned an animal. Livestock lust fractured once close-knit communities. William Bradford, Pilgrim leader at Plymouth, Massachusetts, complained that as his flock's desire for cattle and hogs increased, "there was no longer any holding [settlers] together, but now they must . . . go to their great lots. They could not otherwise keep their cattle. . . . And no man now thought he could live except he had cattle and a great deal of ground to keep them." As a result, his people "were scattered all over the Bay" and their original settlement lay "thin and . . . desolate." Bradford feared such desire would "be the ruin of New England" and bring "the Lord's displeasure" down on them.

And not only the Lord's. As whites migrated to accommodate their livestock, they collided with Native Americans. A member of the Narragansett tribe chanted a common lament: Once upon a time the tribe's ancestors luxuriated in an abundance of "deer and skins." No more. Now "the English" had stolen the land

and allowed "their cows and horses [to] eat the grass; and their hogs [to] spoil [the] clam banks." Cattle tromped through natives' patches of beans and squash, and hogs rooted up caches of corn. Whites in search of fresh meadow and forest for their livestock commandeered land that natives regarded as theirs, encroachment that pushed Indians into territory held by other tribes and nations. More often than not, warfare ensued, especially once white settlers understood that they could use livestock to force Native American dispersion. "Your hogs & Cattle injure Us," lamented one Indian in 1666. "You come too near Us to live & drive Us from place to place. We can fly no farther." He begged the Maryland legislature to "let [his people] know where to live & how to be secured for the future from the Hogs & Cattle." The answer? Nowhere. Courts refused to listen to natives' complaints; assemblies ignored treaties; white settlers deliberately set animals loose in order to push Indians deeper into the frontier.

Natives in their turn used whites' desire for livestock against their enemy. A royal representative who investigated one conflict stripped the event down to its basics: the English settlers engaged in "Violent Intrusions" as a way to seize natives' land; Indians sought "Revenge" by destroying "the Cattel and Hogs of the *English*." In encounter after encounter, Indians stole, slaughtered, tortured, and mutilated livestock, because doing so struck at the heart of what it meant to be white and European. When a group of Narragansetts seized one white man, they forced him to watch as they killed five of his cattle. "[W]hat will Cattell now doe you good?" they asked. After staging a retaliatory raid, another group of Indians warned that they stood prepared to fight for "twenty one years." "You must consider," they told their foes, "the Indians lost nothing but their life; you must lose your fair houses and cattle." During the ensuing two years of ambush, torching, and retribution, seven thousand Indians died as compared to three thousand whites. But the natives slaughtered eight thousand head of cattle.

Other livestock-driven battles would follow, but whites had won the war: they would convert the wilderness, and large chunks of the continent, into a livestock trail epic in size and in its demands on the land and its people. Corn, rather than Bibles, served as the tool of conversion.

As the decades passed, colonists gradually abandoned hands-off husbandry in favor of more deliberate livestock production, prodded in that direction by the growth of a lucrative international trade in meat. Thanks to the British imperial system, North Americans were linked to markets in England, the Caribbean, Europe, and Asia, and they participated primarily by exporting raw materials. Grain was in demand everywhere in the world, but turning that field crop into coin proved difficult. Grain is relatively fragile, and during a market-bound trek of anywhere from one to two months by water or on crude paths and roads, spillage, rot, rain, and rats devoured much of the profit. So colonists learned early that the most efficient way to squeeze income from grain was by converting it into beef and pork (or alcohol, which was bulky but essentially imperishable). Cattle and pigs walked themselves to market, the cattle grazing or feasting on corn at stops along the route, the hogs trailing to feed on kernel-dotted manure. The corn was essential to the system: Cattle that fed on grass alone staggered into sale yards scrawny and exhausted. Corn-fed cattle, in contrast, arrived in better health and bearing more weight and returned greater profit. Once the animals arrived at urban ports, exporters slaughtered the stock and packed it in barrels, shipping most of it abroad. Hinterland farmers responded by paying more heed to their livestock and taking more care with feed and shelter.

One of the most important colonial cattle-producing regions flourished in the valley of the Potomac South Branch in what is now the northeastern corner of West Virginia. There, settlers developed an especially systematic and profitable mode of combining cattle, corn, and hogs. The area consisted of fertile bottomlands suited for planting corn and hilly upland ill suited for crops but thick with forage grass. (That grass had once fed bison, but by the early eighteenth century, those beasts, and the Native Americans who had followed them, were long gone.) In summer, South Branch farmers tended fields of corn while their cattle grazed upland pastures. Come fall, they harvested the corn in the simplest manner possible: they left the ears intact, cut the stalks to the ground, and piled the harvest into "shocks" that they distributed throughout their fields. Every day, hands led the cattle to a collection of shocks. As the cattle fed, they deposited undigested corn (the cattle's digestive systems processed the corn's nutrients, but the kernels passed through intact) and manure, the fertilizer for the next year's planting. When the cattle had devoured the shocks, hands led them to a new location stocked with fresh corn and herded hogs into the first field. Those beasts snuffled up the leavings, including the corn kernels, and deposited their own manure.

This cattle-corn-hog complex was well established before the Revolution, but when that war ended, South Branch farmers joined a vast migration away from the coast and into the interior and the Ohio River valley. There they found ideal terrain in which to grow corn and raise cattle and hogs. For centuries, Native Americans had burned off trees along fertile bottomlands so they could plant corn, beans, and squash in the clearings. Migrating Americans swarmed onto these lush tracts, depositing not just themselves but their livestock. Out beyond the river, at the time the new nation's primary waterway, lay acres of equally rich soil and pasture.

By the early nineteenth century, cattle grazing and feeding operations spread for miles along both sides of the Ohio River and far inland, too. In summer and fall, drovers and herds of as many as a thousand head clogged the overland roads that connected the interior to the ports and markets of the eastern seaboard. The bovine multitude could be seen a mile away, wrote one drover, thanks to "long moving lines of rising dust." The cattle parade marched two by two, each animal plodding through the track left by those ahead. Winter and spring rains turned the ruts into rivers of mud, and when the soil dried, the jagged path claimed wagon and carriage wheels that could not survive the jolt. Despite the bovines' placid natures, keeping so many cattle in line and in motion was never easy, the task exacerbated by the hogs that trailed the drove, rooting through manure as they trotted to market. One drover nearly lost his herd when the crew of a passing steamboat eased their vessel alongside a trail and let loose with the boat's whistle. The ear-piercing shriek sent the cattle "up the river as if the deuce was in them." The drover galloped after his charges and rode for a mile and a half before he managed to make his way to the head of the line and calm the runaways. He'd no sooner restored order than the steamboat caught up with him and the herd, and the crew taunted him with more whistle shrieks. "The name of the captain of the boat I knew not," reported the angry drover, "but I wish to caution the public against a man of such mean and disgraceful conduct."

Difficulties aside, the cattle-and-hog bonanza attracted more settlers, among them young Benjamin Franklin Harris, who had grown up in northern Virginia not far from the South Branch cattle district. There he'd worked for his father hauling goods by wagon to and from Baltimore, and often down into the Ohio Valley, a job that taught him how to handle horses, responsibility, and the rigors of life on the road in early America. In 1832, the family left Virginia for Ohio, where his father bought a farm near Springfield. Benjamin, by then in his early twenties, found work as a drover's hand, helping another man move three hundred cattle from Ohio to Pennsylvania, a trek that required fording two rivers and crossing the Alleghenies. After the drove boss sold the stock, the buyers hired Harris to help run those cattle, plus another five hundred head, to the market at Lancaster. The adventure convinced the young man that a life devoted to cattle trading offered more reward than one spent droving or steering a plow. Within a year, he'd accumulated $1,000 and managed to borrow another $3,000 (that speaks volumes to his character and reputation, and to the importance of cattle and meat: at that time and in that place, banks were few and cash and credit scarce). Harris stashed the money in a belt strapped around his waist, saddled up, and headed for Illinois. There, a handful of prairie "cattle kings" had amassed holdings of hundreds of acres and duplicated the cattle-corn-hog complex. Over the next six years, Harris returned to Illinois five times to buy cattle, driving those back to Ohio where he fed them over the winter on corn, and then herding the fattened stock to markets in Pennsylvania. He earned good money, but it was never easy, especially because the cattle, and the cash that drovers and traders carried, attracted thieves who often used guns to startle the animals into stampede. More than once, Harris barely avoided roadside traps set by armed men. During one trip, he encountered a stranger who offered to accompany him along the road. At one point, the man rode on ahead, and Harris noticed a knife handle poking out of the man's coat collar. Harris asked him about the weapon and the man replied, "I alwase go armed havent you arms on your person?" Harris pulled out his pistol and informed his companion that he "could shoot a man fifty yar distant" and that he kept "watch all the time."

Cattle grazing, feeding, and driving were just three arms of the diverse meat-production industry that emerged in the Ohio River valley in the early nineteenth century. The rich soil produced an extraordinary abundance of corn that allowed farmers to fatten hogs that, in turn, supported a pork-packing industry. Demand for this easily transported protein was immense and global, and American packing flourished. Skilled artisans focused on making quality hams. German immigrants gravitated to the region, transforming meat scraps into sausage, and head, feet, and organs into headcheese. British firms dispatched representatives to set up shop in Ohio. But bacon and ham weren't the only spurs to growth. Hog fat yielded lard, an inexpensive substitute for butter and other fats, and that, too, made its way to ports around the world. In the 1840s, inventors perfected a method of turning lard into light, a development that demolished the trade in whale oil. At a time when metal engines were replacing wooden water wheels, lard oil served as an inexpensive lubricant. Hog processing seeded soap manufacture. Procter & Gamble was born a soap maker in Cincinnati, and Eberhard Anheuser, eventual beer king, earned his first American fortune manufacturing soap in St. Louis, using the leavings of hogs driven there from farms in Missouri and Illinois. Hog bristles and hair ended up in mattresses and hairbrushes. Bone became button, and blood, dye and ink. It was hard to know which was more important: barreled meats or byproducts.

By the 1840s, what had begun as seasonal enterprises run out of rented shacks had mushroomed into a year-round industry housed in purpose-built brick structures, easily the largest buildings in Cincinnati, which reigned for some years as the center of American pork production (and earned the name Porkopolis). In the slaughterhouses that lined that city's streets, hands drove hogs into a pen, packing them tightly so the kill man could walk across their backs as he slammed their heads with a metal sledgehammer. Other workers dumped carcasses into boiling water for soaking, the easier to loosen bristles and hair. Another crew beheaded and gutted what was left, trundling the offal to rendering vats and slinging the carcasses onto iron hooks for butchering into hams and bacon, tongue and rib roasts, some 36 million pounds' worth in 1840. The demand inspired the region's farmers to improve and systematize hog production. They invested in quality breeding stock and, rather than let them scavenge, fed them with intention, and for good reason: a corn-fed hog earned 30 to 60 percent more than a scavenger, and many packers refused to buy the lesser beasts.

By the eve of the Civil War, the meat-making complex of Porkopolis had become world renowned, and so had Americans' prodigious appetite for meat. "There are few things in the habits of Americans, which strike the foreign observer with more force," mused one writer, "than the extravagant consumption of . . . meat." "Truly we may be called a carnivorous people." Thanks to new printing technologies that made newspapers and magazines both affordable and ubiquitous, advisers regaled readers with tips on how to cook, preserve, and serve meats. To use leftovers, advised a contributor to one magazine, chop them fine and season with salt, pepper, and butter. Soak stale bread in milk, chop a few fresh peeled tomatoes, mix, and bake for an hour. One popular cookery book suggested coating meat pieces with egg and flour before frying in beef suet, lard, or butter. A farmer's wife instructed readers of another periodical in the fine art of cooking calf head: Clean "nicely" the "head, pluck [organs] and trotters" of a "*good* calf" until there was not "a hair to be seen upon them." Slice open the head, remove the brains, and boil meat and organs until the flesh fell from the bone. She suggested serving it "plain" with vegetables; mixing it with salt pork, veal, and sage to make meatballs; or mincing it and returning it to the broth in which it had cooked, along with the brains, some fried pork, cloves, thyme, and marjoram, and boiling to make soup (one best served, she added, with some of the meatballs).

But the days of calf head soup were numbered. Time and abundance had solidified the cycle of extravagance and entitlement and Americans' propensity for waste. An Englishman who had emigrated to the United States boasted to his former countrymen that no one but "free negroes" would "think of eating . . . *head and pluck.*" He reported that urban slaughterhouses were known less by their odor than by the remains piled outside their doors: "hundreds of calves' heads, large bits, and whole joints of meat," unwanted and unused, except by "street hogs" that roamed the roads feeding on the leavings of a wasteful society. In "*any other country*" less accustomed to "superabundance," he marveled, all of it "would be sold at some price or other." He likely overstated the case, but there's no doubt that as the century wore on, Americans in general and city people in particular lost interest in head, pluck, and brain thanks to their rising standard of living. The middle class had not yet become the political and economic powerhouse that it would be a century later, but thanks to the relentless growth of the nation's economy, millions of people translated dollars into material comfort: upholstered furniture (the coverings often fashioned from cowhide), walls painted or wallpapered atop plaster (a substance strengthened by the addition of hog bristle), finer clothing, and, of course, improved diets.

Given the surfeit of ham and roast beef, why eat pig's feet or calf brains?

There is perhaps no better testament to abundance than the middle-class fondness for food faddery, especially fads focused on meat, a luxury those yoked to scarcity and want cannot afford. One popular school of thought linked salted meats to salacious behavior; avoid such foods and the masturbatory urge would trouble one no more. Sylvester Graham, food eccentric, graham cracker king, and a man obsessed with denying his (and everyone else's) sexual urges, also linked meat, salted or otherwise, to masturbation, citing as evidence an oversexed young woman, the victim of her mother's penchant for feeding her daughter "highly-seasoned flesh-meat." Graham favored meat abstinence, arguing that eating flesh encouraged the "hunger instinct" and over time, meat eaters developed a voracious nature more animal than human. Graham had the good sense to recognize that few Americans were willing to abandon meat altogether, and he urged his more carnivorous countrymen to stick to roasted or boiled meats (because those were less tasty than fried meats or because long cooking reduced the animality of flesh is not clear). The mid-nineteenth century also marked the onset of a prolonged crusade against alcohol, and many temperance reformers linked meat eating to insobriety. Meat "overload[ed] the stomach," explained one writer, an excess that only the "stimulant" of alcohol could alleviate. Eat less meat and sobriety would follow. "In countries where milk is the chief diet, there is no intemperance," added the author, pointing out that "Arabs," who favored dairy over flesh, were a highly "temperate" people. "Is it not better to be called a milk-sop than a drunkard?"

The reputation of that old colonial mainstay pork suffered from food faddery and from the abundance of beef. A physician writing in one of the era's most popular women's magazines described pork and bacon as "beyond all question the most indigestible" of meats. As far as he was concerned, white Americans should stick to beef or poultry and leave pork to "negroes," who, he explained, enjoyed a peculiar "congeniality" with hogs. As a result, he and others believed, pork and bacon were "peculiarly appropriate for negroes on account of their habits of life, and their defective heat-generating power." But pork had also become associated with the backwardness of farm and frontier. The doctor told readers that Americans living in the southern and western United States, both of which were decidedly rural, were unhealthy in part because of their "excessive use of fat bacon and salt pork." With that last comment, the physician tapped into one of the most important social changes of the nineteenth century: the shift of population off the farm and into cities. That trend is central to our story because urban growth complicated and transformed the business of putting meat on the nation's tables.

In 1820, only about 7 percent of the nation's 9 million inhabitants lived in a town or city. But from the 1830s on, the percentage of urbanites soared, and by the 1860s about a quarter of the then 31 million Americans called the city home. But those averages obscure an important fact that would shape the geography and structure of livestock and meat production for the rest of that century and into the next: urbanization was skewed to the east. In Massachusetts, for example, 60 percent of residents lived in towns. Five percent of all Americans lived in just three eastern cities: New York, Brooklyn, and Philadelphia.

Why does this matter? An important characteristic of urban populations is so obvious that it's easy to overlook: city people don't produce their own food. The more of them there are, the harder farmers must work to feed them (and as a general rule, farmers' numbers decline as urban populations grow). Put another way, cities complicate the task of making and delivering food, and that's especially true of meat. By the late 1860s, the nearly 1 million inhabitants of Manhattan needed 1.1 million animals a year to satisfy their carnivorous appetites. Imagine the logistical complexity of moving that livestock from the countryside to the city's slaughterhouses, transforming them into meat for distribution first to butchers and then to consumers, and disposing of the wastes that slaughter generated. (And that's just meat.

Those million people also needed bread and potatoes, onions and apples. In the late 1860s, New Yorkers devoured 126 million eggs a year; ten years later, they downed 442 million.) Cattle and hog farmers in the Ohio River valley, efficient though they were, could not keep pace, especially as new settlers and entrepreneurs bought up agricultural land and turned it into towns. Squeezed by urban growth and demand, farmers and livestock headed to what was then called "the west," the relatively unpopulated states bordering the Mississippi and Missouri rivers, where rich soil supported the cattle-corn-hog complex. Americans invested millions of dollars in a transportation infrastructure so they could move foodstuffs from west to east. They dredged three thousand miles of canal in the 1820s and 1830s, but those wonders were overshadowed by the great marvel of the age, the railroad. Americans laid seven thousand miles of rail in the 1830s and 1840s, virtually all of it in the northeastern quadrant of the United States, and most of it devoted to moving raw goods, and especially food, to urban markets.

But it was difficult for farmers to keep pace, even with new agricultural technologies like the John Deere plow and McCormick reaper. In early 1852, a Pittsburgh newspaper reported that lumbermen in northwestern Pennsylvania had abandoned their posts, driven away by shortages of meat, potatoes, and even hay to feed teams of oxen. The *New York Times* informed readers that "Eastern demand" had "drained the [western] country of beef cattle." Butchers in Michigan and Wisconsin presided over shops devoid of meat, and in Minnesota, barrels of pork sold for $55 (that's $1,600 today). But meat supplies in eastern markets ran short, too, and city folks cursed high prices and empty meat stalls, blaming, variously, greedy butchers, con men, hucksters, railroad crews, and selfish farmers.

Episodes like these were not uncommon, and not always because of shortfalls on the farm — winter storms often prevented wagon and train travel; drought led to grain shortages. In the early 1860s, the Civil War both highlighted and exacerbated the logistical difficulties of feeding an urban and geographically dispersed populace. Workers raced to lay more rail track in the northern United States, but much of the roads' capacity was devoted to moving troops and materiel rather than food. Combatants destroyed crops and fields and commandeered whatever comestibles they came across, leaving city people to cope with empty shops and pantries. Cattle, whether for meat or dairy products, were in particularly short supply, warned a report from the U.S. Department of Agriculture (USDA, an agency the Union Congress created in 1862). Prior to the war, explained a department analyst, southern states had teemed with cattle, but Confederates had either slaughtered and eaten those, or driven them to safer locations (presumably to Mexico). Geography complicated the deficit: most of the remaining cattle population was located in the northern reaches of the Mississippi River valley, but the bulk of the steak-eating humans lived along the eastern seaboard. Therefore, he concluded, the *"great law of the movement of cattle is here plainly developed. Cattle must be moved eastward and capital westward to supply the pressing demands of our people."* The department reiterated the point a year later in a second report. The "western" prairies of Iowa, Missouri, and Illinois could no longer support the number of cattle needed to feed the nation. The solution? Turn the grassy plains of the "Far West," as Americans then called the region west of the Missouri River, over to cattle. Thus began the project to transform the range into the westernmost outpost of a vast cattle trail that ran from south Texas and Wyoming all the way to New York and Philadelphia, using the railroads to move cattle and meat from west to east.

Few at the time doubted the wisdom of that decision: the Far Western plains were a ruminant paradise, heaven-sent to satisfy the national appetite for beef. For centuries, the plains were populated by bison — estimates put the number somewhere between 30 and 40 million — herds of such mass "as literally to blacken the prairies for miles" on end, wrote one awed observer, their endless rumbling bellows echoing like "distant thunder." Bison, like cattle, are ruminants, and over the centuries their need for food prodded plains ecology toward grasses. Thanks to the

Far West's relatively mild, dry climate, western bison "wintered" on their own, without any special food or shelter; Americans assumed that cattle could do the same. Best of all was the land itself: millions of acres, free for the taking. The logic was as clear as the western sky: if the range could support millions of bison, it could also support cattle, and this otherwise inhospitable terrain — period maps identified much of the region as the "Great American Desert" — could feed millions of Americans. The Far West would preserve and sustain Carnivore Nation.

First, of course, was the matter of eliminating the bison and removing the Native Americans who persisted in roaming the region. Happily — from the perspective of white Americans — the natives relied on the animals' flesh for food and their hides for shelter and clothing. Exterminate the bison and the Indians' way of life would vanish, too. Bison hunting, already a favorite mid-century sport (although *hunting* is perhaps not the most apt term for prey that conveniently stands still for the kill), lured even more thrill seekers, the railroad serving as an ironic accomplice to the slaughter: passengers hung from the windows of their slow-moving cars to shoot at the even slower-moving animals. ("Why," asked one British sportsman, had "an all-wise Providence" created animals "so utterly incapable of self-protection?")

As bison and natives disappeared, cattle and whites rushed in. Many of both came up from Texas. There, thanks to earlier Spanish possession, large cattle herds had long grazed, especially along the state's Gulf coast. Much of that stock had been raised for leather, and the flesh was tough and the "longhorns" more volatile than the placid bovines Americans were used to managing back in Iowa or Ohio. (The "long-legged" beasts, explained one newspaper reporter, boasted "long taper horns and something of a wild look.") During the food shortages of the 1850s, a handful of enterprising traders had driven longhorns to Illinois, where local cattle kings fattened them for shipment to eastern meat markets. The corn rations reportedly did little to improve the finished product. Texas beef resembled venison and was tough when cooked and considered inferior to meat from domestic cattle. During the 1850s and war-torn sixties, tough beef was better than no beef at all, but after the war, a new generation of western ranchers began breeding stock designed to weather the range and produce fine beef when finished on corn.

Moving the animals from west to east was not easy. Cattle drives bordered on the brutal, the trail marked from beginning to end by rain, extreme temperatures, Indians, and rustlers. A man who drove a herd from Texas to Iowa in 1866 recited a litany of woes: eight months of sunburn and stampedes, and long days hunting down skittish and wandering animals or driving them over rain-swollen rivers. "Stampeded last night among 6 droves & a general mix up and loss of Beeves," he wrote after nearly four months on the trail. "Men all tired & want to leave. [A]m in the Indian country [and] am annoyed by them believe they scare the Cattle to get pay to collect them." "Hard Rain & Wind," he wrote a few days later. "Big stampede & here we are among the Indians with 150 head of Cattle gone hunted all day & Rain poured down with but poor success Dark days are these to me Nothing but Bread & Coffee Hands all Growling & Swearing — every thing wet & cold."

Joe McCoy had a better idea. He had seen the future and it consisted of an endless parade of railcars crammed with cattle and headed from his stockyard in Abilene, Kansas, straight to eastern markets and profit. Well, more or less straight there. McCoy didn't much care what happened to the cattle once they departed Abilene, just as long as they did so and someone paid him for the privilege of moving them. McCoy's trail to Abilene started in Illinois, where he and two brothers raised cattle, hogs, and sheep. But McCoy said later that he was not "contented to live quietly at home on a good sized, finely improved farm," even one that yielded as much as a quarter-million dollars in livestock a year. The brothers contemplated the Texas cattle herds, the trails that ran up from the southwest, and a new rail line being laid to Kansas and came up with a plan. In Joe's words, they would "establish a market whereat the southern drover and northern buyer would meet upon an equal footing, and both be undisturbed by mobs or

swindling thieves," the "equal footing" being the McCoys' stockyard, and Joe McCoy the man who would bring North and South
together. After sealing a handshake agreement with the president
of the Kansas Pacific Railroad, Joe headed to Abilene to make the
McCoy fortune. The choice of brother may have been a mistake
(given what we know about Joe, he probably bullied the other
two into sending him). An Abilene resident who knew him well
described him as "a man of hasty temper," a true "Mr Know it all"
who "never asked any Ones opinion of any act of his or any pro-
get [*sic*] . . . his will & wishes were law." As far as Joe McCoy was
concerned, he was "the whole cheese" and the rest of the world
mere "skim milk." (McCoy also possessed a rich sense of humor
and a willingness to poke fun at anyone and anything, including himself. His published writings, including an 1874 account of
his meteoric success and equally spectacular failure, sparkle with
wit and self-deprecating humor.) One fact is certain: Joe McCoy's
ego outstripped his entrepreneurial talents, and over the next
few years, he dragged not just himself but his two brothers into
financial ruin.

At the time, Abilene was a typical no-account western town:
oozing self-importance and ambition, but more or less devoid
of people and profit. By McCoy's reckoning, the townscape consisted of a dozen "log huts," one of which was grandly identified
as the Bratton Hotel, but not much else. He built a stockyard near
the sole rail line then running through town and dispatched mes-
sengers to spread the word along the cattle trails: Drive your herd
to Abilene and Joe McCoy would ship it east. Drivers obliged and
for a few months, all was well — more or less. The cattle carried
"Texas fever," a then-mysterious disease that had no effect on
the Texas bovines but invariably infected and killed other herds
that came in contact with them. During the first longhorn drives
back in the 1850s, Missouri farmers had waged war against
Texas drovers and their infected animals and managed to minimize the damage. But in the wake of the Civil War, with tens of
thousands of longhorns on the move, with men like Joe McCoy
eager to ship them east, and with hungry urbanites clamoring

for meat, the danger of Texas fever loomed large. Even as Mc-
Coy welcomed drovers to his yard, farmers in both Kansas and
Missouri persuaded their state legislators to establish quarantine zones into which the longhorns could not go; and Abilene
sat squarely inside one of those. In McCoy's skewed but colorful
version of events, the Kansas farmers were less disease-fearing
ranchers than crooks, out "to stop the drover by mob violence,
then rob or swindle him out of his stock." If the prairies of Kansas
and Missouri could speak, wrote McCoy, their tales of "carnage,
wrong, outrage, robbery and revenge" would surpass the "annals
of the most bloody savages." But McCoy being McCoy, he simply ignored the quarantine law, which surely didn't apply to a big
cheese like himself. (It helped that in Abilene, as in much of the
West, there weren't enough people, or, more accurately, enough
people who cared, to enforce the laws passed by a state or territorial legislature — a more-or-less willful apathy that contributed to
the reputation of the West as "wild.") So began the great McCoy
cattle parade.

It didn't last long. Joe had made his shipping arrangement
with a single railroad, but within months other rail companies —
bigger roads backed by bigger money — had reached Kansas, and
Abilene's career as the Great Cattle Town of the West ended as
quickly as it had begun. Dodge City, through which ran the Atchi-
son Topeka & Santa Fe, commandeered the McCoy cattle trade.
Having picked the wrong railroad and the wrong cowtown, Mc-
Coy saw his fortune, and his brothers', vanish. (McCoy earned a
bit of it back by publishing an account of his western adventure,
an often hilarious, and always lopsided, view of the West-accord-
ing-to-McCoy. His book did as much as anything to seal the image of the Far West as the land of danger and daring, bad guys,
good guys, saloons, rustlers, and easy women willing to flash their
ankles — and more — in exchange for a drink and some cash.)

But for every failure there were a dozen successes, and money,
people, and livestock poured into the Far West. By the early
1870s, a vast congregation of cattle roamed the western plains

and ranged from the Texas Gulf coast up into what would become Montana and Idaho. Many of those beasts never left the West. In the years after the Civil War, the federal government expanded its presence in the region, and federal agents bought thousands of head for consumption at newly established Indian reservations and military outposts. Mining industries mushroomed, as did railroad construction and the general flow of humanity from east to west. All of it necessitated beef.

But millions of head moved east to stockyards in Kansas City, St. Louis, and Chicago. Indeed, the flood of cattle sealed Chicago's reputation as the nation's premier livestock market. Since that city's founding in the early 1830s, area farmers had sold both cattle and hogs there, and in the early 1860s, its residents stole the title of "Porkopolis" away from Cincinnati. In 1865, Chicagoans confirmed their livestock leadership when a group of investors consolidated the city's many scattered rail lines and stockyards into a unified whole. The Union Stock Yards sprawled over 323 acres and housed rail terminals, animal pens, a water and sewer system, hotels, banks, and restaurants. Surrounding the yards was Packingtown, a dense hodgepodge of manufactories devoted to slaughtering and processing cattle and hogs. For pork packers, raved one member of that tribe, there was "only the one place & that is Chicago," "the greatest provision market in the world." He "never saw a day in Chicago where regular meats could not be sold," and "no place where there is such a selection & steady supply of Hogs." He was right. Chicago was pork purveyor to the world, sending barrels of ham, shank, and bacon to troops in British India, to businessmen in China and the Caribbean; to fishing crews trolling the oceans for cod and sardines; to factory workers in Liverpool and Manchester; to soldiers patrolling the garrisons and forts of the American Far West.

But much of the action revolved around the stockyards and live animals. Every day trains deposited thousands of cattle and hogs, their fates decided by dickering swarms of livestock producers, commission agents, brokers, and meatpackers. Most of the hogs stayed in Chicago, transformed into bacon and ham by

Packingtown's butchers. Cattle traced a more complicated path. Some of the range animals, grass-fed stock that yielded relatively poor beef, were taken to local slaughterhouses where workers packed barreled beef for western mining camps or military garrisons, or for ships bound for Asia, South America, or Europe. But Americans craved fresh beef, and much of the cattle still had miles to travel. Some of the grass-fed western stock was herded onto railcars destined for eastern cities, there to be slaughtered and sold. But a substantial quantity of those western cattle were purchased by farmers from Illinois, Iowa, or Missouri, who fattened the stock on corn and then shipped it back to Chicago for transport to eastern cities, where it was slaughtered and the fresh beef delivered to hungry urbanites.

The task of moving millions of animals a thousand miles east inspired the construction of an infrastructure that stretched from the Mississippi River to the Atlantic seaboard. The stockyard at Chicago was funded primarily by railroad companies, which recognized that livestock represented one of their most lucrative and important categories of freight. But the Chicago yards, and those at St. Louis, Kansas City, and elsewhere, were only one cog in the meat-making machine. Investors, nearly all of them connected to the railroads, built duplicate stockyards at the other end of the line: in Manhattan and across the river in New Jersey; in Philadelphia and Baltimore. An enormous yard at Albany, New York, served livestock dealers in New England. Along the rail routes from west to east lay more cogs, a series of railroad-owned "watering" stations where cattle and hogs could be fed and watered and nearby farmers could load their own livestock for shipment east.

By the early 1870s, the American meat-making machine spanned the continent, grass-rich range of the Far West at one end and slaughterhouses and wholesale markets at the other, with Chicago and "Corn Belt" farmers in the middle. Some Americans paid a steep price for the benefits of this behemoth but efficient machine, while others reaped nothing but profit. East Coast farmers, for example, were all but eliminated from the meat-making equation because, as one man explained, they could not compete with the "great facilities for bringing cattle from the far west at a low price, and in great quantities, at all times of the year." So, too, with hogs: "The number of swine raised . . . in New England, is far less than formerly," noted a report from the commissioner of agriculture in 1861. Between the "high price of grain" in New England on one hand, and the speed with which Corn Belt hogs could be "rushed from the Mississippi to the Atlantic" on the other, eastern hog farming was no longer profitable. The numbers were stark: In 1845 farmers in New York's Harlem Valley, nestled between the Hudson on one side and the Connecticut border on the other, owned 12,000 hogs; by 1875, there were fewer than 4,000. There were 9,000 steer and oxen in the mid-1840s, and just 2,100 three decades later. But western and Far Western farmers and ranchers weren't sure they fared any better. They complained that railroad tyrants imposed unfair freight rates and gouged users for the privilege of using the rails.

The truth was more complex. Railroads, the great wonder of the age, attracted deep-pocketed investors who believed that the profit possibilities were infinite. In reality, they overbuilt the system, especially in the eastern half of the United States, provoking brutal rate wars that threatened to send the entire edifice crashing into bankruptcy. At a time when the railroads were the largest corporations in the world, and their size and complexity both novel and startling, no one fully understood how to manage such enterprises or the competition between and among them. Road owners experimented with "pools" in which they mutually agreed on freight rates and divided the available livestock among themselves. The arrangements rarely succeeded, depending as they did on voluntary cooperation and mutual trust (both in short supply among the railroad kings), but the owners tried the tool often enough that traders noticed and complained that such "cooperation" was nothing more than monopolistic collusion (a criticism echoed over the decades by many historians). Critics complained, too, that the watering yards, stockyards, and slaughterhouses represented another form of monopoly: shippers who wanted to move livestock from west to east were forced to use the infrastructure and to pay rates set by owners who could charge whatever they pleased. But the railroad owners pointed out, correctly, that their stockyard-slaughterhouse-railroad edifice injected efficiency into the project of feeding the cities. Livestock shipping, explained one road representative, "was a business that moved itself— went around on its own feet and legs, and could be driven here and there," and thus was difficult to manage and monitor. Suppose a man contracted to ship hogs from Chicago to Albany but decided to sell the stock during the rest stop at Buffalo. Neither buyer nor seller was required to report the sale. The new owner simply loaded the hogs back onto the train and transported them to the final stop — without paying the railroad. Or suppose a shipper in Chicago arranged with a road to transport five cars of cattle to Philadelphia, but on the designated day a competing road lured him away with a lower rate. When the first train pulled into Philadelphia hauling five empty cars, the traffic manager telegraphed Chicago to ask why. Meanwhile, the road manager who received the unexpected cargo telegraphed his Chicago counterpart demanding to know who owned the cattle and what he was supposed to do with them. Meanwhile, "this butcher and that would go to his ... regular market," discover empty pens and yards, and then "be compelled to run around until he found the cattle." Without established markets and yards, and without pools and other agreements between and among the owners of roads and yards, the system lacked stability and predictability. "The more you can concentrate this business" into just a few hands, argued one railroad executive, "the less expense it can be done with" and thus the less consumers paid for meat.

He was right. Monopolistic though it may have been, the infrastructure provided an efficient mechanism for tapping into the hog farms and cattle herds of the West and Far West and for giving Americans what they wanted: cheap meat and plenty of it. As complex and relatively modern as it seemed, the postwar meat-making colossus was essentially an elaborate version of the colonial cattle-corn-hog complex, albeit one spread over much of a continent. Where the modern system parted ways with that older one, however, was in the cities it served. Back in the colonial era, few Americans lived in villages or towns, and sizable cities were few in number. No one much cared about the livestock parades that tramped the countryside, or about the noisome mess that slaughtering created. Not so in the 1870s and after. Americans wanted cities. They wanted meat, too. But they no longer wanted the one in the other. In modern America, the making of meat would increasingly be out of sight and out of mind.

2

"WE ARE HERE
TO MAKE MONEY"

I N THE SUMMER OF 1882, workmen armed with sledge-
hammers leveled a collection of aging storefronts and sellers' stalls on a wharf near New York City's Washington Market, an enormous wholesale-retail emporium where city residents
bought everything from fish and fruit to bacon and veal. (The
market lay near the Hudson River just north of where the World
Trade Center once stood.) Having demolished the old, crews began constructing the new: a structure that ran eighty feet front
to back, stood two stories high, and was reported to be a giant
"refrigerator." No one knew much about the property's purpose
or owner, but the rumor mill churned with tidbits that pointed
toward a company that planned to distribute fresh beef shipped
from Chicago.

The speculation ended in early October when workers hoisted
a sign into place — G. F. & E. C. SWIFT. A barge crossed the Hudson River from New Jersey and delivered several tons of fresh
beef to the water-side door, and the manager opened the facility to visitors, buyers, and reporters and explained the whats and
whys of the venture. Yes, he said, the Swift brothers would ship

fresh beef rather than live cattle from Chicago to New York; doing so would reduce the price that consumers paid for steaks
and roasts. The shipments of fresh beef would also eliminate
the need to transport live cattle from west to east and to march
them through New York's streets to the nearby slaughterhouses.
Dressed beef, crowed a reporter, promised to eradicate the city of
the "abominable nuisances" of local butcheries, rendering plants,
and "bone-boiling works." Now all of that could stay out in Chicago "where they rather like such things."

If only it were that simple. Within days, the city's stockyards
and slaughterhouses buzzed with new rumors, this time warning of retaliation and warfare. According to gossips, the Swifts'
dressed-beef venture threatened the titans who transported live
cattle by train from Chicago to New York; who owned the trains
that carried the cattle; who owned all or part of the stockyards
in Chicago, New York, and along the route to the East; and who
owned New York slaughterhouses where the animals were turned
into beef for Manhattan, Brooklyn, and other towns and cities in
the region. Surely those men would not allow the Swifts to drive
a wedge between them and their profits. By early November,
newspapers nationwide were reporting that the railroad-stock-
yard-cattle-dealer-slaughterhouse kingpins, led by the powerful Vanderbilt family of New York, planned to destroy the Swift
brothers by launching a rival dressed-beef venture. The old guard
denied the rumors, but they warned the public to beware: the
Swifts were "trying to force their beef on the public," explained
John Dutcher, a major cattle dealer and investor in both railroads
and stockyards. If they succeeded, they would create "one of the
greatest monopolies ever known in this country," and then they
would "put on the screws, and make consumers pay whatever
price they please" for meat. Nonsense, retorted the man who had
designed the Swifts' refrigerated railcars. The brothers were neither monopolists nor "sharks" but entrepreneurs who had developed a "superior system" of supplying beef. Gustavus Swift was a
good "Christian" and a "public benefactor," he told an inquiring
journalist, who wanted to "do good rather than evil" by providing

Americans with inexpensive meat and employing "hundreds" of men with "good and sure pay."

A Boston newspaper reporter took the matter directly to the Swifts themselves in an interview at their offices in that city. Did they believe the rumors? he asked. Did they fear Vanderbilt and his cronies? Gustavus Swift dismissed the fuss. The name-calling and rumors of revenge were inevitable, he said. His opponents had invested millions building an infrastructure to transport live cattle from west to east and had earned "gigantic fortunes" doing so. But in the end, what did they have? Stockyards, and those were nothing more than a few acres of "sheds and fences," property that his "refrigerator business" would render worthless. So, prodded the reporter, would the Swifts back down? Could the "cattle yard railroad ring" stop them? "Stop us!" G. F. Swift reportedly shouted in reply, slamming his fist on his desk. "[N]ot while we have an inch of pocketbook or a drop of blood left!" "We have no fears," he insisted. He and his brother would fight for "their rights, to the last drop of blood." "We shall fight," Edwin Swift added, "till blood stands four inches deep on the floor!"

We can end the suspense here: Gus Swift won the "dressed-beef war." Over the next decade, his beef-filled refrigerated railcars drove many slaughterhouses and stockyards out of business in New York and other cities. For the next century, his name adorned packages of beef and pork sold around the world, and he's typically credited (wrongly) with inventing the refrigerated railcar and (wrongly) with being the first to ship dressed beef. So how did a small-time cattle buyer who boasted neither wealth nor friends in high places transform a centuries-old system of making meat and bring the railroad-stockyard kingpins to their knees? The short answer is that he figured out a way to give Americans what they wanted: not just cheap beef but also large-scale, factorylike slaughterhouses and, what mattered most to Americans at the time, cleaner cities.

Gus Swift was born in 1839 on Cape Cod, where his ancestors had landed some two centuries earlier. In the early 1850s, he began working as a butcher's apprentice, but after a few years he decided he could make more money as the middleman who supplied beef to butchers than he could standing behind a counter cutting it. He began traveling to Brighton, a century-old livestock market near Boston, to buy cattle and sometimes a few hogs, taking them back to the Cape where he sold the stock to local butchers. By the early 1870s, Swift had earned enough cash, and reputation, to invest in partnerships with two livestock wholesalers, one in Fall River, Massachusetts, and a second in Boston, buying cattle for his partners at the markets in Brighton and in Albany, New York. But as was true for everyone on the East Coast who traded in agricultural products, Swift's fortunes were chained to Chicago and the railroads, and like many Americans, he failed to see how the vaunted efficiencies of those roads benefited anyone or anything but their owners. The cattle he bought, whether at Brighton or Albany, came from Chicago, and the more miles livestock traveled, the less profit he earned. To the actual price of the animal the roads tacked on the cost of transporting the stock, the water and feed doled out at the watering stations (whether the cattle ate or drank was irrelevant; the trader got charged anyway), and the sawdust used as bedding. Swift complained that these "simply enormous" fees made other men "immensely rich" at his expense. The yard owners paid $6 or $8 a ton for hay, for example, but charged cattle buyers like himself $40 to $50 for the privilege of using it. The yard paid a penny or two per load of cattle bedding but charged him a dollar a bushel for the stuff. And as he well knew, the pain didn't end there. One of Swift's livestock colleagues, a Boston hog trader and pork packer, learned that the hard way. The packer was infuriated that yard managers charged him $1.50 a bushel for corn that sold "right over the fence [for] 35 cents" and forced him to feed his hogs at the road's yards. Frustrated by the pickpocketing, the man built his own yard at Buffalo. Retaliation was immediate. When his men tried to load his animals, railroad employees refused to ship them because the livestock had not been "fed and watered . . . in their yards." They held the beasts until noon and shipped them to Albany, where he was required to use stockyards controlled by the railroad's partner. But by the time the hogs arrived, the trading day, which began at dawn, was over and buyers had taken themselves off to the stockyard hotel bar to compare notes and boast of deals over drinks. The rebel's agent was left to wander the deserted stockyard, doomed to take whatever price he could get. Lesson for Swift and others: Play by the railroads' rules, or don't play at all.

Swift was as ambitious and profit-hungry as the men who dominated the railroads, and he was not inclined to live his life as the entrepreneurial equivalent of a doormat. In 1875, he moved to Chicago. He would still have to rely on railroads to move his cattle east, but at least in Chicago he could buy his own cattle, rather than rely on an agent to buy on his behalf, and thus eliminate one set of hands snatching his profits.

Had Swift continued to focus on buying and shipping cattle, we likely never would have heard of him; he was, after all, just one of thousands of men trolling the Union Stock Yards in search of a deal. But within a year of moving west, Swift launched a new venture: he would buy cattle, but instead of shipping them east, he would slaughter them in Chicago and ship only the carcasses. That project would make him famous and rich. Because of it, he's been hailed as an entrepreneurial genius. As we'll see, there was genius involved, but Swift succeeded primarily because he constructed a unified system for delivering fresh, cheap beef to urban markets, and because he made his move at an opportune moment. By the mid-1870s, many Americans had decided that the old system of making meat — herding live animals through city streets and slaughtering them on every other corner — was unhealthy, dangerous, and unsuited to life in a modern nation increasingly dominated by cities.

In the mid-nineteenth century, the sights, sounds, and smells of livestock and meat making permeated urban life. Even small towns boasted at least one stockyard, and big cities like New York, Philadelphia, and Baltimore housed dozens. Stockyards ranged from a few hundred square yards to acres of choice real estate, and they constituted swampy mud holes in spring and billowed thick dust in summer. Children straddled fences to watch as traders armed with hooked staffs prodded animals' flanks and *hieeed!* them to and fro for inspection. Moving livestock from rail yard to stockyard to slaughterhouse spawned an endless animal parade. Pedestrians scattered as cattle plodded through streets jammed with carts and horses, top-hatted lawyers and bankers, servants toting baskets and bags, and shopkeepers standing watch over sidewalk displays. Calves and lambs, some only a few days old and prized for their tender flesh, could not be trusted to their own legs or the streets' hazards, so teamsters tossed them onto wooden carts, lacing rope about their feet and necks to prevent them from moving. If a wooden wheel collided with a particularly deep rut or a dried mud hump, an animal or two might fly out of the cart and into the road. Squealing hogs raced through streets and lanes, forcing pedestrians, carriages, and carts to give way. Their drovers used whips to keep them in line, but the more willful swine charged into alleys or through shop doors, chased by boys hired to tackle and drag them back to the parade. The constant march of animals provoked national irritation. "There is perhaps nothing more aggravating," a Milwaukee resident complained, than to trudge home from work "wading through all manner of filth on the sidewalks," only to "find your garden rooted up, your evergreens bitten off and broken," and hanging laundry yanked to the ground and stained with "the marks of muddy cloven feet," all thanks to four-legged invaders.

Slaughterhouses, butchers' shops, and rendering operations enriched the visual and aural feast (if it can be called that). In cities large and small, slaughterhouses abounded, where the proprietors often slaughtered a dozen or more animals a day, selling the carcasses to retailers or vending them at open-air markets where shoppers congregated by the hundreds. But slaughterhouses weren't the only places where blood and stench ran thick. Many retail butchers preferred to cut their own stock; they purchased one or more animals a week, herded them back to their shops, and slaughtered them out back. Butcheries large and small nestled up against residential neighborhoods, shared fences with schools, and backed onto churchyards. Throngs of children hung about to watch with fascinated delight, hanging on every word of the "not very elegant language" of the butchers' world, becoming, critics complained, "habituated to scenes of blood and violence," a gory and three-dimensional nineteenth-century equivalent of the computer games that adults fret about today. The business of making meat cloaked towns in a gag-inducing stench. Blood and urine coursed along walkways into the streets, then meandered toward the local sewer system, typically nothing more than a shallow trough running down the side of the road. Islands of waste landscaped the alleys adjacent to the butcheries and packinghouses. Legs and heads; hooves, ears, and snouts. Intestines and feces. Piles of stomachs, eyeballs, and brains. Winter's cold alleviated the stench but coaxed clouds of steam from the still-warm heaps of entrails. In spring and summer, the air sagged with a thick blanket of stench. A Milwaukee newspaperman commented that pedestrians held their breath and quickened their pace in an effort to escape the assault; horses "snorted and pranced and fled along the streets as if flying from some dread presence," and "mosquitoes, flies and gnats deserted the localities" where butchers reigned. Even the slaughterers weren't immune, said one butcher, who admitted that he "often lost a meal" when passing especially noisome operations.

But stockyards and slaughterhouses were only one piece of a rich mixture of odor, filth, and muck. Imagine, if you will, New York or Des Moines or Tulsa — minus the water supply. Minus plumbing, minus flush toilets. Minus sewer systems and zoning regulations. Imagine block after block of tightly packed wooden structures, each illuminated by candles or oil-filled lanterns. Imagine "tenant-houses," as they were called at the time: two- or three-story buildings crammed with hundreds of people sharing one or two outhouses. Add in teams of horses pulling carts, carriages, wagons, and streetcars, all of them depositing tons of manure each day. Toss in the constant — and bewildering — presence of diseases whose causes no one understood and thus could not prevent: cholera, typhus, smallpox, dysentery, malaria. And to all that add the business of supplying townsfolk with meat, which necessitated moving thousands of animals — a million or more in the case of a city like New York — from train yard to stockyard to slaughterhouse, and thousands of pounds of meat from market to dinner table.

It's no wonder, then, that as cities increased in both size and number, urban Americans pondered their hellish surroundings and acted to improve them. Their efforts constituted one of the great feats of the nineteenth century, one from which we still benefit every day. Urban Americans voted to fund fire, police, and public health departments. They engineered systems to deliver water and remove wastes and invented the technologies necessary to operate them. They created plumbing codes and zoning regulations and built hospitals, all in the name of making urban life both safe and healthful.

And they revolutionized the business of making and delivering meat. Aside from the addition of the railroad, it had not changed much since the colonial days and, charged an official with the newly created Massachusetts State Board of Health in 1870, was "old-fashioned, clumsy and wasteful," as well as a "dangerous source of filth." It was all well and good for farmers to live cheek by jowl with cows and pigs, he argued, but that same situation among a "crowded population" was both "offensive and dangerous." The "nuisances" of meat making "cannot exist in our midst without depriving someone of what he has an inherent right to enjoy," namely, clean streets and pure air. On the other side of the country, a San Francisco newspaper editor agreed, urging residents there to eliminate "cramped [slaughterhouses] and terrible stenches" by banning the "old plan of driving cattle through the city and of hauling the carcasses on wagons through the mud."

In the years just after the Civil War, city councils and (mostly new) boards of health passed ordinances that forced butchers and slaughterhouse owners to move away from crowded neighborhoods and restricted the movement of live animals to late night or early morning. But in hundreds of cities, officials also worked to eliminate as many slaughtering operations as possible by replacing them with what one physician described as "great central slaughter-house[s] [operated] under strict superintendence," meat factories, as it were, whose modern efficiency would replace old-fashioned clumsiness. One of the first of these new "abattoirs," as they were then called (Americans adopted that word because they modeled such facilities after the publicly operated slaughter-houses of France), opened in late 1866 on the New Jersey shore just opposite the southern tip of Manhattan. The Communipaw Abattoir, a fifteen-acre collection of buildings, stock pens, and rail sidings, was built by the New Jersey Stockyard and Market Company, whose owners were intimately connected to a powerful railroad corporation (and, of course, the stockyards owned by that road). Communipaw's yards could hold thirty thousand hogs and sheep (the former greatly outnumbered the latter) and twenty thousand cattle, animals that would no longer need to be shuttled across the river to Manhattan.

Communipaw was a model of modernity. An employee drove a steer onto the killing floor, and another cinched one of its hind legs with a sturdy rope dangling from a winch overhead. A hard yank upended the beast, but just far enough to leave its jaw pressed into the blood-sodden floor and its throat taut and exposed. The "sticker" sliced through the animal's neck to the vertebrae. Another employee aimed a stream of water at the ensuing whoosh of blood. A steam-powered conveyor track whisked the carcass to the dressing tables, where knife-wielding butchers transformed the hulk into sides and quarters. Sixteen minutes from live stock to skinned carcass. The hog operation took place on the second floor. Humans herded hogs up a gangway into one of a series of pens where a man armed with a heavy mallet awaited his victims. He swung his weapon overhead, and — thud. The mallet connected with the hog's skull. Another man shoved the animal, which may or may not have died from the blow, down a short incline and into a vat of boiling water. The gang of "fishers" who ringed the vessel prodded the bloody stew with long iron hooks, shoving the bodies toward a revolving wheel that snagged the carcasses and hefted them onto a workbench. There a line of men armed with bristle scrapers attacked each warm hulk, scraping it clean and pushing it along the table. The last man grabbed the beast's hind legs and tossed the carcass onto an overhead hook. One shove and a pulley system carried its cargo to a duo armed with knife and hose. A quick jab and slice, a barrage from the hose, another shove, and what was left of the animal swayed along the conveyor line to the hanging room, which could hold thousands of carcasses. Thanks to the abattoir's efficient design, raved an observer, the "entire hog can be saved, economized and utilized, from the [end] of his snout to the tip-end of his tail — except the squeal." And, thanks to Communipaw's steam-powered winches, pulleys, and conveyors, employees could slaughter and dress a thousand cattle and another thousand hogs every day, needing but a few minutes to transform a live animal into a market-ready carcass. An attached rendering operation transformed wastes into tallow, lard, and other byproducts. The operation could supply a large part of New Yorkers' meat, and the expectation was that butchers in Manhattan would either shut their doors or relocate to Communipaw, where they could rent space for slaughtering.

If only it were that easy. Butchers and slaughterhouse owners argued that ordinances designed to constrain their work and ventures aimed at replacing private businesses with Communipaw-like factories were "arbitrary, tyrannical and unjust, and contrary to the spirit of . . . free institutions." And why, asked one butcher, would the people of New Jersey or "Long Island, or of any other place" embrace what others had declared to be "an intolerable nuisance"? In Chicago, too, butchers balked at being herded into a central slaughterhouse. The ensuing wrangle landed in the Illinois Supreme Court, which sided with the butchers and dismissed the argument that butchering constituted a nuisance. If that were the case, the judges pointed out, an official slaughterhouse must also be a nuisance and, by the city's own ordinances, must also be banned. Far worse, however, the city's attempt to require butchers to work out of a single, privately owned slaughter-house was "oppressive, and create[d] a monopoly." What would follow? asked the judges. Would the city council grant similar monopolies to sellers of fruit, flour, or vegetables?

The struggle to reconcile property rights, public welfare, and Americans' appetite for meat ended up in the Supreme Court as the "Slaughterhouse Cases," which originated in New Orleans. For years, residents of that city had wrestled with the sanitary and health problems that accompany urban life at sea level in a near-tropical climate. Yellow fever paid regular visits, as did malaria, cholera, and other diseases. The business of putting meat on the city's tables exacerbated those woes because the city's butchers (150 of them by one count) routinely tossed unwanted carcasses, blood, and other wastes into the city's main water source, the Mississippi River. As a result, putrefied offal clung to the mouths of water intake pipes, and one waterworks employee spent his days "skimming the scum" that collected in the tanks that held piped water. In the late 1860s, New Orleans residents reached the end of their sanitary rope and petitioned the city council for a centralized abattoir, arguing that the only way to keep both the river and the city clean was by forcing butchers to work in a sin-gle location. In early 1869, the Louisiana legislature granted a franchise to the Crescent City Live Stock Landing and Slaugh-ter House Company, which laid plans to build a state-of-the-art slaughterhouse and rendering operation.

In an earlier day, New Orleans's white butchers might have co-operated with the project, but in 1869 the wounds of war lay fresh on the body politic. White southerners resented the end of slavery and the presence of 4 million new "freedmen." But they loathed the white northerners who had traveled south to create a new so-ciety there, and the Louisiana legislature that granted the slaugh-tering franchise consisted largely of Yankee "carpetbaggers" and freedmen. When the bill went into effect on June 1, the butchers raised an astonishing $40,000 for legal fees and staged a series of mass meetings to oppose the slaughterhouse. The new law, the butchers argued, threatened "the personal rights of the masses."

We "hold these truths to be self evident," they announced, that "every man in this community has a property in his person and his faculties." They would never "submit" to a law that violated what they regarded as their "natural and constitutional rights." Lawsuits sprouted like mold after a flood, nearly three hundred of them in short order, as butchers, the state, the city, the board of health, and the slaughterhouse franchisees filed suit and countersuit. The gist of those cases echoed others around the country. The state of Louisiana argued that it possessed the right to protect the public health; the abattoir was one way to do so. The butchers, in turn, claimed that forcing them to conduct business at a centralized slaughterhouse violated their rights as defined in the recently ratified Fourteenth Amendment to the Constitution. The legal wrangling ground through local courts to the Louisiana Supreme Court, which ruled against the butchers. The judges argued that the state's "general police power" authorized it to protect the public health, in this case by authorizing construction of the abattoir. "Liberty," said the justices, "is the right to do what the law permits."

The butchers appealed to the Supreme Court of the United States, where their attorney argued that the city's decision to franchise a centralized slaughterhouse was both unreasonable and obstructive because it "compelled" butchers to shutter their own shops. In doing so, the city had violated the butchers' rights in favor of the Crescent City Live Stock Landing and Slaughter House Company. The judges disagreed. Nothing in the Louisiana law, they wrote in their 1873 ruling, "deprive[d] the butchers of their right to exercise their trade." The law merely mandated the location where that slaughtering could occur. The Louisiana statute neither violated butchers' rights nor constituted "deprivation of property." In practical terms, the court ruled that the public's health and welfare trumped private property and "natural" rights.

Butchers weren't the only ones who resisted the new slaughterhouses. In 1874, the managers of the New York Central Railroad, owned by the Vanderbilts, announced plans to build a massive stockyard and abattoir in New York City at West 59th Street, not far from where the Plaza Hotel now stands. City leaders supported the project because the single big meat factory would eliminate the need for many small ones, but property owners living nearby wanted none of it. At the time, the neighborhood marked the northern edge of municipal development and was home to wealthy families who had moved there precisely because it lay far from the factories, butcher shops, and open-air markets that rendered much of Manhattan an intolerable nuisance. A bitter struggle ensued. The editors of the *New York Times*, who sided with the neighbors, pronounced the project an "outrage," the work of "a grasping monopoly." Another man argued that the enterprise was "dangerous" because the ensuing slaughter would "impregnate the air of the surrounding neighborhood with noxious vapors." How could it be otherwise, he asked, given that this one facility would be conducting the "work of about one hundred ordinary-size slaughter-houses"? Another opponent pointed out that even after the city had passed an ordinance requiring butchers to move out of congested areas, fifty-three of them had defied the order. If city leaders could not rein in those "comparatively poor and uninfluential" men, how could they expect to "control this immense corporation"? The arguments were to no avail. The Vanderbilts won, although no one could decide whether to credit that to the project's public health merits or the wads of cash that Vanderbilt agents allegedly stuffed in the pockets of state legislators.

Either way, the outcome was neither unusual nor surprising, nor was the case unique. Around the country, meat men, elected officials, and property owners squared off against city councils, state legislatures, judges, juries, and each other, each party arguing that his or her rights trumped those of others. Courts, legislatures, and city councils consistently demonstrated their approval of big slaughterhouses and the sophisticated technology that came with them: smoke filters, odor suppressors, and conveyor belts and steam engines that hastened the process of slaughtering so that animals were not left standing for hours. Still, the conflict between public good and private interest was real. The contests struck at the heart of a fundamental American dilemma: the need to balance individual rights, including the right to pursue profit, with the public's welfare. Vanderbilt argued that he was entitled to use his property in any way he saw fit, even if doing so intruded on neighbors' right to breathe fresh air. New York health officials had hoped to protect the public health by forcing Manhattan's butchers to conduct their work across the river at Communipaw. Whose rights mattered more? The butchers'? Or the public's? And how did monopolies like the one proposed in Chicago fit into a free-market economy? The debate over slaughterhouses and public welfare highlighted the nature of monopoly, an evil that Americans dreaded more than any other because it struck at the heart of the pursuit of happiness, freedom, and profit. On one hand, a person successful enough to monopolize, say, the manufacture of a good or the provision of a service had demonstrated his or her skill in the pursuit of profit, in capturing and reaping the bounty of America. But having done so, he or she effectively ended others' pursuit of the same goals.

Many Americans favored an alternative route out of the morass of lawsuits and noisome mess: move livestock slaughter out west where the animals were many and the cities relatively few. Keep the cattle and hogs there, and ship the meat to the East. As a bonus, that would also resolve another quandary: by the 1870s, many Americans had concluded that whatever its other merits, the practice of shipping live animals by rail constituted its own threat to the public health. According to common theory, the constant motion and jostling of the two- or three-day journey from west to east provoked "fear and apprehension" in the animals, inducing a "feverish" condition that sparked "chemical decomposition" of muscle fibers and rendered the flesh unfit for consumption. Meat made from such animals, warned members of a commission appointed to investigate the matter, "endanger[ed] the health of the people." A New York physician agreed and explained to readers of the *New-York Tribune* that the "deep red blotches" that decorated many pieces of beef were abscesses caused by blood flowing from "crushed blood vessels" into muscle tissue. The bruises provoked fever in the animal, and as a result the meat was "in a delightful pathological condition when served to your family," as "wholesome" as "liquid scrofula."

The only sure way to eliminate the problem was by shipping dressed beef, as it was called, rather than live stock. But as those who investigated the matter knew, there were other benefits to shipping carcasses rather than live animals. A fifteen-hundred-pound steer lost about two hundred pounds during a railroad trip from Chicago to the East Coast. Given the booming human population and the expense required to move livestock from west to east, Americans could ill afford to lose so much valuable protein. As important, only 50 to 60 percent of the animal was edible. The rest — the bone, hides, offal, and the like — ended up in rendering plants and tanneries to become buttons, leather, and lard. Why ship what could not be eaten?

The unease about urban slaughtering and fear of diseased meat explain why dressed beef had become common in New England even before Gus Swift moved to Chicago. Most of that cargo arrived courtesy of George Hammond, a Detroit butcher-turned-wholesaler, who began making cold-weather shipments of fresh meat from Detroit to the East in the late 1860s. By 1875, the year that Swift landed in Chicago, Hammond had moved to Indiana, and his real estate investments plus his slaughtering operations had blossomed into the busy town of Hammond where his employees processed beef for New England wholesalers. Nor was Hammond alone. In 1871, for example, the owners of the Western Refrigerator Car Company of Missouri slaughtered cattle "right off the grass" from southwestern Texas and shipped it in cold cars to St. Louis. In 1873, the Texas and Atlantic Refrigerator-Car Company of Denison, Texas, shipped one hundred tons of fresh beef from its abattoir to the Erie rail yard in Jersey City, a journey that took eight days. A New York reporter who investigated the delivery described the cargo as being in "excellent condition." And in 1875, the owners of Nofsinger & Co., a Kansas City packinghouse, began shipping beef from Kansas City to the East.

But none of those projects succeeded in breaking the grip of the railroad-stockyard cabal. One reason was that the dressed-beef pioneers encountered the usual bugs and kinks that can derail any new project. They had a hard time finding an adequate supply of cold cars, and railroad employees sometimes failed to add ice along the way. Often trouble developed at the delivery point: refrigerated warehouses could not be secured and the meat spoiled before it reached consumers' hands. According to some reports, those pioneer shippers too often skimped on the raw materials. In 1875, the Massachusetts Board of Health warned that dressed beef arriving in Boston should "be regarded with extreme suspicion" bordering on "aversion": it came from emaciated Texas cattle that had arrived in Chicago reduced to "bone-frame and skin," their meat worth about as much as "a squeezed lemon" and in such bad shape that no one was willing to ship them live.

One other obvious explanation for those early failures is that the railroad-stockyard complex, having invested millions in the business of moving live animals, had no incentive to transport dressed beef. But if that was so, why did Gus Swift succeed when others failed? Because Hammond and other dressed-beef pioneers did not understand the need to create an infrastructure to replace the one built by the railroads, or that beef carcasses were but one factor of a complex equation. Swift, in contrast, saw the beef for what it was: a small part of a vast system that included (among other things) railroad freight charges and rendering facilities; cold cars and warehouses; livestock producers, commission agents, herders, drovers, and stockyard managers; the line workers who "disassembled" the livestock; accountants and the engineers who designed the packing plants; wholesalers, retailers, and salesmen; and the bankers and brokers who controlled the money that financed all of it. In that respect, Swift resembled Thomas Edison and the era's other "system" builders. Consider a decidedly non-meat example: Edison's incandescent light bulb. By itself, it had no worth, other than as a curiosity. The bulb gained value only after Edison and his investors devised an integrated system that included the bulb, a source of electricity, and a means of transmitting that to individual bulbs in a shop, factory, or home. The system also included poles, wire, generators, transformers, and the like; financing packages and contracts; managerial and engineering skill; the willingness of urban residents to grant permission for the construction of the system's physical components; and the political acumen necessary to persuade them to do so. Only then did Edison's light bulb become valuable. The same was true of Swift's plan to ship dressed beef. It succeeded because he envisioned all of the system's parts: an integrated slaughterhouse and rendering plant where animals could be transformed into meat and byproducts; a transportation system to move the meat to a network of refrigerated warehouses and depots; and a network of wholesalers and retailers who were prepared to dispose of the product as soon as they received it.

Swift's first step was to control the refrigeration. This was key to his endeavor because the railroads exerted an unholy control over shipments of perishable goods. Suppose Swift slaughtered livestock on Tuesday and promised delivery to a wholesaler in Massachusetts by Friday. He could not assume that express dispatch services would have refrigerated cars available on Tuesday, and when it came to perishable goods, timing was everything. The only way for him to guarantee the arrival of his shipments was by owning his own cold cars. But Swift did not invent the refrigerated railcar. By the time he needed that technology, Americans had accumulated several decades of experience using ice-filled railcars to haul fish, eggs, produce, and beer from one section of the United States to another. The technology was relatively simple and rested on a basic principle: as air chills, it becomes humid and heavy and drifts downward (warm air rises; cold air sinks). Unless that air circulated, the humidity saturated the car's contents and caused them to deteriorate. So an efficient, functional cold car included not just ice and salt packed along its sides and top but a ventilation system, too. The rest was detail: the contraption had to be simple enough to allow inexperienced hands to add ice quickly during stops en route, and the cargo had to be arranged so that it did not lie directly on the ice.

There were dozens of patented refrigerator cars on the market, and Swift had to decide which one to use. In late 1875, he contracted with George Hammond to slaughter and ship beef on his behalf, not because he was ready to launch his business but because he wanted to test the viability of Hammond's cars without investing his own then-meager funds. He was not impressed and kept looking. A year or so later, he acquired rights to several cold-car patents and arranged for a Michigan company to build cars for him. (Hammond promptly sued him for patent infringement, a common conflict at a time when patent law was relatively unstable. The court ruled in Swift's favor.)

Swift's next step was to contract with a railroad to haul his cars. Swift's hagiographers later claimed that the major railroads refused to deal with him because they regarded dressed beef as a threat. Swift, being his heroic self, fought back and the rest, as they say, was history. But as with much of the Swift mythology, that version contains more fiction than fact. It's true that the roads and their stockyard partners were committed to shipping livestock rather than beef. But it's also true that in the late 1870s, they had no reason to see Swift as a threat. After all, others had tried to ship dressed beef and failed. Moreover, in 1877 and 1878, when Swift was ready to move, the railroad industry was suffering more than its usual chaos thanks to a series of violent strikes that stopped traffic for weeks. Then there were the ongoing demands of maintaining tracks, engines, and cars; the burden of managing the largest workforce in the world; and the thousand other problems that plagued the small group of people wrestling with the first grand corporate venture of the modern age. Swift's failure to arrange shipping contracts with the railroads was probably less a nefarious plot (although the railroaders were capable of those) than it was his inability to capture the attention of people as distracted as any multitasker tweeting, texting, and blogging in the digital age. But the Swift mythology also ignores the most crucial fact: the railroad men who allegedly thwarted him were irrelevant to his plans. The nation's three largest shippers, the New York Central, Erie, and Pennsylvania railroads and their affiliated stockyards and abattoirs, served the New York–Phila-delphia metropolitan area. But Gus Swift planned to launch his empire on his home turf, New England, where he could take ad-vantage of his wide network of business contacts.

That explains why he approached the managers of Canada's Grand Trunk Railway. The Grand Trunk ran along the southern border of Canada and included spur lines that connected it to Chicago. At its eastern end, the route sliced through Vermont, providing easy access to New England towns and cities. As a bo-nus, the Grand's tracks coursed through terrain whose tempera-tures ranged from cool to frigid for much of the year, which would increase the efficiency of his cars. Best of all, the GT's managers delighted in functioning as a boil in the sides of American rail-road magnates and enjoyed nothing so much as a splendid little rate war. They agreed to haul Swift's refrigerated cars from Chi-cago to New England.

Railroad and refrigerator cars in hand, Swift turned to the most crucial component of his system: distribution. Because the meat was perishable, it was imperative that it be unloaded from cold cars into refrigerated warehouses or be transferred to retail-ers for immediate sale. Only then could Swift guarantee that his meat would be fresh and appealing to its final buyers, the men and women who would put it on their tables. Over the previous twenty years, Swift had cultivated a host of relationships with New England cattle dealers, butchers, packers, and wholesalers, and he parlayed those contacts into a network of outlets.

All of it required cash, of which there was never enough. That did not bother Swift. According to his son Louis Swift, who co-wrote a fawning biography of his father, the elder man's "vision" typically "ran far ahead of the money" on hand. The son described his father as a "born expansionist" who operated by the princi-ple of borrowing money whenever possible. Using his "persua-sive enthusiasm," he "hustled" for loans and "wheedled" funds from anyone who would listen. Louis Swift's description of his father's money-grubbing sounds a bit like a Ponzi scheme: Gus routinely borrowed from one source to pay off another. One fact is clear: in those early years, Swift raced from Chicago to Boston to Brighton, from Maine to Massachusetts to Rhode Island, wooing wholesalers, tinkering with refrigerator cars, and persuading people to part with their money. It was, said his son, in what is perhaps the only accurate assessment in a book otherwise devoted to hero worship, akin to juggling a "fish-bowl, a cannon ball, and a live rabbit."

The juggling paid off. In January 1878, Swift and his brother launched Swift & Co. A year later, their "New England Fresh Meat Express" was delivering hundreds of tons of dressed beef to warehouses in Boston, Lowell, Fall River, and other Massachusetts towns. In addition, the Swifts sold meat straight off the railcars to wholesalers in dozens of other locations, buyers who then distributed it to another three hundred other towns and cities from Maine to Connecticut. By 1881, the meat magnate was shipping three thousand carcasses a week from Chicago (about a thousand of which, it's worth noting, landed at the port in Liverpool, England). The company's infrastructure included five hundred refrigerated railcars; forty-eight "coolers" scattered from New England to Washington, DC; and an assortment of warehouses, depots, and ice "farms" that stretched from Chicago to New England. He claimed that his Chicago facility was the largest cattle-slaughtering house in the world. That was likely a bit of promotional hyperbole, but the plant employed five hundred hands and two steam engines and boasted a "refrigerator" that could hold six thousand carcasses.

By 1882, Swift was ready to seek the holy grail: the nation's biggest market, New York City, where he would confront the men who had siphoned off his profits with their overpriced sawdust and hay. He laid the groundwork for his assault by constructing the new warehouse at Washington Market. A newspaperman who visited the facility marveled at the efficient design, which included a "railway" track suspended from the ceiling, the track holding a collection of wheeled hooks from which hung dozens of beef carcasses. The warehouse manager explained that the company's refrigerator cars were equipped with similar ceiling-mounted tracks. When a train arrived in New Jersey, a crew trans-ferred the cars to a barge that floated them across the river to the warehouse. There, workers aligned the door of the train car with the door of the warehouse and slid the dangling carcasses off one track and onto the other. Thanks to such cost-cutting efficiencies, the reporter told readers, the "era of cheap beef" had begun. "Eve-rything with us is systematized," a company representative told another newspaperman. By using the telegraph, employees could respond almost instantly to local changes in demand and adjust prices accordingly, and do so faster than shippers who hauled live animals. "Everywhere we have located," he said, "our success has exceeded our expectations."

The project of shipping dressed beef long distances "has ceased to be an experiment, and . . . has become a demonstrated fact," commented another observer, who predicted that Swift & Co., whose unofficial motto was "quick sales and small profits," would "break down local monopolies and high prices." According to some reports, the opening of Swift's Washington Market refrig-erator provoked a "panicky feeling" among local beef brokers and shippers as well as slaughterhouse owners in Manhattan, Brook-lyn, and Jersey City, who feared that Swift would undercut them on price. That, opined a Chicago reporter, was the least of their worries. A disruption or reduction of New York's live cattle trade would likely destroy local byproduct processors; without cattle, there would be no hides, bones, hooves, and fat. The locals' anxi-ety was justified and surely increased when, just days after Swift opened his New York doors, Philip Armour joined the fray.

Today Philip Armour's name is associated primarily with meat-packing, but he was not a meat man and certainly no butcher. As he once said, "[I]f you showed me a piece of meat I could not tell you what part of the bullock it came from." Armour was only in-terested in meat for the same reason he was interested in wheat, corn, coal, or gold: it offered opportunities for manipulating sup-plies and therefore prices, and thus for earning huge profits.

Armour, who was born in 1832 and grew up in upstate New

York, earned his first serious money during the California gold rush, not by panning for ore but by selling necessities to those who were. In the late 1850s, he landed in Milwaukee, a town boasting a robust and diverse economy, proximity to Chicago, and bountiful natural resources from the region's farms and forests. There he and another man opened a commission house and worked as middlemen selling grain and other provisions. Sensing war on the horizon, the pair bought up a warehouse of whiskey, betting that if war came, Congress would raise taxes on liquor. War came; Congress did; the men profited.

But in the early 1860s, Armour entered into partnership with John Plankinton, a Milwaukee real estate powerhouse and owner of the city's biggest pork-processing operation. Armour promptly impressed the older man with his acumen when the two earned a fortune by cornering the market in packed pork. Corners were Armour's special delight, a fact he would demonstrate repeatedly during his life (to the dismay of his competitors). Plankinton and Armour signed "futures" contracts, agreeing to buy pork from other dealers on a specific date in the future. At the same time, the two men quietly purchased as much pork as they could lay their hands on. When the contracts came due, the saps who had contracted to deliver pork to Plankinton and Armour discovered that there was none to be had — except from Plankinton and Armour, who, having "cornered" the supply, could charge whatever price they wanted. The men holding the futures contracts had to buy from P & A — in order to sell to P & A. The partners reportedly earned somewhere between $1 and $2 million from the (legal) scheme, while many rivals collapsed under the weight of their costly mistake. The men used the windfall to expand their Milwaukee holdings and to fund a second pork-packing operation in Kansas City.

But Milwaukee could not satisfy Armour's ambitions, and a few years later he parted ways with Plankinton (theirs was an amicable separation) and headed to Chicago. There he built a pork-processing plant, annoyed his new rivals by orchestrating corners, and waded into the beef industry by opening a beef-canning facility. Sometime around 1880, he began investigating the possibilities of shipping dressed beef, but he later admitted that his initial effort failed because he and his employees "did not understand the methods of refrigeration and did not get [the] beef to the seaboard in proper condition." But Armour was a quick study, and in October 1882, he pronounced himself sufficiently "confident" to "go into the business on a large scale." The timing was intentional: When Gus Swift marched into the New York market, George Hammond had tagged along. Armour had to make his move or run the risk that the other two would run away with the nation's biggest meat market. A company representative explained that, unlike Swift, who targeted the wholesale market, Armour planned to deal directly with retailers and to sell "refrigerator" boxes of "small cuts" — tenderloins, sirloin, and so forth — rather than whole carcasses. The cost advantage played out at Armour's Chicago packing plant, where employees transformed the rest of the carcass bits into sausage and canned and corned beef and used byproducts on the spot. The company had "no waste at all," explained an Armour executive. "The blood, the bones, the offal, the hoofs, and the horns are all utilized and made profitable here." The equation was clear: Sell direct to retailers. Ship only what they want. Earn top dollar for the rest of the carcass back in Chicago.

The arrival of Swift in Manhattan had been alarming enough. The entry of Armour, whose reputation as a cutthroat corner maker had long since outgrown Chicago, heightened the danger ahead. "There can be only one thing left for all the men who have capital invested here in this business," said one New York meat wholesaler, and that was to "go away." Or, as a less charitable observer put it, "only stupid and sluggish minds" would fail to "heed the signs of the times." Railroad magnates had become "fat and comfortable" on the "toll" exacted from the nation's meat eaters, mused a newspaper editor. But thanks to Armour, Swift, and dressed beef, he told readers, "Mr. VANDERBILT sees in his dreams long lines of his stock cars rotting on disused sidings." "There is really no reason on earth," he added, "why the beef-eaters of New-York should be taxed for bringing hides and horns over Mr. VANDERBILT's roads all the way from Chicago." And should Vanderbilt and other tycoons complain, well, too bad. "[A]ll of this is nothing more than has happened in every trade revolution that has taken place in the country," wrote another observer. "From our standpoint in all this matter, we are only looking at and dealing with the inevitable." Statistics document the speed with which the dressed-beef revolution unfolded: In 1880, Chicago trains carried 416,000 head of live cattle and 31,000 tons of dressed beef to eastern markets. Five years later, the number of live cattle had dropped to 281,000 and dressed-beef tonnage had risen to 232,000. A journalist who covered commodities markets for the *Boston Journal* reported in 1883 that three-fourths of the dressed beef sold in that city came directly from Chicago, sixty train cars a week delivering nearly 1.8 million pounds of "bright and sweet" beef. Those shipments, he reported, had "materially curtailed" slaughtering operations at the Brighton market.

By any measure, the packers' rapid conquest of the American beef market was extraordinary; in less than a decade they upended a long-standing system of distributing meat and beat the powerful railroads at their own game. Part of the reason, it's clear, is that the dressed-beef men offered a superior alternative. But in the 1880s, the newcomers also benefited from rising demand for beef, not just in the United States but around the world, and from a cattle bonanza in the Far West that glutted stockyards and drove down the prices the packers paid for their raw material.

In the last thirty years of the nineteenth century, Americans benefited from an expanding economy and a proliferation of clerical and managerial jobs as well as factory work that often paid high wages. The rising standard of living shaped shoppers' demands, and people in every economic class developed an insatiable appetite for fresh beef. But not just any cuts. Families satisfied with tongue or cheek twenty years earlier now demanded finer cuts, a Wisconsin butcher explained to a newspaper reporter in 1882. His customers snapped up porterhouse, sirloin, and rib roast, but the rest of the carcass, he grumbled, landed in his account books as a loss. "Even a laborer on the street or a negro will come in and ask for a porter-house steak," groused another butcher. "[N]obody wants anything else." A Boston meat seller confirmed that observation. Among his regular customers was a young seamstress who purchased only tenderloin. He explained to her that she could save money by buying round steak instead. The woman took offense. "Do you suppose because I don't come here in my carriage I don't want just as good meat as rich folks have?" she demanded. From the butchers' perspective then, Swift and Armour offered relief, Swift because he delivered carcasses to wholesalers who sold butchers only the pieces they wanted, and Armour because he offered boxes of choice cuts.

But the demand for beef stemmed from more than a desire to emulate "rich folks." In the late nineteenth century, widely accepted theories linked food to national power and racial superiority. According to this set of ideas, a nation's diet predicted whether it would dominate or be dominated. That goes far toward explaining the era's obsessive exploration of the science of nutrition and of agricultural production: if diet and national might were linked, it was crucial to understand which foods delivered strength and health and, as important, how to wring every last ounce of nutriment from every last inch of soil or, if need be, the laboratory. (In 1894, one chemist predicted that by 2000, fields of corn and wheat would be a thing of the past because humans would manufacture flour and other foodstuffs in laboratories.) More than for any other food, however, access to meat both denoted and endowed power, and of the meats, beef reigned supreme. Meat-rich diets had made Europeans and Americans masters of the planet. In contrast, the "rice-eating" Japanese, Chinese, and "Hindoos," as one typical essay phrased it, were an "inoffensive" collection of people from whom not much could be expected. The cultural and nutritional significance of flesh-based protein explains why Europeans invested heavily in public slaughterhouses and eliminated tariffs that hindered the importation of cheap (and mostly American) meats. Doing so ensured

that citizens — many of whom, after all, would likely become soldiers — would have meat on their tables.

In the 1870s and 1880s, however, a series of epidemics ravaged
cattle herds in Europe and Great Britain. The resulting meat
shortages prompted government officials and private investors to
look to Americans for supplies. Britain's Parliament, for example, sent two men to investigate the livestock situation in the Far
West; the pair returned to London intoxicated with not just the
numbers of cattle they found there, but the potential for wealth.
A western livestock producer "makes an enormous return" on his
investment, they reported, reaping an "average profit" of "fully 33
per cent." Another promoter claimed that, assuming "good business management," a herd of western cattle returned 25 percent
a year. A correspondent for the London *Times* told readers that
ranching consisted primarily of "riding through plains, parks,
and valleys," pleasant jaunts interspersed with livestock round-
ups conducted by "masters and men, well mounted." "The cost of
both summering and wintering [livestock] is simply the cost of
herding," claimed one Wyoming rancher, "as no feed nor shelter
is required." Or, in the western vernacular popular at the time:
Graze 'em, round 'em up, ship 'em out, pocket the proceeds.

These hyperbolic promises of easy wealth spurred a race to
capture both beef and profits. Hundreds of English, Scottish, German, French, and American investors dived in, scooping up land
and livestock. Cowtowns swarmed with men on the make. The
editor of the *Laramie Boomerang* described that burg's cattle district as "a young Wall Street" where buyers, sellers, and madmen
talked of "millions" as if they were "nickels." Corporate ranching
ventures laid claim to cattle lands from the Canadian border to
the Rio Grande. Some were legitimate and well managed. Others existed only on paper and served as "clever bait," observed a
reporter with a Denver newspaper, with which to separate "suck-
ers" from their money.

One of the loonier ventures was a Dakota Territory slaughtering operation launched by Antoine-Amédée-Marie-Vincent
Manca de Vallombrosa, known to all as the Marquis de Morès.

Born in France into a lush background suitable to his highfalu-
tin name, he married a wealthy New York woman in 1882. He
worked briefly for her banker father, but then decided he needed
a stake of his own. He set out for the Dakota Territory, surveyed its possibilities, and hatched a "ranch to table" scheme, as
he called it. "We propose," he explained to a reporter, to eliminate "the middleman and send meats direct from the producer
to the consumer." How he planned to slaughter enough livestock
to compete with Swift and Armour, find buyers for the mounds
of byproducts, ship from Dakota to New York City, and still earn
a profit was not clear. (It's unlikely he wasted much time pondering such trivia.) He dumped his and his wife's inheritances as
well as funds from a collection of gullible investors into an abattoir, a byproducts-processing facility, and a town, which he chris-
tened Medora, after his wife. Morès proved to be a brilliant pub-
licist, and newspapers around the country regaled readers with
updates on the Frenchman ("distinguished scholar, gentleman,
millionaire and cowboy"): his conflicts with ranchers who tried to
scare him away (one of whom he reportedly killed in a shootout;
self-defense, decided the jury that acquitted him); his home on
the range — "an agreeable cross between a Newport cottage and a
hunting lodge"; and, of course, his efforts to bring industrial capitalism to the range. When the end came, the Marquis was dodg-
ing creditors (and was eventually arrested for fraud).

It's not surprising that the cattle bubble went the way of all
such bubbles. If nothing else, the western plains could not support the burden. In 1870, a steer could survive on five acres of
land; by 1880, thanks to overgrazing and grass depletion, those
same animals needed fifty to ninety acres. President Grover
Cleveland compounded the problem in 1885 when he ordered
livestock owners to remove more than two hundred thousand
head of cattle from federal lands in the Indian Territory (now
Oklahoma). There were only two directions the herds could go:
east to the slaughterhouses, or west to a range already teetering
on the brink of disaster. Thousands poured into the stockyards
in Kansas City, Chicago, and elsewhere, scrawny range cattle that

provided cheap raw materials for beef canners and packers alike. Thousands more flooded the overcrowded plains. Then came the winters of 1885–86 and 1886–87, with frigid temperatures and a string of brutal blizzards. Tens of thousands of cattle perished, a cruel rebuttal to the notion that they could fend for themselves and that ranching consisted of a roundup romp and a jaunt to the bank. Cattle companies large and small collapsed. The disaster coincided with, and exacerbated, one of the periodic economic slumps that punctuated an already unpredictable economy, and bankers began calling loans. Small ranchers and corporate cowboys alike stared foreclosure and bankruptcy in the face and sold their livestock for whatever price they could get. It was not much. "I have tried everybody," an agent for a British company reported to his superiors. "I tried every possible means I could to cause a sale by personal favor, commission, etc. . . . There are simply no buyers." The stockyards at Chicago and Kansas City could not "contain the enormous car-loads of . . . cattle . . . pouring in from all directions," reported another observer. "The thing has been overdone, the market is glutted and collapse is imminent." The disaster enraged a veteran cattle buyer from south Texas, who denounced the invasion of "men who did not know what they were doing," representing as they did "large capitalists" rather than knowledgeable livestock producers. "I do not think I ever saw a business that was as prosperous . . . that went down as quick and fast, with no confidence left in it at all." From Iowa to Texas, livestock producers watched as prices plunged and their livelihoods disintegrated.

The reasons behind the collapse are obvious to us now — overgrazing, incompetence, greed, weather — but in the volatile economy of the 1880s, those whose fortunes vanished were convinced that someone or some group must have manipulated the market and pushed cattle prices into an abyss. Blame focused on the dressed-beef men, and rumors of a "Big Three" and a "Big Four" swirled about the stockyards and drifted through the smoky bars that lined the streets of Dodge City and other cowtowns. One man spoke for many when he denounced Swift, Armour, and Hammond as a rapacious "monopoly" and a "dangerous power": "They antagonize the railroads, the butchers, the stock yards, the cattle raisers, and the beef consumers; they seem to want the whole earth." A Texan complained that the upstart packers constituted a "dressed beef syndicate" that colluded to control cattle prices. "A man from the range arrives with a train load of beef on the hoof at Kansas City," he told a reporter, and receives an offer from a member of the "combination." "The offer is not a good one," so the seller ships the stock to Chicago — and discovers that no one there will offer more. Why? Because the meatpacker's Kansas City agent telegraphed the Chicago office, warning the boss that the rancher had not cooperated. The packers made "an example" of him by offering a price lower than the one in Kansas City. The Texan calculated that the dressed-beef packers earned $15 profit on each head. "We [ranchers] think that if the slaughterers made a profit of from $2 to $5 on every steer they ought to be well satisfied, and so would we be, and the consumers, too."

Swift and Armour likely howled at the idea of earning that much on cattle or anything else. They knew what the public did not: on its own, dressed beef returned almost no profit thanks to the layers of expense that stood between the live animal and the shipped carcass. When packers bid on livestock in Kansas City or Chicago, they were paying for a beast that had already moved hundreds of miles and devoured money in the form of water, feed, and care, all of which figured into the price on the hoof. Once purchased, the animal had to be fed and watered until it was time for slaughter. The finished carcass was stored in a refrigerator (that contained tons of expensive ice) before being loaded onto a railcar (also filled with ice) for shipment east, where it was unloaded and stored again. All of it necessitated owning and maintaining an enormous infrastructure of railcars, warehouses, and ice farms as well as office space and hundreds of employees. Every step devoured money, and when the final sale was made, it had to be at a price customers would pay. If not, the carcasses rotted. Assuming all the relevant variables — including weather, the size of the corn crop, and the health of the overall economy — aligned, at best sides of beef returned 1 percent profit and usually less. In bad times — if the corn crop failed, if inflation forced consumers to choose between beef and bread — the packers lost money. That slender line between profit and loss, and meat's perishable nature, explains why the dressed-beef kings obsessed over the three factors they could control: efficiency, volume, and byproducts.

Swift, Armour, Hammond, and a handful of other beef packers understood that they had to slaughter huge numbers of cattle in order to keep their plants operating at capacity, and that spurred them to outbid everyone else at the stockyards. They needed every animal they could lay their hands on. Huge numbers of cattle translated into mountains of waste in the form of blood, bone, hide, and marrow that could be converted into money. Hides, for example, could be sold almost anywhere in the world for a profit. So, too, "oleomargarine," an animal-fat-based butter substitute the packers developed in the 1880s and shipped around the world. Byproducts subsidized beef.

But neither demand nor volume nor byproducts could keep that infrastructure afloat, which is why the beef packers used other, less obvious tools in their search for profit. Simeon Armour, Phil's brother and manager of the company's Kansas City operations, explained the problem and the solution at which the packers had arrived: Suppose a dealer arrived at the stockyard with a herd of cattle, only half of which suited Armour's needs on that particular day. The dealer, however, insisted on selling the entire herd as a whole. "I want part of those cattle," Simeon Armour explained, "and perhaps my neighboring packer wants part of them. I may go to that [packer] and say 'Here, there is no use of our bidding against each other; I will take half of them and you half.'" In the meatpackers' minds, the activity was less collusion than justifiable necessity: beef was perishable and supplies and demand fickle. Why not divvy up supply to match demand? But there the "cooperation" stopped, Armour added. "We are the biggest fighters, and have the biggest time in cutting each other's throats of any class of business that is done in America." In markets where the brothers competed head to head, Simeon groused, "we are cutting each other's throat all the time in the way of competition. I am sorry to see it." As for setting prices, that, too, was the child of necessity: in the 1880s, Swift, the Armours, and a few others competed most directly against each other in the urban Northeast, but in those early years, there was not yet enough business for all of them, or, more accurately, not enough business to pay for the investment each had made in plant, warehouses, and railroad cars. The men recognized that until they could build up their operations in other parts of the country (as Armour was doing in the Deep South), it made sense to cooperate, in this case by setting prices for meat sold in northeastern cities.

The packers were not alone in cooperating in order to manage markets and avoid ruinous competition. "Combinations" and trusts spanned the diversity of American commerce: railroads, oil refining, cottonseed oil, and whiskey; rope and cord, window sashes and frames; pig iron, wallpaper, and barbed wire; stoves, beer, and gunpowder. Most of these arrangements were little more than gentlemen's agreements, unenforceable in court and so almost always doomed to failure. Only a handful followed John D. Rockefeller's example in the oil-refining industry, devising binding partnerships cemented by pages of complex contracts. The rationale for these transactions was obvious to those who created them: many businessmen of that era believed that competition was inefficient because it hindered the smooth functioning of an industry and thus of the economy as a whole. That had been the lesson of the railroad industry, where relentless competition provoked rate warfare that threatened to destroy the entire transportation infrastructure. Moreover, many Americans embraced the view that bigger was better: operating a large factory lowered the cost of manufacturing and thus prices that consumers paid for goods, just as, in the minds of many, a single, giant abattoir was more cost-efficient than many small slaughterhouses.

Still, the rise of giant corporations raised troubling questions, and the proliferation of trusts and combinations seemed to indicate that, left to its own devices, competition devoured itself, leaving only a string of monopolies to mark its grave. Was competition thus inherently inefficient? What would happen if monopoly won the day? Would monopolists control supply and thus price, leaving consumers at their mercy? By their nature, monopolies barred opportunity for others. Was that the price Americans had to pay for a free-market society? Or was there, as some suggested, a natural limit to competition? If so, how to identify and impose that limit without also destroying the pursuit of opportunity that was the bedrock of American life?

Until answers could be found, many Americans opted to counter the power of the Rockefellers and Swifts of the world with their own cooperative ventures. In 1886, skilled workers organized the American Federation of Labor in order to amass the clout necessary to meet their corporate employers on a level playing field. (Those employers argued, no surprise, that unions hindered their right as owners to operate their companies as they saw fit.) Butchers did the same: when Armour and Swift began selling dressed beef in New York, Philadelphia, and other cities, meat cutters complained that the invaders were trying to monopolize and control the fresh meat business, leaving not just them but consumers, too, "at the mercy of . . . soulless corporations," as one put it. The butchers responded with their own "counter-combination." The president of the Butchers' National Protective Association argued that the tactic was a necessity in "an age of organizations," because those who failed to combine would "fall far behind in the race for business success."

Fears of monopoly had already inspired thirteen states to pass or ponder antitrust legislation, and in 1885, the U.S. Senate held hearings on alleged collusion in the railroad industry. Witnesses regaled senators with complaints about the railroads' wily methods of dispensing special rates and rebates, and details of the railroad men's cooperation in setting those rates and rebates. The testimony seemed proof positive that tycoons like Vanderbilt — and Swift and Armour — rarely acted in the public's interest and ought to be reined in. Those hearings resulted in the creation of the Interstate Commerce Commission, a first tentative effort to manage the new national economy with regulations aimed at mitigating the chaos in the railroad industry (regulations that, it should be noted, the roads supported: here, finally, was a way to end chronic rate wars).

So when cattlemen complained about a Beef Trust, their words resonated with politicians who had discovered that antimonopoly rhetoric played well with voters, especially in western states and territories. In 1888, the Senate opened hearings to examine the dressed-beef industry. An array of the aggrieved showed up to testify, from ranchers and livestock dealers to butchers and packinghouse employees. Most of them unloaded complaints in the vein of an Iowa cattle feeder who was convinced that the packers colluded to destroy his profits. The man explained that he received Chicago price reports via telegraph and knew when stockyard supplies were running "light," a signal that cattle prices would rise. When that happened, he loaded his livestock and himself onto the next train to Chicago. And it never failed, he complained: by the time he got there, receipts were running heavy and he couldn't get the price he wanted for his livestock. He was convinced that the Big Four were manipulating supplies so as to manipulate price. It did not occur to the man that other cattle farmers read the same telegraph reports and made the same decision to head to Chicago, thereby turning a cattle shortage into a glut. Another witness had gone to Arizona in 1883, hell-bent on grabbing his share of the cattle bonanza. By his own admission, he was "entirely unfamiliar with the business," but that did not stop him. He bought cattle and took them to Kansas City, where the dressed-beef kings offered him what he regarded as an insultingly low price. More experienced sellers advised him to take the offer, but the would-be cattle king decided to outsmart the packers by taking his livestock straight to the East Coast. No one would buy it there, he complained, and that, too, he blamed on the long arm of the "Dressed Beef Trust," which he believed shipped its cheap beef east and employed a "local stool-pigeon" to pass the goods off to butchers. That kind of testimony, which

dominated the hearings, confirmed what the committee's members, all of whom represented cattle-producing states, already believed: the packers were robbing cattle producers at one end and
driving up consumer prices at the other, all to satisfy their greed.

Phil Armour begged to differ. He and the other packers had
been subpoenaed by the committee, but only Armour showed
up. After days of hearing complaints from ranchers, farmers, and
butchers, and given that the senators had thus far demonstrated
little understanding of how stockyards, meatpacking, and meat
retailing worked, Armour's testimony must have sounded like the
words of an alien being. Where other witnesses focused on their
small piece of the stage — the butcher shop, the ranch, the stockyard — Armour described an industry that was international in
scope and boggling in its complexity. He regaled the committee with statistical evidence of the global demand for cowhide;
discussed the taxes that hindered the manufacture and sale of
American oleomargarine; described livestock production in New
Zealand, Australia, and South America; explained changes in
consumer demand in foreign markets; and tallied the amount of
beef and mutton imported into the United Kingdom in 1888 as
well as the price of tallow in New York City and "oleo oil" in Rot-
terdam.

A no-doubt statistics-dazed committee finally managed to
steer Armour toward what it viewed as the main point. Had he
and the other beef packers practiced collusion in order to monopolize the nation's meat supplies? No, said Armour. There was
no monopoly and no collusion. The beef men "combined" for the
same reason as railroads and livestock shippers: if they did not,
price wars would drive them to ruin. What outsiders regarded
as collusion, insisted Armour, was simply smart business. The
prices he paid at Kansas City or Chicago were based on the supply
at hand, the supply en route, and the type and number of cattle he
needed. If someone showed up in Chicago "with a couple of car-
loads of steer from Kansas," and Armour knew that "a thousand
more" were "coming in from the West," he behaved as would any
smart businessman: he adjusted his buying price. "We do the best

we can to buy cattle as cheap as we can," he said. "We are here to make money. I wish I could make more. If I knew of any method of making more out of cattle I should certainly do it." And, he added, had he "not been a little inventive and enterprising," he wouldn't have made any money at all. "I know I couldn't do it in the old fashioned way," he said.

Armour denied that the dressed-beef men were responsible for driving down prices paid for live cattle. Simple math said otherwise. Between 1880 and 1887, he explained, the nation's cattle supply had risen 37 percent (thanks mainly to the cattle bonanza), but the human population had increased just 20 percent. Cattle supply outstripped demand, and so prices for live cattle had dropped. Rather than criticize packers, he argued, ranchers and farmers ought to thank them for opening new markets for beef among factory workers, in the Deep South where pork once ruled, and in Europe, where American imports rose annually. Without those markets, cattle producers would be in even worse shape.

Armour also explained that packers weren't hoarding meat in order to drive up the price paid by consumers; rather, they stored it so they could sell it year-round at a stable price, a point he explained with the example of tenderloins. The packers procured those choice cuts during just two months of the year, when corn-fattened cattle from Iowa and Missouri arrived at the yards. If the packers dumped every tenderloin on the market as fresh meat, prices would fall while the supply lasted, and then soar as it dwindled. So Armour's employees stored those cuts in freezers, dispensing them as ordered by his customers throughout the year. Nor was he gouging anyone. The choice cuts that Americans demanded constituted only a small portion of a carcass. Inevitably, demand for choice cuts outstripped supplies, and so prices for them were high. Prices of the less desirable cuts, in contrast, remained low because carcasses yielded large quantities of a product that few people wanted.

He dismissed the claim that the packers had plotted to dominate and control the stockyards. Armour explained that with-

out access to the well-organized terminal markets like the stockyards in Chicago and Kansas City, the incorporated ventures that
dominated cattle ranching would find it impossible to sell their
enormous herds in a timely and efficient manner; those yards
guaranteed that the livestock would find buyers. Moreover, those
ranchers were dependent on the global marketplace to which Armour served as a conduit. The complex mechanisms of the national and foreign markets, he argued, justified the so-called conspiracy of which he and the others were accused. The "trust" he
was charged with operating was simply a means by which he and
other big packers managed the domestic and global market for a
desirable, perishable good.

Armour's nuanced argument was lost on the committeemen,
who had begun the hearings with their minds made up: the "artificial and abnormal centralization" of livestock markets, especially at Chicago, they concluded, had spawned a Beef Trust
whose members intentionally engaged in actions aimed at robbing cattle ranchers at one end and consumers at the other. But
there was little they could or would do about it. In the late 1880s,
few Americans, and certainly not members of Congress, understood how to manage the nation's rambunctious economy, and
many weren't convinced that it should be managed. Despite the
ubiquity of trusts and combinations, many people feared that
government regulation would destroy the lifeblood of the economy: competition. Nor was it clear that "trusts" were inherently
evil: the price of sugar, oil, and meat, for example, had dropped
in the hands of alleged trusts. Indeed, economists since have calculated that during the age of robber barons and monopolists,
the industries accused of colluding to restrain trade actually increased their output, and prices for their goods fell rather than
rose. In the case of the alleged Beef Trust, the Senate investigators failed to grasp the way built-in expenditures, from wages and
maintenance to shipping and fuel, drive up the prices of goods in
a national economy. Their belief that Armour and other packers
earned excessive profits was based entirely on the fact that the
prices butchers and wholesalers paid for beef appeared to be high

relative to the prices those packers paid for cattle at the stock-yards.

In 1890, the packer hearings and the outburst of antimonopoly fever resulted in the passage of the Sherman Antitrust Act, which banned any activity that restrained trade. But the law proved a milquetoast piece of legislation that appealed to voters and eased politicians' consciences and did little to stanch corporate power. It oozed loopholes, and in the decade after its passage, merg-ers, syndicates, and holding companies proliferated as corporate managers sought ways to create efficiency and earn profits. More to the point, however, it also left the dressed-beef packers free to expand their empires, and that, in turn, saddled them with a reputation for playing foul with the nation's stomachs and placed them on a collision course with a president and a novelist.

3

THE (HIGH) PRICE OF SUCCESS

IN 1902, A MYSTERIOUS and short-lived "beef famine" drove meat prices into the stratosphere. "BEEF TRUST SQUEEZES POOR FOR $100,000,000" announced a headline in the *New York Herald* in March 1902. The *Herald* reporter told readers that a "Beef Trust" "dominat[ed]" the nation's food supplies by using "despotic and aggressive" tactics that had "killed" competition. Readers who stayed with the story — and who could resist? — learned that the trust controlled 75 percent of the nation's egg and poultry supply. Swift executives had "secretly" stashed 43 million eggs in cold storage and planned to release or hold the cache "as suits their convenience in manipulating the market." The trust (whose membership numbered either four, five, or six firms, depending on the whim and knowledge of reporters) practiced collusion through a hired hand who maintained a secret office somewhere on Madison Avenue in New York City. The trust controlled the stockyards, cheated livestock producers, fixed prices for steak, and woe be to anyone or anything that tried to stop it. Americans' only hope of escaping the trust's "grip," concluded one reporter, was by becoming "rigid vegetarians."

Cooler heads tried to explain that the "famine," which was less a famine than a temporary shortage of preferred cuts like tenderloin, had more to do with weather conditions and tight cattle supplies than the evil machinations of corporate tycoons. Agriculture Secretary James Wilson, himself an Iowa farmer and livestock producer, blamed high meat prices on a bad corn crop. "Cattle and meat," he explained, "like all other commodities, have to follow the laws of supply and demand"; supplies of corn and cattle were low and prices of meat high. "Corn is the corner-stone of the livestock industry," explained the author of an essay in *Century* magazine. When the corn crop was "off," beef prices rose. He added that farmers could not bring cattle or hogs to market weight fast enough to keep pace with consumer demand caused in part by an increase in national population; meat prices would remain high until cattle and hog herds increased.

Logic and facts be damned. The *Herald*'s exposé, which was reprinted in hundreds of newspapers and read into the *Congressional Record*, ran long on supposition and rumor and short on substance and facts. Many of its most dramatic revelations came from anonymous sources alleged to be former employees of one or another of the packinghouses. But its accuracy, or lack thereof, mattered not a whit to readers predisposed to believe the worst of corporations in general and the meatpackers in particular, and who were increasingly suspicious about foodstuffs that came from factories, especially their meat. Although the meatpackers did not yet know it in 1902, the famine uproar would land them in the crossfire of a then-unknown novelist named Upton Sinclair.

The standard version of the passage of the Pure Food and Drug Act, signed into law in 1906, goes like this: In that year, Upton Sinclair published *The Jungle* and exposed horrific sanitary conditions in American meatpacking plants. Outraged citizens demanded that Congress do something. Congress complied and passed legislation aimed at safeguarding the nation's food supply. As is often the case with historical events, however, that account bears little resemblance to the facts. The Pure Food and Drug

Act had little to do with meat, and *The Jungle* was a last straw, not a first blow. By the time Sinclair's book appeared, Americans had been fretting about food safety and debating food and drug regulation for more than fifty years. Back in the 1880s, for example, when the dressed-beef men first threatened the power of the railroad-stockyard-abattoir stronghold, their enemies lobbed accusations of tainted meat precisely because they knew such charges would resonate with consumers already wary about their food supply system. Opponents accused the meatpackers of processing diseased cattle and dousing their beef with ammonia and other toxins. The author of one widely disseminated story denounced Chicago beef as "wholly unfit to be eaten. It can only feed fever and foster disease."

Why did Americans wait so long to act on food safety? One reason is that in the United States, the legislative machine grinds slowly, and food producers resisted efforts to regulate and constrain their businesses. Consider, briefly, the (not-at-all-brief) conflict in the 1880s over the manufacture and sale of oleomargarine, the butter substitute that meatpackers manufactured from beef byproducts. Oleo found a ready market both in the United States and abroad because it was cheaper than real butter and appealed to consumers trying to stretch meager food budgets. But dairy farmers, whose incomes depended in part on butter sales, denounced oleo as a dangerous product sold by greedy capitalists for the purpose of driving honest farmers like themselves to the poorhouse. They asked Congress to tax its manufacture and sale, hoping to price oleo out of the market. The dairymen's chief supporter, Robert M. La Follette of Wisconsin, then in his first term in the House, denounced margarine as a fraud. "It is made to look like something it is not; to taste and smell like something it is not; to sell like something it is not, and so deceive the purchaser." Nonsense, replied oleo's supporters. Margarine was an improvement over butter and evidence of the march of commercial and scientific progress. Then why, queried a real-butter advocate, was "oleomargarine sacred? Why may we tax manufactured whiskey and not tax manufactured butter?" In the end, Congress passed and President Grover Cleveland signed a watered-down version of the original proposal, one strong enough to make the point, but not enough to tax margarine out of existence.

Competing interests like these stalled the food safety debate, but so did legitimate and complex questions of constitutionality. Since the colonial era, Americans had relied on local governments, primarily municipal authority, to legislate matters relating to food: municipal ordinances mandated weights and measures, for example, and banned the sale of putrid or poisonous foodstuffs. Given that long-standing local tradition, many people were justifiably wary of using either state or federal authority to dictate the ingredients that manufacturers could and could not use in making, say, mustard or coffee. If the federal government imposed food standards, argued a member of the House during one of dozens of debates over the issue, "how long will it be before he will say what kind of clothing we shall wear in summer or in winter, what kind of horse [we] shall drive" or how a man ought to "run [his] farm[?]" Another congressman feared that the enforcement of food safety laws would require "a pestilential lot of spies, meddlers, and informers" whose actions would render the government itself "a great deal more impure than any food or drink." (A few years later, anti-Prohibitionists made that same argument against the amendment to ban alcohol.)

In the late nineteenth and early twentieth centuries, these long-standing arguments lost much of their clout. The germ theory and other then-new medical and scientific tools and ideas, including the growing use of the microscope, altered Americans' understanding of the way disease functioned and spread, and challenged the notion that local control of the public's health was either possible or desirable. But as more Americans exchanged country for city, and plow and hoe for typewriter and assembly line, their relationship with food itself changed, and that, too, forced many people to ponder what an earlier generation would have found unthinkable. "We are no longer a nation of farmers living in sight of our food supply," a writer reminded the readers of a women's magazine. "The journey between us and [our] food supply, once only as long as from our own field and garden to our back door, has been lengthening year by year." In modern America, food traveled "through the hands of more and more middlemen. It is time we found out what happens to it along this journey." No wonder Americans fretted about their food supply and wrangled over how to monitor it. When families set their tables with foods that were shipped halfway across the country, local governance alone no longer made sense. But who should decide what could or should go into a can of tomatoes? The states? Congress? Were Americans doomed to eat mystery foods prepared at the whim of giant corporations? Were Americans' stomachs the servants of private interests and corporate profits?

But Americans coupled their fears to a sense of entitlement. Any increase in the price of porterhouse or roasts, even if only a penny a pound, as was the case during the so-called beef famine, provoked outrage. Urban Americans didn't care that meat comes from animals, or that food for those animals, like its human counterpart, depends on weather. Never mind the price of corn that determined the cost of raising hogs and cattle. Never mind the push-pull of the global demand for American beef and pork, demand that drove up prices paid by consumers at home. Never mind that the making of meat, like the making of steel, shoes, or chairs, depended on the cost of fuel, power, labor, and the like. As far as consumers were concerned, the price of meat was connected only to their own pocketbooks, to an intangible price defined not in dollars or relative to rainfall, but simply as "affordable."

The relationship between the nation's food production system and the people who ate that food embodied a contradiction: Americans insisted on access to cheap food, regardless of its true cost, but believed the worst of those who made that cheap food possible and abundant. And in the early twentieth century, the meatpackers processed and distributed not just meat but a host of other foods as well. It's not surprising that they became the primary targets of the public's outrage over food prices.

• • •

By the 1890s, all of the big packers had followed Armour's lead and added hog slaughter to their activities, and bacon, ham, and fresh pork to their offerings. They also sold sausages, bolognas, and "luncheon" meats, and a host of other meat-based foods like canned gravy. They built laboratories and hired scientists in an effort to squeeze as much profit as possible from a carcass, whether bovine or porcine. They operated glue factories, sold animal oils as gun lubricant, and transformed byproducts into billiard balls, chess pieces, buttons, sandpaper, and fertilizer. Thyroid, thymus, pancreas, and spleen could serve as ingredients in tonics and elixirs, or as compounds used to tan hides and print fabric. A bemused commentator described the packers as magicians who sold beef and pork simply "for the purpose of getting [the meat] out of the way" in order to perform "tricks" with their byproducts. They eyed cattle and hogs "with distrust," suspicious that the animals were holding back a source of profit. There was money in that magic, lots of it. The more byproducts a packer had, the lower the price at which he could sell his beef and still earn a profit. The larger the packer, the greater his volume of wastes, and the bigger his cost-cutting advantage.

But the meatpackers had also discovered the magic of diversification, and they performed tricks with vegetables and fruits, milk, cheese, and eggs. And why not? They owned thousands of refrigerator railcars and continent-wide networks of warehouses chilled by mechanical refrigeration (a relatively new technology that spread quickly in the 1880s and 1890s). They had developed the expertise necessary to deliver large quantities of perishable goods to retailers and wholesalers, skills that were relatively rare at the time. Having constructed this technological and managerial infrastructure, it made sense to use it for other goods as well. Moreover, the meatpackers found a ready market for these services. In California, for example, industrial farmers — "growers," they called themselves — clamored for the one thing that hindered both profits and expansion: reliable, speedy transport to carry their tomatoes and lettuce, grapes, oranges, and plums from West Coast to East. When Gus Swift moved to Chicago back in 1875, he would have been hard-pressed to find a fresh orange any time of year, and if he had, he would have paid dearly for it. By 1900, oranges — and bananas, plums, and peaches — had become year-round staples. Some of that produce arrived as canned goods (the packers owned many canning factories), but a great deal of it was delivered fresh, carried in the packers' railcars and stored in their warehouses. The packers' ability to centralize and organize distribution injected efficiency into what we take for granted today but what was new then — a national food system — with the result that Americans enjoyed access to more food, and a wider variety of foodstuffs, than at any time in their history — food provided, it should be noted, by a shrinking number of farmers.

So the *New York Herald*'s claims that the Beef Trust controlled both food and prices rang true with many people. The reporting prompted the U.S. attorney general to launch an investigation, but he found nothing to support the newspaper's charges. Ten or twenty years earlier, this particular scandal might have gone the way of so many *causes célèbres* and day-old newspapers, or been overshadowed by other, bigger journalistic exposés — the *Herald*'s series landed on newsstands just as Ida Tarbell published her investigation into the inner workings of the Standard Oil Company. But in 1902, the man in the White House shared Americans' rage about corporate mischief and, ever the savvy politician, understood that in an urban nation high food prices could knock even the most beloved of elected officials out of office.

President Theodore Roosevelt's considerable historical baggage includes his reputation as a "trust buster," but his view of corporations was nuanced and complex. On one hand, he shared Americans' mistrust of corporations and harbored no illusions about the greedy self-absorption of many corporate titans, as demonstrated by what happened when his Department of Justice filed an antitrust suit against a proposed railroad merger masterminded by a collection of Wall Street financiers. None other than J. P. Morgan, the biggest of the big financiers, descended upon the White House to straighten things out. "If we have done anything wrong," he told Roosevelt, "send your man to my man and they can fix it up," believing, apparently, that Roosevelt was simply another tycoon who played by the same rules as himself. The president declined the suggestion, describing the encounter as an "illuminating illustration of the Wall Street point of view. Mr. Morgan could not help regarding me as a big rival operator who either intended to ruin all his interests or else could be induced to come to an agreement to ruin none." On the other hand, Roosevelt had no desire to dismantle the corporate-industrial structure. Like many Americans, he recognized that large, national enterprises drove what he described as "the wheels of modern progress," and he was less interested in busting trusts than in using federal authority to corral corporate power and manage an economy that was as temperamental as it was robust.

So it's no surprise that as president, Roosevelt engaged in battle with a variety of business behemoths, including the railroads, steel makers, tobacco manufacturers, Standard Oil, and, of course, the alleged Beef Trust. Indeed, from a political perspective, Roosevelt's war on the Beef Trust was his smartest battle. Voters blamed meat makers for high food prices, and packers were an easy and visible target. (It was also the meat men's misfortune that the president had owned and worked a cattle ranch in Dakota Territory in the 1880s; he understood and sympathized with cattlemen's woes.)

Initially, Roosevelt went after the packers on the grounds that they violated antitrust and interstate commerce laws, a challenging angle of assault. In 1902, the Sherman Antitrust Act remained what it had been at the time of its passage in 1890: a model of flabby political expedience that did little to clarify the distinction between mergers and trusts; between corporations that were simply large and those that monopolized industries; between "good" trusts and "bad" ones (the latter being a distinction in which Roosevelt firmly believed). Worse, neither that law nor any other had cornered that elusive animal known as interstate commerce. The Constitution granted Congress the authority to "regulate commerce . . . among the several states," a principle affirmed by the Supreme Court in 1824. There certainty ended. Neither the states nor Congress, neither chief executive nor judiciary (indeed, the judiciary least of all), knew for certain what constituted interstate commerce. Suppose a packer bought cattle at the stockyards in Kansas City, transformed the animals into carcasses in the same city, and then shipped those to Indiana. Where did his business end? In Missouri? Or in Indiana? What body ought to regulate said business? The state of Missouri? The federal Congress? The packers themselves? Did Congress have all the authority over interstate trade, or only part of it? How much authority could or should remain with the states? For that matter, what marked the distinction between "commerce" and "manufacturing"? Questions abounded but answers would not be found anytime soon. In early 1903, and in response to the *Herald*'s reports, a judge issued an injunction forbidding the packers from fixing prices and from engaging in "combination"— unless it was necessary to do so. The ruling allowed the packers to withhold meat from the market whenever necessary in order to "prevent the over-accumulation" of those "perishable articles." In short, the judge affirmed the point Phil Armour had made fifteen years earlier about the difficulties of making and selling perishable foodstuffs for a national market.

But not long after that ruling, and in a case of excruciatingly bad timing (at least in terms of public relations), officials at Armour, Swift, and Morris, another major dressed-beef outfit, made a move that confirmed the public's suspicions: they merged most of their assets and created a separate entity, the National Packing Co., to manage those shared holdings. There was nothing illegal about the venture, but that was irrelevant to an angry public; the merger seemed to confirm the belief that the packers wanted the whole earth. When Gus Swift died a few weeks later, the manager of the company's Trenton, New Jersey, facility lowered the building's flag to half-staff. An enraged delegation of neighbors promptly descended upon his office. Swift did not deserve the honor, the group's spokesman informed the manager, because he was "simply a dead multi-millionaire, a trust magnate." Raise the flag, he warned, or the crowd would "make trouble." As the neighbors "shout[ed] in triumph," the Swift employee hoisted the flag.

The combination of public outrage and the new holding company encouraged Roosevelt to move forward with his plan to force the packers into submission, if not through the courts then by some other means. "Daylight," he believed, was a "powerful discourager of evil." Shine enough light on a situation, its evils would be revealed, and lawmakers would cure them. To that end, he prodded Congress to establish a Bureau of Corporations whose employees would gather information about corporate activity, analyze the results, and present Congress with recommendations for action. With his usual bull-in-a-china-shop enthusiasm, the president pronounced it an important step toward solving the problems posed by "the great corporations and corporate combinations" and the relationship between them and the public well-being. The bureau's information, he assured the skeptical, would be deployed "in a spirit of absolute fairness and justice and of entire fearlessness."

The bureau's first (and, as it turned out, only) task was to flood the packers' operations with daylight. Roosevelt asked James Garfield (son of the former president) to launch a full investigation into meat making in general and the packers' firms in particular, including company files and account books. Alas, the report that Garfield delivered to the president in the spring of 1905 failed to satisfy TR or to mitigate the public's outrage. It consisted of three-hundred-plus pages packed with tables, statistics, charts, graphs, and excruciatingly detailed descriptions of American livestock production and meat processing, all couched in equally excruciating prose. It was, remarked one newspaper editor, not the kind of thing "young ladies will take to the seashore for perusal during vacation days." Nor, Roosevelt knew, was it a document that would captivate a public accustomed to the sensationalism of yellow journalism. Worse, instead of confirming the public's suspicions, Garfield concluded that high meat prices had nothing to do with cabals and conspiracies and everything to do with crop failures and corn prices. He confirmed what the agriculture secretary had tried to explain three years earlier: the corn crop in 1901 had been "exceptionally poor," and so meat prices had gone up in 1902. When crop conditions improved the following year, prices paid for livestock fell, and so had the cost of meat for consumers. Garfield also affirmed what packers had long insisted: Americans enjoyed quality, affordable meat because the packers subsidized its production and distribution with other components of their operations, especially the processing and sale of byproducts.

Garfield's conclusions mattered not the least to the public, whose reactions alternated between outrage and uproar. As one newspaper put it, the public had no interest in "tedious and voluminous reports. It only wants to know why its steaks and roasts cost more than they did a short time ago." Few people bothered to wade through Garfield's charts and tables, so the press performed its usual magic, simplifying his complex analysis, contents, and conclusions to the point of distortion and portraying Garfield as a patsy who'd been bought off by the packers. Garfield himself shrugged off the calls for his job (and his head). He knew that his findings failed to accord with "popular demands — but it is the truth," he wrote, and "I care not for popular clamor."

Fortunately for Theodore Roosevelt, prices for all foods, and especially meat, continued to climb, keeping the pot of public rage at full boil, and not long after Garfield delivered his report, a Chicago grand jury indicted the packers for antitrust violations. Even better, the editors of the national publication *Everybody's Magazine* ran a multipart exposé on the meat industry or, as the series' author, Charles Edward Russell, termed it, "the greatest trust in the world." The series ran for much of 1905 and detailed the inner workings of a "greedy monopoly" aimed at crushing anything and everyone in its path and "follow[ing] to its logical conclusion the idea of the survival of the fittest, the right of the strong to annihilate the weak." But Roosevelt knew that so far, the courts had delivered nothing but disappointment, and it was possible that neither the new exposé nor high prices for steak would be enough to bring the packers to heel. "The experiences that [the attorney general] has had in dealing with these beef trust people convinces me that there is very little that they will stop at," he fumed. And so TR added another weapon to his arsenal: the public's demand for federal legislation to guarantee the safety of the nation's food supply.

Up to that moment, Roosevelt had not been particularly interested in the pure food and drug crusade, preferring to devote his first term in office to attacking trusts, monopolies, and arrogant tycoons. By the start of his second stint as president, however, the demand for food safety legislation had reached a ferocity that he could not ignore, thanks in part to a string of journalistic exposés that regaled readers with tales of poisoned medicine, adulterated coffee, tainted canned foods, and the like, all of it, according to investigative reporters, the work of greedy, unscrupulous corporations. The president invited food reformers to meet with him and used his State of the Union message to ask Congress to protect American stomachs from conscience-deprived manufacturers. In true Rooseveltian fashion, he also traveled the highway of political expedience, asking for a law that would safeguard both consumers and "legitimate" manufacturers. Then, in early 1905, *The Lancet,* a respected British medical journal, ran a series of articles written by Adolph Smith, an Englishman with medical expertise, who detailed unsanitary conditions in Chicago packinghouses; the articles' contents were widely reported in the American press. Here, Roosevelt realized, was a way to couple the pure food campaign with his assault on the packers. And that explains his temporary alliance with Upton Sinclair, an impetuous, publicity-starved writer who had recently completed a novel about life in Packingtown, the neighborhood surrounding the Chicago Union Stock Yards.

Sinclair, who was then in his late twenties, had thus far stomped through life burdened by a chip on his shoulder: he believed that the world owed him not just a living but fame and fortune, too. To his disgust, the rest of humanity had failed to cooperate. He routinely asked others for financial support so that he could write, always reminding those he hit up that he had a wife and child to support. At one point, he badgered novelist Owen Wister, who had written the bestseller *The Virginian,* for money. Wister suggested that Sinclair get a job; Sinclair dismissed the idea. Casting about for a way to boost his sagging morale and fatten his bank account, the author latched on to socialism as the tonic that would rejuvenate both.

In our time, socialism has come to be viewed as more of a punch line than a substantive political stance, but a century ago, many thoughtful Americans embraced all manner of communal and "cooperative" ideologies, politics, and projects as a way to mitigate the stress of urban industrialism. Women from all backgrounds banded together to operate communal child care programs and kitchens. Factory workers organized benevolent associations to support each other in times of injury and poor health, and at death. So it's not surprising that an American version of socialism gained favor among voters interested in mitigating corporate power, in eliminating disparities between rich and poor, and in promoting social justice. The American Socialist Party enjoyed its greatest popularity in the first fifteen years of the twentieth century. Its presidential candidate, Eugene Debs, won 3 percent of the popular vote in 1904 and 1908 and 6 percent in 1912. Eighteen cities had socialist mayors, and socialists sat in the New York and Rhode Island legislatures and in Congress, too. Americans still enjoy the benefits of one popular socialist project: in many cities, voters in the early twentieth century transferred ownership of utilities — water and sewer systems, and gas and electrical services — from private companies to municipal authority.

Among the converts to socialist politics was Upton Sinclair, whose upbringing had introduced him to economic extremes. He had grown up in poverty thanks to his father's fondness for drink (which eventually killed the elder man) but was exposed to great wealth thanks to his father's relatives. Sinclair claimed he wanted nothing that smacked of the easy life that led, in his view, to corruption both moral and political. The wheeling and dealing of the nation's rich, he wrote, constituted "invisible governments" that undermined democratic institutions. But Sinclair's personal desire for fame and fortune undercut his enthusiasm for socialist reform. "One feels," commented a man who was asked by a potential publisher to read the manuscript that became *The Jungle*, "that what is at the bottom of his [political] fierceness is not nearly so much desire to help the poor as hatred of the rich." Still, the writer's newfound political passion fired his literary ambitions. "I am going to do my share," he wrote. "I am going to write a Socialist novel . . . I am going to write it with the feeling that a million readers are following it and demanding that it be well done" — a million readers who would, presumably, buy his book and thus relieve him of both his poverty and his anonymity. He latched on to the packing industry as a framework for the book and in 1904 traveled to Chicago during a meatpacking strike to gather material for the new book. There he met packinghouse workers as well as social reformer Jane Addams, who introduced him to Adolph Smith, then in Chicago gathering material for his *Lancet* series.

Sinclair began writing his manuscript in late December 1904, and in late February 1905, the editor of a socialist magazine, *Appeal to Reason*, started publishing the work as a serial. The magazine had a paid circulation of nearly three hundred thousand readers and offered Sinclair $500 for the rights. But even socialists, it transpired, weren't sufficiently interested in the great American diatribe; the magazine's editor declined to publish the entire manuscript because readers had lost interest. Sinclair began hunting for a mainstream publisher. One editor expressed interest but complained that the novel's emphasis on "blood and guts" detracted from the "vital human interest" necessary to carry the story. When the novelist refused to make changes, the editor canceled the contract. Five more publishers turned him down. The tide turned when Sinclair visited the offices of Doubleday, Page & Company, which published books and a popular national magazine, *World's Work*. An editor and publicist there decided that the combination of Sinclair's bravado and the novel's gory details marked a sure winner, and in February 1906, the book arrived in stores. The publicist, enthusiastic despite being "seriously embarrassed at times" by the novelist's impetuous behavior, hauled Sinclair from one interview to the next, determined to make a bestseller of the polemic.

Among those who perused the book's pages was Theodore Roosevelt, who received at least four copies, including one from Sinclair himself and one from a senator. After reading it, the president invited the novelist to a meeting at the White House. Roosevelt's enthusiasm stemmed more from his determination to battle the packers than from his approval of the novel. As a rule, he despised the sort of half-baked rabble-rousing that filled its pages. ("I have such awful times with reformers of the hysterical and sensational stamp," he once wrote.) "Personally," he would later tell Sinclair, "I think that one of the chief early effects" of socialism "would be the elimination by starvation . . . of the community on whose behalf [it] would be invoked." Despite the novel's flaws and Sinclair's politics, however, Roosevelt recognized that *The Jungle* was tailor-made for generating publicity to power his anti-packer battering ram.

By the spring of 1906, he needed the help. His administration's most recent attempt to convict the packers in court had ended, like every previous effort, in failure. Government attorneys had based this most recent case on documents compiled in 1904 during the Garfield investigation. The packers argued that the material was inadmissible: they had cooperated with Garfield because he assured them that the information they provided could not and would not be used by the Justice Department. The presiding judge agreed with the packers and granted them immunity, a move that effectively ended the trial. The "charitable view . . . of the Judge's action," groused Roosevelt, "is that he has lost some of the powers of his mind." Worse, although both the House and Senate were then debating food safety legislation, as usual, bills in both houses were mired in debates about the limits of constitutional authority. Once again, a food bill seemed destined to drown in a sea of politics, and TR's campaign against the packers doomed to failure.

And so an egomaniac socialist became Roosevelt's weapon of desperation, and the president got busy with plans to use it. In response to both the *Lancet* articles and *The Jungle*, agriculture secretary Wilson had decided to send his own team to Chicago to investigate the packinghouses, and Roosevelt insisted that Sinclair be brought in to aid the cause. A "merely perfunctory investigation" would not suffice, the president told Wilson, and instructed the secretary to recruit a "first-class man" to meet with Sinclair and obtain from him a list of witnesses who could verify what Roosevelt still regarded as wild exaggeration. "You must keep absolutely secret your choice of a man," he added.

Keeping secrets, however, was not on Sinclair's agenda. Having gained the attention of the White House, he intended to use that clout to boost the book's sales, even if doing so interfered with the president's plans. He bombarded Roosevelt with letters and telegrams demanding that the chief executive mount a more public and vigorous defense of *The Jungle*. "My dear Mr. Sinclair," Roosevelt wrote on April 11, "you seemed to be a good deal more agitated than the facts warrant." "Keep quiet," he demanded, in a futile effort to contain his loose cannon. "I cannot afford to be hurried any more than I can afford to be stopped from making the investigation," which, he added, might take "months." It was all wasted on the novelist-genius. In the time it took Roosevelt to write that letter, Sinclair had dashed off another missive plus a telegram. The barrage prompted the president to add a postscript to his letter: "Your second telegram has just come; really, Mr. Sinclair, you must keep your head," the president wrote.

Roosevelt's ire increased when Wilson's men handed over their report in early April. The document, detailed, thorough, and systematic, concluded that meat inspection could and should be improved, but it also refuted most of the charges made in both *The Lancet* and *The Jungle*. Its tone and content were not much different from those of the tedious affair submitted by Garfield a year earlier and therefore no competition with Sinclair's sensational novel when it came to convincing the public that American meat was safe. Caught between a potential media bonanza and the turgid prose of government bureaucrats and fearful that Congress would once again push food safety back into a closet, Roosevelt sent yet another team of investigators to Chicago, this time men of his choosing. A few weeks later, they handed over a study that contained precisely what the president wanted and needed: confirmation of Packingtown's evils, couched in graphic detail but in language that avoided the reckless hysteria of *The Jungle*. But having gotten what he wished for, Roosevelt realized that he needed to handle it with care. American livestock producers and packers had grown accustomed to large foreign demand, but in recent years, other governments had used meat imports as tools for political bargaining with the United States. Roosevelt feared that if he released the document's contents, an already contentious diplomatic situation would be made worse and that panicky foreign buyers would cancel orders for meat. But he also wanted Congress to pass food safety legislation, and he preferred that it do so without prodding from him. He decided to withhold the report and use it as a big stick in case the House and Senate leaned toward dismissing food safety yet again.

But Sinclair managed to lay his hands on a copy of the document, and he regarded its contents as proof that his novel was no fiction. He demanded that Roosevelt publicize the findings. The president refused. Doing so, he explained, might satisfy "the apostles of sensationalism," but it would damage the livelihoods of "stock-growers, ranchers, hired men, cowboys, [and] farmers," people who were "guilty of no misconduct whatever." Upton Sinclair, fair-weather socialist to the end, was not interested in cowboys or hired hands. He leaked the contents to the *New York Times*, and newspapers around the country picked up the story.

Roosevelt was furious, although as events unfolded, he would have been forced to release the report anyway. A member of the Senate had introduced legislation that would expand federal meat inspection, but the bill had then been trapped in the House agriculture committee, whose chair came from an old livestock-producing family and who had no intention of sending it to the House floor. Nor did the committee member from Illinois, William Lorimer, a seasoned political boss who represented the district that contained the stockyards. A meat inspection bill, he announced, would never get out of committee, "not if Little Willie can help it."

But Little Willie had met a bill — and a president and a novelist — he could not stop. Thanks to publicity generated by the new report and Sinclair's hunger for publicity, Congress could no longer avoid the issue of food safety. In late June 1906, Roosevelt signed both a pure food bill and a meat inspection act. In theory the nation's stomachs were now protected from doctored maple syrup and tainted meat. Upton Sinclair got what he wanted, too: fame and fortune, as his novel became a bestseller (proving, perhaps, the publicity power of congressional hearings and bureaucratic reports). Ironically, beef consumption rose. Sinclair's book had prejudiced the public against processed meats — canned goods, sausage, bologna, and the like — so consumers satisfied their carnivorous urges with fresh beef. In 1908, Americans consumed eight more pounds per capita than in 1906.

In the end, neither Roosevelt nor Sinclair inflicted much damage on the packers. In 1912, Armour, Swift, and Morris dissolved their jointly owned holding company, but only because it had proved to be more trouble than it was worth. They divvied up their holdings, which had grown during National Packing's short life, and dumped the profits into expanding their respective companies, buying out smaller packing operations and building new plants. Swift and Armour also set up shop in South America, building what were at the time some of the largest meat-processing facilities in the world. Their motivation for doing so was connected directly to U.S. agriculture: American cattle ranchers and farmers could not keep pace with the demands of both U.S. consumers and the global market. The packers hoped to ease the burden on American meat supplies by using South American cattle to fill export orders. Some people even recognized that whatever crimes the packers may or may not have committed, their focus on cost cutting, efficiency, and diversification made it possible to eat well at a low price. As an essayist wrote in a magazine

THE (HIGH) PRICE OF SUCCESS

article about the Swift empire, "We make great outcry against the concentrated bigness of the packers, yet the probability is that we would make yet greater outcry if the modern system of food supply were suddenly cut off and we were put back on the basis of local butcher-shops." He was right. In the United States, the mechanisms of food supply were so efficient that they had become taken for granted — and when it came to food, Americans took nothing for granted so much as low price. In the end, it was the high price of meat that fashioned the snare that tripped the packers.

American food prices had risen steadily since the beginning of the century thanks to a growing population — up by a third in the first decade or so of the century — and high demand for foodstuffs in the United States and around the world. American farmers, however, could not keep pace, and the chronic gap between supply and demand pushed prices for all foods up, ever up. In 1910, millions of Americans joined a meat boycott to protest what they regarded as exorbitant prices. But when war broke out in Europe in 1914, demand for American grains and meat soared, as did the prices and public fury. In 1916, Congress convened hearings on high food prices, but as had been the case in 1888 and 1902, Americans were not interested in relationships between and among food prices, war, weather, global demand, agricultural technology, and population size. They only knew they were paying more at the butcher shop, a fact to which an Armour vice president was resigned: when summoned to testify at the hearings, he commented that there were "a hundred and one million people in this country" with no interest in the price farmers received for cattle. They cared only about "how cheap they [could] buy their beef steak."

True enough. In early 1917, just weeks before the United States officially entered World War I, food riots erupted in several cities. "We shall have in this country a political revolution, if not something worse," warned one government official, "unless the question of the furnishing of foods to the people at the lowest possible price is taken up." President Woodrow Wilson, then starting his second term in office, could not ignore the outrage. He ordered the Federal Trade Commission (FTC) to investigate the national food supply system, from farming and food processing to food storage and retail sales.

The commission's analysts ignored Wilson's orders. Most of them supported socialist ideals or were progressives who favored using federal authority to foster both economic efficiency and social justice. They were convinced that the Beef Trust was to blame for the nation's food woes, and that the packers had escaped legal prosecution because they had bribed judges, jurors, or both. What was supposed to be a general analysis of American food production and distribution morphed into a microscopic analysis of the meatpacking industry. FTC researchers combed through packers' company records, hoping to accomplish what courts had failed to do: find evidence that the meat men had violated interstate commerce and antitrust laws, or used cold storage to hoard food and thus control prices. The resulting six-volume report, which often oozed the biases of its authors and sometimes merged fact and fiction in order to score points, concluded that the sheer size of the "trust" rendered it so inefficient that it functioned as a drag on the nation's food supply; that, analysts concluded, had caused rising food prices. They recommended that federal authorities seize the railroad and stockyard facilities used to transport, buy, and sell livestock, as well as the packers' refrigerator railcars and cold-storage facilities, and combine all of it into a meat production system owned and operated by the federal government. Doing so, the analysts contended, would break the trust's lock hold on the nation's food supply, allow smaller packers to compete, and drive down food prices.

The idea was not as far-fetched as it sounds. The transition to an industrial economy had provoked a deep-rooted anxiety about capitalism and free markets, expressed in part by the middle-class embrace of socialism. Advocates of nationalization argued that government ownership and management would create a more efficient, productive economy and equalize the distribution of wealth and prosperity. When the United States entered World War I, the government had taken over the nation's transportation and shipbuilding systems, and the American Federation of Labor, one of the nation's most powerful unions (at a time when unions commanded attention), favored a plan to allow railroad workers to share management duties and profits with company owners.

In late 1918 and early 1919, the House of Representatives held weeks of hearings on legislation that would nationalize meatpacking and livestock trading. Fortunately for the packers, those hearings coincided with a "red scare" sparked by pitched battles between workers and employers. Many people blamed the violence on Bolsheviks who were believed to have infiltrated American factories and mills as part of a larger Russian plot to convert the world to communism. (The Russians had entered the war as a monarchy and departed as a communist state.) Socialism was one thing; in Americans' hands it had become a comfortable middle-class belief. But the prospect of communists running amuck in the streets and on factory floors was too much to bear. When persons unknown bombed the homes of public officials around the country, opinion turned against anything and everything that smacked of socialism, nationalization, or communism. The Justice Department launched a crusade to root out infiltrators, and the Senate delved into alleged communist-sponsored activities. An Indiana senator demanded that the FTC analysts who had penned the meatpacking report be investigated for "sedition and criminal anarchy." The Senate obliged with an internal witch-hunt that included sifting through the trash at the homes of several FTC staff members.

That ended the effort to nationalize meatpacking, although the packers did not escape unscathed. Attorney General A. Mitchell Palmer, whose political ambitions outweighed his scruples, seized the opportunity to have his reds and his packers, too. Although most of his attention was devoted to tracking down and deporting communist sympathizers, he let the packers know he was preparing a new criminal case against them. The companies' leaders, weary of endless court battles, fended off what was sure to become a noisy and expensive contest by agreeing to divest their companies of most of their non-meat-related holdings: according to the consent decree they signed, they could no longer own shares of stockyards and newspapers, they could not function as retailers, and they could use their cold-storage facilities only for meat. In exchange, Palmer dropped his case.

The consent decree proved a mixed blessing for the packers. Louis Swift, who had taken control of the family business after his father's death in 1903, shared the elder Swift's eye for detail, cost cutting, and opportunity. In the wake of the decree, he and his colleagues streamlined operations and focused on extracting profit from what remained. Armour's post-decree fortunes proved more fragile. When Phil Armour died in 1901, leadership had passed to his son, J. Ogden, who expanded what his father had begun but committed the one sin the old man had warned against: he funded that growth with debt. Worse, he dumped company funds into firms that had nothing to do with meat or food and everything to do with his (mostly unwarranted) belief in his skills as a magician of profit. Burdened with a bewildering array of holdings and a mountain of debt, in 1923 the company went into receivership and ended up in the hands of its bankers. They nursed the money machine back to health; acquired Nelson Morris's packing company, which was also teetering on the brink; and combined the assets, eliminating dead weight.

The consent decree wasn't the only woe the packers faced. Per-capita meat consumption spiraled downward during the first two decades of the twentieth century, and for that, ironically, the packers had themselves to blame. They had built an efficient infrastructure for processing, transporting, and distributing an array of foodstuffs. As a result, Americans' plates were filled with so much food and such a variety of it that meat no longer dominated the nation's diet. But the kinds of food Americans wanted changed, too. Consider the breakfast cereal mania that gripped the nation in the first decade of the century, as shoppers snapped up new products like Corn Flakes, Cream of Wheat, Malta Vita, and Granula. Critics complained that those cereals were no more nutritious than crackers or bread, and because they were highly processed, consumers paid anywhere from $5 to $12 for the privilege of eating a bushel of wheat that sold for a dollar. "It is not so much that the new foods are better than the old," argued the editors of a national weekly magazine, than that Americans had "been persuaded to eat them" thanks to advertising that featured "kindly old gentlemen, pretty maidens and chubby children" urging Americans to "partake of their diet and so to share in their health, beauty and benevolence." But the critics missed the point. Urban Americans wanted what the cereals offered: convenience. Why waste time cooking and eating when there were so many other ways to spend it? The early-twentieth-century city offered a host of entertainments, from nickelodeons and vaudeville to beer gardens and amusement parks. The great wonder of the age, the automobile, of which Americans purchased some 9 million in the first twenty years of the century, allowed the nation to move faster and do more. The new breakfast foods may have been processed and (relatively) expensive, but they epitomized convenience. Open the package, pour some into a bowl, add a splash of milk, and eat. What could be simpler?

The national cornucopia wasn't the only reason for the decline in meat eating. In the early years of the twentieth century, new ideas about diet and nutrition diminished the value of a meat-centric diet. The first blow arrived courtesy of Horace Fletcher, a wealthy businessman who devoted most of his time to exploring dietary fads and ideas. He conducted a series of self-experiments and concluded that eating less was better than eating more, and that one key to optimal health lay in chewing one's food to a liquid state. Doing so, he claimed, amounted to a predigestive process that boosted stamina and endurance. (Upton Sinclair and his wife tried "Fletcherizing" but gave up on the diet because they lost so much weight.) Fletcher's work attracted a surprising amount of attention from scientists, among them Yale University faculty member Russell H. Chittenden, who was intrigued by the small amount of protein that Fletcher consumed. For several months, Chittenden fed low-protein diets to a collection of soldiers and athletes, and his subjects demonstrated a marked increase in muscle tone, strength, and endurance. Chittenden concluded that Americans could and should eat less meat, certainly less than nutrition experts advised. The professor's work, noted one admirer, "herald[ed] the collapse of a fundamental fallacy in diet."

Had Chittenden's research remained closeted in his university ivory tower, it and he might not have mattered. But he was a skilled promoter, and news of his work reached deep into Americans' daily lives. Those who ate meat at every meal courted disaster, one writer told readers of *Cosmopolitan*, at the time a national general-interest publication, because excessive meat consumption led to "proteid (meat) poisoning," and that, in turn, caused "brittle arteries." A meat-rich diet was "utterly abnormal and must lead inevitably to disaster." A professor at Columbia University explained to readers of *Good Housekeeping* that excessive meat consumption led to "gout, rheumatism and other 'uric acid disorders,'" and, worse, meat proteins putrefied in the intestines, spawning bacteria and "poisonous" byproducts. She advised women to feed their families less meat and more milk, eggs, and cheese. The advice, and its shaky science, earned an official seal of approval from C. F. Langworthy, the director of nutrition investigations at the federal Office of Experiment Stations: meat, he announced in a 1910 report, was "not essential to a well-balanced diet," and he advised Americans to eat more eggs and cheese, legumes and nuts.

The onset of World War I hastened the exit of meat from the center of the plate. Herbert Hoover, who served as the Wilson administration's wartime food manager, asked citizens to support the Allies by changing their eating habits. Europeans needed food, he explained, and it was up to Americans to provide it. "We have a great surplus of potatoes, vegetables, fish, and poultry," he explained, but those foods were difficult to ship, and the government planned instead to export "concentrated foodstuffs — grain, beef, pork, fats, and sugar." Fill up on eggs and cheese, he implored the nation, but leave beef and pork for the war. Americans complied (more or less) and learned they could live on less meat than they had once done.

But vitamins delivered meat its biggest blow. Scientists had long suspected that besides protein, carbohydrates, and fats, foodstuffs also contained a mystery substance that in some equally mysterious manner contributed to health. Scurvy, for example, was cured by eating certain fresh foods, especially citrus fruits. Why? What did those foods contain? In 1912, Polish chemist Casimir Funk offered an answer: a substance that he labeled "vitamines," the "vita" for life and the "amine" because he believed they were amines. (Some are and some are not, and within a decade or so, the final *e* vanished from the word.) A year later, several American researchers working in different laboratories demonstrated that milk fat also contains a life-essential substance, what we now call vitamin A, "incontrovertible evidence," rejoiced one of the men, of a "hitherto unsuspected nutrient indispensable for health and . . . the maintenance of life." Over the next few years, the vitamin publicity engine cranked into full gear as information once buried in scientific journals became fodder for the pages of newspapers and magazines eager to explain the virtues of spinach, lettuce, tomatoes, and other once-lowly foodstuffs. "Feed your body vitamines," urged a typical magazine essay published in 1919. The body demands these "Unknowns," "mysterious substances that have defied chemical isolation and analysis, but which have a powerful and determining effect on growth." Another writer warned readers by way of example, relating the tale of a mother and father determined to nourish their son, little Willie, with a diet "carefully balanced" in proteins, fats, and carbohydrates. Alas, little Willie "languish[ed]; he failed to grow; he whimpered and fell away." A friend recommended that the parents feed the boy raw cabbage, advice "the father took for offensive humor and the mother for an insult." Still, desperation knows no bounds and they piled Willie's plate with cabbage. Lo and behold, he "began to grow and shout. . . . Little Willie is now nearly six years old, and he shows every promise of becoming a great football player."

What was good for the little Willies of America proved a disaster for the meat industry. In 1926, the New York City school board banned frankfurters from lunchrooms on the grounds that the food was "unsuited" to students' nutritional needs. The board's lunch director explained that sausage was so "heavy" that when children ate it, they "neglected to eat green stuff" and milk. "This is an open attack on the frankfurter," fumed a writer for a butchers' trade newspaper. The lowly frank was one of the meat industry's "best foods" because it provided "the most nutriment for the money." The decision "puts us back ten years, at least," sighed one manufacturer. Children were told by teachers that frankfurters were "unwholesome," they carried that message home, and their mothers banished sausages from "the home table." The United States Department of Agriculture sided with the sausage. Frankfurters are "wholesome, appetizing and economical," said a department spokesman. When served on bread and with a drink, "they provide lunches that are hard to beat when time is a factor and the pangs of hunger are to be fully satisfied." (The packers, by the way, insisted on the term *frankfurter* as a more palatable alternative to a moniker they loathed: "hot dog.")

The meat industry responded as special interests do when threatened: by launching a campaign to counter what it termed "propaganda." The Meat Institute, a packers' trade organization, and the American National Livestock Association mounted a pro-meat publicity campaign, sending lecturers hither and yon, placing pro-meat articles in newspapers and magazines, and bombarding teachers with instructional material. Industry representatives commandeered microphones at the nation's newest media outlets, radio stations, to tout meat's virtues. During "Meat for Health" week, the industry's publicity arm cranked out 3 million pieces of literature, including pamphlets and advertisements and posters for windows and meat wagons, and sponsored informational programs at butcher shops and grocery stores. The Milwaukee Meat Council, made up of packers and retailers, hired an actor to portray a caveman, presumably because such a figure epitomized brute strength and good health. He strolled up and down one of the city's busiest streets, carrying a cavemanlike club and wearing a "shabby mane and beard, bear skin, [and] sandals" as well as a sandwich-board sign that read "I EAT MEAT."

But the industry's most important efforts unfolded behind the scenes. In the first half of the 1920s, meat makers urged officials at the USDA to promote and protect not just meat, but the entire meat production system. The department obliged, contributing statistics for use on promotional posters, thus giving the "eat meat" campaign an official stamp of approval. The packers' Meat Institute persuaded eighteen of the nation's agricultural experiment stations, which were attached to land grant colleges and universities, to fund meat research coordinated by the institute and the USDA. In this way, explained the institute, "the nation's best brains and equipment [could] be utilized to the full in bringing light to bear on the problems to be studied." The meat men also put their money where their mouths were, funding university fellowships to support meat-based research.

These efforts forged a permanent alliance between the meat industry and the land grant establishment, a relationship that would become increasingly important—and problematic—in the years to come. But those links between and among the USDA, schools, farmers, and meat processors also provided the underpinnings of a long-term project that fundamentally altered the way livestock was bred, raised, and fed. Factory farming, as it was called, was intended to support livestock producers and other farmers and satisfy Americans' demand for low-cost food, especially meat.

4

FACTORIES, FARMERS, AND CHICKENS

I N THE MID-1930S, Jesse Jewell, a businessman living in Gainesville, Georgia, was forced to confront an uncomfortable truth: thanks to a series of catastrophes, both natural and man-made, his family's seed-and-feed company was, as he put it, "shot." Unless he could find another way to sell what he had to offer — seed stock, livestock feed, fertilizer, basic farm tools — the business would go under and he, like so many other residents of north-central Georgia, would be bankrupt and unemployed. That prospect did not appeal to the ambitious, entrepreneurial Jewell, and he soon latched on to his new approach to profit: he bought a load of live chicks on credit and loaned those, plus bags of feed, to unemployed and mostly destitute local farmers, who raised the chickens to market weight (anywhere from two to four pounds). Jewell then hauled the birds to Atlanta and other regional urban markets, sometimes live and stashed in wooden crates, sometimes slaughtered and packed in ice. When he had sold the birds, he paid the farmers their share of the profit (after deducting payment for chickens and feed).

The rest was profitable history: over the next three decades, Jewell expanded that unassuming start into a broiler-making empire. (The term *broiler* referred to a bird's size. Broilers ranged from two to two and a half pounds, fryers weighed about three pounds, and roasters were anything larger.) He contracted with hundreds of "growers," as they were called, who agreed to feed thousands of chickens at a time in factorylike conditions. The growers employed automated watering and feeding equipment and used carefully calibrated "inputs" that included commercially manufactured mixtures of feed and antibiotics. Jewell integrated those chicken-growing operations into his larger corporate structure, which included processing plants where his employees slaughtered and packaged the chickens, mills where he manufactured the chickens' feed, and hatcheries where other Jewell employees cranked out the basic raw materials: chicks and eggs. He diversified beyond the basic bird into ready-made convenience foods such as frozen fried chicken and chicken potpies. By the time he sold J. D. Jewell, Inc., in the early 1960s, both he and the company were worth millions. Along the way, chicken had been transformed from an expensive, seasonal luxury into a dietary staple, and integrated, "industrial" livestock and meat production had migrated from the chicken house to the hog pen and cattle barn.

Factorylike livestock production extended the food infrastructure pioneered decades earlier by the dressed-beef men. Armour, Swift, and other meatpackers had designed slaughterhouses that emulated factories and incorporated those into complex, nationwide distribution systems. Jesse Jewell and others carried the factory model to the farm and built integrated corporations that connected farm to slaughterhouse to food processor to retailer. Two motives inspired the project of taking the factory to the farm: a desire to keep food costs for consumers low and a need to ensure that farmers enjoyed an adequate standard of living. Both were inextricably linked to the emergence of a consumer economy in the early twentieth century. Because the subject of factorylike livestock production will dominate much of the rest of this book, it's important to understand the context in which it took shape.

A consumer economy thrives on the making, selling, and buying of nonessentials — think cars and cosmetics, shoes designed for style rather than function, iPads and televisions. That economy, so familiar to us today, was preceded by and built upon the "producer" economy that dominated the nineteenth century, when Americans built factories where they manufactured goods that furthered industrial development: rail ties and sewer pipes, machine tools and steam engines. By the end of the nineteenth century, that foundational structure was in place and they shifted their attention to manufacturing consumer goods — clothing, cosmetics, radios, and cars. Americans bought such goods prior to the twentieth century, of course, and they continued to invest in and manufacture producer goods after consumers gained supremacy. But in the twentieth century, the economy revolved around making and getting (relatively) unnecessary "stuff."

The health of a consumer economy depends on disposable incomes that allow people to spend money on nonessentials. One way to ensure that consumers consume is with credit, which became widely available in the 1920s. General Motors, for example, created the General Motors Acceptance Corporation (GMAC) to provide low-interest loans so that Americans could purchase cars. But another crucial factor in sustaining a consumer economy is ready access to low-cost food. The less money Americans must spend on food, the more they can spend on video games, books, and cell phones. When food is abundant and supplies are greater than demand, consumers enjoy low prices, but food producers — farmers — earn little profit. If the reverse is true and demand outstrips supply, food prices rise. Farmers profit, but consumers howl. Thus the fundamental contradiction of a consumer economy: the paradox of plenty (or, as farmers call it, the pain of plenty). Urbanites demand that farmers produce an abundance of foodstuffs. But if farmers comply, they earn little profit and so either can't or won't produce more. And so the consumer economy has grown hand in hand with one of the great balancing acts of American politics: the need to guarantee cheap food on one hand and income parity for farmers on the other, a need that spawned the programs and policies known collectively as "farm subsidies." This balancing act was and still is complicated by the fact that most Americans live in cities and don't produce their own food.

Americans experienced their first significant encounter with the paradox of plenty during an agricultural crisis sparked by World War I and its aftermath, an episode that served as the seedbed for factory farming. The outbreak of war ratcheted up demand for American agricultural products, whether wheat or meat. President Woodrow Wilson, his food administrator, Herbert Hoover, and USDA officials urged farmers to produce, produce, produce; to feed not just Americans but the warring nations of Europe, too. Farmers obliged, increasing their output by the fastest means possible: they bought more land so they could plant more acres or feed more livestock. Most could not afford to pay cash, so they took out mortgages and then borrowed more money to pay for barns and silos, for additional draft animals (tractors had not yet become common), for feed, fuel, and tools. As food czar, Hoover encouraged farmers in that decision, arguing that Germany had "sucked the food and animals from all those masses of people she has dominated and left [them] starving." Even when the conflict ended, he said, Europeans would need twice as many imported fats and proteins as they had during the war.

Hoover was wrong. When the fighting stopped, military officials and foreign countries alike canceled contracts for everything from cotton to corn. Desperate to find buyers for what they had produced, farmers dumped crops and livestock on the market, and the ensuing glut caused prices to collapse. The price farmers received for corn fell 78 percent, and returns on both beef and wheat dropped by more than half. Demand vanished, but farmers' debts did not. They could not sell their output at prices high enough to pay their bills, so they responded in what seemed, to them, a logical manner: they increased their output, hoping that volume would pay off their debts. But because every farmer did the same thing, agricultural products glutted the market and prices plunged again.

As the crisis deepened, many farmers slid into bankruptcy and threatened the vitality of the banks that had loaned them money. Economists, agricultural experts, sympathetic politicians, and leaders of farmers' organizations warned that fewer farmers would mean less food and even higher food prices. They argued that if urbanites were entitled to cheap food, farmers were entitled to an adequate return for their labor and an income that would allow them to maintain economic parity with city folks. The moment prompted some advocates, including farmers, implement manufacturers and seed dealers, and agricultural economists to propose a radical solution: they urged lawmakers to detach agriculture from the free market and use federal legislation to support crop prices and farmer income; to subsidize agriculture so that farmers could enjoy the same standard of living as city people. Many Americans were (and still are) horrified by the idea and railed against the plan of using taxpayer dollars to circumvent marketplace mechanisms, arguing that therein lay the path to socialism, communism, or worse. But supporters pointed out that in war-ravaged Europe, high food prices had already sparked social unrest and contributed to the spread of fascism and communism. If American food prices soared, the same thing could happen in the United States. Government "interference" in agriculture, they argued, would save the republic. In the 1920s, that argument was not enough to carry the day. Urbanites, who made up a majority of the population, wanted nothing to do with the burdens of subsidies. Twice in that decade, Congress passed parity legislation, and twice President Calvin Coolidge vetoed it. As we'll see, the Great Depression demolished resistance to subsidies, but in the 1920s, many farm advocates touted a different plan for ensuring farmers' profits and maintaining low food prices: factorylike farming.

The idea was neither new nor unusual. As early as the 1890s, Wilbur Atwater, at the time one of the nation's best-known nutritionists and head of a federal nutrition program, maintained that applying factory methods to farming was both logical and inevitable. He pointed out that historically, as human societies shifted from agricultural to urban, demand for manufactured goods increased. Inventors had responded by devising tools and machines designed to produce goods on a large scale at a low price. Atwater argued that modern urban societies required "a cheap and abundant food-supply," and so it was time for Americans to "manufacture" basic foodstuffs — corn, wheat, beef, and pork — by applying to agriculture the "principle which has proved itself true . . . in the factory." His choice of model was not surprising. The factory lay at the heart of the American economy. Mass-produced goods were inexpensive goods, far less costly than those made by hand by artisans. Thanks to factory production, most Americans owned more than one shirt or skirt and multiple pieces of furniture. The factory had made America great. Why not extend its combination of automation and organization to the farm? If manufacturers could build high-speed assembly lines to manufacture huge quantities of low-priced goods, farmers could do the same.

Factory farming also dovetailed with a cultural value prized by Americans living in the late nineteenth and early twentieth centuries: efficiency, of which the factory was a primary embodiment. Americans believed that a powerful, successful nation was one that practiced efficiency because doing so ensured maximum productivity from people, machines, and institutions. In pursuit of that goal, universities turned out cadres of experts — engineers, sociologists, statisticians — trained to analyze, dissect, and codify every aspect of American society, from kindergarten instruction to intellectual testing to bookkeeping; from housekeeping and cooking to filing systems and traffic management. Anything and everything could be quantified and thus managed for maximum efficiency and productivity. By the turn of the century, only farming had escaped the drive toward efficiency. It remained, in the felicitous phrase of one historian, the nation's "last great nest of chaos," an inefficient backwater that prevented farmers from keeping pace with consumer demand, a state of affairs experienced in the form of rising food prices. Economists reasoned that bigger harvests would yield cheaper food and a healthier, more productive workforce (and stave off anarchy, socialism, and other evils). But the urge to improve agriculture stemmed from more than just a desire to keep food prices low. In an age of imperial expansion, many feared that the relatively primitive state of agriculture would leave the United States behind in the food race or, worse, force Americans to rely on imported foods, which would be tantamount to abandoning a cornerstone of the American ideal. "When a nation depends on other nations for its food," argued one writer, its relationships with those others must inevitably consist of "either subordination or control. Whether a nation becomes a dependent or dominant nation depends upon the ability of its agricultural population to provide for the whole population." "The wars of the future," predicted an employee at the Department of Agriculture, would depend less on weaponry than "upon the ability of the people, not only to produce largely, but to live cheaply." Unless agriculture became Fordized, Americans would be reduced to the status of the rice eaters in Asia, the worst imaginable fate for an industrial (and racist) society. High time, then, to tame the backward beast of agriculture and transform it into a model of systematized, mechanized efficiency.

The farm crisis of the 1920s inspired a new generation, including many farmers, to embrace factory farming as a way to manage the paradox of plenty. In their minds, factorylike efficiency in field and barn would reduce farmers' costs of production. The less money farmers spent to grow corn or feed cattle, the more profit they could earn when it came time to sell. An agricultural economist conceded that in the short run, "industrial agriculture" might "have a demoralizing effect" on rural Americans, but over time, weaker farmers would leave the land and those that remained would enjoy "a higher standard of living"—and, of course, reduce the amount of money Americans spent on food and thus maintain the health of the consumer economy.

Two decades (and a depression and another world war) would pass before factory farming reached full flower, but during the crisis of the 1920s and the Great Depression of the 1930s, Americans embraced factory farming as a way to manage the peaks and troughs of agricultural production and to integrate farming into the larger economy. The USDA, the land grant schools, lobbying groups like the then-new American Farm Bureau, and interested corporations developed and supported policies, technologies, and products designed to help farmers increase yields, maximize efficiency, and reduce production costs. Those efforts spurred livestock research, the manufacture of commercial fertilizers, and the development of herbicides, fungicides, pesticides, and hybrid corn.

So it's no accident that when Jesse Jewell cast about for a way to save his business, he latched on to this new model of farming. If nothing else, its focus on integrated, centralized organization appealed to his businessman's sensibilities. Jewell had spent much of the 1920s working as a surveyor in Florida during a real estate boom there. But when the boom went bust in the late 1920s (a harbinger of the bad times to come), he headed back to Gainesville and his mother's feed store, where business had evaporated, thanks to the agricultural crisis.

In many ways, Georgia and other southern states had never recovered from the devastation of the Civil War, when northern troops destroyed both crops and livestock. That war ended slavery, but most southern black farmers, and many white ones, too, traded legal enslavement for the chains of sharecropping: they worked land but did not own it, "paying" rent with the crops they grew, typically either cotton or tobacco. Sharecropping fueled a cycle of debt and poverty that left rural Georgians chained to the land and to debt. Tenant farmers started the planting season by borrowing seed, tools, and even basic food supplies such as flour, cornmeal, and bacon from local merchants like the Jewells. At harvest, sharecroppers all dumped their crops on the market at the same time, and the ensuing glut drove down the prices they received for them. There was never enough profit to pay rent or the debts owed to merchants.

Then came the farm crisis of the 1920s. Prices for both tobacco and cotton collapsed. Sharecroppers sank deeper into debt and prayed that their landlords would not evict them and that merchants would not deny them credit for food. A boll weevil infestation exacerbated the despair, devouring cotton crops as they stood in the field. Landowners evicted their croppers. Furnishing merchants, having lost the crops that paid their own bills, went bankrupt. Banks shut their doors as landowners and merchants defaulted on loans. Such was the situation that Jesse Jewell faced when he returned to Gainesville in the late twenties.

Almost immediately, his predicament and almost everyone else's worsened thanks to the onset of the Great Depression. That was particularly true for farmers, as their plight shifted from bad to horrific. Demand for foodstuffs dwindled, but farmers' debts did not. Many families lost their farms. The growing disaster, plus the election of Franklin D. Roosevelt in 1933, finally demolished resistance to the idea of subsidizing agriculture. Much of Roosevelt's New Deal legislation aimed at restoring health to consumers: his alphabet agencies — the Works Progress Administration (WPA) and the Civilian Conservation Corps (CCC), to name two of many — created jobs that provided paychecks so that ordinary Americans would have money to spend. Farmers, Roosevelt recognized, were consumers, too, and shortly after his inauguration, Congress approved the Agricultural Adjustment Act (AAA), the first direct subsidy program. The AAA was designed in part to eliminate surpluses of key commodities, including hogs, dairy products, cotton, corn, rice, and tobacco. The bill authorized the USDA to buy those products, thereby removing them from the market and fueling a short-term scarcity. In theory, as those commodities became scarce, their prices would go up and farmers would earn more money. Then they could spend that to pay debts and to buy manufactured goods like shoes or gasoline, thus providing work for shoemakers, sales clerks, refinery workers, and gas station attendants. Or, as officials with the Roosevelt administration phrased it, shortages of hogs and cotton would "prime the pump" of the nation's economy and help consumers get back to the business of consuming.

Initially the arrival of the AAA in Georgia drove Jesse Jewell closer to bankruptcy. Federal agents began paying farmers (or, more accurately, landowners) to plow up part of their cotton fields; what little remained of demand for the seed, feed, and fertilizer sold by Jewell evaporated. That's when he turned to the project that would make him a multimillionaire. Some historians and industry insiders have credited Jewell as one of the inventors of the modern broiler industry. In fact, he and others were influenced by a similar industry being built at Delmarva, the spit of land where the borders of Delaware, Maryland, and Virginia meet, where federal and state agricultural experts, bankers, and feed manufacturers were helping residents switch to large-scale chicken farming. In addition, by the 1930s, employees of the USDA and the nation's land grant schools, as well as geneticists, animal nutritionists, and other scientists, had laid the groundwork for factorylike livestock production. A more accurate assessment of the broiler industry's early years is that Jewell was less its inventor than a man who maximized opportunities presented by new research and a bounty of free expertise. But the nascent industry emulated the factory model in part because prior to the 1930s, making chickens for meat was less an industry than it was the work of a haphazard collection of entrepreneurs operating in scattered locations and according to rules of their own devising. So those who built the broiler industry started from scratch; it's not surprising that they were inspired by the new model of farming and replaced the haphazard with factorylike structures.

Chickens had long been a ubiquitous presence on the American landscape; every farm family kept them, and until the twentieth century many city folks did, too. Unlike hogs and cattle, chickens needed little by way of care. Barnyard and backyard fowl foraged their surroundings, eating corn, food scraps, and insects. But prior to the twentieth century, a chicken's primary purpose in life was to supply eggs, efficient packages of protein that could be easily preserved and transported long distances. In contrast, once slaughtered, chickens had to be eaten immediately, so in those days before mechanical refrigeration had become common, chicken meat was a rare treat. (The trait that makes poultry attractive to the health-conscious — its low saturated fat content — renders the flesh highly perishable.) As a result, fresh chicken was a seasonal food, available primarily in summer and fall. After hens laid eggs in spring and early summer, farmers culled the cockerels — young males — keeping a few to eat and hauling the rest, live and stashed in wooden crates, to the nearest town market, the makings for the summertime treat of fried chicken. In the fall, new supplies of poultry arrived at market as farmers rid their flocks of worn-out hens, aged roosters, and males kept on hand to raise to "roaster" size (about four pounds). These birds' relatively tough flesh made for hearty winter soups and stews. Birds were sold whole so that shoppers could study the head and feet for clues to the carcass's age and health. Spurs, for example, indicated an old male. Spoilage was impossible to disguise because poultry flesh turned green as it decayed, and "green-strucks" often ended up in the hands of merchants who specialized in cut-rate poultry for those with thin wallets.

But a growing urban nation demanded protein, and in the first decade of the twentieth century, the Armour and Swift companies tried to transform chicken from seasonal treat to dinner plate staple. In the spring, buyers scouted farms, especially in the Midwest where most eggs came from, in search of young birds. They delivered those to packer-owned feeding stations, which consisted of stacks of wire cages, "batteries," each cage sized to hold four or five birds. Troughs attached to the sides allowed the birds to feed at will. For ten days to two weeks, the chickens feasted on ultrarich and fattening diets of corn, oats, and buttermilk. Some packer-processors accelerated the feeding process with cramming mechanisms: a wooden tripod equipped with a foot pedal and a rubber tube attached to a bag of feed. An operator shoved the tube down the bird's throat and then pressed the pedal to force food from the bag into its gut. "Under the machine system," explained one man, they "have to eat, and they must take on flesh. Then there is no waste of food." When the animals reached a weight of two pounds, plant employees slaughtered them, leaving head, feet, and innards intact; scalded the carcasses to ease the removal of feathers; froze the carcasses, at that time a process that required three to four days; and packed them in wooden crates for immediate shipping or for storage in freezer warehouses.

Armour and Swift built their poultry operations primarily in the Midwest, where farms contained literally millions of laying hens. On the urban East and West coasts, a small number of entrepreneurs raised chickens specifically for meat and sold those to butchers in nearby cities, particularly ones who catered to the massive influx of Jewish émigrés from eastern Europe. Chicken figured heavily in their diets — observant Jews don't eat pork and beef was a rare luxury — and many ate diets based on Talmudic law, including the stipulation that meat animals be slaughtered according to ritual. The *schochet* — the authorized religious representative — grabbed the bird by the wings with his left hand, then used that same hand to grab the head and yank back the neck. Using a sharp blade held in his less-occupied right hand, he slit the animal's throat and tossed the bird into a barrel where, one observer noted, "it remain[ed] with others in the same condition until the death struggles" ended. When the barrel was full (and the "death struggles" presumably completed), an assistant dumped its contents onto the floor. The poultry was ready for buyers.

An altogether different market centered around specialty chickens like the "Philadelphia" broiler (born and raised in southern New Jersey). "Of all the toothsome, appetizing poultry," raved one commentator, the Philly "most appeals to our palate." "They are plump, tender-meated, juicy and sweet flavored," a delightful combination created by an especially rich diet and by confining the birds to a small area so that they avoided "violent exercise" that led to "hardened muscles." They were also, he added, "often beyond our pocketbook." Indeed. Few companies specialized in raising chickens for meat, and because those birds required freezing and packing or, like the Philly broilers, were hand-raised on special diets, meat chickens were too expensive for most budgets. A Philadelphia broiler typically cost 50 cents a pound; in today's money, that two-pound bird would cost $22. As long as the price was high, owners of butcher and grocery stores were reluctant to spend money on refrigerator or freezing equipment. Why bother when so few people could afford to eat chicken?

Without mass outlets and a mass market, there wasn't much incentive to mass-produce chickens. Even Armour and Swift found it difficult to achieve economies of scale that would lower the price of poultry to the level of pork or beef. They sold virtually their entire output to a narrow market: high-end hotels and restaurants, posh resorts, railroads that offered first-class dining services, and caterers that specialized in serving what one broiler industry analyst called "swell spreads." That narrow market also explains why the packers chose to invest in feeding operations: those customers demanded a uniform product, which could be achieved only by controlling the birds' diet. "Hotel men and restaurant keepers," one poultry man explained, "have found through experience that it does not work well to serve one banqueter half a large chicken and the next man a small one." But size mattered, too: commercial kitchens prized two-pound broilers because those could be halved and cooked without subjecting impatient diners to a long wait. Finally, as a USDA employee explained, the packers' "juicy, milk-fed" birds were superior to barnyard "ranger" chickens.

In the 1920s, the poultry industry was barely an industry. Production was limited, the price was high, and few Americans enjoyed access to chicken on a regular basis. When members of the Republican Business Men, Inc., ran a full-page advertisement in the *New York Times* in the fall of 1928 touting the virtues of their party and presidential candidate Herbert Hoover, they promised that Republican prosperity would put "A Chicken in Every Pot." (Hoover himself, it should be noted, never made such a promise.) The Republican businessmen were wrong: the job of putting a chicken in every pot would ultimately have little to do with Republican prosperity and much more to do with factorylike efficiency and taxpayer subsidies.

When the agricultural crisis hit Georgia in the 1920s, many businessmen and employees at the state's land grant school, the University of Georgia (UGA), latched on to both chickens and eggs as replacements for cotton and as resources that would revive and diversify the ailing economy. They lobbied the legislature for funds to support a new program aimed at increasing livestock production, especially poultry. UGA faculty helped organize a poultry trade association that coordinated the production and marketing of both chickens and eggs. Bankers encouraged these projects with loans to businessmen, and a railroad line sponsored "poultry specials," train cars loaded with chickens and headed for northern cities. Forty-one hatcheries opened in Georgia during the first half of the 1920s, and executives at Swift and Company encouraged the trend by buying up every broiler and fryer that company agents could find and slaughtering them at an existing packing plant. But the new chicken boosters weren't interested in simply populating farms with barnyard birds. Rather, they specifically promoted an industry based on science and modeled on the factory, urging struggling farmers to build modern chicken coops that included electricity and heating. Officials at Georgia's Department of Agriculture helped entrepreneurs build hatcheries and encouraged poultry growers to start with purebred stock rather than barnyard "scrubs."

But all that cost money, and that was the one thing that local farmers didn't have. That's why so much of the new poultry industry ended up in the hands of people other than conventional farmers: bankers were willing to offer the loans needed to get the project off the ground, but they preferred dealing with borrowers experienced in business. Enter men like Jesse Jewell. In many respects, his migration from shopkeeping to poultry production amounted to a one-for-one substitution: for decades, merchants like him had provided farmers and sharecroppers with feed, seed, or fertilizer in advance of the growing season, taking payment when the crop was sold. Jewell simply swapped chickens for feed and seed, benefiting from the research and expertise provided by UGA faculty. He also enjoyed assistance provided by the manufacturer of the feed he sold: the company extended credit so that he could buy the feed and chicks that he loaned to local farmers, helped him establish a modern bookkeeping system, and dispatched a salesman to accompany Jewell on tours of the countryside to recruit farmers. Moreover, by the time Jewell settled on chickens as his salvation, there was new cash floating around the region. The AAA had paid out $8 million for the cotton plow-up, money that landed in the pockets of landowners who were looking for ways to invest it. The New Deal also offered other, indirect agricultural subsidies: in 1935, the USDA launched the Poultry Improvement Program and committed manpower and intellectual capital to the study and control of poultry disease. Thanks to the Tennessee Valley Authority and the Roosevelt administration's investment in rural electrification, southern farmers obtained access to electricity that enabled Jewell's growers to install automated feeding and watering devices. Those tools, which were often designed at land grant engineering programs, saved labor and allowed growers to increase the number of birds they could feed.

Other subsidized research also shaped the new broiler industry. In the then-new field of genetics, researchers studying how and why traits passed from parent to offspring often used chickens as their research subjects because they were small and easy to handle, and they matured in weeks rather than months. Compared to other animals, hens have a short reproductive cycle, and their offspring develop not in the womb but in a separate container, the egg. By the 1920s, the chicken was one of the most studied of all domestic livestock. Even before the broiler industry took shape, scientists had learned a great deal about how to increase egg yields and raise healthier chickens. The ubiquity of laboratory chickens also led, inadvertently, to a central component of factorylike livestock production: confinement. Researchers who worked with chickens studied their subjects in a confined setting so that they could control light, temperature, and humidity and monitor the birds' food intake. Scientists soon realized that confined hens lived longer and laid more and healthier eggs than their free-ranging farmyard cousins. Confinement also eliminated the primary obstacle that stood between poultry producers and efficient, large-scale production: flock size. Chickens are highly susceptible to disease, and every farmer knew that the bigger the flock, the higher the incidence of disease, and the harder those outbreaks are to control. In a confined setting, however, growers could quickly identify and remove sick birds. The major obstacle was that confined birds invariably developed rickets, or "leg weakness" as farmers called it, leaving them unable to walk and preventing chicks from maturing and hens from laying. But in the early 1920s, researchers discovered that adding vitamin D to chicken feed eliminated the need for sunlight. That "phenomenal" discovery, raved one expert, opened the door to "specialization and the application of factory methods" to poultry production.

All these factors — expertise, research, money — shaped the new broiler industry, thanks to which, wrote one man, chicken farming was headed toward "commercialized production on an efficient and . . . large scale." Jewell was no farmer, and that was fine with the people who urged him and others to build the new industry. What supporters wanted was an agricultural sector that operated more like a factory than a farm.

Jewell spent the late 1930s expanding his business. He contracted with more growers and sought out quality chicks for them to raise, and he cultivated outlets where he could sell the birds, which he continued to drive to market himself. But the onset of World War II presented an unexpected opportunity for rapid expansion and solidified the industry's reliance on contract farming, automation, large scale, and integration of livestock production with processing. As had been true during the previous world war, demand for all goods, especially foodstuffs, rose sharply (and ended the depression), but few industries benefited more than the one devoted to making broilers. At the outset of the conflict, federal officials decided to set aside most of the nation's pork and beef for the troops, in part because of their value for both nutrition and morale, but also because those could be shipped as, say, smoked hams or canned beef stew. But the commercial poultry industry was so new that an infrastructure for packing and processing its meat was limited, and bureaucrats charged with managing the nation's food kept the chickens at home. (Turkeys, however, were shipped to troops for morale-boosting Thanksgiving and Christmas meals on the front lines.) USDA officials launched a "Grow More Poultry Program," the public feasted on chicken fixed every which way, and military buyers grabbed as much as they could to feed to men and women stationed stateside.

World War II also drained American agriculture of its labor supply, a fact that, as we'll see later, would have a profound impact on the way farmers raised livestock. Even before the United States entered the war, factories had geared up to supply warring countries with materiel, and men and women decamped from the farm for jobs those factories provided. In Georgia alone, between 1937 and 1941, 30 percent of agricultural workers left farm for factory. The shortage worsened after the United States declared war in late 1941. Everywhere in rural America, from dairy farms to cattle-feeding operations, from Corn Belt hog lots to rural Georgia chicken coops, labor vanished. When labor cannot be found, humans make a logical decision: they replace it with machinery. Americans had a long-standing tradition of doing so. For most of the nineteenth century, for example, the country suffered chronic shortages of labor that fostered a national passion for mechanization and automation. So, too, in the 1940s. Factory farming already had plenty of support both in and out of agriculture, and World War II affirmed that enthusiasm. Nowhere was this more true than in the broiler industry.

Faced with record demand on one hand and lack of labor on the other, Jesse Jewell tightened his control over the broiler-making process. Back in the 1930s, his growers had cobbled together coops from scraps of brick, sheet metal, or wood. Now Jewell required them to replace those with purpose-built structures outfitted with electricity and automated feeding and watering systems, buildings that contained thousands of chickens housed in long rows of stacked wire cages. Jewell helped his growers finance those improvements: he borrowed from a local bank and then reloaned funds to growers. He replaced verbal agreements with written contracts that gave him outright ownership of chicks and required farmers to use feed supplied by him. He based payments on the growers' efficiency as measured by the number and size of birds they raised per pound of feed. Other Georgia broiler makers made the same decisions, and similar contracts ruled in burgeoning poultry industries at Delmarva and in Arkansas and other (mostly southern) states. The change unnerved some observers. A poultry extension agent at the University of Delaware feared that Delmarva growers did not understand the implications of these arrangements. As long as they could pay for feed "and have a few dollars left," they "figure they are making a little profit," he complained. They seemed not to realize that their profit had been earned at the expense of interest payments on debt. But faced with relentless demand — and, of course, the potential for profit — integrated poultry production built on the factory model became entrenched.

The processing side of the equation changed, too. When Jewell signed contracts to supply chicken to military buyers, he also agreed to meet federal regulations in his factory. The contracts mandated, for example, that carcasses be subjected to a high-temperature scald and that he ship packaged, precut pieces rather than whole birds. Eventually the War Food Administration decided that federally purchased poultry must be shipped frozen. All of it required Jewell to redesign his plant and to invest in processing, packaging, sanitizing, and cooling equipment. It wasn't cheap: the required scalding machinery increased production costs by 50 percent, forcing Jewell to compensate by reducing expenses elsewhere in his facility. But here again, Jewell got help: USDA and military staff provided engineering expertise and ensured that equipment manufacturers, already burdened by war demands and materials shortages, honored nonmilitary contracts such as those from broiler processors. Faculty at land grant schools and extension programs contributed research in the form of new freezing techniques, for example, and disease management strategies. The assistance infuriated small operators who couldn't (or wouldn't) shoulder the necessary expense. One man complained that the system was "arranged to help big business and discourage little business." He was right: the USDA, military buyers, and land grant experts encouraged large-scale, efficient, machine-based production as a way to manage the paradox of plenty and to produce food as inexpensively as possible. By war's end, broiler production had become a highly mechanized, science-based, integrated industry. The results were extraordinary: In 1939, Georgia producers put 1.6 million chickens on the market, well up from the 400,000 they had raised in 1934. In 1945, they sent nearly 30 million to market.

But labor wasn't the only shortage that afflicted agriculture during the war. Everyone who raised livestock, whether chickens, cattle, or hogs, struggled with feed supplies that ranged from scarce to nonexistent. Corn, for example, was in short supply. So, too, were fish meal and cod liver oil: Americans had long imported the former from Japan and the latter from Norway. The Nazi invasion of Norway and the bombing of Pearl Harbor closed supply routes. The results were predictable: farmers spent more to feed livestock, and the relatively scrawny animals they took to market yielded less meat and translated into higher prices at grocery stores. (That, by the way, was one rationale for wartime price controls on meat: without them, retail prices would have soared and shoppers would have raised hell — the last thing any politician wanted, especially those who remembered the food riots that preceded American entry into World War I.) Unless Americans could find substitutes for conventional feedstuffs, warned one official, a "serious bottleneck" would eliminate meat from many tables and from camps on the front lines. Those shortages led directly to the use of antibiotics in livestock production.

To understand why, we need to look briefly at barnyard nutrition. Single-stomach animals like chickens and hogs thrive when their diets contain animal-derived proteins, such as fish meal and cod liver oil, or "tankage" (the byproducts of rendering plants). Deprived of those proteins, animals are more prone to disease and weigh less at maturity. Less flesh on the animal translates into less meat on the table. By the time World War II began, scientists had been studying the mysteries of animal-derived proteins for more than twenty years, and their research had fostered the development of the commercial feed industry. Ralston-Purina and Quaker Oats, for example, manufactured feedstuffs that included fish meal and cod liver oil. But those ingredients were expensive; if scientists could find substitutes, they could help farmers reduce their production costs.

Thus the search to understand why animal-based proteins are more powerful than ones derived from plants, and to identify the so-called animal protein factor (APF) that differentiates fish oil, say, from plant-based proteins. The wartime feed shortage intensified the need for answers, and university, corporate, and USDA researchers (themselves short-handed as scientists and graduate students headed off to war) doggedly conducted feeding trials with sweet potatoes and other plants, as well as vitamins, minerals, amino acids — anything that might replicate the effects of APF. An employee at one agricultural experiment station chided his colleagues for their lack of imagination. There was no time "to repeat feeding trials for five successive years before conclusions are drawn." The emergency of war, he argued, demanded "newer and more effective research." He urged them to follow the lead of biologists, chemists, and geneticists engaged in basic research, especially those studying the fundamental physiological processes of life. How, precisely, did growth happen? What internal mechanism caused plants, for example, to reach for sunlight?

"The ultimate objective" of such research, explained one scientist, was "growth control." Once humans understood the mechanics of growth, they could manipulate and control it and even encourage "abnormal growth." That explains the interest in colchicine, a substance derived from the crocus plant. Historically, it had been used to treat gout, but in the 1930s, biologists discovered that it accelerated "evolutionary changes," transforming conventional plants into "giant" specimens. Some researchers believed that colchicine could have the same effect on animals. In 1940, a scientist at the University of Pittsburgh injected it into chicken eggs. The birds that hatched grew "abnormally large" combs and wattles, and males crowed three months earlier than usual.

In the late 1940s, scientists finally unraveled the mystery of APF, arriving there as researchers so often do: by accident and via a circuitous path, in this case research aimed at curing pernicious anemia, at the time a deadly global menace. Pernicious anemia cripples its victims, leaving them too weak to move, and eventually attacks the nervous system. At the time, the only way to alleviate or cure it was with hefty doses of liver — a half-pound or more a day — or injections of liver extract, both of which were expensive. (Nor, it must be admitted, was the prospect of eating a half-pound of liver a day particularly inviting.) But as with APF, it wasn't clear how or why that cure worked, or which component of liver played the crucial role. Scientists knew that if only they could identify that mystery ingredient, they could design a cheaper substitute. The answer came in 1948 when scientists working at the pharmaceutical company Merck announced that they had isolated liver's anti-anemia ingredient, which they named vitamin B_{12}. A dose weighing less than a single strand of human hair was sufficient to set patients on the road to good health. But even that was expensive: one ton of liver yielded just twenty milligrams of the vitamin. A few months later, scientists at Lederle Laboratories, owned by American Cyanamid, announced that they had extracted the vitamin from common bacteria, and not long after, the Merck group developed a technique for making large quantities at a low price. Merck manufactured antibiotics, bacteria-killing substances that were then relatively new, in enormous vats of fermented microbes. The process generated gallons of waste in the form of organism-soaked residues, and those could be used to make B_{12}.

The final step in this convoluted chain of discovery came in 1950. Two researchers at American Cyanamid were testing the impact of B_{12} on livestock with the expectation that the vitamin would improve the animals' health. It did — and then some. To the men's astonishment, B_{12} manufactured from the residue of the antibiotic Aureomycin acted as a superaccelerant. Animals that ate it grew as much as 50 percent faster than animals fed B_{12} extracted from liver. Nor did it take much to produce that effect: about an ounce of antibiotic per ton of feed. The implications were obvious. Feeds laced with a synthetic vitamin-and-antibiotic product cost less to manufacture than those based on fish meal or tankage, and livestock that ate it would reach maturity faster, which meant farmers could spend less on feed. For broiler producers like Jesse Jewell, the combination produced a 10 percent trifecta: chickens needed 10 percent less time to reach market weight, they ate 10 percent less feed, and mortality rates dropped about 10 percent. The discovery blew "the lid clear off the realm of animal nutrition," noted the editors of a farming magazine, and left "animal nutritionists gasping with amazement, almost afraid to believe what they had found." Farmers would "[n]ever again" have to contend with the "severe protein shortages" that plagued them during World War II. From the perspective of both farmers and consumers, antibiotics were as valuable as tractors, combines, and agricultural subsidies.

Enthusiasm for antibiotics and other components of factory farming increased after World War II thanks to three factors. First was the ongoing shortage of agricultural labor. When the war ended, most men and women did not return to the farm. The cold war, a dire need for housing, and the baby boom pushed the economy into hyperdrive. Factory assembly lines, whether in weaponry, building materials, furniture, or automobiles, absorbed record numbers of workers, as did offices, schools, and other non-agricultural employers. American farmers dumped their wartime profits into technologies that replaced human labor.

Second, postwar politics transformed agricultural mechanization into a patriotic imperative. From the 1940s on, American food served as a weapon, first against the Axis enemies, and then in the cold war struggle against communism. U.S. General Lucius Clay, who served as the governor of occupied Germany, summed the equation in blunt terms: one way to "pave the way to a Communist Europe," he said, was by forcing citizens of the former warring nations to choose "between being a communist on 1500 calories and a believer in democracy on 1000 calories." If food, scarce nearly everywhere in the world except the United States, could help win this new war, American farmers must do whatever was necessary to support the cause. There was no time for dallying and no place for laggards, of which, economists grumbled, agriculture harbored entirely too many. Most farmers were "moving forward" into more mechanized, factorylike farming, noted a reporter summarizing one of the many hearings and investigations into the problem of agricultural "underemployment." But many persisted in "standing still" and in relying on the "methods of their grandfathers." By refusing to do their share, they imposed a "heavy burden" on the nation.

The third factor that contributed to enthusiasm for factory farming lay well beyond the chicken coop and battlefield. In postwar America, large grocery chains emerged as major power players in the nation's food supply system, and factory farming, and especially the integrated broiler industry, was well suited to meet their demands.

The ascendance of chain grocery stores can be traced back to the agricultural crisis of the 1920s. As beleaguered farmers glutted the market with their corn, cotton, and cattle, prices of those commodities collapsed, and in theory, consumers should have benefited. Instead, food prices soared, and a baffled public demanded an explanation. Dozens of studies examined the entirety of the American food system, from farm to table. Most analysts arrived at the same conclusion: Basic agricultural foodstuffs were cheap — and farmers weren't making much money — but consumers were paying high prices at grocery stores thanks to two unrelated factors. The first was consumers' insistence on convenience. One USDA analyst pointed out that more women were working outside the home and they had neither the time nor the inclination to spend hours in the kitchen. A contest between, say, a cooked-from-scratch roast and canned beef stew was no contest at all.

But convenience was neither cheap nor free, and the demand for "[t]ime-saving, convenience, comfort, and satisfaction," explained a congressional commission appointed to study rising food costs, had "reached a point where it costs more to distribute and serve [food] than it does to produce [it]." The price of store-bought bread, for example, included "a maze of service costs." Its manufacturer invested in equipment needed to mix and bake the bread and employed an army of salespeople and advertising copywriters to persuade shoppers to buy it. Moving the bread from factory to table necessitated hiring truck drivers, machine operators, packing crews, and deliverymen. Those layers of expense provided jobs and paychecks, but they also drove up the final price of bread and other foods.

But the dismal state of food retailing also contributed to the high cost of eating. In the 1920s, most Americans still shopped for food the same way their grandparents had, buying dry goods like flour and spices at one store; perishables such as potatoes, onions, and apples from another; and meat from a butcher shop. The average food retailer catered to a limited neighborhood clientele and purchased supplies in small lots from multiple food jobbers, each of whom carried a narrow line of goods. One analyst used lettuce to calculate the resulting inefficiencies: Suppose a wholesaler bought a carload of lettuce, or 320 crates. A typical jobber purchased 1/16 of that load; a retailer 1/320; and the consumer "one head or 1/7,680 of a car." Each subdivision of the original carload added to the cost of the final product. Worse, complained critics, the grocery business was too often the refuge of the incompetent and the inexperienced. A study of grocers in Oshkosh, Wisconsin, revealed that most of them lacked any experience in retailing, and their numbers included a policeman, a shoemaker, and a musician, which, said one observer, explained why so many of them failed. In Louisville, Kentucky, a third of grocers failed after a year; in Buffalo, New York, 60 percent went under.

These inefficiencies created an opening for large, centrally managed chain grocers who could drive down costs through volume buying and streamlined distribution. Even before the 1920s, a handful of chain grocers had made inroads into retailing, mostly in large cities and mainly on the East Coast. Chief among them was the Great Atlantic and Pacific Tea Company, or A&P, which began life in the nineteenth century as a purveyor of tea and coffee but whose owners gradually expanded their offerings to include a full line of grocery items. By 1900, A&P operated two hundred stores. The original outlets offered delivery and credit, but not self-service; clerks gathered items for shoppers. But in 1913, A&P launched a collection of "Economy Stores." The new shops abandoned in-home delivery and other frills in exchange for low prices that company executives believed would generate high-volume sales. Manufacturers of national brand products like canned foods and dry cereals initially objected, arguing that A&P's policies besmirched hard-won reputations by treating branded goods as cheap stuff. They changed their minds once they recognized that shoppers who patronized modern stores like A&P's were more willing to try to buy branded goods.

In the wake of the agricultural crisis of the 1920s, those charged with studying and reforming the American food system touted chain grocery stores as a way to modernize and improve food distribution. The chains streamlined the task of shopping by providing an array of foodstuffs, from produce to canned goods, in a single location. A&P and other grocers also emphasized the pleasures of consumption by providing clean, well-lit environments, wheeled carts, low prices, and, thanks to self-service, maximum convenience. But chains made their biggest impact behind the scenes. Unlike neighborhood shops and independent grocers, chains ordered directly from manufacturers and in bulk, which kept their costs low. Food manufacturers benefited, too; by dealing with a single grocery chain rather than hundreds of individual retailers, they reduced bookkeeping and accounting expenses, to say nothing of costs associated with selling and delivery. All of it added up to efficiency that translated into lower food prices, and by the time World War II ended, grocery chains dominated food retailing.

Their dominance of *meat* retailing unfolded more slowly. Back in the 1920s and 1930s, the chains had struggled to learn how to sell meat. As one grocery executive admitted, "[c]hain store merchandising is founded on control," and meat, with its unwieldy carcasses, fat, gristle, blood, and bone, resisted control. An A&P executive begged the nation's packers to make meat behave less like itself and more like easy-to-manage canned peas. "It is now possible to buy bread already cut in slices," he argued, so surely it was "logically and economically" feasible to supply grocery chains with precut, prepackaged meats. If only it were that simple. "The packaging of coffee, crackers, [and] cereals is child's play compared with packaging of fresh meats," marveled a reporter in 1929. "A whole new technic [*sic*] must be worked out." Even when the packaging succeeded, customers weren't always sure what to do with it. One retailer recounted the day an angry customer marched into his store and demanded a refund for a package of bacon she'd bought three weeks earlier. The meat was spoiled, she told the man. The puzzled grocer asked her where she'd stored it. On top of her icebox, she replied, but that "should be of no significance" because the bacon was in "a 'sealed package' and should not require special care." (Presumably the woman's refund included a quick lesson in packaging and refrigeration.)

By the 1950s, chain grocers had solved those problems, in large part thanks to wartime research that resulted in new packaging materials and improved refrigeration equipment, and so they extended their command and control to meat sales as well. Their power allowed them to dictate terms to meatpackers and processors. That was especially true in the broiler industry. Chain stores nationwide used packaged chicken as "loss leaders," calculating that shoppers lured by low poultry prices would stick around to load their carts with higher-priced goods. Selling chickens below cost quickly became a requirement for any grocer who wanted to lure customers. If a competitor across town sold broilers for, say, 29 cents, lamented one grocer, "we've got to sell at 29 or lose our customers for everything else we sell in the store." The more dependent the chains became on cheap chicken, the more they pressured Jewell and other processors to supply broilers at a low price. Jewell had no choice but to comply, and he in turn pressured his growers to increase production. The resulting output glutted the market, and grocers snapped up cheap poultry for use as loss leaders. "This starts the price-cutting sale cycle all over again and everybody gets hurt!" complained a merchandiser for a major chain.

The pain wouldn't end anytime soon, as the chickens themselves got a dose of modernity that gave shoppers even more meat for the price. In 1945, the Dekalb Company of Illinois began developing hybrid birds that would mature and feather quickly, produce two hundred or more eggs a year, and provide meaty flesh. They weren't alone. In 1946, a tour guide at a USDA research facility boasted about the changes scientists there had wrought in the basic bird. "See that batch of pullets over there?" he asked a visitor. "They're practically all white meat, tender and delicious." But few did more than A&P to encourage and sustain the broiler boom. The grocer sponsored "Chicken of Tomorrow" contests that rewarded breeding innovations. Thousands of breeders and growers participated, and in 1950, the USDA calculated that nearly 70 percent of the 625 million chickens raised for meat descended from Chicken of Tomorrow bloodlines. By the early 1950s, the American broiler was meaty and big-breasted, boasted hefty drumsticks, and arrived at maturity faster and on less feed than chickens sent to market just a few years earlier. Modern chickens converted feed into meat more efficiently than did cattle, and nearly as efficiently as that master of conversion, the hog; and pound for pound, chicken offered a less costly form of protein than its two competitors.

During the fifties, in part because of the chains' demands but also because so many investors wanted a cut of the action, the broiler industry resembled nothing so much as a gold rush, complete with boomtowns, fast wealth, and spectacular collapses. Even so, output soared, and production costs, and the prices consumers paid, dropped. Genetics, breeding for meat, and antibiotic-laced feeds helped, of course, but so did the integrated production-processing structure developed by Jesse Jewell. Indeed, the broiler industry was dominated by the same people who had invented it: integrators like Jewell who exercised control from egg to chick to packing plant to grocery store. "Integration has made chicken the cheapest meat on the market," Jewell said, "and we want chickens to stay cheap." His centralized decision making also allowed him to manage the price gyrations ignited by grocery chains' use of broilers as loss leaders. He balanced the up-down prices of basic broilers with more stable income from "value-added" products like chicken sticks (a takeoff on another popular innovation of the 1950s, the fish stick) and chicken-based frozen TV dinners, the latter an innovation introduced during the decade by the Swanson company, another major broiler maker. Frozen, canned, and refrigerated foods satisfied consumers' demand for convenience and taught shoppers to think of chicken as something other than a basic commodity sold at below-profit prices. Jewell could manufacture those value-added products because he controlled the number and types of chickens that flowed into his processing plants. Analysts applauded Jewell and other integrators, arguing that they were more business-oriented and "cost-conscious" than traditional farmers who operated on "a smaller scale."

Here, then, was modern farming of the sort so many people had envisioned back in the 1920s. It was subsidized, thanks to government research and poultry improvement programs. Production was automated and large-scale. Critics complained that poultry growers were mere hired hands rather than farmers. But, for better or for worse, that was precisely the goal: to make the farm function like a factory. Supporters pointed out that contract farming was neither new nor unusual. For decades, commercial vegetable and fruit farmers had raised crops under contract for food processors who required produce of uniform size and grade. Moreover, every farmer who participated in a federal subsidy program worked, in effect, as a contract producer, and as many supporters of integration pointed out, most Americans worked for a contracted price. "As a whole," commented one analyst, "agriculture stands alone as the only major industry that still clings to its glorious past and holds out for a 'free price.'" In time, another predicted, integration would "revolutionize the production of animal products," and contract farming would be the norm rather than the exception.

The story of the mid-twentieth-century agricultural revolution is less one of malevolent corporate capitalism than it is the struggle to balance the welfare of the producing minority with the demands of the consuming majority. The middlemen in this case were federal policies aimed at protecting the few in order to benefit the many, as well as the tools and ideas aimed at reducing the costs of feeding a nation. For decades, the farmer epitomized the rugged American individualist, living on the land, beholden to no one. But in the 1950s, farmers shouldered heavier burdens, charged as they were with feeding the world, preventing the spread of communism, and paving the way for consumers to spend money on televisions, vacations, and college educations. An urban majority screamed bloody murder if the price of steak rose 5 cents a pound, blamed lazy farmers and ignorant politicians for that woe, and threatened to vote said politicos out of office. So midcentury farmers employed the ideas and tools that empowered them to make low-cost food and earn a decent living doing it. They fed their livestock antibiotics and caged their

chickens. They accepted the federal government's goal of eliminating "marginal" farmers and subsidizing large, efficient ones.
In the 1950s, those who wanted to stay on the land had to play by
the new rules; that was the price of survival.

Jewell's chicken-based empire was just one manifestation of
that midcentury revolution. Farmers who started their careers
in the 1920s went from horse-drawn plows to agile, powerful
tractors. From dousing crops with Paris Green to watching an
airplane drench fields with DDT. From shoveling feed and manure to pushing a button and letting a machine do the work. A
half-century later, "pro-food" activists would argue that Americans have paid a high price for that revolution, and at the time,
many farmers reacted with trepidation. But far more responded
the way Americans would, fifty years later, to the digital age: with
amazement, awe, and delight.

Among those who experienced the revolution was John Davis
(born in 1904), who grew up on Corn Belt farms, first in Missouri and then in Iowa. During his childhood, his family relied on
horse-drawn plows and cultivators and a steam-powered thresher
(which they shared with their neighbors), and they butchered
and processed their own hogs. He graduated from high school in
1923, a moment when the farm crisis hammered even relatively
prosperous farm families like his. By then, the Davises were living in central Iowa, not far from Iowa State College (now Iowa
State University), one of the nation's premier land grant schools.
The proximity allowed Davis to attend school and help on the
farm, but after earning a bachelor's degree in economics, he, like
so many other young rural Americans, migrated away from the
farm. During the 1930s, he watched the nightmare of the Great
Depression from a small Iowa town where he taught school, but
in summers he headed to the University of Minnesota for course-
work that earned him a master's degree in agricultural economics. He finished in 1935 and never returned to full-time farming,
choosing instead to take a series of white-collar jobs, including

two stints at the USDA. In 1954, he accepted a position at Harvard, where he directed an agriculture program at the university's business school.

By that time, the fifty-year-old Davis had spent his entire life immersed in agriculture, albeit from a variety of perspectives. Those vantage points inspired a simple, but powerful, observation: farmers and their work could not be isolated from the rest of the economy. Viewing "agriculture as an industry in and of itself" may have made sense a century earlier when most Americans lived and worked on the land, he wrote, but in the mid-twentieth century, that perspective was both foolish and shortsighted. Davis observed that modern farmers had handed over the tasks of "storing, processing, and distributing food and fiber" to "off-the-farm business entities," like trucking companies and grocery chains. A different set of "off-the-farm" companies designed, built, and manufactured the inputs on which modern farmers relied, whether tractors and combines or antibiotics and poultry cages. Together, these three sectors — agricultural production, processing-distributing, and input manufacturing — constituted an interlocked whole, no part of which could survive without the others. Similarly, the triad's manufacture and distribution of food and fiber constituted one of the overall economy's largest components. Davis and a collaborator calculated that in 1954, consumers spent $93 billion on agriculturally based "end products and services" — food, paper, restaurant tabs, textiles, and so forth — a figure that didn't include dollars spent to grow, process, manufacture, or distribute food and fiber. Americans could not afford to conceptualize agriculture as an enterprise distinct from the rest of the economy.

Davis also understood that agriculture constituted the weakest link in the triumvirate because its individual units — farmers — lacked the power and the information needed to make market decisions. Input manufacturers and output processors, in contrast, executed financial and production decisions based on internal factors largely under their own control. Even if commodity prices fell, the price a farmer paid for, say, a tractor typically remained high because that price was based on factors controlled by the manufacturer, not the farmer. Davis argued that over time, the market stabilized this "cost-price" squeeze, but always at the expense of farmers and the taxpayers who subsidized that weak link. The more subsidy programs that Congress created to protect farmers, the more those programs entangled other members of the triad. Manufacturers of grain silos, to use a simple example, had a vested interest in ensuring that farmers produced surpluses that needed to be stored in those silos.

But like other economists and politicians at the time, Davis distinguished between farmers who practiced "commercial" agriculture and those "low-income" farmers who did not. He argued that marginal farmers — men and women who worked the land but either refused to or could not commit to thinking like factory managers — contributed nothing substantive by way of food and fiber; as a result, society lost "the value of their productive potential." Worse, when policymakers and politicians pondered solutions to the "farm problem," they invariably characterized that quandary in terms of those two poles — commercial farmers on one end and low-income farmers on the other — rather than seeing the two as connected to each other and to the other two members of the triumvirate. Until and unless Americans grasped the complexities of providing food and fiber for a non-agricultural population as well as the intimate connection between agriculture and the economy as a whole, and until they made hard choices about what constituted a "viable" farm, the agricultural problem would never be solved. Davis urged Americans to think of the production of food and fiber not as agriculture but to perceive it instead as "agribusiness." If that included abandoning adulation of the "family farm" and rethinking the myth of the sturdy yeoman, so be it. Only then would the nation come to terms with the fundamental conundrum of how to feed an urban majority and sustain a consumer economy.

Americans should have paid more attention. Over the next fifty years, agriculture in general and the production of livestock and meat in particular would become even more complex. Global politics, new dietary ideals, inflation, and environmental concerns would inspire farmers and meatpackers to devise ever less expensive ways to raise animals and transform them into meat. And in the late twentieth century, the logic of factory farming played out to a perhaps inevitable conclusion as large corporations demolished the boundaries between and among the triumvirate that fed the nation.

5

"HOW CAN WE GO WRONG?"

I N 1966, A REPORTER WHO visited Monfort Feed Lots, Inc.,
near Greeley, Colorado, marveled at the combination of
sights he found. A "touch of the Old West" was delivered
by Monfort veterinarians who ambled through the lots on horse-
back to monitor the well-being of the sixty thousand head of cattle fed there, but otherwise the ambiance was more suited to astronauts than cowboys. One building contained an electronic
device that looked like a "control board at the Cape Kennedy mis-
sile site." Employees fed it punch cards that contained vital information: minutely calculated feed formulas for the company's livestock, whose daily diets required a thousand tons of alfalfa, corn,
meat scraps, vitamins, minerals, antibiotics, and hormones. To
the tune of "clicks and clatters," the machine read the cards and
transmitted their data to a second machine housed at a nearby
silo, a three-hundred-foot-tall structure subdivided into vertical
bins, each bin containing one ingredient. The electronic signals
tripped the bins' gates, releasing feedstuffs into a truck equipped
with rotating drums that mixed the goods en route to the feed
bunks. When the driver neared his destination, he slowed to fifteen miles an hour and flipped a switch that opened the drum.

The contents spilled onto a conveyor belt and from there into a feed trough, ready for the cattle that milled around on the Monforts' three hundred acres. When the cattle were thirsty, they served themselves, using their noses to trip an automatic fountain fed by underground pipes.

The Monfort feedlot is another example of the factory farming ideal. But in the 1950s and 1960s, the proliferation of such operations — the Monforts' was the nation's largest, but it was just one of many — were driven by many factors: soaring demand for beef, which strained the capacity of the western range; the emergence of the "hotel, restaurant, institutional" food industry; and population growth in the western United States. In the years just after World War II, these factors inspired farmers and entrepreneurs to invent new modes of raising not just cattle but hogs, too. As in the broiler industry, these livestock systems embraced large scale, confinement, and the use of drug-laced feeds. But in cattle and hog production, innovations came primarily from traditional farmers working in conjunction with land grant schools; only later did large outside corporations commandeer the model. A half-century later, that midcentury version of livestock production still stands — and has become a target of considerable criticism — so it's important that we understand how and why these changes took place. There is no better way to do so than by tracing the history of the Monfort family's beef empire.

Warren Monfort was an unlikely cattle king. In the early twentieth century, his parents migrated from Illinois to Weld County in northern Colorado, where they bought a farm just a few miles from Greeley. Warren attended college there and worked briefly as a high school teacher. But the classroom wasn't enough to satisfy his ambition, and by 1919, he was back at his parents' farm with his new wife. He focused first on raising sheep, a common source of agricultural income in Colorado, but in the mid-1920s, he made a risky but ultimately profitable decision: he would feed cattle.

Historically, cattle feeding had been the domain of the Corn

Belt. Farmers there bought western, grass-fed range cattle and "finished" the livestock for market by feeding the stock a corn-rich diet, a practice that yielded "Prime" beef marbled with fat and endowed with a toothsome richness that grass feeding rarely provides. Those feeders bought their stock from ranchers in Colorado, Wyoming, Texas, and other western states, men and women who specialized in raising young stock on grass for about two years before selling their herds either directly to packers or to Corn Belt feeders.

But during the agricultural crisis of the 1920s, faculty at Colorado's land grant school, what was then Colorado Agricultural College (now Colorado State University), and its affiliated experiment station urged local ranchers to diversify into feeding. They pointed out that motorized trucks and networks of paved roads had given Coloradans better access to urban markets like Los Angeles and Salt Lake City, where consumers otherwise relied on beef shipped in from the Corn Belt. Why not give those Corn Belt farmers some competition? They also noted that although Coloradans produced little corn, there was an alternative: at the time, one of the major industries in Weld County and northern Colorado was sugar manufacture, an industry that relied on locally grown sugar beets and that generated mounds of waste in the form of beet tops and pulp; tests at CAC's experiment station indicated that cattle thrived on it.

Warren wanted to give feeding a try even though his father, Charles, opposed the project. Like most Colorado farmers, the elder Monfort grazed a few cattle, but he couldn't see the point of wasting time or labor on them. But when Charles died in 1930, the younger Monfort faced a choice: sell what had been, thanks to his father's lackadaisical management, a mostly failed farm ("During the 20s we thought we would go under about every year, but somehow we managed to hang on," Warren said later), or find a way to turn the eighty acres to profit. Warren decided to keep the land and try his hand at feeding, calculating that he'd be able to compete with more experienced Corn Belt feeders. At the time, those midwestern farmers typically practiced what agricultural economists called "in/out" feeding: When corn prices were low, they bought cattle and fed them grain, gambling they could make more money from cattle than from corn. When grain prices were high, they bought fewer cattle, or none at all, and sold their corn for cash. Put another way, feeding was a sideline to the main project of raising corn. Feeders were more interested in unloading cheap grain than in making high-quality beef, and so the meat's quality varied widely. Monfort also knew that Corn Belt farmer-feeders dumped their fed stock on the market at the same time in the fall, which produced a temporary glut that lowered the price they got for their cattle.

Monfort envisioned a number of ways to compete. Cattle gain weight more quickly in warm weather than in cold, and during snowy winters and wet springs they lose weight because they burn energy trying to keep their footing. The climate in Weld County, however, was more temperate than that of the Midwest; northern Colorado boasted mild, dry winters and relatively cool summers. His cattle could gain weight more consistently and he could feed and market them year-round, most importantly during those months when there were no midwestern cattle available. He had access to alfalfa, beet tops, and pulp, which, unlike corn, had little value other than as feed; that would allow him to compete on price. Finally, because he planned to specialize in feeding, he could focus on quality rather than quantity. Still, the project was risky, not least because Corn Belt farmers had dominated the finished-beef market since the 1860s; Monfort would have to convince packers that he could offer a product as good as or better than his competitors'. But he thrived on risk — others described him as an "aggressive" businessman — and so why not?

By the end of the brutal 1930s, cattle had paid off the farm's mortgage and Monfort had persuaded local bankers that he was a candidate for more credit. Wartime demand offered an opportunity for expansion, and by the early forties he was sending three thousand head a year — a remarkable number of cattle — to a single buyer, a national grocery chain. He maintained his focus on quality, which allowed him to compete where it mattered most:

at the Chicago stockyards, where he earned a reputation for shipping cattle that consistently yielded Prime beef, stock that rivaled, and often exceeded, anything sent to market by his Corn Belt competitors. During the 1940s, he also expanded his repertoire of feedstuffs and built networks of suppliers. He shipped shelled corn in from the Midwest, but he also contracted with farmers nearby to grow corn silage, feed composed of the entire corn plant — kernels, cobs, leaves, and stalks — chopped fine. Monfort provided his growers with hybrid seed and sold them, at cost, fertilizer that he bought in bulk. When it was time to make silage, Monfort's employees showed up with Monfort equipment and cut and chopped the crop, hauling it to storage pits near the feedlots.

But as the forties wound to a close, Warren Monfort sensed that change lay ahead. He believed that beef consumption was about to rise but that the Prime-grade product on which he'd built his reputation would decline in popularity. If so, he said, his future success would depend on using "a slightly lower grade cattle" that yielded a lesser cut of beef "that would appeal to the tastes and the pocket books of the general public." He was right on both counts. Historically, Americans have eaten more beef as their incomes rise, and in the 1940s and 1950s, the thriving economy drove incomes up even as prices for all foods remained low. During the 1940s, despite the constraints of war, ongoing rationing, and "meatless Mondays," the nation's appetite for beef rose ten pounds per capita. In the 1950s, it jumped another ten pounds, and during the 1960s, another twenty. There were more meat eaters to feed as well: the nation's population rose by almost 20 million during the 1940s, and another 50 million from 1950 to 1970. The ascendance of King Beef fostered midcentury clichés: suburbanites grilling burgers at backyard barbecues, and white-collar workers feasting on three-martini lunches punctuated with steak. But Americans did not live by fresh beef alone. More than ever, convenience mattered, and sales of canned beef goods soared. "Our products are like cake mixes and canned soup," explained a happy purveyor. "They're selling well because housewives are looking for quick, easy ways to fix food." Canned beef stew or corned beef hash, tamales and chili, and "sandwich steaks" (precooked steak slices ready to meet bread) offered a harried housewife an easy way to get a meal on the table. When the family tired of beef stew, Mom could turn to Kri-Pi, a pre-packaged meat pie sold in two cans taped together to make a single package, dough in one can, "meat, vegetables and gravy" in the other. The nation's millions of "war babies" (or, as we now call them, baby boomers) feasted on canned strained beef and other beef-based commercial baby food; in the early 1950s, Swift alone sold thirteen meat-based baby foods. Canned meat products were inexpensive, too, because they were manufactured from the lowest grades of grass-fed beef, tough, stringy stuff that is most tasty when cooked for long periods and paired with other ingredients and spices. Perfect for Chef Boyardee spaghetti in meat sauce.

Even as record numbers of Americans downed record amounts of beef, they turned their backs on expensive Prime cuts. The nation's longtime obsession with weight watching had fallen off during the hard times of the Depression and wartime rationing, but in postwar America, calorie counting became the national sport it remains today; grocery shelves sagged under the heft of artificial sweeteners, weight-loss aids, and low-calorie beer. Prime beef with its high fat content lost its appeal. But so, too, did its high price: buyers for the grocery chains quickly learned that Americans, true to form, demanded not just lots of meat, and good meat, but meat at a low price. They wanted "Choice" grade, which, like Prime, came from grain-fed stock but contained less fat than its higher-grade cousin.

Shoppers and grocery chains weren't the only ones demanding the step down from Prime. By the late 1940s, Warren Monfort and other cattle feeders were accommodating a new power player: the burgeoning hotel, restaurant, and institutional industry. The HRI behemoth, ubiquitous now, is primarily a product of the mid-twentieth century. Ongoing military operations, first in World War II, then in Korea, Southeast Asia, and elsewhere, fueled the growth of the armed services and the bureaucracy that supported them (the food service at the Pentagon, built during World War II, dished up thousands of meals a day). The baby boom fueled another kind of growth as children filed first into school lunchrooms and then into university and college dining halls. Americans funneled record amounts of money into medical research, and hospitals and affiliated health care enterprises proliferated, as did their food services. Hotel chains that offered restaurant service flourished as an affluent society spent more of its disposable income on travel for both business and leisure. HRI included federal and state prisons, airports and airplanes, corporate and factory cafeterias. All of it added up to an immense demand for food, especially beef, served outside the home. In the mid-1960s, one Chicago purveyor packaged a staggering 3 million hamburgers a day for its HRI customers, mostly schools and hospitals.

The "R" part of the HRI equation accounted for a significant chunk of demand. Prior to midcentury, restaurants primarily catered to the well-to-do at one end and urban workers on a budget at the other. But in postwar America, consumer demand spawned a collection of chain enterprises aimed at every conceivable market niche, not least of which was the one devoted to supplying a busy nation with "fast" food, an industry segment that grew 79 percent in the second half of the 1960s alone. By the mid-sixties, Americans could choose from over four hundred fast-food chains; the two hundred largest of those operated more than forty thousand outlets. McDonald's grew from one shop in 1955 to 228 just five years later. Over the next decade, founder Ray Kroc opened new shops at a rate of a hundred a year. By 1970, the company was the sixth-largest food server in the United States, after the army, the USDA, the navy, Kentucky Fried Chicken, and Marriott. But McDonald's was not alone. The much smaller Mr. Steak chain, for instance, dished up 150,000 steaks a week, all of which had to look and weigh the same. What linked these new food outposts (and by the sixties, Americans were eating a third

of their beef someplace other than at home) was their need to ca-
ter to a mass audience, and that audience wanted Choice or Good
beef, not Prime. Cattle feeders like Monfort had to adapt or die.

Given these changes, we might assume that demand for grain-
fed beef declined. After all, feeding cattle to Choice grade rather
than Prime required less grain, not more, and canned meat products came from grass-fed stock. But consider these numbers: In
1950, 47 percent of the beef Americans ate came from "fed" cattle. By 1968, that number had risen to 71 percent (and held steady
for the rest of the century). The explanation for this apparent conundrum lay out on the western range. It could no longer support the number of cattle needed to meet demand. "Just to raise
the calves we buy every year [to feed] requires an area the size
of Delaware," said Warren Monfort in 1952, and as he and every other cattleman knew, the nation's supply of grazing acres
was shrinking even as beef demand rose. In the fifteen years after 1935, 9 million acres of federal grazing lands were closed or
shifted to other uses. The Pentagon, for example, commandeered
thousands of acres for use as airfields, bases, and weapons testing
grounds. All that military development and affiliated industry attracted workers who needed housing, and New Deal projects like
the Grand Coulee Dam encouraged landowners to use once-arid
soil for crop farming rather than grazing. Planted fields and suburban houses flourished where cattle once roamed. All told, 45
million acres of the western range were removed from grazing
during the 1930s and 1940s.

Nor did Monfort and other ranchers believe that the number
of available acres would grow anytime soon. Federal officials had
dumped money into reseeding projects aimed at increasing range
capacity, but there was no guarantee that even those acres would
be available in the future, thanks to a bitter, ongoing conflict between Washington bureaucrats and western grazers. Ever since
the cattle disaster of the 1880s, federal authorities had monitored
ranchers' use of the range and in the early twentieth century began requiring them to pay a (minuscule) fee for their access to it.

Ranchers did not own the property outright, but many behaved as if they did, and relations between federal bureaucrats and cattle and sheep growers were contentious, to say the least. Many officials believed that ranchers should not use the land at all but, if they did, ought to pay more for the privilege. Most ranchers disagreed. As far as they were concerned, their use amounted to ownership. Over the years, tensions between the two sides routinely flared, died down, flared anew, and faded again. But in 1934, Congress passed the Taylor Grazing Act; the law, which most ranchers supported, set aside 142 million acres for grazing, established a collection of grazing districts, and granted administrative control over them to ranchers. Unfortunately, the new law also sparked a ferocious turf war in Washington, as the officials charged with managing public lands sought to exercise greater control over them, especially the acres devoted to grazing. That conflict in turn alarmed many ranchers, who, fearing they would lose their rights, abandoned support for the Taylor Act and urged Congress to turn the range over to the states.

During the 1940s, the tension spawned a series of lengthy and well-publicized congressional hearings into the use (or, as many argued, abuse) of the range that drew attention to grazing practices of which, until then, few Americans had been aware. Conservationists seized the moment, arguing that ranchers were freeloaders and that the range in general and grazing land in particular belonged to the American people. Not to the ranchers; not to the government. To all Americans. Critics charged that ranchers defrauded the public by using what amounted to subsidized land to reap profits from cattle and abused the range, which could no longer support the herds grazing it, let alone the numbers needed to keep Americans in beef. Bernard DeVoto, a well-known writer and a Utah native devoted to both conservation and the West, charged that the ranchers' "lust" for land could "bring the United States to the verge of [environmental] catastrophe in a single generation."

Those conflicts and the ongoing pressure of urban development in the western United States did not bode well for cattle ranchers or consumers. As grazing acres shrank, so would the ability to raise cattle, and beef prices would inch upward. What to do? "More of the growing period will have to be in feedlots," Warren Monfort argued, and less on the range. Instead of keeping cattle on grass until age two or three, as was customary, ranchers would have to sell them as yearlings in order to make room for new stock. Those yearlings would go to feedlots. Put simply, if American consumers wanted to keep eating beef at a price they would pay, cattle would have to spend more time eating grain than eating grass.

And so Warren Monfort began the journey that led him to become the nation's largest cattle feeder. In the late 1940s he remodeled and expanded his feedlot in order to accommodate younger cattle and more of them. He installed equipment that automated the feeding process and configured feed formulas designed for cattle of various ages. But Monfort did not reinvent the wheel. The model he emulated, he told a journalist some years later, could be found "across the mountains" in California. "Out there they didn't have to unlearn anything such as we do in changing from the small farm feedlot" to a factorylike, automated operation.

It was true. The commercial feedlots that emerged in the plains states in the 1950s were based on ones built in the 1940s along the Pacific coast, especially in California. Californians had been breeding and grazing cattle for two centuries, but when World War II broke out, West Coast ranchers found it impossible to keep up with demand. Between 1940 and 1955, California's population doubled from 6 to 12 million. Despite the state's well-established commercial farming industry, food of all sorts, and especially meat and milk, was in short supply. But conventional feeding and dairying operations could not keep pace for two other reasons: as was true elsewhere in the United States during the war, agricultural labor was in short supply, and in California, farmland was being devoured by factories, airstrips, and housing. To adapt, landowners converted conventional farms into factorylike operations designed to yield maximum quantities of food using minimal labor and land. Cattle feeders replaced human labor with machinery and pasture with fenced, and often paved, lots. Conventional livestock feed was scarce, so feeders relied on alfalfa and barley, as well as sugar beet tops and pulp, citrus rinds, almond husks, and other wastes from canning plants. Add vitamin and protein supplements designed to replicate the nutritional value of corn, toss the ingredients into a machine and mix, and feeders were in business.

During the 1940s, that combination of high demand, alternative feedstuffs, and shrinking supplies of both labor and land fostered the construction of dozens of mechanized commercial feedlots across California. Consider the McDougal Livestock Company, located halfway between Sacramento and San Francisco. The feedlot held fifteen thousand animals; in a year, McDougal turned out about forty thousand market-ready cattle. But McDougal's proprietors were not conventional cattlemen. They were contractors who fed cattle for owners who paid to board their livestock at McDougal and who collected the animals once they were ready to be sold. At any one time, a third to half of the feedlots' inhabitants were owned by packing companies and traveled directly from feedlot to slaughterhouse, no stockyard or middleman needed. That, too, was a California innovation, and by the late forties, 90 percent of California feeder cattle were sold directly to packers. As urban pressure squeezed land prices, many California feeders transferred their operations to Arizona, where there was still plenty of relatively cheap land as well as other big feedlots. Consider the Tovrea Land and Cattle Company near Phoenix. The Tovrea family had been raising cattle in the area since the 1880s and over the years had built a small packinghouse and feed mill. But in the late 1940s, the family sold the packinghouse in order to focus on feeding, thirty-five thousand head at a time. An adjacent company-owned mill churned out eighty-two thousand tons a year of feed made from hay, milo, barley, cottonseed hulls, and cottonseed meal. A network of conveyors and augers transported the rations from mill to feedlot, where another set of augers mixed the feed to precise specifications and carried it directly to the feed bunks. The number of hands needed to manage the stock? A mere seventeen. And like the McDougal venture, Tovrea owned almost none of the animals. Instead, it provided "custom" and "specification" feeding to its clients, some of which were meatpackers and grocery chains.

Warren Monfort studied those West Coast models and he understood the new dynamics of making beef: take stock off the range at a younger age, feed it to specifications dictated by either a meatpacker or a grocery chain, and use mechanization to slash expenses at the "beef factory," as he called it. Monfort started the 1950s with eight thousand head of cattle, turning the stock over at least once a year so that he marketed between sixteen and twenty thousand head a year, sending cattle to market every week. By decade's end, he owned one hundred acres of feedlots that held twenty-two thousand cattle at a time, lots designed to accommodate machinery that reduced the need for human labor.

By that time, Warren's son Ken had joined the family business. As a boy, Ken had worked around the farm and shown animals at livestock competitions. At Colorado State University he majored in animal nutrition, although he was more interested in writing than in farming (for years, he wrote a column for a Greeley newspaper). But his beloved older brother died during World War II, and when Warren began his great expansion, Ken left college without a degree and returned home to help. Ken Monfort was born for business. He was an imposing man. (This was in part because of his exuberant personality, but also because of his height: nearly six and a half feet tall. The company's Japanese customers adored him: here was the Marlboro man come to life.) Like Phil Armour, he kept one eye on business and the other fixed on events national and global, contemplating the way in which, say, monsoons in India or labor strikes in Milwaukee might affect his Colorado company. He had the brain of a mathematician and an endless fascination with turning ideas and opportunities to profit. He was famous (or infamous) among friends and acquaintances for his indifference to his surroundings, known for wearing two different shoes or the same shirt many days in a row. But the chain-smoking, coffee-swilling Monfort (a small mountain of disposable cups obscured the back seat of his car) loved his work, and his ambition equaled if not exceeded that of his father. Warren Monfort had always been "a heck of an asset to the industry," mused a cattle-feeding neighbor, but "when the young fellow came along he just went ape."

The Monforts operated the biggest feedlot, but theirs was just one of many new ventures that opened in the western and southern United States at midcentury. From California to Texas to Kansas, entrepreneurs ran fencing, constructed feed bunks, and outfitted trucks with mixers. In 1962, commercial feeders — defined by the USDA as feeding a thousand or more head of cattle — accounted for just a third of the fed cattle sent to slaughter. Eleven years later, two-thirds of the nation's fed cattle came from such lots, and a mere 1 percent of feedlots put out nearly half the nation's fed cattle. Nowhere was the boom more evident than in Texas. In 1950, Texans fed a mere quarter of a million cattle; twenty years later, they turned out 3 million. Among the Texas feeders was Paul Engler, who opened his gates in 1961 with just five thousand head and doubled his feedings in a year. (Twenty years later, he would rule as the world's cattle king.) Engler credited location for that growth. His lots lay a few miles southwest of Amarillo, long a busy cattle market but now a depository for range cattle that, a few years earlier, would have been shipped to the Corn Belt. "I can walk into that town at any time," said Engler, "and find the type of cattle I need." The cattle buyer for the Swift packing plant in Fort Worth was delighted. "We used to have to ship in a lot of choice-grade carcasses from the Corn Belt to meet the consumers' demand for meat," he said. "Now we have choice cattle all year around [sic] fed right in this area." The manager of the tony Amarillo Club applauded the change. For years, the steaks he sold came from Chicago; now he could serve T-bones and fillets from animals born, raised, fed, and slaughtered nearby.

The midcentury birth of commercial feeding operations had little to do with corn. As we've seen, western commercial feeders used everything from almond husks to citrus pulp to sugar beet

tops. But the grain that drove feedlot expansion in the mid-twentieth century was sorghum. The grass was not new to the West
and Southwest, but prior to the 1940s, it played a small role in
those regions' agriculture. That changed when federal allotment
programs reduced acres that could be devoted to cotton. Western
and southern farmers latched on to sorghum as a substitute, and
it became the primary ingredient in feeders' rations, its production increasing markedly after a hybrid version became available
in the late 1950s. A sign at the Hillcrest Cafe in Tulia, Texas, testified to the change: "Our feature— Texas sorghum-fed top sirloin
steak, $2." "Those sirloins really move," boasted the happy owner.

As had been true of the California feedlot pioneers, many operators fed livestock on contract for specification buyers like meatpackers and grocery chains; those direct purchases eliminated
the need for stockyards, whether in Chicago or Fort Worth. Some
packers and grocers even operated their own feedlots, a tactic
that allowed them to exert maximum control over the quality of
beef they sold. South of Denver, for example, a grocery chain operated several mammoth feedlots and processed the animals at
its nearby company-owned slaughterhouse. The number of packers that fed their own beef was small, but skewed to the West. By
the mid-1960s, meatpackers fed about 7 percent of all the cattle
slaughtered in the United States, but the number was higher in
the West: 38 percent in Washington state and 22 in Idaho. Forty-
three percent of all packer-fed cattle came from just three states:
Texas, California, and Washington. Without those feedlots, said
a Utah packer, he and his peers as well as regional grocery chains
would have found it "impossible" to lay hands on "year-round
supplies of finished animals in sufficient volume" to meet their
contracts and, more important, to keep consumer prices low for
shoppers.

The movement of cattle off the range and into western feedlots
was a transformative moment in American livestock production.
Nowhere was the impact felt more keenly than in the midwestern Corn Belt, where, as had been true for the previous century,

agriculture rested on the cattle-corn-hog complex. During the 1950s and 1960s, and even aside from the new competitors, turmoil unsettled that long-standing triad, in part because new subsidy programs for corn and other grains diminished the appeal of livestock production. Livestock feeders headed for the exit. "I'm getting out of the cattle business," said an Iowa feeder in 1953, a man who'd been marketing about twelve thousand head a year. "I'm going to plow up my pasture, put it in corn and then sell the corn to the Government at $1.55 a bushel." Two Nebraska feeders also decided to "dry up" their operations. "We're going to grow about 90,000 bushels," said one of them, and then "seal it [in a silo] and go fishing."

Western competition squeezed those who stayed in, as cattle that once traveled to Chicago or Kansas City stayed in the West. "No question," sighed one Illinois feeder, "but that competition's driving [up] prices" that he and other farmer-feeders paid for cattle. And not just prices: as Warren Monfort had expected, the temperate plains climate and westerners' access to cheap feedstuffs gave midwesterners headaches. Monfort was right about something else: Corn Belt feeders weren't specialists, and in the 1950s, that could be fatal. Any ten Iowa cattle (or hog) farmers gave their livestock ten different types of feed and ended up with ten lots of livestock that varied in weight, musculature, fat, and marbling. Specification buyers like Armour and Swift, Safeway and A&P weren't interested in those grab bags. They wanted uniform cargoes of carcasses with specific ratios of lean to fat at a specific price. Commercial feeders like the Monforts obliged, exercising razor-sharp focus to achieve uniformity, providing not just more consistent beef but huge quantities of it, far more than the average Corn Belt farmer-feeder could muster.

In 1959, an analyst with the Federal Reserve Bank offered a blunt assessment: western competition was driving "the small, one-or-two-carloads-a-year cattle feeder in the Corn Belt out of business." A western meatpacker had little sympathy for the losers, pointing out that professionals like the Monforts focused on "only one aim and that was to produce an animal of desired quality as quickly and as economically as possible." By comparison, Corn Belt feeding practices were "wasteful and unscientific." Put a bit more charitably, midwesterners were nonspecialists in a specialized world. A Missouri man got the message: "As in most any business, the fellow who produces the cheapest will stay in." If he and other Corn Belt farmers hoped to survive, they would have to reduce their costs by joining the Monforts in putting "beef feeding on a factory basis."

Midwestern hog farmers experienced even more turmoil in part because pork's future looked none too bright. In a 1956 Roper poll, many interviewees described pork as "less nourishing" than beef or poultry and more fattening than both. Those polled associated beef with "athletes, bankers, [and] slim and beautiful women" and pork with "poor people, truck drivers, [and] large families." Between that, grain subsidies, and the labor shortage, many hog farmers wanted out. A Minnesota man who abandoned hogs in favor of corn in 1958 told a reporter that as grain subsidy programs reduced the risks of crop farming, hogs became "more of a gamble." And, he added, "When I raised hogs, I didn't have time for anything else." "Hog-raising is not only hard work but it's also a year-round chore," one made increasingly difficult by the lack of labor. "Now I'm free in the winter. Last year, we made a two-week trip to Florida and Washington."

But Corn Belt hog farmers also faced new competition, in their case from entrepreneurs in the southern and southeastern United States. As federal allotment programs reduced cotton and tobacco acres in the South, landowners there hunted for alternatives and many turned to hog farming. Despite the region's historically pork-centric diet, southerners had little experience raising hogs because landowners had traditionally devoted their land to cash crops and imported pork from northern states. So when southerners turned to hogs in the 1950s and 1960s, they started from scratch and, not surprisingly, built enterprises modeled after the broiler industry. Hurdles abounded. Southerners competed against experienced Corn Belt hog farmers, and they had to ship corn in from the Midwest. On the plus side, however, were weather — hogs gain weight faster in warm climates — and in states like North Carolina, proximity to the East Coast's metropolitan markets. As in the broiler industry, the new hog producers tended to be entrepreneurs rather than traditional farmers, and as in broiler making, they relied on contract growers and assistance from affiliated industries. Swift, for example, had taken advantage of North Carolina's relatively cheap land and labor and built a packing plant there but had trouble buying enough hogs to keep it running at capacity. To encourage local farmers, the plant's managers leased sows to farmers who agreed to take at least fifty of them and to sell the offspring to Swift. "Inherent in all this are the principles of the industrial production line," explained a reporter in 1959. "The businessman at one end of the line ships out standardized pigs to farmers who'll feed them according to a set pattern." Regular production schedules would stabilize supplies and prices, and consumers would get "cheaper, better pork." "This is the beginning of a revolution in swine raising," raved a Missouri slaughterhouse owner who tried to transplant the model to his state.

Many midwestern farmers cringed at such praise, fearing that contract farming would reduce them to the status of hired hands. But an executive with a Missouri agricultural consulting firm advised doubters to keep an open mind. "If you don't want [outsiders] to take over your traditional product," he said, "don't spare the horses." Translation: Modernize your operations.

At least hog farmers had antibiotics to help keep costs in line. Cattle feeders had seen the results those high-tech inputs provided, and that's why they applauded a 1954 announcement from Iowa State College: Wise Burroughs, an ISC faculty member, had discovered that feeding cattle the synthetic hormone diethylstilbestrol, known as DES, accelerated growth and thus lowered feed costs. At last cattle feeders had their own version of a pharmaceutical miracle worker.

As noted earlier, the war-era search for new feedstuffs had led to the use of antibiotic-laced feeds on broiler and hog farms. But antibiotics had limited value for cattle feeders: unlike chickens and hogs, bovines have multiple stomachs and they don't chew their food so much as they moisten it to ease its trip to the first stomach, the rumen. Those multiple stomachs also complicated scientists' understanding of bovine nutrition. Researchers had figured out that cattle manure contained some substance — an X factor — that satisfied the nutritional needs of hogs and chickens. They also knew that the rumen harbors immense colonies of microorganisms that transform roughage into carbohydrates. Beyond, that, however, and even in the 1940s, bovine digestion and nutrition were little understood, and precisely what transpired in the rumen and the other stomachs was a mystery.

In the 1940s, bovine nutrition research centered around institutions in Indiana and Ohio, including the Ohio State Agricultural Experiment Station where Wise Burroughs was employed. Burroughs's team included a nine-month-old Hereford named Christopher Columbus. A visitor to the laboratory in 1948 described Chris as an exceptionally "happy" and healthy animal — despite his two-legged colleagues' habit of rummaging through his rumen via a hole cut in his flank. (After a local newspaper touted Chris's unusual contribution to science, a representative from the Society for the Prevention of Cruelty to Animals descended on the lab. He concluded that Chris was in neither danger nor pain and not likely to become a "charcoal-broiled steak" anytime soon.) Burroughs and his colleagues fed Chris combinations of feedstuffs and then pulled those back out of the rumen for analysis, hunting for nutrition-rich combinations that maximized rumen activity. They studied urea (nitrogen-rich but converted to protein by the rumen) and molasses (which sweetened the mix and added carbohydrates), but corncobs, a source of cellulose-rich roughage, provided a particularly tantalizing line of research. Cobs piled up by the billions on American farms; if those could be used as cattle feed, livestock producers would save money.

Burroughs's work with corncobs intrigued Roswell Garst, an Iowa hybrid corn producer (and, in 1959, host to visiting Soviet premier Nikita Khrushchev). In the late 1940s, Garst conducted corncob experiments with his own herd and discovered that cattle fed a mixture of cobs and cornmeal fared as well as those that ate shelled corn, and that using the cobs cut his feeding costs by half. Eager to know more, and worried that Iowa cattle feeders like himself were losing market share to western feedlots, Garst prodded officials at Iowa State College in Ames to devote more resources to the study of bovine nutrition and to hire Burroughs.

By 1951, Burroughs was ensconced in his new laboratory at ISC and had obtained a research grant from Rath Packing Company, located in eastern Iowa. He built an artificial rumen and, using sheep rather than cattle, continued to study the mechanisms and nutritional demands of bovine digestion. (Burroughs switched to sheep, also ruminants, because they cost less, ate less, and were easier to manage than cattle.) Some of his subjects received conventional feed and some ate feed supplemented with antibiotics. But Burroughs dosed one group with DES.

There was nothing unusual about his decision to use the hormone in his research. As we saw earlier, midcentury scientists were determined to unravel the mysteries of growth, whether in plants, animals, or humans, and many of them studied the impact of hormones on growth, aging, and death. In the early 1940s, for instance, a scientist at the University of Chicago created hormone-based substances to destroy Japanese rice crops, and by the time the war ended, Americans were using hormone-based herbicides on their lawns and farms. DES had attracted the attention of researchers studying hormonal changes in women. As women age, their hormone levels gyrate and decline, a process that produces hot flashes, headaches, and the other miseries of menopause. For years, physicians had relied on hysterectomy to alleviate those woes, but some scientists believed that replacing those hormones would be a more effective (and presumably less intrusive) tactic. Natural hormones were expensive, so researchers sought synthetic substitutes. Among them was DES, an exceptionally powerful estrogenic substance that could be manufactured from coal tar derivatives. Like natural estrogens, DES is potentially carcinogenic but there the similarities end, not least because DES is about three times more powerful than natural estrogens. In addition, while the body breaks down and eliminates ordinary estrogen, DES residues linger for some time, and even when they're excreted, they retain their estrogenic power. Despite these drawbacks, physicians used DES to counteract the effects of menopause and prescribed it to pregnant women; manufacturers added it to breast-enhancement creams.

During World War II, animal nutritionists latched on to DES for the same reason they focused on antibiotics: as a way to accelerate livestock growth and thus reduce the costs of production. In the early 1940s, a poultry scientist at the University of California–Davis discovered that DES altered the life cycle of male birds: when he implanted hormone pellets in roosters, their combs shrank, they sprouted "female feathers and a layer of fat," and they "lolled around like capons." Most important, at least from a marketing point of view, their ordinarily "stringy" flesh "became light and tender." In 1947, the Food and Drug Administration (FDA) approved DES for use as a chemical castrator in the form of pellets implanted in the birds' heads or necks. (Those parts of the anatomy were removed at packing plants and in theory, there was no danger that the pellets would end up in human stomachs.) By the time Burroughs began tinkering with DES, a team of scientists at Purdue University had already tried feeding it to both cattle and sheep.

Burroughs assumed that the sheep he dosed with DES would grow faster than those in his control groups. To his surprise, however, all the animals grew at the same rate, regardless of what they'd eaten. The only feed common to all the subjects was clover hay. Burroughs prowled the pages of scientific journals and discovered that, indeed, common livestock forages such as clover and soybeans contain estrogenic substances. He theorized that estrogen somehow improved the rumen's digestive mechanism and maximized its nutritive output. If so, adding hormones to feed would provide cattle the same growth boost that antibiotics gave chickens and hogs. DES was inexpensive to manufacture and DES implants cheaper than clover grown on expensive pasture. In February 1954, Burroughs announced that cattle growers, like their hog and poultry counterparts, could reap the benefits of a growth-promoting additive.

Not that DES was a precise counterpart of antibiotics, if only because it posed more risks. In the early fifties, mink growers who fed chicken heads to their animals complained that DES residue rendered females barren. In New Jersey, a man who worked with DES at his job with a pharmaceutical company sued his employer because of side effects. Despite his wearing a respirator and rubber gloves, the DES had "poisoned" him, he complained; he'd "suffered effemination" and "been rendered permanently impotent" and therefore deprived of "the rights and benefits of marital relations." He wasn't the only one. The owner of another chemical company told FDA officials that male employees who worked with DES experienced breast development and impotence. (The FDA urged him to hire older workers, men who might not be as concerned about DES's "devirilizing effect.") Even meatpackers weren't convinced of the wisdom of adding DES to cattle diets. One complained that hormone-fed cattle failed to "cut out a carcass that's as good as they look on the hoof." He worried, too, that "short-cut, cheaper fattening methods promoted by every agricultural college around" were doing more harm than good. "The beef we're seeing today doesn't measure up to the old corn-fed beef. It looks plump and good on the outside, but when you cut it open the quality isn't there. The way things are going, corn-fed beef will be a thing of the past in four or five years."

But many Corn Belt feeders dismissed those concerns. "My family and the tenants' families have been eating the meat for months," said an Illinois cattleman. "It's completely safe." An agricultural reporter pointed out that farmers didn't have to handle much of the stuff: one ounce was sufficient to "fortify" rations for 2,800 head of cattle, and that small dose translated into "an extra half ton of beef." DES had "become the bright hope of feed dealers and cattle feeders alike." Still, he and others advised farmers to use common sense and caution so that they didn't end up looking like "sweater girls." By early 1955, 2 million cattle were ingesting Stilbosol, a premix manufactured and marketed by Eli Lilly and Company, which had secured five-year exclusive rights to the patent. "Amazing? You bet it is!" enthused a writer for *Farm Journal*. "Nothing has ever hit the meat-animal business with the impact of stilbestrol," he opined, not even the much-ballyhooed antibiotics. Nor was DES the only new cattle feed. Burroughs and other researchers engineered a host of products designed to reduce Corn Belt feeders' costs: molasses and corncobs, for example, became standard components of the feed toolbox, as did plastic pellets, which generated friction and boosted rumen efficiency.

DES and antibiotics helped Corn Belt feeders hone their competitive edge. But they still faced one obstacle that weighted the game in favor of western and southern feeders: weather. That explains the enthusiasm for another tool that Corn Belt feeders adopted just after World War II: confinement.

The roots of confinement date back to the wartime emergency of the 1940s. In California, the combination of labor shortages and the pressure of urban growth on farmland forced cattlemen not just to feed rather than graze their livestock but to keep the animals confined to a relatively small, fenced area. Many of those feeders kept their animals on paved lots in order to reduce the labor needed to move manure out of the way. Those first steps toward confinement intrigued agricultural specialists searching for ways to help farmers elsewhere reduce production costs and cope with lack of labor. Farmers and agronomists alike were also influenced by the example of the broiler industry, which had relied on confinement to manage large flocks, and analysts began crunching the numbers to determine if taking animals off pasture could pay. A study conducted in the 1940s at Iowa State College revealed that in wet spring weather, cattle struggling to maneuver in inches-deep mud burned so many calories that they lost as much as three pounds a month, loss that negated weight gains and turned expensive feed into a "complete loss" in the account book. Add in mud-related injury and disease, and analysts calculated that mud cost midwestern farmers money, time, and labor. When the ISC team moved its livestock onto a paved lot, the animals lost less weight and had fewer injuries; profit margins increased by as much as $10 a head. The pavement also allowed the team to move manure using tractors and blades rather than shovels and shoulders, and to spread it where it was needed rather than where livestock deposited it. "You can't *afford* a muddy barnyard," a reporter told readers of a farm magazine. "If yours is, it's costing plenty."

In the years just after the war, Americans explored confinement's possibilities, building on studies like those conducted at ISC but also borrowing ideas from European farmers, many of whom had long coped with lack of land and labor by confining their livestock. By the late 1950s, many American farmers, especially hog growers, had moved beyond the initial confinement concept of paved surface plus fencing and carried the idea to its logical conclusion: moving swine not just off pasture but completely indoors, using heating, cooling, and ventilation technologies to replicate ideal outdoor conditions. Confinement protected animals from predators and weather and enabled livestock producers to automate feeding and to exercise complete control over animals' diets, something that was impossible when livestock ran on pasture.

Those who took the plunge regarded the money as well spent. Two Indiana brothers who moved their cattle from pasture to confinement reduced per-head feeding time from four hours to just fourteen minutes a day, and cleanup from three hours to twenty-four minutes. That in turn enabled them to increase the number of cattle they fed from 82 to 257. A South Dakota man raved about his neighbor's confinement operation. "He's got what I call a beef factory for the 60s!" said the man. "Slickest set-up I ever saw." He just "pushes a few buttons and feeds 300 head in 20 to 30 minutes." Thanks to that equipment, the penned animals ate a "complete ration" of "silage, corn, protein pellets, [and] molasses," all of it so thoroughly mixed that "every mouthful a steer [ate was] alike," a crucial benefit given that meatpackers and grocery chains demanded animals with specific carcass attributes. The owner confirmed that he was pleased by the switch from pasture to confinement. "You should have been here last winter to appreciate fully what it means," he told a reporter. Multiple storms dumped a "17-inch snow pack on the ground." While his neighbors' cattle lost weight trying to navigate the treacherous terrain, his enjoyed "good gains." Indeed, confinement mitigated the role of climate and enabled Corn Belt farmers to compete with year-round feeders like the Monforts. "We were getting killed selling twice a year," said an Iowan who moved his cattle into confinement. "Now we're marketing every month, averaging the ups and downs, and making money." A Michigan farmer was blunt about what drove him to invest in confinement: "I can't afford to pasture cattle on high-priced Corn Belt land." From the 1950s on, and even in the relatively rural Midwest, urban sprawl and burgeoning networks of highways and interstates gobbled agricultural acres and pushed land prices into the stratosphere. Many farmers sold their holdings to developers, but those who did not were forced to farm intensively rather than extensively. Pasture grazing had always imposed an upper limit on the number of animals the grasses could feed, but with confinement, farmers could increase herd size on a small parcel of land, allowing them to turn what had been pasture to other uses, such as planting grain crops.

Hog farmers were even more enthusiastic about confinement. Consider an Illinois man who marketed about seven hundred head a year, feeding them with corn he grew. In the late 1950s, he sat down and reconsidered. "I analyzed my work schedule," he said, "and found that raising corn brought me in only 10 per cent of my income, but took 50 per cent of my time. That was the turning-point of my farming career." He rented his corn acres to another farmer, increased his hog herd, and invested in automated augers that carried feed from bins to mixing floor to hog pens. By 1960, he'd upped his output to seventeen hundred head and was aiming for two thousand. "With 700 hogs, my gross ran about $30,000," he mused, and he'd "had to work as long and as hard as any farmer." By "modernizing," he doubled his gross and "with far less work." Confinement benefited hog farmers in two other ways. First, it helped them reduce the otherwise high mortality rates that cut into profits. An Iowa farmer learned that. Year after year, his pasture-based swine suffered dysentery. In the early 1950s, he adopted antibiotic-laced feeds in hopes of reducing disease-related mortality, but the drugs made no difference because, an agent from Iowa State College explained, the soil in his pasture teemed with parasites and bacteria. Moving the hogs indoors significantly reduced his losses from disease. Second, confinement protected hog farmers' investments in expensive breeding stock. As grocers and meatpackers became increasingly specific in their demands, many midcentury farmers replaced older stock with breeds engineered to produce leaner hogs, and some invested in "Specific Pathogen-Free" stock: animals bred and born in sterile environments. Having invested their money, farmers were loath to let the animals run free. Confinement also enhanced the possibilities of specialization. A Wisconsin hog farmer decided that instead of raising hogs from birth to market, he would focus on inseminating and farrowing sows, selling the offspring — "feeder pigs" — to farmers who only wanted to feed for market. Because he conducted his new operation entirely indoors, he could breed his sows more often and sell feeder pigs year-round. Demand was so high that he contracted with other farmers to produce feeders for him. Another Corn Belt family — a father, two sons, and a son-in-law — also shifted to confinement as a way to streamline their hog farm. One family member specialized in breeding, another in farrowing; a third finished the hogs for market; and the fourth stayed in the farm's office, keeping the books and arranging sales. Mimicking the division of labor found in a factory or corporation, they argued, enhanced their profits and protected them in the market.

Land grant faculty and USDA officials urged midwestern feeders to specialize and invest in confinement to reduce costs and hone their competitive edge. Packers and feed dealers who wanted Corn Belt producers to stay in the game supported the new technologies, too. A Kansas City feed manufacturer contracted with packers on one side, and hog farmers on the other, preselling the farmers' hogs to the packers. The manufacturer provided "technical assistance" to farmers who agreed to use its feed and raise hogs according to contracts that stipulated every detail, from feed formula to breeding stock to the design of breeding pens and farrowing huts. Another midwestern feed company rented boars, sows, and gilts (young females that have not yet reproduced) to Corn Belt farmers. The farmers bought feed from the manufacturer and paid swine "rent" only after they'd marketed their animals, often for a premium and on contract, to packing companies that regarded those hogs as higher quality than those from conventional farms.

Assistance like that eased the pain of the transition from conventional to factory farming, but more was involved than simply a fatter bank account. An Illinois man who moved his hogs into confinement reported that he'd reduced his labor by half even as he doubled his output. "You don't have to go to confinement feeding and slats to stay in the hog business, but it surely takes a lot of the drudgery out of raising hogs!" he said. His two sons applauded the move: both were in college; both planned to come back to the farm; neither wanted the "drudgery" of old-fashioned farming. One man reported that new-style confined hog farming required "more power, more interest, and more insurance. The tax assessor was there before the roof was even on." But he had no desire to go back to the past: he was making more money, but as important, his operation was easier to manage and more comfortable for him and the animals. "It boils down to our being able to take better care of more total cattle with less labor," said another Iowan. "At the same time, the cattle are doing better. How can we go wrong?"

Make no mistake: farmers who wanted to ease their workloads weren't lazy; they were realistic. No one believed that the labor shortage would end, and even hands who could be persuaded to get on board weren't interested in the sunup-to-sundown, seven-day weeks of the past. Many people believed that confinement would lure a younger generation of farmers. Confinement did not cure all ills, and no one expected it to do so. But for many, it was a welcome departure from the past.

But confinement also forced livestock producers to contemplate what had once been deposited on pastures: manure. "You need some kind of manure handling system," mused an Indiana man, "or it'll drive you nuts." In the fifties, most farmers trying to incorporate confinement into their operations used a tractor and blade to push the stuff to one side and, when the pile warranted, loaded it onto a truck bed and either spread it on fields or sold it as fertilizer. Others borrowed a European solution: they hosed solids and "float[ed]" them into a nearby pit, pumping the goop into a tank every few weeks and hauling it to a field.

But in the early 1960s, a new idea swept the countryside. The manure "lagoon" was promoted by Ralph Ricketts, an agricultural engineer at the University of Missouri. During the course of his research, he discovered that ordinary pond bacteria could digest and thus eliminate hog wastes, leaving "hardly a whiff of foul odor, flies, or even sediment." The use of lagoons to capture and transform manure spread quickly from Missouri to other states. When two *Farm Journal* reporters investigated in 1962, they found more than two hundred hog-farm lagoons in Missouri, and dozens more elsewhere, from Pennsylvania to Illinois, from Kentucky to Utah to California. In that last state, a chicken farmer built a lagoon after neighbors complained about flies and odor. The five-foot-deep pit occupied an acre of his land, and thanks to it, he said, his problems (and his neighbors') were over. "County health officials came by once after I finished it," he reported. "They haven't been back since." When a Kansas hog farmer wanted to water his fields, he "just pull[ed] the plug" and his lagoon's contents drained into an irrigation ditch below. "Works perfectly," he said.

Not everyone was convinced. "How stupid can you folks get, anyway?" asked a reader of one farm magazine. Why would anyone "dump manure into lagoons, and thereby destroy organic matter, rather than put it back into the soil?" he asked. "Lagoons, the magic way to get rid of manure? Better say: Lagoons, the magic way to poverty!" "You can call it a lagoon if you like," groused another man. "For my money, it was an open, stinking, septic tank. Nobody would go near it." By the mid-sixties even enthusiasts were questioning the magic, in part because it was clear that a successful lagoon (although plenty of people regarded that idea as an oxymoron) required more land than most farmers were willing to sacrifice. An employee of the U.S. Public Health Service calculated that an anaerobic lagoon required seventy-eight cubic feet per hog, and a truly odor-free pit required nine acres per thousand hogs. Even then, warned a reporter, lagoon operators "faced all the problems of a sanitary engineer operating a sewage works for a town of 1,000 people, without the engineer's training and staff."

Ironically, in the 1960s, the greatest resistance to confinement came not from farmers or their rural neighbors but from city folks as urban growth narrowed the geographical divide between town and country and urbanites got a whiff of modern farming. A reporter who investigated manure odor litigation in 1965 found that nearly all the complaints lodged against farmers came from residents of new housing developments. "You've got a stick of dynamite in your hands if enough people living near you decide they don't like your barnlot smells," warned a reporter for one farm magazine. "They can close you up!" "It's the number of animals being kept in one place that's doing it," said an official with the Illinois Department of Public Health. But as another observer mused, farmers were "caught in the middle": consumers "demand[ed] more red meat" even as they insisted on "less pollution from its production."

Ken Monfort was one of those caught in the middle. For years, the family had collected liquid runoff and used it for irrigation or sold it to local farmers. But in the 1960s, some Greeley residents complained that wasn't enough and that the Monforts' considerable contribution to the local economy was outweighed by the nuisance their operation created. The matter came to a head late in the decade when Ken proposed building a 125,000-head feedlot south of town. A group of homeowners near the site organized opposition to the plan, and the spokesman for "Operation Fresh Air" argued that feedlots had become a drag on Greeley's economy. "If you were [an employer] and you wanted to come to Colorado and the clean, Western fresh air, would you locate in Greeley between two feed lots?" he asked. A city councilman agreed. Whenever visitors came to town, he said, "they invariably inquire [about] the strange odor" and ask "how do you stand it." The editor of one local newspaper sided with the Monforts, pointing out that in the previous year, the company had purchased $2.5 million worth of feedstuffs from area farmers, and that property taxes on the new lot would contribute almost a half-million dollars to local revenues. Unsure how deep the opposition ran, Ken Monfort announced that he would abandon the project. That prompted an outpouring of support in favor of the expansion and he decided to proceed, but as a concession, he closed his father's original feedlot and built a second new one farther from town.

The problems of manure management and urban opposition raise an obvious question: Why didn't government officials — city, state, or federal — ban confinement operations? The answer is deliciously ironic: in the 1960s and 1970s, many Americans, and especially environmental policymakers, regarded confinement as an efficient method of pollution control and as environmentally superior to conventional pasture grazing. In the 1960s new concerns about air, water, and soil pollution prompted Congress to pass a series of environmental laws. Among those was a bill that required the states to establish pollution standards; state governments, in turn, ordered polluters, including farmers, to add antipollution measures to their operations, and in many states, livestock feeders were required to develop waste-management technologies. All of it pointed toward confinement as the best way to manage and control wastes. An Ohio State University professor of environmental engineering told a reporter that thanks to environmental regulations, there was "no question but that a lot of the livestock industry is ultimately going to have to go to enclosed systems."

And so the new model of livestock production — confined, large-scale, automated — thrived and spread. In the early 1960s, feedlots of fewer than one thousand head put out 61 percent of grain-fed cattle. A decade later, only 35 percent of fed cattle came from such small lots. During the sixties alone, the number of feedlots dropped from 164,000 to fewer than 120,000, and about 400 giant lots put out half of the nation's fed cattle. The number of livestock producers dropped, too. In 1950, 2.1 million American farmers sent hogs to market, the majority of them raising fewer than a hundred head of hogs a year. Twenty years later, the nation's hog farms numbered fewer than a half-million. The geography changed as well. In the early 1970s, a team of University of Missouri researchers found that of the 141 largest hog operations, 95 lay outside the Corn Belt.

The new model of cattle and hog production satisfied the inextricably linked goals of making cheap food and creating factorylike, integrated agriculture, the one the demand of millions of urban Americans, the other the embodiment of the early-twentieth-century vision of farmer-as-businessman. Over the next twenty years, that model would become firmly entrenched thanks to upheaval in the meatpacking industry and economic turmoil that permanently altered the face of American agriculture.

6

THE VACUUM AT THE TOP

I N THE 1960s, a small group of meatpacker revolutionaries reinvented the industry. They moved slaughterhouses out of cities and into rural areas, built plants designed to eliminate the need for skilled labor, and introduced a new product called "boxed beef." The revolution forced other packers, whether regional small fry or national giants like Swift and Armour, to make a choice: adjust and adapt — or go out of business. Few achieved the former, and so most suffered the latter.

Ken Monfort guided the revolution's battering ram. In the late 1950s, he realized that his company's future was, as he put it, "at the mercy" of the ten meatpackers then operating in the Denver area. Three of the ten were owned by a national grocery chain that fed its own cattle and rarely bought any from the Monforts. Of the remaining seven, four were owned by national packers and three were local independents. None of them, Ken complained, were interested in buying the quality cattle that the Monforts produced. If father and son wanted to expand their feedlot operation — and they did — they needed to find additional buyers. But that would mean shipping their cattle longer distances and paying yardage fees and commissions to distant stockyards. The better alternative, Ken decided, was to persuade one of the giant packers to build a plant in Weld County. He tried but failed. "Most of the big packers would go as far as Denver," Ken said later, "but just wouldn't consider a plant in Greeley."

So he turned to Plan B. We should build and operate our own meatpacking plant, he told his father. Warren Monfort was aghast. Even by his aggressive standards the idea was flawed, not least because neither of them knew anything about operating a slaughterhouse. The one thing Warren did know about meatpacking was that it was a crazy way to earn a living: the Monforts typically earned three to four times as much as companies like Swift and Armour, which were lucky to reap a 1 percent profit. What made Ken think he could do a better job? And, too, like most cattle feeders, Warren Monfort disliked and mistrusted packers on principle, and the idea of becoming the enemy did not sit well with him. But Ken was convinced that the future lay in integrated operations of the type that characterized the broiler industry, and he would not be deterred. As a compromise, Ken offered to minimize the risk by bringing in other investors. He tried to persuade local cattle feeders, and by that time there were plenty of them in Weld County, to invest in the project, but they were scared off by what he described as the "legal hassles" the project necessitated. Eventually he persuaded the Averch brothers, who owned Capitol Packing Co. in Denver, to enter into a joint venture: the Monforts would build the plant; the brothers and their employees would manage it.

The slaughterhouse that opened next to the Monfort feedlots in the spring of 1960 bore little resemblance to a conventional packing plant. It flowed horizontally rather than vertically, and most of the killing and cutting operations took place on the ground level. Natural light spilled onto the kill floor, thanks to an expanse of green glass on the building's north face. Instead of hanging carcasses on hooks, Monfort installed an automated, ceiling-suspended rail-conveyor system that carried carcasses from one butcher station to another. Workers stood on adjustable platforms that allowed them to move up, down, and around a carcass with a minimum of bending or stooping. No one humped carcasses from one location to another, a traditional practice that made men old before their time and bruised and damaged the meat. Another conveyor carried wastes to rendering operations located in the basement. The hides landed there, too, deposited into two circulating, automated brine tanks that cured the skins in just six hours.

Two factors drove the design. First, the layout and automated equipment eliminated the need for skilled labor, a must because Ken insisted on hiring local residents. "When we opened our plant," he said later, "we were advised to advertise for butchers in Omaha, Kansas City and other cities, but we refused to do it." He wanted his employees "to be from Greeley, not only to help local people but to get men who would stay with us." Weld County farmers had long relied on seasonal labor, much of it Mexican American. From Kenny's perspective, the local economy would benefit if those men (and, as was typical of that time, he hired only men) enjoyed full-time work and steady wages. Thus the plant's design: rather than have skilled union butchers carve an entire carcass, each man would make only one or two simple cuts, tasks that could be learned quickly even by novices. In 1962, the union came calling, and Kenny supported his employees when they voted to join the Amalgamated Meat Cutters and Butcher Workmen of America. In true maverick fashion, however, he persuaded them to eschew the master contract that governed other unionized packing plants in favor of an agreement that included cost-of-living increases as well as a profit-sharing plan designed to fund the employees' retirements. It's unlikely anyone complained: the Monforts paid the highest wages in Greeley.

The second factor that shaped the plant's design was byproducts or, more accurately, the lack of them. As we saw earlier, dressed-beef pioneers like Armour and Swift learned early on that byproducts paid the bills, whether as bone and hide, or margarine and medicines. They had designed slaughterhouses that accommodated the rendering and processing operations necessary to extract profit from hoof, bone, hide, and other animal parts. But in the 1940s and 1950s, demand for those products dwindled and their profits evaporated. Synthetic body soaps and detergents replaced ones made from animal fats. Lard was an antique curiosity in the age of calorie counting and convenience foods. The value of hides, long one of a meatpacker's best friends, plunged as manufacturers of shoes, purses, and furniture substituted fabrics and plastics for leather. In the early 1940s, 78 percent of shoe soles were leather; by the early 1950s, more than half were fabricated from synthetics like Neolite. New drugs and commercial fertilizers eliminated the need for hog thyroids and dried blood. Ken Monfort recognized that without those byproducts, he faced a hard climb toward profitability. One way to compensate for them was by eliminating every possible inefficiency and expense, from the number of steps workers took during the day to the number of light bulbs needed to illuminate the interior of the plant.

Monfort struggled to master the intricacies of the new venture, which in those early days, he admitted, "was something less than a howling success," thanks to recalcitrant machinery and his own inexperience; so unsuccessful, in fact, that within six months, the Monforts' partners wanted out. Despite his woes, he refused to expand into value-added, processed meat products — canned beef stew and TV dinners — to which other packers had turned as replacements for byproducts. Slaughtering cattle and making beef was one thing; figuring out how to sell branded, packaged foods to grocery chains was another business entirely, and not one he was prepared to tackle, at least not while he was still learning how to slaughter and pack. Indeed, he was so wary of the grocery business that he focused entirely on the HRI market. Still, if he wanted to survive, he had to add additional value to his beef. Like his father before him, Ken Monfort found an opening that he could exploit: his customers' dissatisfaction with unions and with carcass beef. In early 1962, he announced plans to build a second plant where employees would "break," in industry jargon, whole and half carcasses into "primal" cuts and box them for shipping.

Thus began the boxed-beef revolution (which another meat-packer, IBP, is credited, wrongly, with launching), a pivotal moment in the American meat industry, and one we can best understand by looking at the problems that inspired first Monfort and then other packers to offer this service. Consider the path that fresh beef traveled from a meatpacker to, say, a chain grocery store. Packers shipped whole or half "swinging carcasses" by truck or train to a grocery warehouse. There, in-house butchers broke the carcasses into primal cuts such as flank or loin and boxed them for delivery to individual grocery stores. At the store, meat department butchers cut the primals to order for shoppers or broke them into individual steaks or roasts that were wrapped and packaged for sale in self-service cases. Every step drove up the final retail price, a fact confirmed by a 1966 study commissioned by the grocery industry. On average, workers handled a beef carcass nineteen times before shoppers dropped the meat in their carts to take home: five times at the packinghouse, eight times by various middlemen, and another six once it arrived at a grocery store warehouse. Worse, the prolonged shipping and handling contributed to "shrinkage": in the first forty-eight hours after leaving the packing plant, a carcass lost 2 percent of its bulk and during the nine days needed to move beef from slaughterhouse to grocery store, lost more than 5 percent of its weight, or thirty-three pounds in a typical six-hundred-pound carcass. Union wages and work rules added another layer of expense, in part because butchers resisted innovations that would eliminate their jobs. In Chicago, union butchers employed at grocery stores stopped work at six p.m., and no fresh meat could be sold until they returned the next morning. No wonder, then, that beef returned minuscule profits but gobbled about 60 percent of a typical meat department's labor costs. Add in the equipment — slicers, power-driven saws, oversize refrigerators — and it's not surprising that many grocery meat departments operated at a deficit. The situation was no better for the HRI industry, where buyers faced the same layers of middlemen and expense.

Grocers begged meatpackers to help eliminate not just those

lost profits, but the odor and mess that in-store butchering spawned (and to which customers objected) by making more cuts to carcasses before those left the packing plant. One analyst urged packers to stop thinking of carcasses as commodities and see them as a "vehicle for selling services." Only then, he argued, would they "reap the . . . true profit which the market offers." Many established packing companies had a hard time grasping this idea, and their longtime relationships with unions made it difficult to institute new work practices. But newcomer Ken Monfort was wedded to neither meatpacking's past nor its entrenched unions. In his mind, it made sense to add value to his beef at the plant; thus the new breaking operation. By shipping only edible beef, and by shipping it in vacuum-sealed bags packed in stackable boxes, the Monforts chopped $3 to $4 off their transportation costs, eliminated the bruising that lowered the value of a swinging carcass, and, most important, extracted maximum profit from their beef.

By the late sixties, the Monfort processing operation looked like something off the set of a science fiction film. The action revolved around a giant electronic control board—the heart of the facility's "automated electronic beef handling system." With a push of a button, the dispatcher directed a carcass—whose weight and meat ratio met the buyer's specifications—to, say, rail fifteen, where it hung awaiting the rest of the buyer's order. When all the items had arrived, a click of a switch sent them rolling along a track to the loading area or to a conveyor that carried them to the breaking room where crews reduced them to the primal cuts that the customer had requested. Employees packaged the pieces in boxes dosed with carbon dioxide to keep the beef chilled, or bundled them in vacuum-sealed plastic film before boxing them for shipping. The investment in electronics, automation, and fabrication was a necessity, said Ken Monfort, because "the only way to stay alive in this business is to continually improve your efficiency." He had transformed the family business into a mechanized, automated, integrated beef factory, the feedlots a model of Fordized production, the packing plants a futuristic wonderland that bore no resemblance to the aging hulks that dominated Chicago's old Packingtown.

In the 1960s, the Monforts' main rival was another maverick packer. A year after Ken flipped the switch at his packing plant, Andrew D. "Andy" Anderson did the same at Iowa Beef Packers, Inc., known to all as IBP. (The company's formal name changed several times but was always referred to by its initials, which became its official name in the early 1980s.) Like Ken Monfort, Andy Anderson was a commanding figure: six feet four inches tall and typically dressed in jeans and an "LBJ hat"— a good ol' Texas cowboy hat — that enhanced an already uncanny resemblance to President Lyndon Johnson. He was also smart, talented, and ambitious. "Andy's a genius," said one of his colleagues. "He has an idea every 15 seconds, some realistic and some unrealistic." Two urges fueled those ideas: profit, of course, but also a passion for transforming ideas into tangible ventures. Indeed, Anderson is best described as a serial entrepreneur: as soon as he launched one venture, he was itching to tackle another. In his case, success inevitably bred success, and he never lacked for investors. His association with meatpacking dated back to the 1930s, when he worked at a West Coast slaughterhouse. In the early 1950s, he and two partners opened a packing plant in Boise, Idaho, which they sold eighteen months later. Anderson stayed to manage the plant, but when the new owners sold it to Swift in the mid-fifties, Anderson left Idaho for his home state of Iowa and Denison, a small town in the western part of the state. There IBP was born.

It's not clear why Anderson landed in Denison, although it's possible that he was responding to an advertisement that the town's chamber of commerce placed in the *Wall Street Journal* in 1956: "DENISON, IOWA. With every natural advantage for industry, offers excellent sites and build-to-suit plans! If you, Mr. Industrialist, are planning expansion or relocation, INVESTIGATE DENISON, IOWA NOW!" The invitation was born of desperation: the postwar years had not been kind to Denison and the surrounding area. Fordized farming had left some farmers under-

or unemployed, a damaging drought had wreaked havoc on corn crops, and the growth of western feedlots had hammered the local cattle industry. In the previous fifteen years, some three hundred farm families had left Crawford County; nearly every issue of the local newspaper included at least one full-page advertisement for a farm sale. Fewer farmers translated into fewer patrons for Denison businesses.

Not long after he arrived in town, Anderson proposed building a hog packing plant that would utilize livestock from area farms, a project that town boosters promoted with an appropriate slogan: "A farmer a day is moving away; Let's build the plant and help him stay!" Local residents contributed $300,000 to the venture, and Anderson obtained a matching amount in the form of a loan from the federal Small Business Administration. Crawford County Packing Company opened its doors in the spring of 1958. A year later, the shareholders, all of them area residents, sold CCPC to Consumers Cooperative Association, a thirty-year-old farmers' cooperative with more than $100 million in assets, including oil wells and a refinery. The slaughterhouse shareholders earned a 123 percent return on their investment, not bad for a small-town venture and confirmation that Andy Anderson knew how to turn ideas into profit.

True to form, a few months later, Anderson launched his next project: IBP. Within weeks, Crawford County residents had pledged $400,000 in support. (Five years later, those backers were millionaires, some of them several times over.) Again Anderson supplemented that with funds from the Small Business Administration, this time a government participation service loan: of the $350,000 requested, the Denison Federal Savings and Loan would provide 10 percent and the American taxpayers the rest. The money paid for 140 acres west of town, a site that included plenty of water (the operation would consume millions of gallons a year) and abutted a line of the Illinois Central Railroad. As had been the case with the hog slaughterhouse, Anderson, a self-taught, and by all accounts talented, engineer, designed the new plant to achieve maximum efficiency and accom-

modate minimal skill, adopting many of the ideas Ken Monfort
had implemented at his Greeley slaughterhouse, including adjustable platforms and an overheard conveyor system that transported carcasses from the kill room to the refrigerator or directly
onto a refrigerated truck or railcar. Like Monfort, the people at
IBP relied on unskilled, local labor and focused on one product:
fresh beef. "We don't believe in highly complex situations," said
one IBP executive by way of explaining why, in an age of convenience, IBP eschewed processed foods.

The company's buyers bypassed stockyards and auction
houses and purchased cattle directly from farmers and feedlots.
As soon as a buyer completed a transaction, he used his in-car
radio to relay the animal's weight and price to a dispatcher back
at the plant. IBP production managers used that information to
decide when they needed more cattle, when buyers should pull
back, and whether the buyer's price was in line with that day's
needs. Line managers always knew exactly how many cattle were
headed their way and when those would arrive, and cattle were
slaughtered within hours, and often minutes, of their arrival at
the plant. IBP saved money because it spent little to feed and water the livestock. At IBP, everyone, from cattle buyers and jan-
itors to line workers and Anderson himself, worked six days a
week. The goal that united employees was profit, a point Anderson drove home by adopting green (the color of money) as the
unifying theme of the company's public face. Inside and out, the
packinghouse and office walls were green. So were the carpets.
Secretaries sat at green desks and cranked out letters and memos
on green typewriters. The company motto: "Think Money."

Green thinking paid off. By the end of the first year, employees
were slaughtering a thousand cattle a day, and IBP had acquired
a second plant in Fort Dodge, Iowa, where Anderson installed another state-of-the-art processing line. Denison's pockets weren't
deep enough to support Anderson's ambitions, and in October
1963, IBP went public. (That alone testified to the demand for
a new meatpacking model: two years after the initial offering,
an IBP share was worth sixty-three times its original value.) By

1964, IBP was the tenth-largest packing company in the United States and had landed on *Fortune* magazine's 500 list. In the late 1960s, IBP followed Monfort into boxed beef, with the goal, as one company executive put it, of breaking the "chains of history that . . . confined the retailing of meats to the dark ages."

Revolutions invariably disrupt the status quo, and in this case, labor unions understood that the new model of making meat was designed to eliminate them. As a result, IBP slaughterhouses often resembled a war zone. During a months-long strike that began in 1969, persons unknown toppled the towers that anchored IBP's in-house radio communications system, and an arsonist destroyed the home of a company executive. One gun-wielding striker confronted an IBP secretary who was believed to be providing information about the union to her bosses. He shot and wounded her, but killed her sixteen-year-old sister. Andy Anderson, who made no secret of his loathing for unions, and his colleagues refused to back down. "We're trying to revolutionize beef packing," said a company spokesman. "The union is trying to prevent this." Company executive Currier Holman packed a tear-gas gun, boasting that "business as we pursue it here at IBP is very much like waging war." IBP responded to the strike by importing workers from California and Mexico, offering them not just jobs, but housing, too. In mid-April 1970, after fifty-six bombings, two hundred tire slashings, more than twenty shootings, and one death, the strike ended. IBP agreed to pay 20 cents more an hour than the union had originally asked for but compensated for the loss of that battle by winning the war itself: the company refused to agree to the master contract rate paid by other unionized packers. By comparison, peace prevailed at Monfort in Greeley, but only because unions and meatpacking had a much smaller presence than in Iowa, where unionized packing plants abounded.

Unlike Monfort, IBP focused on the grocery trade, and there, too, the company battled the unions, especially in large cities, as grocery butchers resisted the invasion of boxed beef because the product eliminated jobs (a goal that grocery chain executives supported). That was especially true on the East Coast, where IBP leaders were determined to break into the lucrative big-city markets. But butchers' unions there enjoyed intimate connections with the Mafia, and so IBP had to deal not with union officials, but with Mafia henchmen. Frustrated by the Mob's nearly impenetrable wall, Andy Anderson consulted with the owner of one of the country's biggest broiler companies, a man who'd managed to gain access to New York–area grocery chains. The chicken man's advice was simple: Pay the bribes that the unions demanded; it was the only way in. The bribes opened the way, but Currier Holman, who was IBP's president at the time and handled the negotiations, landed in the snare of a federal investigation into Mafia-union connections and was convicted of conspiracy. "I never bribed anybody in my life," Holman told a reporter. "It's all a damned lie." He got lucky: the judge who tried him viewed Holman as a "victim of the extortionate practices" of the very people he had bribed. There were, he told Holman, "few people in American business who would have acted differently in these circumstances." Holman avoided jail, and IBP paid a $7,000 fine and, it should be noted, went right on paying the bribes necessary to win grocery contracts. In the end, the packer-revolutionaries had their way. Over the next decade, unions vanished almost entirely from packing plants and grocery stores. There was no room for them, literally in the case of the new streamlined slaughterhouses, in meatpacking's future.

The clearest evidence of the rebels' success can be measured in the declining fortunes of the old meatpacking kings, especially Armour, Swift, and another of the old giants, Wilson & Co., who remained chained both to the unions and to what Ken Monfort dismissed as "ancient and obsolete plants." He was right. Armour's Chicago operation consisted of 7.6 million square feet of floor space in 121 buildings spread over eighty-seven acres. Inside, workers moved from carcass to carcass, beef slabs that still hung, as they had for eighty years, from iron hooks. Employees shoveled offal and tossed hides into wooden handcarts, trundled their loads to an elevator, waited for a car, boarded, pushed the cart off at the designated floor, unloaded it, and then retraced their steps, this time pushing an empty cart. Currier Holman, who'd grown up around packinghouses in the 1930s, recalled that "people would stand waiting for elevators . . . for fifteen minutes at a time." That had not changed by the 1950s and 1960s, and soaring labor costs — up 80 percent in the 1950s alone — exacerbated the old packers' woes.

The aging titans' problems went beyond creaky elevators and empty handcarts. By the 1960s, much of their infrastructure stood idle. Their packing plants had been designed back when farmers sent stock to market only once or twice a year, a schedule that required huge facilities to handle the onslaught. But twentieth-century feeders like Monfort sent cattle to market every month, leaving packers with real estate that gobbled electricity and contributed nothing to profits. The cavernous curing and refrigerator rooms stood mostly empty, too, as packers adopted methods that reduced curing and smoking time from two months to as little as thirty minutes. New technologies reduced by 25 percent the time needed to chill a carcass to the required sixty degrees. The "Turbo-chill" technique surrounded the carcass with waves of "supersaturated" cold air; as a bonus, the rapid chilling also prevented shrinkage. The new methods reduced expenses but left older packers saddled with idle square footage. Add the declining value of byproducts and high union wages, and the costs added up.

The giants struggled to adapt. They pulled out of Chicago (the stockyards there closed in 1971) and sold off their urban slaughterhouses in favor of new or newly remodeled plants in rural locations in Iowa or Nebraska, New Mexico or Texas. "We're going to spend several million dollars to replace our 1910 plant in Oklahoma because we can't afford not to," said a spokesman for Wilson. "With wage rates the way they are now, we can't go on paying people to wait for elevators." But as one onlooker put it, the old guard "moved from very big obsolete plants in the city to very small obsolete plants in the country." They had little choice:

unlike IBP and Monfort, Swift, Wilson, and Armour were wedded to union workers who resisted innovations that eliminated
jobs, whether plant layout, processes, or machinery. So when
Swift built a new plant in, say, Fort Worth, it looked different
from its aging one in Chicago, but it "worked" the same. Consider
two small but telling differences between old and new: In 1963,
Armour constructed plants in Kansas and Nebraska. At both of
the new facilities, workers shoveled offal into "gut buggies" and
trundled those from kill floor to rendering department. At the
Monfort packinghouse, in contrast, offal fell from the carcass directly onto a conveyor belt that whisked it away. Consider, too,
the shrouds used to cloak carcasses while they chilled in the refrigerator room. At the Armour plants, workers removed those by
hand and dumped them into pushcarts. At IBP's Denison packinghouse, a mechanical arm plucked the shrouds from the carcasses and deposited them in self-propelled carts that conveyed
them to the laundry. In 1967, Armour abandoned its attempt to
wring profit from the two plants and sold them to IBP, which gutted them and installed automated processing systems, upping capacity from twenty-five hundred head a week to eight thousand.

The old-timers even dragged their feet when it came to the
meat itself. Armour and Swift balked at the idea of frozen meats,
let alone boxed beef, because their union employees resisted. But
even when they manufactured value-added products, they often
proved too timid to venture from familiar ground. In the 1960s,
for example, Swift developed foods like "compressed bacon bars"
that American astronauts carried into space. What should have
been a marketing boon was not to be. Swift executives decided to
keep the company's connection to space travel locked in a closet
because, as one employee said, "Suppose the moonshot fails and
those guys die up there." The astronauts didn't, but Swift's opportunity did.

Ironically, for a brief time those failings made the biggest packers an attractive target. In the late sixties and early 1970s, Armour, Wilson, and Cudahy and Morrell, two survivors of the pi-
oneering nineteenth century, were taken over by conglomerates

with no experience in making meat. Why? Because, explained the president of the packers' trade group, adding a mere "half a cent [additional] profit" to pork or beef carcasses could jack up earnings by $50 million, a prospect that proved irresistible to corporate managers seeking diversification and new ways to bolster their bottom lines. (And probably their egos, too. Who wouldn't want to be the wunderkind who finally taught meatpackers how to make money?) Not everyone was impressed. "What meat packing assets are best equipped for," scoffed one analyst, "is the luring of lambs to slaughter." Ken Monfort had little sympathy for his bigger brethren. "After World War II," he said, when they "should have modernized, they didn't. When they should have changed location, they didn't." So he and IBP and other revolutionaries had seized the moment. He had proved "money [could] be made in modern plants, operated well, in the right locations." "The big packers," he said, "follow us now, rather than lead us."

He was right. The moment, and the future, belonged to Monfort and his fellow rebels, whose numbers multiplied as more upstarts, many of them former employees of IBP, opened their doors, most of them in plains states where they enjoyed close proximity to big cattle feedlots. Their relentless pursuit of efficiency smashed unions and dealt fatal blows to conventional packers, but it also enabled them to survive the catastrophes of the 1970s. During that decade, a combination of inflation, high grain prices, a global famine, and changing consumer tastes roiled the meatpacking and livestock industries. Many packers, large and small, shut their doors, and a new kind of factory farmer altered the nature of livestock production as well.

It's nice to think of the 1970s as the decade of disco, bad TV, and cringe-inducing clothing, but those who lived through it are more likely to remember the misery. Energy prices soared, thanks to a short-lived but gut-punching embargo on the part of oil-producing nations. Motorists lined up at gas stations, but the more significant impact was less obvious: rising energy expenditures increased the cost of doing business — whether as higher heating bills at an insurance company or soaring electricity costs at an automobile plant — and that, in turn, drove up the tab for all goods and services. At the same time, the United States was losing its dominance as manufacturer for the world. The project to rebuild war-torn Europe and Asia had succeeded, and workers in western Europe and Japan were cranking out an array of goods — steel, clothing, radios, toasters, and automobiles — that were cheaper than those made in the United States. For the first time in eighty years, the United States recorded a trade deficit. The deluge of inexpensive manufactured goods battered the foundations of the American manufacturing economy; factories closed their doors, many never to reopen, and unemployment soared. The dollar declined and consumer prices marched up, as did inflation — about 5 percent a year in the early 1970s — and interest rates. Unemployment doubled during 1970, topped 9 percent five years later, and bounced up and down, mostly up, during the decade. Any one of these factors would have affected the making, selling, and eating of meat — farmers passed rising fuel costs on to packers who handed them off to consumers — but the event that whipped all of it into a perfect storm and fundamentally altered the business of meat was a global famine whose economic and political consequences played out for the next two decades.

The famine took shape in the late sixties and early seventies when drought in some parts of the world and monsoons in others destroyed crops, and people living in those areas experienced food shortages. Historians and economists still argue about the extent of those scarcities, and scholars disagree about the severity of the famine and even whether a true famine occurred. But whether the famine was "real" or not is irrelevant; at the time, world leaders believed it was and acted accordingly. In the early seventies, officials with the United Nations' Food and Agriculture Organization (FAO) announced that global food supplies were at their lowest levels in twenty years. Economists predicted that unless world leaders responded immediately, food shortages would result in mass starvation and political turmoil. Rising affluence aggravated the situation: the same Asians and Europeans who were turning out cheaper cars, radios, and steel also enjoyed higher incomes that enabled them to eat more. At a moment when the world's poorest needed food, the world's wealthiest were demanding more of it. Because postwar global trade and political networks were more intertwined than ever, the consequences of Indian monsoons or Russian drought inevitably played out on American soil. Indeed, after Russian wheat crops failed, Soviet leaders staved off potential unrest by buying billions of bushels of grain, a purchase that nearly wiped out American stockpiles. The "grain grab," as many called it at the time, unfolded entirely in secret, conducted by a handful of powerful grain dealers and unbeknownst to most American officials. But anything and everything connected to agriculture and food was complicated by the fact that since the 1940s, global politics and American foreign policy had become inextricably chained to food largess, and the famine provoked tension between the United States and some of its allies.

In the United States, all these factors, from famine to oil embargo to inflation, wreaked havoc on the business of making meat. In 1972, Colorado cattle feeders paid $50 for a ton of corn. A year later, the price had more than doubled, and it rose again in 1974, including a 40 percent increase during the summer alone. Cattle and hog feeders alike responded by cutting back on the number of animals they fed. Those decisions, in turn, influenced the calculations of western ranchers: fearing they would not find buyers for their cattle, grazers culled their herds, sending cattle to market whether the animals were ready or not. For a brief moment, feedlots ran thick with a glut of exceptionally cheap, young, underfed stock, but their low price wasn't enough to balance feed costs. "A year ago we bought two-thirds of [cattle] weight and added one-third," said Ken Monfort in the summer of 1973. "Today we're buying 58 per cent and adding 42," and he paid exorbitant prices to add that 42 percent. Monfort slashed his cattle numbers by twenty thousand, a stunning turnaround for the nation's biggest feeder, but it wasn't enough to stem the tide. By early 1974, he was losing as much as $125 a head on each animal he sent to the packing plant, where his overhead costs climbed as the oil embargo sent fuel prices soaring. When he tallied the numbers, Ken Monfort calculated that he had lost $2 million. "We've taken beatings before," he mused, "but this is the biggest loss in my experience." That $2 million, however, was a mere drop compared to the $50 million he'd lost on paper: In 1970, he'd taken the company public. Initial shares sold for $16. By early 1974, they were worth $4. "It seemed like a good idea at the time," he said of the decision, and he still believed it was. "We're not going to back down now." IBP emerged from the chaos in better shape, in part because company executives established partnerships with a number of western cattle feeders, contracting in advance to buy a feedlot's entire output. And, too, IBP's size — by the mid-1970s, it was the largest cattle slaughter operation in the world, and three times bigger than its nearest American competitor — gave it economies of scale that outstripped those of the smaller Monfort operation.

But even IBP could not escape the turmoil of the seventies. The Nixon administration responded to soaring food prices by imposing ceilings and freezes, but those did little to ease the pain, and as the impact of the Russian grain deal rippled through the economy, outraged consumers staged protests and organized boycotts. As had been the case during World Wars I and II, high meat prices drew most of their fire. An organization called Fight Inflation Together organized a "housewives" boycott and urged shoppers to leave beef and pork at the store and eat poultry instead. "I'll boycott until I grow feathers from eating so much chicken," vowed one woman. Another told a reporter that her entire family had voted to join the boycott, although given that her household included "two men with good appetites," she added, "it won't be easy." "Don't Eat Beef!" read newspaper advertisements paid for by a group of New York City restaurateurs. "Join us to fight against those ridiculous beef prices." The lure? A 10 percent discount when diners ordered something other than beef. The boycotts and consumer fury aggravated Ken Monfort, who was "appalled by how little consumers know about the real world." Why, he asked, were shoppers willing to "pay $2 a pound for certain fluff like Sara Lee cakes, and argue about paying $1 a pound for chuck roast?" They didn't understand that food came attached to "basic costs," he complained, and "the more they want us to do for them, the less value they're getting." Meanwhile, butchers blamed high meat prices on packers; packers blamed grocers; and everyone else was convinced that the culprit was either farmers, the Russians, mysterious middlemen, or the equally mysterious "them" in Washington, DC, who seemed not to care about average, hard-working Americans. "We've got a worldwide food panic on our hands, and unless something is done we're going to have shortages in this country," insisted an executive with a Kansas City grain mill.

But deciding what that something should be was not easy. The United States could not afford to appear indifferent to global starvation, but the State Department was more accustomed to wielding food aid as a diplomatic cudgel than to giving it away for free. And suppose farmers gassed up their tractors and cranked out bigger grain surpluses than usual, but the predicted demand failed to materialize? Grocery store prices would drop, but farmers would be furious and taxpayers would be stuck paying more for agricultural subsidies. If economists were correct about global demand, however, domestic food prices would rise even higher and citizen-consumers would be out for blood, which, of course, they would extract on election day. At the White House, in Congress, in offices strung along the corridors of the Departments of Agriculture, State, and Treasury, the debate raged: Should the United States stockpile food to protect Americans from future shortages? Should it do as some poor nations demanded and give it away? Should Congress reduce tariffs on imports? Raise them? And what to do about rising food costs? Stick with price ceilings? Freeze wages? Expand and extend unemployment payouts? "Let's just say we're, well, a little befuddled," an employee at the Treasury Department confided to a reporter.

In the end, befuddled bureaucrats agreed on two points. First, the food famine was real and action must be taken. Economists calculated that over the next decade, American farmers needed to increase production of food and fiber by a third. Second, Nixon's advisers concluded that agriculture "had become far too important to be left to the agriculturists." As long as the crisis persisted, agricultural policy would come not from the USDA but from the White House or State Department. Earl Butz, secretary of agriculture under Presidents Richard Nixon and Gerald Ford, was not persuaded that the world's billions would starve to death anytime soon, but his opinion didn't matter. The State Department and White House ordered him to board the famine express, and so Butz urged farmers to get busy making food.

"We're on the threshold of the greatest age of agriculture that this country has ever known," crowed the president of the American National Cattlemen's Association. In an echo of the 1950s, many farmers unloaded their cattle and hogs, in part because of soaring feed costs but also because they believed that grain, especially wheat, would return higher profits. In Iowa alone, two thousand cattle feeders called it quits in 1973 and 1974; nationally, the number of cattle feeders fell 11 percent between 1975 and 1981. But farmers weren't the only ones hoping to cash in on the famine. One of the most significant consequences of that moment, one that would play out for decades to come and reshape agriculture in general and livestock production in particular, was that, as one analyst put it, the "farm belt" became the "new IBM." Deep-pocketed investors and corporations prowled the countryside looking for land with which to reap the profits of the greatest age. Insurance giant John Hancock bought thousands of acres of farmland in Nebraska and in North Carolina. The cheap land and temperate climate of that eastern state attracted a number of profit seekers, including chemical manufacturer American Cyanamid as well as investors from Japan, Australia, and Italy.

The belief that the world was about to starve was so widespread, and the potential profits of alleged starvation so attractive, that it inspired a modern version of the Marquis de Morès. In late 1973, one Charles McQuoid showed up in Kahoka, Missouri, a dot of a burg in the northeast corner of the state, announcing plans to spend at least $300 million to build a vertically integrated hog and pork production complex. He told townspeople that his would be the largest such facility in the United States, cover nearly seven thousand acres of land, include a slaughterhouse capacity of 2.5 million hogs a year, and employ two thousand people. McQuoid promised big money all around: An annual donation to the University of Missouri, half for swine research, half to the football team. A million dollars to the local school district and an area hospital. An eighteen-hole golf course, a swimming pool and country club, and an airstrip to accommodate the "foreign dignitaries" who would visit the area. That was enough to convince the Missouri commissioner of agriculture, who approved the project in early 1974. He waved aside objections from farmers and Missouri Senator Thomas Eagleton, who persuaded a Senate committee to investigate the project's potential for antitrust violations. The naysayers were outnumbered, or at least outvoted. "I don't think, as I view the situation today, that this will be the demise of the small hog farmer," said the commissioner. Businessmen in Kahoka praised McQuoid's vision, and the town's mayor dismissed fears that the facilities would generate pollution, arguing that McQuoid's backers would ensure that he complied with any and all environmental legislation. The farmers had the last laugh. McQuoid, a former insurance salesman (and occasional visitor to a Chicago bankruptcy court), was fake from start to finish. His alleged backers were nonexistent, his collateral bogus. After borrowing $155,000 from two local bankers, he skipped town.

McQuoid was a fake; Don Tyson was not. In 1977, Tyson, who headed what was at the time one of the nation's biggest broiler companies, made an investment that transformed him into the biggest hog farmer. A reporter who visited Tyson's eastern North Carolina hog operation found a ten-thousand-acre facility that included farrowing, breeding, and feeding operations and a half-million porcines housed in a "glimmering row of buildings that . . . seem[ed] to stretch forever," each building overseen by a professional manager. "It's got all the advantages of working in a factory right here on the farm," explained one of the barn managers, the barn in this case being a temperature-and-humidity-controlled structure where odor, waste, disease, and farrowing were managed like so many factors in an equation. "Those aren't just hog buildings up there in those hills," said another employee. "They're Cadillacs." The editor of a national farm magazine was blunt about the implications: Tyson's move, he wrote, "ought to scare the hell out of every hog farmer in the country."

That didn't bother Tyson, who thrived on risk, large scale, and success. Tyson Foods began in the early 1930s when Don's father, John, a Springdale, Arkansas, truck driver, began hauling live chickens from northwest Arkansas to Kansas City, Chicago, St. Louis, and other northern cities. Over the next few years, the elder Tyson followed the same trajectory as Jesse Jewell, building an integrated operation for the raising, processing, and sale of broilers. By the time the World War II poultry boom began, Tyson owned a hatchery, feed mill, and feed dealership. A friend of John's once described him as "a very ambitious man. There is a thin line between ambition and greed. I don't think John ever got over the line, but he was pretty ambitious."

His son Don, on the other hand, made no distinction between greed and ambition; as far as he was concerned, both were essential components of a businessman's toolbox. A "gregarious, voluble fellow," he augmented his ambition with an optimist's outlook and greeted the world with "an easy, cherubic smile" (the resemblance to a cherub enhanced by his billiard-ball-shaped head). The angelic facade concealed a brilliant entrepreneurial brain. In the time it took an ordinary soul to notice a possible opportunity, Don Tyson had already calculated its risks and profit potential and devised several possible scenarios in which that potential might play out. He coupled that genius with a ruthless disregard for anything but profit. "If it makes money, we expand it," he said late in his career. "If it doesn't, we cut its throat. . . . The 11th Commandment is that you need to make a profit." He also believed that one sure route to profit lay in power; friends in high places equaled money in the bank. "The business of politics consists of a series of unsentimental transactions between those who need votes and those who have money," he once said, "a world where every quid has its quo." Those traits propelled his company's ascent and won him many admirers. "[T]here is," said one devotee, "only one Don Tyson. There is no man in the world quite as sharp in the poultry business." "He's one of those that comes along once in a lifetime," raved a Tyson Foods executive. "I have him on a pedestal. He's Superman." Admiration was not universal. "Don Tyson," said one company truck driver, "is a lying, thieving S.O.B.," a view others shared in large part because Tyson hated unions and worked relentlessly to eradicate their presence among his growers and employees. One example makes the case: In the spring of 1962, a group of Arkansas broiler growers met to organize an association, hoping their combined numbers would give them more clout when negotiating with Tyson and the region's other integrators. Don Tyson dispatched some of his employees to the scene. Driving company trucks, they lined the road to the courthouse and recorded the license plate numbers of the men and women who showed up for the gathering. Once the meeting began, the driver of one truck, his vehicle conveniently lacking a muffler, raced his engine to drown out the speakers inside the building.

Don joined his father's company in the early 1950s, a boom-town moment for the broiler industry, thanks to high demand and chronic overproduction. The turbulence taught him a valuable, if obvious, lesson: safety lay in size and market share. He said later that he and his father faced the entrepreneur's classic dilemma: they had to either "expand or expire. There was no middle ground. We had to grow or die." But he also learned that chaos and bad times represented opportunity. When competitors failed, the Tysons snapped up their plants and equipment, a strategy that allowed them to avoid the expense, in both dollars and time, of building new and, more important, to move quickly during upswings. In 1963, Don convinced his father to take the company public. He knew that doing so opened their books to greater scrutiny, and that shareholders might challenge his steamroller approach. But in Don's mind, the benefits of a Wall Street presence and the opportunities for funding, mergers, and acquisitions outweighed the risks. And Tyson wanted it all. "We're not committed to the broiler business as such," Don explained in 1964. "We're not overlooking ducks, geese, or anything else that will make us money! . . . We intend to be 'Mr. Poultry' in every sense of the word to our customers." (Turkeys proved the exception. "I've had two turkey plants, and two red-headed women in my lifetime," he said later, "and never done good with any of them.") Like Jesse Jewell, Tyson believed that as long as grocery retailers treated broilers as loss leaders, his industry would remain stuck in the "commodity" category, and, like Jewell, he believed that the way to change that — and to mitigate the industry's manic gyrations — was by transforming the broiler from basic commodity to consumer product.

The 1970s offered fertile terrain for his vision. The broiler business flourished in the wake of the famine. Foreign countries compensated for protein shortages by snapping up American chicken products, which were less expensive than beef or pork and, thanks to new freezing technologies, easy to ship. In 1976, the Soviet Union ordered 2,500 tons, and the Iraqis 35,000, of frozen chicken from U.S. manufacturers. Tyson parlayed his long-standing presence in the HRI industry into profit as beef-centric restaurants struggled. High-end restaurateurs added chicken *cordon bleu* and chicken Kiev to their menus, and fast-food chains, from Long John Silver's to Burger King, supplemented burgers and fried fish with chicken sandwiches.

Tyson seized the moment to diversify into hog farming. Hogs appealed to his calculator brain because they would complement his broiler operations: he could use the company's feed mills to manufacture hog rations. By doing so, he would increase the volume of his raw materials purchases, which would lower their cost. Because hogs took longer than chickens to reach market weight, he could use their birth-to-market cycle to balance the volatility of broiler production. Tyson had taken small steps toward hog

production in the late 1960s, but he'd backed off once he realized that hogs weren't like chickens. It's not "easy to grow pigs
in confinement like broilers because of the disease problems," he
explained to a reporter. "It takes tremendous capital and management knowhow [*sic*], as we know it in the broiler business,
is not as available." By the mid-1970s, however, he was confident
those obstacles could be overcome, and he announced plans to
enter hog production "on an integrated basis." What better time
to do so than when the world demanded more food and Americans were complaining about high prices?

He built one hog facility in Arkansas not far from company
headquarters, but in 1977 he forayed into North Carolina. The
facility he bought there had been built by another investor hoping to cash in on the famine, Malcolm McLean, a multimillionaire and North Carolina native who'd made a fortune from
his trucking business. In 1974, McLean shelled out $60 mil-
lion for 375,000 acres of land in eastern North Carolina where
he planned to grow corn and feed a million hogs a year. "It's a
question of supply and demand," explained one of McLean's employees. "People are starving. It's just like the energy crisis except
that people are going to find it difficult to wait in line for food."
McLean's First Colony Farm (named for its proximity to the settlement established by Sir Walter Raleigh nearly four centuries
earlier) bore "the same relation to a farm that a computer does to
an abacus," observed a newspaper reporter. This being the early
1970s, environmentalists pounced, and rightly so. First Colony
occupied a large chunk of North Carolina's Dismal Swamp, an
environmentally complex area that lay between the Pamlico and
Albemarle sounds. But no one in state government was inclined
to stop the project, because, explained an official with the state's
Department of Natural and Economic Resources, "the food crisis
is up and coming, and I guess the feeling is that it's just not good
to stop and do an environmental study when it will take so long
and cost so much." McLean proceeded with his project, but when
Tyson came along with an offer, he sold the hog facility and ten
thousand acres to the Arkansas broiler king.

Satisfied that hogs would pay off, Tyson expanded his porcine empire. By 1980, he was also operating a breeding facility in Nebraska, selling the piglets born there to another corporate hog farmer, National Farms, Inc. NF was owned by the Bass family of Texas, whose immense fortune was dispersed among global corporations, huge chunks of Fort Worth, horse ranches, apartments and hotels, and oil wells, to name just a few. During the 1970s, NF owned and farmed (or leased to other farmers) forty thousand acres scattered across Texas, Nebraska, and Kansas, raising grain and processing alfalfa-based feeds for its cattle operations, all of it fueled, explained NF's president, Bill Haw, by the belief that food producers and farmers had "a God-given mission to feed the world." As part of that "mission," Haw built a couple of small experimental hog farms to assess the profit potential of converting part of National's corn crop to pork. Satisfied with the results, he announced that NF would join the "leading edge" of modern hog farming. By 1984, employees at National's Nebraska facility were feeding 350,000 hogs a year — purchasing the pigs from Tyson — an output then worth about $40 million.

Tyson and National Farms weren't the only big companies hunting for gold buried in the turmoil of meatpacking and livestock production. "We think the basic food industry is a hell of a place to be," Mike Harper told a reporter in 1981. Harper, an imposing hulk of a man (between his height — six-six — and his "booming voice," noted one observer, he "looks like a truck coming at you"), had recently embarked on a buying spree, his goal being to transform ConAgra, the company over which he presided, into a farm-to-table powerhouse. ConAgra had begun life in 1919 as Nebraska Consolidated Mills Co., a collection of formerly independent grain mills that joined forces to go public. Over the years, Nebraska's managers tried, with little success, to move into other food-related businesses, most notably with Duncan Hines cake mixes (which it sold to Procter & Gamble in the 1950s). By the early 1970s, ConAgra, as it was then named, teetered on the verge of bankruptcy. Harper was hired to salvage what he described as an "awful, awful disaster."

He dumped assets and streamlined management, but he calculated that global grain shortages, rising energy prices, and inflation would crush ConAgra unless the company reduced costs through integration and diversification. Harper decided that the company's survival depended on control of assets, whether cattle, corn, or chicken Kiev (frozen and ready to eat, of course). Harper bought river barges and terminals as well as grain elevators (the better to move raw materials from farm to factory to overseas port) and a grain-processing outfit (the better to keep prices low on the feed needed for the livestock in his portfolio). Harper also loaded his shopping cart with food manufacturers, including Chun King and Patio Mexican, often buying at rock-bottom prices because their owners didn't know what to do with them. "The guy buys things you wouldn't get a wooden nickel for and gets change back," one observer marveled. Consider one of his first major acquisitions: Banquet Foods, Inc., then the country's largest purveyor of frozen processed foods and owned by RCA, which specialized in electronics and media equipment and content. RCA's leaders had no idea what to do with food, frozen or otherwise. ("They were thinking of Skylab when Banquet was talking chicken pot pies," said one amused onlooker.) At the time, financial analysts predicted that rising energy costs spelled the end of the frozen-food market; grocery chains would balk at spending money keeping the cases cold. Harper believed otherwise: consumer demand for convenience would keep the lights on and the temperature low.

Harper was less interested in Banquet's packaged foods than in its integrated poultry divisions, which supplied the protein for many of the company's frozen-food products (processed, of course, in Banquet-owned factories). Harper had cut his corporate teeth on broilers — he'd headed Pillsbury's broiler operations before moving to ConAgra — but he also believed that even beef and pork could return a profit as long as he sliced production costs to the bone and turned basic carcasses into convenience foods. So he set out to conquer meatpacking. In 1978, he went after MBPXL, a beef-packing behemoth born of the merger of two Monfort/IBP-style clones. He shook hands on the deal, which would have given him a company whose sales outnumbered ConAgra's by two to one. But Cargill, a privately held, fabulously rich dealer in, among other things, global grains (it had made millions on the Russian grain deal), swooped in, snatching it from Harper's grasp and renaming it Excel. The acquisition transformed Cargill into the nation's second-largest meatpacker. (Cargill's maneuver was not as out-of-the-blue as it appeared: it already owned Caprock Industries, a giant cattle-feeding operation that existed primarily to sell livestock to what had been MBPXL.)

Mike Harper wasted no time bemoaning his failure. There were plenty more packers to choose from; the upheaval of the 1970s had pushed dozens of small ones into bankruptcy and Armour, Swift, and Wilson to the edge of collapse. A Swift executive conceded that management had stumbled — or, more accurately, slumbered: "We should have moved quickly to match" Monfort, IBP, and other new packers, he conceded. "Instead, we sat back and read the 1913 annual report and didn't change anything." Executives at the three ailing giants embraced the same survival strategy. They shut down their hog-slaughtering operations and dumped their dwindling capital into processed convenience foods. But that move put each of them in direct competition with Oscar Mayer and Hormel, both of which were financially stable and boasted decades-long track records selling processed pork products. To no one's surprise, the tactic failed to save any of the three, in part because their corporate owners had no idea how to make food.

Their failure opened the door for Harper, who went after Armour. Since 1969, it had been owned by Greyhound Corporation, a company more accustomed to operating buses than packing plants, and whose managers floundered in the turbulent world of food making and especially meatpacking. Greyhound's chairman groused that he never had a chance with Armour because Monfort and IBP, with their highly efficient plants and nonunion employees, were "like a bunch of piranhas cutting away at [Armour's] base." Once Armour's managers realized that they could not compete in processed foods, they pivoted back to basic slaughter — only to find that their former customers were swimming with the piranhas. "Armour's dead in the water," said an onlooker. Harper swooped in with an offer. The purchase provided ConAgra with two slaughtering plants, one each for pork and beef, and, more important, nineteen facilities primarily devoted to the manufacture of value-added foods like hot dogs and frozen entrées. A few weeks later, ConAgra reopened what had been Armour's doors with a nonunion workforce.

Harper wasn't finished. Four years later, he flew to Greeley, Colorado, and persuaded Ken Monfort to sell him the feedlots, the packing plants, and the brand. Monfort needed little persuasion. He had never recovered from the bloodbath of the 1970s, and by the end of that decade, production costs at his Greeley plant were 50 percent higher than those at IBP, thanks to Monfort's desire to play fair with unions. When he finally asked his employees for concessions, workers struck. The confrontation was ugly and painful for both sides. Monfort argued that in the age of IBP, union work rules and high wages were driving the company toward ruin. Nonsense, replied union leaders. "Monfort wants to return to the industrial dark ages of starvation wages and destructive working conditions." Employees vowed they would "not surrender to Monfort's selfish demands." The strike ended after seventy-three days, but the plant did not reopen. Ken Monfort closed it and one of his feedlots and began carving the fat from his operations, laying off management, dumping assets, and revamping the packing plant. In 1982, he reopened the slaughterhouse, minus a union contract, but he never caught up with his competitors. So when Mike Harper presented his offer, Ken grabbed the lifeline. Harper, he said, was "the 'big friend' I was looking for." Monfort of Colorado, Inc., would remain a separate entity within ConAgra, and Ken would stay on as its head.

Monfort's fellow meatpacking pioneer, IBP, also changed hands, not because it was struggling but because that company wanted to move into hog slaughter and pork processing. "Pork has been there for 25 years waiting for someone to automate and upgrade," said IBP's president, Robert Peterson, in 1980, and grocery chain executives were pressuring him to give them an IBP version of pork. If anyone could reinvent hog slaughter, it was Peterson, an Andy Anderson protégé, but he, too, needed a big friend to foot the bill. Peterson found his partner in Occidental Petroleum Corp., a global behemoth with holdings in, among other things, oil, ammonia, pesticides, fertilizer, and cattle. Oxy's chair, Armand Hammer, explained that his corporate strategy for the 1980s was to "increase world food production 'to see that all people are fed.'" Or, as an Oxy vice president put it, "We think food will be in the 1990's what energy has been to the 1970's and 1980's." What better way to pursue that strategy than by owning the biggest beef processor in the world? The folks at IBP wasted no time marching into the disarray that was hog slaughtering in the early 1980s. The plan was to produce boxed pork and sell it to the IBP customers who relied on its boxed beef. IBP executives outfitted the venture with pork-related expertise by wooing top managers from Wilson and Oscar Mayer. As for packing plants, those were (almost) a dime a dozen, thanks to the turmoil of the previous decade; Iowa, still the national leader in hog production, boasted a bouquet of idle slaughterhouses. IBP bought a shuttered Hygrade plant in northern Iowa, gutted it, and renovated it into a marvel of streamlined efficiency. Capacity: 3.5 million hogs a year. Within months, IBP announced plans to build the world's largest hog slaughter plant in either western Illinois or eastern Iowa. (Two small towns — one with a population of 1,100 and the other 600 — duked it out for the honor. Stanwood, Iowa, won.)

IBP's invasion of the pork industry pushed the remaining member of the old Beef Trust, Wilson Foods, as it was then called, over the edge. In the late 1960s, a corporate conglomerate with holdings in electronics had bought Wilson, but no good had come of it, and a decade later, the meatpacker was gasping for air. The firm's president placed the company's last bet on pork and "branded" fresh pork cuts, but that plan unraveled once IBP entered the pork market. In 1983, bleeding a million dollars a week, Wilson's executives filed for bankruptcy and used that protection to cancel its labor contracts. (The union sued, but the Supreme Court sided with Wilson.) Wilson unloaded plants, laid off workers, and dumped its employee retirement plan. It wasn't enough. "I just don't see how they can stay in business," said one analyst. They couldn't. In 1985, Wilson put itself up for sale. Tyson, ConAgra, Cargill, and Swift all looked — and passed. IBP wanted it, but the bankruptcy judge refused that offer. In the end, Wilson found a buyer in Doskocil, a Kansas sausage manufacturer whose major customer was Pizza Hut.

It was inevitable that the new titans would test their prowess and collide in the process. In 1988, ConAgra and Tyson Foods battled for ownership of Holly Farms, one of the oldest and most solid of the broiler companies. Tyson made the first move, announcing it planned to spend $900 million in stocks and cash to acquire Holly. Most analysts assumed that Tyson was after the chickens. Those were attractive, but they weren't Tyson's primary target. A few years earlier, the Arkansas giant had moved into processed pork products, a natural move given its investment in hog farming, and Holly owned a subsidiary that manufactured hot dogs, ham, and other pork-based foods. "We are confident that this proposal will be extremely attractive to your stockholders," Don Tyson wrote in a letter to R. Lee Taylor, Holly's president. Nothing doing, replied Taylor. According to analysts who knew both men, the refusal stemmed from personal relations or, more accurately, lack of them: Taylor did not like Tyson and had rejected a similar offer three years earlier. Don Tyson wanted what he wanted, however, and he marched forward; indeed, Taylor's recalcitrance likely whetted his appetite for battle. (A year earlier, he'd introduced a meeting with a poster of Rambo-chicken, a bird outfitted with "battle helmet, grenades and machine gun.") After weeks of Tyson's pestering, Holly's board informed Don that it had agreed to a "friendly" takeover by Mike Harper and ConAgra. Tyson responded with a sweeter deal. Months of warfare ensued, but in the end, Tyson, the nation's biggest poultry processor, snatched Holly, the number-three, away from Harper, the number-two man on the chicken totem pole, for a final price of $1.29 billion, well above his original offer of $900 million. "This is a very tasty morsel for us," cackled Tyson's general counsel.

By the late 1980s, the new food powerhouses dominated meatpacking, but their gigantic operations required massive quantities of raw materials: cattle and hogs. The beef packers formed partnerships with big cattle feedlots or bought them outright because those feeders could provide not just large quantities of cattle, but, as custom feeders, the precise kinds of livestock that ConAgra or IBP wanted. Paul Engler, the man who'd opened a feedlot near Amarillo, Texas, back in the early 1960s, enjoyed personal connections to IBP's leaders and those links led to profit. Cargill owned Excel as well as a collection of feedlots.

Hogs, however, posed a more complicated problem because companies like ConAgra, IBP, and Tyson had to satisfy two different markets. First were the global buyers, especially in Asia, where pork was the most popular meat and where local farmers couldn't supply enough to feed rapidly growing urban populations. American hog producers dominated that export market, but there was a catch. "[I]nternational customers," explained an agricultural economist at Oklahoma State University, "don't buy and view meat the same way we do domestically. It's not a commodity to them. It's a very specific quality, value-added product to them and they will force us to market it that way." Japanese customers, for example, demanded marbled pork that oozed flavor and fat. But Tyson and other hog growers also supplied the U.S. market, and Americans wanted lean, fat-free, low-cholesterol pork. If Tyson, for example, hoped to sell ham to McDonald's for its McMuffins, it had to give the fast-food chain precisely the lean meat it wanted. Food processors and grocery chains also demanded low-everything pork that could be used to manufacture low-fat, microwaveable, processed pork products, whether sausage, bacon, or frozen, low-calorie entrées.

As a result food processors, meatpackers, and farmers — and by the 1980s, these were often one and the same — could no longer afford to think of hogs (or cattle or chickens) as basic commodities whose price depended on supply, demand, and the cost of corn. Those traditional "fuzzy" price signals, explained two economists, had been supplanted by ones transmitted by consumers who made purchases based on calorie and cholesterol count and a product's "convenience" quotient. Put another way, packers and processors didn't want hogs. They wanted four-legged sources of specific types of pork: low-fat, low-cholesterol for diet-crazy Americans; fattier cuts for the Asian market. The most cost-effective way to lay their hands on such animals in the huge quantities needed was by demanding that farmers add value to a hog from the moment of its inception. By the late eighties, "value-added" referred not to, say, boxed pork or microwaveable sausage, but to a hog bred with specific genetic traits and raised on a combination of computer-designed rations and biotechnologies, such as porcine somatotropin (pST), a drug that increased weight gain per pound of feed and reduced fat accumulation by as much as 80 percent. But all those hogs also had to be identical. Said one packer: "I can do well with lean hogs. If I have to, I can get along with fat hogs. What I can't stand is two fat hogs, then a lean hog and then another fat one coming down the chain. It's impossible to merchandise the mixed shipments we get today." Small wonder, then, that the new food-and-meat giants constructed their own hog-and-pork supply chains. It was the only way to guarantee a consistent product, volume, and price. Nor was it any wonder that in the world of meat, wrote two analysts, "product development" now began "on the farm, rather than in the processing plant." When packer-processors had to buy hogs outside their own supply lines, they replaced fuzzy signals with contractual detail, telling farmers, "We will buy X number of hogs with X amount of fat and at X weight, and we want uniformity, not just sometimes but always." But because most conventional in/out farmers could not meet those demands, processors and packers relied on corporate farmers who understood the rules of the game, new-style farmers like Premium Standard Farms. "We want everything to be consistent," explained an official with PSF, "and that's part of our name."

By the early 1990s, corporate hog farms had become the norm: operations defined by large scale (not hundreds of hogs, but hundreds of thousands), extensive automation, confinement, antibiotics and other drugs, and contract growers. Among the companies that jumped into the business was Seaboard Corporation, another mongrel conglomerate: it was born in 1918 as a flour miller and followed a meandering path in and out of related areas. In the early eighties, the company shifted its focus to building a global empire based on grain and food, including chickens and hogs, the latter an effort to conquer Asian markets. (The shift from flour mills to chickens and hogs fit Seaboard's mission as an "entrepreneurial organization": "We could produce chairs for conference rooms," a company vice president said, as long as those chairs made money.) Seaboard built one hog facility in Colorado, already home to fellow hog producers Tyson and National, and hunted for a second location where it would build another hog farm and a slaughterhouse. Oklahoma fit the bill. Tyson operated a breeding facility in that state and contracted with local farmers to raise the resulting pigs. More important, in 1991, the Oklahoma legislature nourished the state's nascent hog industry (Oklahomans typically raised cattle, not hogs) with a bill that allowed corporations to operate breeding facilities, feed mills, and processing plants, and to provide "technical . . . assistance" to farmers — a euphemism for contract farming of the sort introduced by the broiler industry.

City leaders and business owners in Guymon, Oklahoma, a small town (population about ten thousand), wanted in on the action. In recent years, that town and surrounding county had suffered a string of economic hits, including the 1987 closure of a Swift packing plant. Local movers and shakers wanted to replace lost industries before the area's economy spiraled down the path of decline. Guymon wooed Seaboard and won, thanks in part to a package of incentives that totaled more than $30 million. The project was spearheaded by townspeople, to the dismay of many farmers and other residents of nearby rural areas. "Now why do the poor people of Guymon Oklahoma . . . have to subsidize a corporation of that size and magnitude[?]" asked one farmer. Another found the situation both frustrating and comical. "I'm sure those executives were saying — What? They want to do what? Oh, boy. Just so we'll locate there?" From Seaboard's perspective, Oklahoma made good sense, so off to Guymon went Seaboard, another factor that turned an unlikely location — Oklahoma? — into a new hog powerhouse.

Seaboard's arrival created hundreds of jobs and attracted other hog-related, job-producing companies, but the ensuing stench — giant hog farms generated as much odor as they did pork — turned neighbor against neighbor, and locals engaged in that oldest of American activities: defining the distinction between personal liberty and community well-being. "The trouble is that the odor goes across the fence and that doesn't seem right at all," mused a local cattle rancher. "That can ruin somebody's property values and make it so they can't enjoy their own property. It seems like a real infringement to me." But a cattle feeder who'd seized Seaboard's arrival as an opportunity to diversify into hogs scoffed at that view. The "pigs came and you don't like it," he said. "My attitude is — leave!" As far as he was concerned, "you control your own life, you can live anywhere you want, you can do anything you want. You can use your property in any fashion you feel proper. And the government should stay the hell out of it." Others weren't so sure. "I'm an advocate of individual rights, but there's a limit," said an Oklahoma state legislator. "You can't just let mass pollution happen. And in some cases you are going to be stepping on individual rights when you regulate." Another man marveled at the way Seaboard's arrival had turned his worldview upside down, to the extent that "a group like the Sierra Club" had become "popular with conservative Republicans." "I thought I was a conservative Republican," he mused. "I'm not sure what I am now. I thought conservative Republicans were pro-growth, pro-business" and "wanted to build things and sell them. Instead they are hugging trees." In 1993, the Oklahoma legislature decided that the well-being of the state's economy trumped individuals' rights to odor-free air. It approved a measure that allowed corporate farmers like Seaboard to operate without a permit. But if the company opted to apply for a permit, it gained permanent protection from nuisance suits.

As it turned out, residents of Guymon and the surrounding county weren't the only ones arguing over the impact of corporate hog farms. By the 1990s many Americans in both town and country were questioning the power of the new food giants, arguing, as others had nearly a century earlier, that they exercised too much control over the nation's plates. In the Midwest, political activists organized to oppose the encroachment of corporate farms, and other critics challenged the dominance of meat in the American diet. That backlash announced the arrival of the newest power player in the meat and livestock industries: public interest groups that advocated on behalf of consumers, the environment, and what was left of "family farmers."

7

THE DOUBTERS' CRUSADE

I N THE SPRING OF 1981, Mike Douglas, who hosted a day-
time talk show (its popularity on par with that of Oprah
Winfrey's twenty years later), welcomed two guests to the
program. One was Ralph Nader, a household name thanks to
two decades of advocacy on behalf of American consumers. The
other was Michael Jacobson, a Nader disciple who founded (and
at this writing still heads) the Center for Science in the Public
Interest, an organization that specializes in attacking food manufacturers and reforming Americans' eating habits. Nader and
Jacobson regaled viewers with the horrors of modern meat and
inducted bacon and hot dogs into a "Junk Food Hall of Shame,"
commemorating the moment by throwing meat onto the floor.
Their showmanship did not go unnoticed. Officials with the National Pork Producers Council and the American Meat Institute
(AMI) filed complaints with Douglas's producers and with the
Federal Communications Commission, arguing that Nader and
Jacobson had used the airtime to promote "innuendo, implication and unsubstantiated information" and foment "consumer
distrust in the nation's food supply." The show's producer, no
doubt sensing a ratings bonanza in the make, offered meat equal

time. On the appointed day, representatives from trade groups showed up — but so did Nader and Jacobson; Craig Claiborne, a widely published food writer who had recently embarked on a low-sodium diet; and The Captain and Tennille, a then-popular singing duo who touted the virtues of vegetarianism. With the stage stacked against them, the beef and pork representatives changed few viewers' minds.

Such theatricality was part of Nader's stock-in-trade, and by that time he'd been using it against meat makers for almost two decades. He'd launched his anti-meat crusade back in the late 1960s when he attacked the manufacturers of hot dogs, at the time the unofficial food of American childhood (thanks to the postwar baby boom, hot dog consumption soared 75 percent in the twenty years after the end of World War II). Using statistics he'd wrangled out of the USDA, Nader reported that in 1937, the typical dog contained about 19 percent fat and 20 percent protein. A 1967 hot dog, however, was nearly a third fat but less than 12 percent protein. Prodded by the publicity — Nader's was already a household name thanks to his best-selling book *Unsafe at Any Speed,* an exposé of the automobile industry's devotion to profits rather than consumer safety — in the summer of 1969, the USDA agreed to consider new regulations to govern the dog's fat content and held a public hearing so that consumer advocates and meat industry representatives could weigh in on the proposals. The meat men asked for 35 percent, explaining that fat yielded a juicier, more toothsome dog. More like coronary delights, insisted the packers' foes, and toxic to kids and grownups alike; they demanded that hot dogs contain no more than 25 percent fat. Then Virginia Knauer, President Richard Nixon's consumer adviser, stepped in and issued an ultimatum: 30 percent and no more. The consumerites were delighted; USDA officials and meat industry representatives, flummoxed. Was the White House telling the Department of Agriculture what to do? Yes, Knauer assured them, it was. (Nixon later phoned Knauer to affirm that he backed her "100%" on "the hot dog issue." He was on a low-cholesterol diet, he explained, but he identified with the dog because of his "humble origins." "Why, we were raised on hot dogs and hamburgers. We've got to look after the hot dog.")

That hearing and the appearance on *The Mike Douglas Show* were all in a day's work for Nader and his Raiders, activists who dedicated their lives to the cause of "consumerism." For the rest of the twentieth century, Naderites would challenge the safety of meat products, the nutritional value of meat, and even how farmers raised the livestock that produced that meat. Those crusades, and others like them, changed the dynamics among government, private corporations, and ordinary citizens and fueled the growth of a consumer-interest infrastructure.

From the 1960s on, Nader was the most prominent face of a consumer activist movement that had begun back in the 1930s and grown steadily since then, an inevitable byproduct of the consumer-based economy. After all, if consumption made the economy go 'round, consumers themselves surely constituted one of society's most important groups, a view confirmed by the events of the 1930s and 1940s. Much of President Franklin Roosevelt's New Deal, for example, was designed to foster consumer activity. During World War II, federal officials enlisted shoppers as homefront warriors, urging them to monitor prices and report retailers who violated price control regulations. Organizations of "citizen consumers," and there were many, adopted the language of rights to demand the same recognition and protection granted to other interest groups, such as labor, agriculture, and business.

Ralph Nader, who was born in 1934, intended to further the cause. He believed that consumers were among society's most vulnerable groups, their needs and wants too often ignored by politically motivated government bureaucrats, elected officials, and profit-driven corporate managers. Nader, the son of Lebanese immigrants, grew up in a small Connecticut town where his father owned a restaurant. The elder Nader was opinionated and argumentative and expected both his customers and his children to give and get the same. The younger Nader was by all accounts bright to the point of precociousness, studious, and, when interested, capable of intense concentration and focus. Ralph left his hometown to attend first Princeton and then Harvard, where he obtained a law degree. Along the way, he became obsessed with a need to combat corporations, which he dubbed "private governments," a phrase that echoed Upton Sinclair's phrase of choice, "invisible governments," and which, in his mind, wielded power to an extent that was unhealthy for a democratic society. The sales of *Unsafe at Any Speed* and income from a lawsuit against automakers earned Nader enough money to expand his crusade against corporate evils. Driven by zealousness that bordered on fanaticism, Nader — tall, lanky, gaunt to the point of being a bit spectral, and a reclusive workaholic — exuded charisma that inspired others to follow.

Nader may have been eccentric, but his attitude toward corporations was shaped by the era in which he lived. The 1950s are typically thought of in terms of McCarthyist anticommunism and *Leave It to Beaver* conformity, but it was also a decade in which the dangers of an atomic and chemically saturated world bombarded the American psyche. In 1953, for example, more than a thousand sheep died under mysterious circumstances in Utah, deaths that angry stockmen blamed on fallout, as it was called, from a Nevada weapons test site. The Atomic Energy Commission denied the charge, but that assertion lost authority the following year after drifting residue from a weapons test in the Pacific Ocean deposited a coating of white ash on twenty-three men aboard a Japanese fishing boat. The men became ill and one of their group died. This time it was impossible to pretend that fallout was not to blame. Worse, analysts determined that the dust contained a substance called strontium-90, and a few years later, the editors of *Consumer Reports* (founded in the 1930s to alert Americans about unsafe products and fraudulent manufacturing practices) informed readers that Sr-90 was embedded in the nation's food supply, especially in milk. Then there was the Nightmare Before Thanksgiving: just days before the Novem-

ber holiday in 1959, the secretary of health, education, and welfare warned consumers that some of the nation's cranberry crop
was contaminated with the residue of aminotriazole, a herbicide
and a known carcinogen. Most Americans celebrated that holiday season cranberry-free. Even the suburbs, that postwar haven from the city, weren't safe, a fact millions of homeowners discovered when their backyard septic tanks turned lawns into toxic
soup and new synthetic detergents rendered tap water undrink-
able.

In the fall of 1960, *Time* magazine summarized the nation's
fears in a cover story titled "Environment v. Man." The author
told readers that every year, more than four hundred new chemicals were unleashed on an unknowing public, substances that
wormed their way "into the air people breathe, the water they
drink and the food they eat." The "invisible" invaders "damage
plants, kill fish, slip undetected through sewage-treatment plants
and blanket entire cities with clouds of noxious vapor." A medical expert calculated that 15 percent of cancer diagnoses were
likely due to environmental causes. Nor were chemical assaults
the only such woe. In 1965, eighteen thousand residents of River-
side, California, became ill, and several died, after drinking municipal water contaminated by salmonella, a word most Americans had never heard until then. The head of epidemiology at the
National Communicable Disease Center described the rise in salmonella poisoning as "a major national problem." He and other
experts blamed food-processing plants where workers manufactured enormous quantities of everything from frozen TV dinners to dried milk to boxed cake mixes. One careless move at just
one factory, the epidemiologist explained, could spawn an "infection that [could] spread throughout the country." There was,
it seemed, nowhere to run and no place to hide from the dangers of modern life. The relentless onslaught explains the robust
sales and gut-punching impact of Rachel Carson's 1962 book *Silent Spring*. Her work has been credited with inspiring the modern environmental movement, but a more accurate assessment

is that the book was less a launching pad than a tipping point, as Carson articulated fears shared by many Americans. (It helped, however, that Carson was one of the best-known writers in America, thanks to two earlier, best-selling, prize-winning books about nature and science.) Had *Silent Spring* been released in, say, 1952, it's unlikely that it would have had the same impact. Instead, it landed in the hands of a public well versed in the dangers of DES, DDT, and Sr-90.

Confronted with unpronounceable food additives, salmonella, and toxic milk — to say nothing of unsafe cars — Americans longed for someone, anyone, to voice their concerns. No wonder, then, that the circulation of *Consumer Reports* more than doubled in the second half of the 1960s, that so many people regarded Ralph Nader as a hero, and that so many law students abandoned conventional careers to join his crusade. In 1969, not long after the hot dog campaign, Nader landed on the cover of *Time* magazine, his face presented as a Warholesque collision of orange and green, that image sliced by a banner announcing "The Consumer Revolt." "Evidently there's a dearth of causes right now," grumbled a vice president at the Jewel grocery chain. "Consumerism has become like motherhood and the flag, with everybody jumping on the bandwagon." Nader thought that critic had it backward. "Other issues such as Vietnam and civil rights have divided the country into camps," he argued, and those who had something to sell would always be divided from those who wanted to buy. But among consumers, there was "no split." Everyone, black or white, young or old, rich or poor, was a consumer, and consumerism was a "people's movement." Nader tapped into that collective identity and into the frustration and fear that afflicted the most affluent society in history. He also understood that because consumers were voters, he could always count on some politicians to support him. But Nader's genius lay in his ability to particularize the war on corporate power. Unlike Teddy Roosevelt, who battled meatpackers using the arcana of antitrust laws and courtroom maneuvers, Nader taught Americans to think about consumer protection in terms of the stuff of daily life, whether baby food or automobiles.

Nader's war on the hot dog is a good example of the way he framed corporate evils in terms that resonated with the public. When he launched the hot dog crusade in the late sixties, he knew that Americans were already unnerved by a string of reports about the alleged relationship between fat and disease, thanks to another face from the cover of *Time* magazine, Ancel Keys, then one of the nation's most famous scientists and primary perpetrator of the fat-is-bad theory. Time and again, Nader and his colleagues would use Keys's ideas to educate the public about the evils of corporate power and the way in which corporations sacrificed the public health in favor of profits — but also to warn Americans about the dangers of meat.

Keys's influence and the "fat is bad" mantra took shape after World War II, when medical experts began warning Americans about a heart disease epidemic. The evidence for the alleged epidemic was (and is) shaky, based as it was on anecdote rather than fact. It was true that physicians were diagnosing more heart disease, but that was because they had better tools with which to identify it. Moreover, thanks to medical advances like antibiotics, life expectancy rates were rising and more Americans were experiencing the ailments that afflict aging hearts. Rather than tout those explanations, however, many in the medical establishment linked the epidemic to diet. Once again, the connection was flimsy: during the 1940s, the rates of heart disease and heart attack had declined in Europe but gone up in the United States. At the time, and thanks to war-related food scarcities, Europeans ate diets low in protein, fat, and calories. That was enough to convince the easily persuaded: people living in "poor" countries experienced fewer heart attacks than affluent Americans who feasted on foods rich in fat, sugar, salt, and protein. Therefore, rich diets and rich people reaped rich numbers of heart attacks. Never mind that this leap into cause and effect rested on virtually no research, and none that controlled for other factors, such as whether postwar Europeans walked more than Americans or engaged in more physical labor. In 1948, Congress responded to the fear-mongering by creating the National Heart Institute and the National Heart Council. As is often the case, Congress offered the organizations little in the way of money, so staffers at the new agencies launched public relations campaigns designed to prove the heart disease danger and thus persuade senators and representatives to part with the public's money. Worried that it might be left behind in the scramble for financial support, the American Heart Association (AHA), a decades-old but moribund organization of physicians interested in (medical) matters of the heart, hired a public relations firm that transformed the AHA into a fundraising powerhouse devoted to broadcasting the evils of heart disease. The ensuing publicity generated research proposals from scientists looking for a share of public and private money, and so began the search for facts with which to flesh out the phantom epidemic.

Chief among the researchers was Ancel Keys, who argued, based on evidence that ranged from sketchy to nonexistent, that high-fat diets elevated serum cholesterol, which led to atherosclerosis ("hardening of the arteries"), which led to heart attack, an equation dubbed the "diet-heart hypothesis." From there, Keys leaped to two conclusions: Fat is bad. Because meat contains fat, meat is bad for your health. His claims were both simplistic and incorrect. Fat is essential to human well-being, and the body contains plenty of it in the form of cholesterol, a substance it uses to manufacture hormones, among other things. Over time, cholesterol can build up in arteries and cause them to "harden." Saturated fats, which come primarily from animal products, can also deposit fat in arteries, so eating excessive amounts of that class of fats can contribute to atherosclerosis. But not all fats come from animals; plants contain fat, too, and some fats are unsaturated, even in animal-based foods. Half the fat in beef is saturated, for example, and half unsaturated. But Keys, to the regret of his peers, colleagues, and opponents (of whom there were many), was an intellectual bully and a relentless self-promoter of the World According to Keys. Having decided that his view was correct, he promoted it, the facts be damned. Other scientists and even officials at the American Heart Association challenged his lack of evidence, but Keys ignored critics (and elbowed his way into a position of power at the AHA and turned its machinery to his cause) and rebutted challengers by arguing better safe than sorry. Even if there wasn't any proof, if there was a chance that fatty foods caused heart disease, Americans ought to be told. The ever-savvy Keys also knew that he who controlled the medium also controlled the message, and his ability to explain his ideas in simple language appealed to journalists, who dutifully reported theory as fact. In 1961, editors at *Time* magazine solidified both Keys's reputation and his ideas by putting him on the magazine's cover.

Ralph Nader wasn't interested in scientific squabbles or questions about Keys's credibility, but he recognized an opening when he saw it. The "fat is bad" claim gave him a reason to wage war on meatpackers, with the hot dog as his weapon of choice. The frankfurter war heated up in early 1972 when *Consumer Reports* published a behind-the-scenes — or, more accurately, under-the-skin — look at the dog. "Once upon a time," *CR*'s reporter told readers, the frankfurter had been "a reasonably honest product" composed of meat, a bit of water, a dollop of fat, and plenty of protein. No more. The 1970s edition contained as much as a third fat and a lot of water — legally, as much as 54 percent. A dog labeled "All Meat" could, and likely did, contain a combination of any number of animal parts, such as lips and tongues, pork, beef, chicken, mutton, or goat, as well as cereal and dried milk or soy meal. And then there was the plastic package that housed the dogs. If it was airtight, no problem. If not, the water provided a breeding ground for bacteria. A safe threshold, the reporter noted, was 10 million bacteria per gram, but 40 percent of the samples tested by the magazine surpassed that number, and one contained 140 million bacteria per gram. Add in some sodium nitrite — newsworthy at the time because of its allegedly carcinogenic qualities — salt, spice, monosodium glutamate, corn syrup, sodium ascorbate, and/or ascorbic acid, and there it was: the all-American hot dog.

Those revelations and continuing pressure from Naderites prompted USDA officials to ponder still more regulatory rules for hot dogs, including a ban on meat byproducts in their manu-facture. Department protocol mandated that it request public in-put before making changes to existing rules, and under normal conditions, the "public" consisted of spokespersons for whatever industry's products would be affected. But normal had been Na-derized, and to the horror of hot dog makers and meat indus-try lobbyists, the actual public weighed in. A Maryland schoolgirl took pencil in hand to make a polite but firm request: Please stop adding "pig swill" to hot dogs, she wrote. "We get bad lunches at school as it is and I would hate to have to turn down hot dogs if you put it in. And besides I would starve the whole day!" P.S., she added, "If you really have to put pig snouts in, could you blow their noses first, please??" The young lady had company. A New Jersey woman complained that it was bad enough that meat mak-ers added "cancer producing" preservatives to their products. But making hot dogs from "the same meat that they now put in dog food" was too much. "How much more does the American con-sumer have to take?" she asked. "Let us get off the dollar band-wagon and get back to eating pure foods. Our children ask the in-dustries to stop polluting their bodies."

The "wiener is being clobbered," mourned the president of the American Meat Institute as hot dog sales plummeted. Oscar Mayer Jr. interpreted the attacks as "personal affronts to him and his meat-packing forebears." The Mayer family had been manu-facturing sausages and other processed pork products since the late nineteenth century and had built a global company by fo-cusing on convenience foods and by inventing packaging mate-rials and processing technologies for them. In the early 1960s, its hot dog, already an all-American bestseller, gained new fans thanks to what is arguably one of the most memorable advertis-ing ditties in history: the so-called Wiener Jingle ("Oh, I wish I were an Oscar Mayer wiener"). A colleague reported that Mayer

Jr. was "absolutely stunned" by the uproar. Other meat makers were less stunned than infuriated. "I have an answer to the stupid jerks in Washington, including Nader," said the president of an Illinois meat-processing company. "I would suggest that all packers stop buying [livestock] for a two-week period to show the American people what these jerks in Washington are doing to the farmer and packer and, in the end, the American consumer. It's time someone tells these jerks where they fit." The president of another meat company offered a more measured response in a letter to Richard Lyng, the assistant secretary of agriculture, suggesting that rather than ban protein-rich byproducts like tongue, liver, and lips, the USDA should educate the public about their nutritional value. A ban based on emotion and "aesthetics," he argued, would propel the USDA down a slippery slope. Gelatin, for example, was manufactured from bone. Did the department also plan to ban "gelatin desserts" such as Jell-O? Mushrooms were "grown in manure" and typically eaten raw. Was it also going to ban mushrooms?

In the end, both sides got something they wanted as the USDA hewed to the middle road rather than the slippery slope: under new rules, sausages manufactured from just one type of meat would wear a label boasting that fact. Those that included the dreaded snouts, eyes, and lips would be labeled as containing byproducts or "variety meats," terminology that was blessedly vague by packers' standards and too vague by those of consumer advocates.

Naderites had less success with another project, one carried out in partnership with environmental advocacy groups (another new feature of the political landscape): an assault on the use of hormones and antibiotics in livestock production. In 1970, newspapers carried an Associated Press report that steaks and burgers probably contained traces of DES, long since identified as a carcinogen. Federal inspectors pulled tainted carcasses from meatpackers' lines, but a spokesman for the FDA assured Americans they had nothing to fear. "Most of us can't get too excited about the occasional animal showing up [with] two parts per billion of stilbestrol," he said. That comment sounds callous, but his dismissal stemmed less from indifference than from a belief in his own expertise. Unlike average Americans — the ones reading the newspaper report — he and other experts understood the fine points of DES, animal nutrition, and physiology, including the fact that bovines' bodies contain natural estrogens. In his mind, minute traces of DES residue were nothing to worry about. A human would have to eat tons (literally) of residues before suffering any damage. The FDA was so confident about the safety of DES that it granted cattle feeders permission to double the amount they could use. What the public heard, however, was the word *cancer* coupled to an airy dismissal from an official seemingly indifferent to the public's health, which was more than enough to keep consumer advocates in attack mode. In response, the FDA and USDA announced they would use more sophisticated tests for residues and prosecute those who violated federal regulations; in early 1971, both the House and Senate investigated the use of DES and other chemicals in the nation's food supply. There the matter might have ended, but not long after those hearings, the *New England Journal of Medicine* published a study of the so-called DES daughters, a group of young women who had been diagnosed with a rare form of vaginal cancer. The women's mothers had been prescribed DES while pregnant (in the mid-twentieth-century, doctors used the hormone to prevent miscarriage), and that, hypothesized the researchers, had caused the cancer. After that, it was impossible for the FDA to ignore the matter. In 1973, the agency banned DES, although the prohibition did not go into effect until 1979, stalled by a series of court challenges. Although DES left the farm, the FDA allowed livestock producers to use other, noncarcinogenic hormones.

The Naderites also tried to eliminate antibiotics from livestock production. On the face of it, science appeared to affirm the need for a ban. In the late 1950s, scientists had discovered that bacteria could and did develop immunity to antibiotics and that, more troubling, resistant bacteria could pass that trait on to their offspring and even to other, unrelated bacterial species nearby.

Scientists and physicians believed that resistance was exacerbated and encouraged by steady, regular ingestion of the drugs, which was precisely how most antibiotics were administered on livestock farms. In 1966, the editors of the *New England Journal of Medicine* described the resistance effect as "intellectually fascinating and therapeutically frightening." Unless humans began taking more care with how and when they administered the drugs, the editors warned, physicians treating infectious disease would "find themselves back in the preantibiotic Middle Ages." By that time, however, the entire food industry had found uses for antibiotics and had no desire to let go. Processors, for example, used Aureomycin to preserve fish and poultry. Still, it was hard to ignore either the facts or pressure from scientists and consumer advocates, and as the 1960s ended, the FDA commissioned an investigation of nonmedical uses of the drugs and recommended that food manufacturers limit their use of antibiotics to ones not used on humans. Beyond that, however, the investigators' advice amounted to timid banalities: Gather more information about drug use in livestock production. Add stiffer warning labels to drug packaging. Collect data; exercise caution. To be fair, the committee's members — physicians, veterinarians, bacteriologists, and biologists — explained that they were reluctant to issue stronger recommendations because they lacked evidence that pointed to a different conclusion. They believed that long-term doses of antibiotics provoked bacterial resistance, but as yet, they noted, scientists did not understand how or even if those doses affected humans who ate meat from drug-treated livestock. Barring definitive data, they argued, there was no reason to ban the drugs.

Even so, in 1972, FDA officials announced that antibiotic-laced livestock feeds constituted a "potential health hazard" and that manufacturers would henceforth be required to demonstrate the "safety and efficacy of their products." Translation: For the time being, antibiotics were safe from the meddling of Nader and his Raiders. The "bad news," groused the editor of a livestock industry magazine, was that manufacturers would be forced to spend millions on research, an expense they would surely pass on to farmers and consumers. An official with the National Livestock Producers Association was equally irritated. There was no "better research" available, he fumed, "than the 200 million healthy Americans eating 200 pounds of red meat and poultry per capita annually, thanks largely to low-level use of antibiotics. I'd say that ought to be enough research."

It's easy to conclude that federal officials caved to pressure from pharmaceutical manufacturers and meat industry trade groups, and there's no doubt that both groups lobbied to protect their interests. But that alone does not explain why Naderites failed to oust antibacterials and hormones from the barnyard. At the time, two other factors carried more weight. First, although scientists had affirmed the reality of antibiotic resistance, for better or for worse, none of the available research produced concrete, irrefutable evidence that linked antibiotic-laced feeds to specific cases of human antibiotic resistance. In the words of the FDA's commissioner, the available data was "grossly inadequate." No one had died from eating meat from animals raised on antibiotics (or DES), so no one could be certain beyond a doubt that the drugs posed a danger. If 100 percent certainty was the relevant criterion, certainty lay on the side of the status quo. Second, the scientific community had more at stake than did farmers and pharmaceutical manufacturers: their professional credibility. Imposing a ban based on no evidence was a cure worse than the disease, because it undermined the authority of science. In this case, science trumped knee-jerk fear.

Another Nader-driven project, the 1967 Wholesome Meat Act, also produced a mixed victory. That law imposed federally mandated inspection at slaughterhouses operated by intrastate meatpackers, companies that slaughtered livestock only within a state's borders. Prior to the law's passage, they had not been subject to federal inspection — and, as often as not, no inspection at all. But 15 percent of the animals slaughtered in the United

States came from such facilities, as did a quarter of all processed meats. Prodded by Nader, Congress passed the 1967 law, which required those packers to adhere to the same federal inspection standards that governed interstate packers. To Nader's dismay, the final bill gave states little incentive to comply. If they ignored the stipulated deadline, federal officials, using taxpayer money, would show up and do it for them — and then hand administration of the inspection program back to the state. Consumer activists complained that those inspectors, beholden to neither state legislatures nor federal officials, would become pawns of meatpackers who would encourage them to look the other way when tainted meats passed along the line. Even worse, however, the law spawned a consequence that Nader never intended: it drove many intrastate packers out of business. As the industry's smallest and most vulnerable members, few could afford to comply with the regulations that the law imposed. Such was the case with United Packers in Opelousas, Louisiana. An inspector told the owner that he would have to replace his plant's floors, walls, and ceilings at a cost of at least a quarter-million dollars, and even that, the inspector warned, might not be enough to meet compliance. United's vice president complained he could understand if such regulations enhanced consumer safety and improved food purity, but as far as he could tell, that was "the furthest from being the situation." "Is there a conspiracy between big business and USDA to put small independent companies out of business?" he asked. "Needless to say, if the giants in the meat industry are the only ones left in business, then the consumer will certainly suffer and the farmer and rancher . . . will be forced to accept the prices the giants are willing to pay." There wasn't a conspiracy, but in the economic turmoil of the 1970s, every packer struggled to survive, and the financial requirements of the Wholesome Meat Act pushed smaller ones over the edge. If nothing else, the lesson Naderites learned was that good deeds could have unintended consequences, hardly surprising given that, at the time, consumer advocates were still learning how to navigate the murky terrain of federal bureaucracies, of which there were many: by the late seventies, thirty-three federal agencies housed four hundred sub-agencies and bureaus that managed more than one thousand programs aimed at consumers' needs.

But navigate they did, and setbacks and disappointments were not enough to stop the growth of public interest and consumer advocacy. Nader-inspired activism spread beyond the Washing-ton Beltway, as crusaders settled in rural areas and devoted their energy to protecting small farmers — "family farmers," they were called — from the clutches of agribusiness, a term that, in the hands of reformers, became a euphemism for "corporations try-ing to control agriculture." The critique of agribusiness and cor-porate farming was initiated by the Nader-inspired Agribusiness Accountability Project, founded in 1970 and dedicated to dissect-ing and publicizing the relationships that linked corporations, agriculture, and the nation's land grant colleges and universities. The group was best known for a report (later published as a book) titled *Hard Times, Hard Tomatoes*. Lead author Jim Hightower argued that corporate interests had commandeered land grant research in the name of transforming farms into factories and re-placing family farms with Big Ag. The book was a classic exam-ple of muckraking journalism in the Naderist mode and justified the squirming it induced among land grant officials. But High-tower and his colleagues overlooked, or more likely didn't un-derstand, the larger context in which American agriculture had changed since World War II. Family farmers had pioneered the shift toward large scale, confinement, and the use of livestock ad-ditives because they wanted more efficient, profitable farms and a lifestyle on par with that of city people. That history mattered not a whit to those trying to save the family farm, and from the 1970s on, a network of rural activists battled corporate involve-ment in agriculture. In 1972, for example, crusaders persuaded a Nebraska state legislator to introduce a bill that would outlaw farms that produced or sold more than $5 million worth of goods (roughly $27 million today). Nebraska was "relatively free of the cancer" of corporate farming, he argued, and his bill would ensure that it stayed that way.

That legislation went nowhere, but by the early 1980s, Nebraskans were more receptive, thanks to a devastating agricultural crisis that roiled farming in the plains and Midwest. During the 1970s famine, farmers had heeded the call to increase their output, and many did so by borrowing money to buy land and equipment. All too often, the bet did not pay off. Crop yields outstripped global demand, leaving farmers stuck with debts they could not pay. Foreclosures, bankruptcies, and, most tragically, farmer suicides followed. (If this sounds familiar, that's not surprising. The farm crisis of the eighties mirrored that of the 1920s.) Hunting for a scapegoat, farmers and their advocates latched on to a familiar culprit: corporate farms, an appealing bogeyman and as good an explanation as any for the crisis. Once again, opponents lobbied for laws to prevent corporations from owning or operating farms. In one important instance, Nebraskans campaigned for Initiative 300, a constitutional amendment designed to stop the spread of corporate farms. If ratified, it would allow existing corporate ventures to remain but prohibit them from buying any more land. The initiative's supporters aimed their sights directly at National Farms and Bill Haw, who had announced plans to expand the company's Nebraska hog-farming operation. Should he succeed, warned an analyst with the Center for Rural Affairs, a farm advocacy group, the state's hog prices would drop by a dollar or more per hundredweight and cost "small" farmers about $2,400 a year in income. "Do you get the feeling that we small producers — dumbly and blindly, like a sheep being led to slaughter — are being forced out by the greed of those high-rollers?" asked one farmer. "Have you stopped to figure out how many 100-sow farm units will be replaced by 24,000 sows?" A spokesman for Tyson, which supplied NF with pigs and would also be affected by the amendment, reacted with little sympathy and more than a bit of outrage: "If the people of Nebraska want Tyson to get the hell out, we will do that."

The people did. Voters approved the amendment, and Bill Haw, unable to expand in Nebraska, moved on to South Dakota. Back in 1974, that state's legislature had passed a law designed to protect family farmers from corporations. But the bill exempted livestock feeders, and Haw assumed he would be able to build a new facility there. He was wrong. Opponents were ready and waiting. The South Dakota Pork Producers Council urged the legislature to amend the law to include hog farms and circulated petitions demanding a special election on the issue if the legislature did not act. The South Dakota Farm Alliance, a coalition that included such strange bedfellows as the National Farmers Organization, the South Dakota Meat Promoters, and the Catholic Rural Life Conference, launched a separate campaign to force National to abandon its proposed site near Pierre, the state's capital and one of its largest cities. The alliance succeeded — Pierre's residents were not happy about having a giant hog farm so close — and Haw homed in on an alternative location near the (tiny) burg of Doland. The town council voted unanimously to support Haw's project, but other townspeople were less enamored. A few days after the vote, a resident told one councilman that he would no longer patronize the man's hardware store if NF came to town. Doland avoided what could have turned into a local civil war: in late 1988, South Dakotans voted to ban corporate hog farms.

Identical scenarios unfolded in Iowa, Minnesota, and Missouri as networks of rural activists spread the gospel: corporate farming must be stopped. Those efforts, and the larger story of the farm crisis, garnered attention beyond the Midwest thanks to dramatic expansion of the media universe. Cable television had only recently become a mainstay, as had the twenty-four-hour news cycle that came with it. The new medium provided ample opportunity to cover stories that broadcast networks could not always fit into conventional half-hour newscasts. The depth of the farm crisis also attracted journalists working for big-city newspapers, and in 1985, singer-songwriter Willie Nelson amplified the cause when he staged his first Farm Aid concert. The rural activists had been tutored in the ways of Nader, and they greeted journalists with facts and figures that made reporters' work easier. Ironically, much of that data came from the land grant schools that Jim Hightower had condemned a decade earlier. The Hightower critique, as well as the political activism that demarcated the sixties and seventies, inspired a generation of university faculty to embrace research projects rooted in real-world problems, such as the impact of corporate farming on rural incomes. And, too, by the 1970s, scholars and political activists were able to draw on the work of land grant economists who had compiled extensive databases that tracked the changes in agriculture since the end of World War II.

Make no mistake: not everyone opposed corporate farming. Consider this: in Nebraska, National Farms employed 150 full-time people, and more hands during busy seasons, and bought most of its inputs from local businesses, the exception being fertilizer. That didn't bother the man who managed the fertilizer dealership. "They can get [it] cheaper elsewhere. If I was their size, I'd do it the same way. You have to be good businessmen," he said. National's employees weren't complaining either. The company paid higher-than-average wages, and workers enjoyed health insurance and pension contributions. Jobs at NF offered another benefit many people valued: leisure time. One man told a reporter that he had begun farming right out of high school, but after he married and started a family, he resented the seven-day-a-week schedule that his farm demanded. He signed on with National so he could work regular hours and enjoy more time with his wife and children. Nor was everyone convinced that corporate farming represented an economic dead end. After hog producer Premium Standard Farms was denied a permit to build a confinement operation in central Iowa, the company moved to friendlier terrain across the border in Missouri. The director of the Missouri Rural Crisis Center denounced the state's willingness to support PSF. Missouri's leaders had demonstrated that they would "stoop to anything for economic development," he complained, "and the family farmer be damned." Others disagreed. "It's going to be a big help here," said the owner of a farm equipment dealership not far from PSF's new location. "This area has just been devastated by the poor farm economy in the past four years." Finally, many thoughtful people questioned the wisdom of anticorporate farm laws because they feared those bans would have unintended, and negative, consequences. They were right to worry. In 1990, John Morrell & Co. closed its Kansas packing plant, at the time the state's biggest slaughtering operation, throwing some seven hundred people out of work. Why the closure? Because a 1981 state law had banned corporate farms, and the state's "family" farmers couldn't supply enough hogs to keep the plant operating at capacity. Morrell, already struggling to compete with behemoths IBP and Tyson, had to either import livestock from other states or close the plant. Morrell's CEO opted for the latter and relocated to Colorado, where Bill Haw had already built a new hog farm. "We don't need to do business in a populist, antibusiness environment," Haw had said in explaining the move. Colorado wanted his two hundred jobs and $3 million a year, so that's where he went.

As these last two examples indicate, pro-family-farm laws provoked fundamental alterations in the geography of hog farming as Corn Belt states ceded dominance to Oklahoma, Colorado, North Carolina, and Utah. But by the 1980s, this too was true: the creature that rural activists identified as the family farm was more myth than reality. Family farmers had led the agricultural revolution of the 1950s, and many had embraced large size and scale. As they did, and over time, the agricultural infrastructure that supported farmers had changed, too. Two USDA analysts affirmed that in a report published in 1985. Small-scale hog farmers faced a steep trek toward survival because the food-making infrastructure supported big farmers, not small ones. Meatpackers and food processors wanted to buy bigger lots of livestock than most small farmers could provide. Moreover, in hog production as in the rest of farming, life and death "rest[ed] largely with those who provide the capital," and banks were no longer willing to fund small ventures. Even relatively big hog farmers — two to ten thousand head a year — could see the writing on the hog barn wall. When the editors of *National Hog Farmer* surveyed readers in 1987, 29 percent of the respondents — most of whom marketed at least two thousand hogs a year — identified "large corporate hog farms" as their biggest threat. Another 23 percent feared encroachment from vertical integrators who raised hogs for use in their packing plants and food factories. The owner of one of the nation's largest independent hog farms predicted that "within 10 years, [his] operation probably [would] be considered very small." Like the Tysons back in the 1950s, he recognized that he'd reached a fork in the road; he had to get bigger or get out.

But there was another, less obvious but significant reason why the family farm, whatever it may have been, faced extinction and why big farms, corporate or otherwise, had moved center stage. During the 1970s and 1980s, demographic and social changes transformed Americans' relationships with food, changes that would ripple across the culinary landscape for decades to come and lead, eventually, to enthusiasm for organic and "local" foods and inspire a new generation of small farmers. But in the 1980s and 1990s, large-scale, corporate livestock production surged because that model of meat making was best suited to the demands of a fragmented and demanding nation of eaters.

There's no better place to launch a survey of that new terrain than the American home. In the last quarter of the twentieth century, record numbers of households were headed by adults, married or single, who worked outside the home, among them members of the core grocery-shopping, food-preparation demographic, women in their thirties and forties. Cooking was low on many households' agendas, and fewer Americans were interested in buying raw materials that had to be transformed into meals. They preferred foods that were ready to eat or, as economists phrase it, preferred to trade money for time. Back in the 1920s, shoppers regarded canned soups and quick biscuit mixes as gifts from the convenience gods. Fifty years later, Americans had moved beyond such basic processed foods, which, after all, still required some "making" in order to eat, to paying someone to fix their food for them. In 1960, Americans spent about 27 percent of their food dollars outside the home. By the early 1990s, that share had risen to nearly 50 percent, about half of which went to fast food.

Late-twentieth-century eating habits were also shaped by consumer consciousness, which matured to a logical conclusion: consumers reasoned, however unconsciously, that if their actions greased the economic engine, they were also the economy's most important players, ones whose demands must be met. What had been a relatively homogeneous consumer market splintered into myriad fragments, or, as analysts labeled them, "niches," defined by age, income, race, ethnicity, geography, and a mysterious but important inner drive for self-satisfaction. In clothing, for example, consumers expressed both desire and identity by wearing jeans adorned with "designer" labels or T-shirts emblazoned with logos or slogans that linked the wearer to a specific niche. So, too, food became a consumer good that conveyed image and status and provided (instant!) gratification. To name one example, in the 1980s, "yuppies," a teensy demographic segment that briefly captured the admiration of economists and media, boosted sales of imported beer because drinking that carried more cachet than drinking conventional American brands. At the same time, an even narrower demographic scorned imports in favor of "craft" beer whose niche appeal stemmed from both its artisanal source and its relative scarcity. Several years later, another cohort of consumers flipped that equation on its head, expressing a "hipster" image by scorning imports and craft brews in favor of mainstream beers like Pabst Blue Ribbon.

Such fragmentation played out in the food industry as a whole, as the hordes demanded foods and menus that satisfied individual tastes and whims. Some in the restaurant-going public, for example, wanted steak. Some wanted chicken. Some wanted chicken grilled with teriyaki sauce, and others wanted it on a pizza. The health-conscious demanded salads (perhaps to compensate for indulging in "all-natural" ice cream the night before), and the budget-conscious wanted all-you-can-eat buffets (a gastronomic free-for-all that required restaurants to seek rock-bottom prices on everything from lettuce and tomatoes to pickled beets and precooked meats). Cooking-averse consumers expected grocery stores to function as personal chefs capable of satisfying every craving. Aging baby boomers wanted low-salt foods. Busy parents wanted (cheap) food that could be combined with, say, hamburger or pasta and turned into a meal for four. Even better? A package that contained both burger and pasta. The diet-conscious demanded low-calorie, fat-free foods. (SnackWell's, a line of low-fat crackers and cookies, was one of the biggest food success stories of the 1990s because it allowed Americans to eat out of both sides of their mouths, pronouncing themselves "healthy" eaters with one side while satisfying junk-food desires with the other.) Teenagers and twenty-somethings wanted anything and everything that could be microwaved, the teenagers because they were hungry after school or too busy working jobs to eat at home or because their working parents were too tired to cook, and the twenty-somethings because they didn't know how to cook and didn't realize that cooking from scratch was cheaper than toasting a Pop-Tart. "Nichification" fueled technological innovation that fueled more nichification. Consider the microwave oven, arguably the most important food preparation technology of the twentieth century. A convenience-crazed nation recognized its value immediately: it enabled them to zap foods to fork-ready condition in minutes. It was up to manufacturers, however, to supply zappable foods, from conventional TV dinners to pizza to chicken nuggets.

Fragmentation plus convenience fueled a self-perpetuating cycle: the easier it was to put dinner on the table without cooking, the less relevant cooking skills became. Kids who grew up in homes where no one cooked became adults who didn't know how to cook and relied on manufacturers, grocery stores, and microwave ovens to do it for them. Nor, it's worth noting, did economic upheaval derail the long-term trend. In the mid-1970s, even amid inflation and unemployment, a manufacturer of plastic packaging materials was delighted by soaring sales — delighted, but puzzled — and conducted a study to determine what drove its good fortune. The answer: grocery stores were installing "deli" departments to meet the demands of "young and leisure-oriented shoppers" (read: young adult baby boomers) who subsisted on prepared foods like fried chicken, macaroni and cheese, and presliced meats and cheeses. Hence the demand for take-it-home packaging. "The supermarkets are crying for anything new that will stop people from going out to eat," mused a Tyson executive in 1979. The company embraced the new niches and dumped millions into the "precooked frozen" market, moving beyond conventional TV dinners with their tinfoil compartments of sliced chicken and pasty mashed potatoes into chicken-based hot dogs, corn dogs, and bologna; packaged, presliced chicken; chicken and turkey "ham"; boneless turkey breasts; chicken patties and steaks; and frozen, ready-to-cook chicken Kiev and pre-fried chicken that only needed to be heated before eating. "I think my mother could cook it better," Don confided to a reporter who asked about the fried chicken, "but I'm not sure my wife could." Nor did it matter in an era when convenience trumped taste: "People who eat precooked frozen today are not as fussy as the previous generation," he added, and predicted that "succeeding generations" would prove even "less discriminating."

What's most remarkable is how little Americans spent to satisfy their desires. From 1960 to 1990, the cost of food fell by a third; even during the inflation-dogged 1970s, and the passion for eating away from home notwithstanding, Americans spent a minuscule amount on food. In the early 1990s, on average, consumers paid out just 11 percent of their disposable income to feed themselves. Obviously many households spent more. People earning less than $10,000 a year, for example, devoted about 35 percent of their income to food. But even those in what was then the lower range of the middle class — households with incomes of $20,000 to $30,000 — spent only about 17 percent; the wealthiest spent less than 9 percent. And of course that was good for the economy: people had money left to buy other consumer goods.

But more than demographics roiled the culinary landscape. By the late 1970s, Keys's fat-is-bad theory had become gospel, and the nation's medical experts urged the public to cut back on fat and cholesterol, a message many Americans interpreted as "Don't eat beef and pork." That view got a federal stamp of approval in 1977 when a Senate committee chaired by George McGovern of South Dakota issued a report recommending that everyone eat more poultry and fish and reduce their intake of "meat," by which it meant pork and beef. The report also documented the extent to which the political establishment had embraced consumer activism and Naderist ideas, complete, it must be said, with an establishment-like dollop of hypocrisy. Naderites had long criticized government agencies for relying on information and advice from industry insiders trying to protect their turf, but when it suited their cause, they did precisely the same. In this case, Nick Mottern, who wrote the McGovern report, was a Nader acolyte eager to challenge the powerful meat lobby. Mottern relied on expertise provided by D. M. Hegsted, a Harvard professor who endorsed and admired the work of Ancel Keys. The staffers who assisted Mottern gathered information primarily from newspaper and magazine coverage that affirmed the view the committee wanted to promote, namely, the Keysian version of the relation between diet, fat, and good health. ("We really were totally naive," a staff member later conceded.) The press conference to introduce the committee's final findings was a masterpiece of glib assertion. Senator McGovern summarized the document's largely unsupported claims about the relationship between diet and health and then introduced experts who espoused still more assertions as if those were fact, all of which reporters dutifully recorded and passed on to the public.

Beef and pork producers as well as meatpackers took offense at the document because it specifically indicted meat (as a man involved in the fracas put it, all "hell broke loose"), and McGovern released a revised version that avoided that word. But opposition to the report came from more than just the meat industry. In 1980, for example, the National Academy of Sciences published a study that challenged the heart-healthy mantra. Consumer advocates denounced the academy's findings as biased because one of the report's authors had once worked as a consultant for the egg industry. The man pointed out the lunacy of that criticism: during his career he'd received a quarter-million dollars in grants from industry sources, but $10 million from government agencies. How could he be a corporate patsy because of $250,000, but not a government stooge thanks to $10 million? (It's worth mentioning that Hegsted, the Harvard scholar who tutored Mottern in the "correct" view, devoted his later career to research funded in part by Frito-Lay.)

But the damage was done; in the minds of many Americans, beef and pork had become public enemies one and two, and the bad news kept coming. In the early 1980s, several widespread, and widely reported, disease outbreaks were traced back to beef tainted with a newly discovered and exceptionally virulent form of an otherwise common bacteria, *Escherichia coli* O157:H7. After investigators tracked one of the episodes back to a South Dakota cattle herd, they concluded that feeding antibiotics to livestock had potentially fatal consequences for humans. There could no longer be any doubt, argued the researchers, that "antimicrobial-resistant organisms of animal origin cause serious human illness." No doubt in their minds, but plenty in other people's. In the wake of the findings, a consumer advocacy group petitioned the FDA to ban drug additives in livestock feed, but a hearing on the request ended like every other discussion of the subject: it raised more questions than it answered, and the scientists' seemingly irrefutable evidence proved to be both debatable and refutable.

Between lethal bacteria on one hand and heart disease on the other, beef and pork consumption plunged. A 1983 consumer poll documented pork's woes. Those surveyed complained that pork contained too much salt, cholesterol, fat, and calories. Forty-five percent said they'd cut back on fresh pork for "health reasons," and nearly a quarter said they'd reduced their consumption of all pork products, fresh or processed. Even McDonald's, the wizard of food, couldn't work its magic on pork. In the summer of 1980, the company began testing a "McRib" sandwich, rib-shaped slabs of ground and chopped pork slathered with barbecue sauce. The pork industry salivated at the potential of this new menu item, but the McRib proved a no-go; the company pulled it from the menu in 1983. Part of the problem lay in preference: Kansas City–style barbecue sauce leans toward sweet, and North Carolina's toward tart; McDonald's one-taste-suits-all could not overcome those regional differences. The condiment also made for messy eating, a detriment to Americans accustomed to eating on the run and in their cars. But in the end, McDonald's conceded that the McRib succumbed to consumer resistance: good taste and low price could not overcome pork's bad reputation. McDonald's fared better with its Egg McMuffin, which also contained pork, apparently because it suited a consumer niche: when analysts dissected the ten-pound-per-capita drop in pork consumption, they discovered that Americans would eat pork as long as it was processed and convenient — whether as bacon, "lean" microwaveable sausages, or Egg McMuffins.

The toppling of King Beef was more shocking. Per-capita consumption dropped from 131 pounds in 1976 to 105 in 1980 to 97 pounds a decade later. "A story about the beef industry belongs in the obituary column," mourned Ken Monfort. A Nebraska cattle raiser agreed. "Nobody eats beef anymore," he mused. "Sometimes I wonder if I would be better off not getting out of bed in the morning." Cattle feeders pooled their funds to support pro-beef advertising campaigns — "the Mercedes of Meat" and "Somehow, nothing satisfies like beef" — but those did little to bolster the king's sagging reputation. In desperation, members of the California Cattlemen's Association petitioned the national cattlemen's group to end the use of low-level antibiotics. "We thought everybody would always eat beef," said the California organization's director, "but it turned out not to be true"; his group's members reasoned that eliminating antibiotics might persuade some people to come home to beef. The National Cattlemen's Association refused to go along, but Paul Engler, whose cattle-feeding operation was by then the largest in the world, announced that he would stop using two controversial antibiotics. He didn't believe that antibiotic-laced feeds were dangerous, he explained, but many consumers did. The "inference" of danger was already out there, he argued, so "why jeopardize the demand for your product?" "By dropping antibiotics," added a company vice president, "we are trying to teach the public that beef is healthy."

But Engler's decision had no effect on beef sales, although how much was due to fear of fat and calories and how much to potentially lethal bacteria was not clear. A financial analyst warned cattlemen that it was time to accept "the harsh reality that the collapse in consumer taste for beef is permanent." "It's a declining industry," he emphasized, "and the only question is how far it will decline." Even the president of the National Livestock and Meat Board conceded that the days when meat makers could take consumers for granted were over. "It's the younger, more highly educated, high-income people who are turning away from beef toward more vegetables and white meat in their diet," he said. "These are the opinion leaders that are eventually going to be influencing the eating habits of our bread and butter customers."

It's not clear what role income and education played in the shift, but he was correct about the ascent of "white meat," by which he meant chicken. Every report about heart disease, fat, and cholesterol touted the virtues of poultry (and, to a lesser extent, fish) as a healthy alternative to beef and pork. Consumers didn't need much convincing, in part because chicken consistently cost less than the other two meats, a factor of biology: cattle and hogs needed months of expensive grains to reach market weight, but a broiler was table-ready in eight weeks or less. As important, chicken was everywhere shoppers and diners wanted to be. From its inception, the broiler industry had worked the convenience angle more aggressively than its pork and beef counterparts, and packaged chicken products abounded. Don Tyson hit the broiler jackpot in the early eighties when he won a contract to supply McDonald's with its newest offering: the Chicken McNugget, which consisted of a bit of chicken, a lot of "filler" and batter, and even more calories and fat. McNuggets were an instant success — and drew instant fire from Michael Jacobson: in a complaint filed with the FTC, Jacobson's Center for Science in the Public Interest accused the chain of false advertising. Mc-Donald's described the McNugget's contents as "delicious chunks of juicy breast and thigh meat," but Jacobson pointed out that the bites also contained sodium phosphate, chicken skin, and beef fat. Who cared? Want to eat healthy? Eat chicken. Eat a McNugget: a bit of chicken and a lot of calories and fat. All of it added up. In 1960, Americans ate twenty-eight pounds of chicken per capita; by 1970, that had risen to forty. In 1980, they put away forty-eight pounds, and in 1987, broiler makers squawked with delight as poultry toppled King Beef. It's no accident that in the late eighties, pork producers adopted an ad campaign that touted pork as "the other white meat."

But even broiler producers couldn't take their market for granted, not in an era of media bloat and heightened consumer awareness. The final decade of the century dished up plenty of evidence that when it came to meat, whether beef, pork, or poultry, whether on the table or on the farm, something had gone wrong.

In 1993, scores of people became ill, and some died, in a food-poisoning episode traced to undercooked hamburgers purchased at Jack in the Box, a northwestern fast-food chain. The culprit proved to be the same one scientists had linked to bacterial resistance a decade earlier: *E. coli* O157:H7. The tiny organism became a household name after the Jack in the Box incident, and the tragedy highlighted the flaws in a food safety system designed for a premicrobial era. Federal meat inspection dated back to 1906, when inspectors were trained to look for diseased *livestock*, not diseased meat. They were right to do so: back then, epizootic diseases routinely ravaged poultry flocks and cattle and hog herds, and the USDA poured money into researching and eradicating those scourges. That work proved so successful that by the 1950s, many once-common vaccinations were no longer necessary. Indeed, researchers theorized that *E. coli* O157:H7 had flourished because cattle ranchers and feeders had reduced or eliminated once-routine vaccinations. But meat inspection procedures had not kept pace with science. Federal rules allowed inspectors to condemn foods that were "so infected" that eating them might "give rise to food poisoning," but the men and women charged with monitoring slaughterhouse output had few tools for identifying microorganisms. A 1974 court ruling made that even more difficult: bacteria were not an adulterant and inspectors were not required to consider their presence when giving a carcass the thumbs-up or -down. But the proliferation of O157:H7 and the Jack in the Box episode amounted to a line in the sand. Critics demanded that meat inspection be overhauled. Strategies that worked back when slaughterhouse lines moved at the pace of a single-load rifle were useless on kill lines that operated at machine-gun pace, and speed, many argued, contributed to cross-contamination that led to tragedies like the one at Jack in the Box.

Leaders of the meat industry's primary trade group, the American Meat Institute, conceded the point, but they argued that federal inspectors were also part of the problem. "They don't know where they'll fit [in a new system]," argued an AMI spokesman. "They're not microbiologists." Not so, retorted an official with the inspectors' union. He and other inspectors were "not against technology, and we're not against moving forward." But they objected to proposals that would replace conventional inspection with a "science-based system." Nor were packing plants the only problem. The Jack in the Box episode was blamed less on *E. coli* than on line workers who had failed to cook hamburger to the required temperature. But state and city food and restaurant inspection systems suffered from that most common of ailments, lack of funds. Consider the case of Kansas: Its inspectors were charged with traveling to and inspecting thirty-two restaurants a week. Any one inspector might manage a cursory search for, say, cockroaches and overflowing dumpsters, but it's unlikely they'd have time to do much more.

Changes were needed, but what those should be, and how to implement them, was open to debate. Some critics argued that the USDA should shift its mission from agricultural cheerleading to consumer protection. Easier said than done. For over a century, the department had tried to be, and often succeeded at being, all things to all people: it had led the way in eradicating crop and livestock diseases and in promoting improved agricultural and livestock management. But it was also the cheerleader-in-chief for the nation's food industries, and employees promoted both production and consumption of everything from steak to broccoli, from poultry to cantaloupe. Asking the department to support and promote the interests of farmers, manufacturers, and consumers was bound to generate power struggles and gridlock. Worse, the work of the FDA and the USDA typically either overlapped or collided. In the wake of the Jack in the Box case, one reporter pointed out the looniness of a food safety system that required the USDA to inspect canned soups that contained meat, and the FDA to inspect soups without. Reforming the status quo was easier to imagine than do; there are few human endeavors more entrenched than bureaucracies.

The Jack in the Box incident cast doubt on the USDA, on meat safety, and on food inspection, but a different disaster highlighted the role that agriculture played in putting meat on the table: the North Carolina manure spills of the late 1990s. Those marked a turning point; after that, it was hard for anyone to ignore the costs of factory farming.

No state had benefited more from the new geography of hog farming than North Carolina, and no group more than Murphy Farms, one of the biggest hog farmers in the United States. Murphy Farms was the brainchild of Wendell Murphy. After graduating from college in 1960, he taught high school briefly, but like that other schoolteacher-turned-agricultural-power-player, Warren Monfort, Wendell Murphy wanted a different life. In the early 1960s, he bought a corn mill, which he operated with his father and brother. From there it was a short leap into feeding hogs. In 1964, the Murphys recruited their first contract "growers," and as in the broiler industry, the Murphys functioned as banker and coordinator, loaning their growers the money needed to buy piglets and feed, and selling the hogs when they were ready for market. Over the next twenty years, the family embraced confinement production, signed up dozens of contractors, and built farrowing operations. In the late 1980s, they expanded into Iowa because, said Wendell, "we wanted to find out if we ought to be in the hog business in Iowa or North Carolina." He concluded that North Carolina had more advantages, especially weather, but that didn't stop the family from establishing additional outposts in Missouri and Illinois. But as had been the case with the Monforts back in the 1950s, the Murphys' desire for growth collided with lack of outlets: Murphy Farms produced more hogs than North Carolina packers could process.

Deliverance arrived in the form of Smithfield Foods, a Virginia-based hog slaughter and pork-processing company. Like Murphy, Smithfield's president, Joseph Luter III, wanted to expand but couldn't lay his hands on as many hogs as he needed. Urban sprawl had devoured Virginia farms, and he was trucking a third of his kill from the Midwest, a logistical burden that raised his costs relative to midwestern slaughtering operations. His problem became the solution to the Murphys'. In early 1990, Luter announced plans to build the world's largest hog slaughterhouse in North Carolina, not far from where Murphy and other hog-farming giants raised millions of animals. When the new plant opened in 1992, it ignited North Carolina's already robust hog-farming industry: in 1991, the state turned out 2.8 million hogs; in 1994, the number hit 7 million, nearly all of them clustered in the southeastern corner of the state.

But even in hog-friendly North Carolina, hogs, pork packing, and the jobs both created came at a price, and critics dug in their heels. "We are not against the smaller farmer," explained a spokesman for the Alliance for a Clean Swine Industry, but he and other opponents objected to "the bondage of feces and urine" created by big hog farms. But what mattered more? Jobs or odor? According to many residents in that part of the state, jobs did. When Bladen County officials held a hearing to consider Smithfield's request to build, more than a thousand people showed up, many of them wearing "I support Smithfield" buttons, and a "wildly cheering" crowd roared its approval when the state's commissioner of agriculture urged county officials to let Smith-field move forward. As hogs, and jobs, proliferated, local media tracked the turmoil and the debate. In February 1995, reporters at the *Raleigh News & Observer* published a series of reports on the impact of the state's hog industry, little of which was flatter-ing, especially the portrayal of Wendell Murphy as "Boss Hog," the legislative kingpin who called the shots and built the industry. (Murphy, who served in the state legislature from 1983 to 1992, was not insulted. "All of a sudden, I found myself a hero," he said later. "It was like all of a sudden people really started coming to me: 'Man, you are really good. We didn't know you were doing all this stuff.'") The series, which won a Pulitzer Prize, described the complaints of people who loathed the industry's odors and feared the pollution, detailed the way the legislature had smoothed the path for hog farming and the world's biggest slaughtering house, and noted the gratitude of those who saw impoverished counties gain jobs and income. It captured, in short, the complexity, para-dox, and unease that was meat in late-twentieth-century America and drew attention to agriculture, an economic sector whose ef-ficiency had rendered it all but invisible in the eyes of the general public. In the wake of the coverage, the state's legislators pon-dered changes to the legal structure that had long supported and empowered Murphy and other hog producers.

And then came the storms. In the summer of 1995, and not long after the Pulitzer series ran, torrential, prolonged rainfall in-undated large parts of the state. Water swamped a dike on an "in-dustrial swine" farm, and nearly 30 million gallons of feces and urine poured into the New River. Hog waste stood eight inches deep on a nearby road, and sludge coated crops in the fields of nearby farms. "Didn't nobody mean for it to happen," said one of the owners of the company that had built the lagoon. "It just happened." Maybe, maybe not, but reporters discovered that the farm, which was less than two years old, had been the first one built using a new set of strict environmental guidelines designed to protect citizens, land, and water from industrial hog wastes. Over the next few weeks, several more lagoons, including one at a chicken farm, collapsed, washing more waste into waterways. The "environmental Alamo," said one reporter, destroyed the illusion that giant hog farms were benign. The environmental Alamo had siblings: In 1999, Hurricane Floyd struck the North Carolina coast. Four rivers flooded and thousands of hog carcasses littered the state's countryside. The ensuing stench and mess, and detailed reporting about it, fueled the debate about livestock production and meat.

So did the 1998 trial of Oprah Winfrey, one of the most powerful people in American media. Her journey to a Texas court room began in the mid-1990s, when bovine spongiform encephalopathy, or mad cow disease, ravaged cattle herds in England. Winfrey dedicated a program to the subject and listened as her guest, a former Montana cattle rancher, railed against the dangers of meat in general and diseased meat in particular, arguing that if mad cow struck American herds, the outbreak would make "AIDS look like the common cold." He explained that scientists believed that the British outbreak erupted after cattle ate feed manufactured from diseased sheep meat. Winfrey responded by announcing to her audience of millions, "It has just stopped me cold from eating another burger! I'm stopped!" Whether by coincidence or cause, within a day cattle futures plunged, dropping so low that trading was halted. A few weeks later, a group of Texas-based cattle ranchers and feeders, including Paul Engler, sued Winfrey, using a 1995 False Disparagement of Perishable Food Products Act as the basis of their suit. (A number of states had passed such "veggie libel laws" in the early 1990s after a television news program warned about the dangers of Alar, a coating used by apple growers to protect their fruit.) The judge who heard the case ruled that the disparagement laws did not apply, forcing the cattle groups to prove that the talk show host had intended to damage the industry. They could not, and she walked out of the Amarillo courtroom cleared of any wrongdoing. But Oprah Winfrey was Oprah Winfrey, and her fears of hamburger cast still more doubt on meat and the farms and factories that produced it.

Manure spills, dead hogs, and bacteria-tainted meat high-lighted Americans' contradictory relationships with their food and their values: they wanted cheap, low-fat meat, and they wanted it from a drive-up window, but satisfying those desires carried costs in the form of environmental damage and real threats to health. But nothing says more about the paradoxical nature of the American character than this: even as hog factories and fast-food chains flourished, some Americans began building an alternative food system based on diametrical opposites: small-scale, traditional livestock production and "organic" meats that contained neither antibiotics nor corporate fingerprints.

8

UTOPIAN VISIONS, RED TAPE REALITY

WHEN COLORADAN MEL COLEMAN'S first "natural" cattle carcass rolled off a slaughterhouse line in 1980, he was there waiting for it, his new, $300, custom-made ink roller in hand. The carcass came to a stop and Mel rolled the stamp over its surface, and there it was: a side of "Coleman Natural Beef," ready to change the world and improve the condition of the Coleman bank account. Or not. The local USDA inspector happened to be on site that day and he ordered Mel to stop. "I don't have papers on that roller," he said. "Do you have permission to roll that carcass?" "Permission?" said Coleman. "This is my roller ... What more permission do I need?" Much more, explained the inspector, in the form of paperwork and official USDA sanction. Mel scraped the ink off the carcass and set out to master the byzantine USDA regulatory process. He made an appointment with the department's regional inspector and explained that he wanted permission to use the words *natural beef* on his labels. "What the hell are you talking about, Coleman?" she asked. "Cattle are natural — all cattle are natural!" Mel encountered one dead end after another in Colorado and eventually took himself to Washington, DC, and the heart of the USDA maze. Two years and a two-foot-thick file of paperwork later, he received permission to use the word *natural* to describe his beef products. By the time Mel died in 2002, his family's company was the largest purveyor of natural and organic meat in the United States.

The founding and growth of Coleman Natural Meats is an important element of the story of meat in the late twentieth and early twenty-first centuries, but it's not the only one. As the Colemans built their company, whose structure mimicked that of conventional meat makers, a group of activists far from the Colemans' rural Colorado valley were laying the foundations of an alternative food economy, one that they hoped would not be dominated by Big Ag and Big Food. They succeeded, but they, like Mel Coleman, had to rely on the USDA to gain the regulatory mechanisms, research, and retail markets necessary to foster that project. By the start of the new century, they'd been so successful that alternative foods had captured the interest of middle-class consumers, and fringe had moved into the mainstream.

Mel Coleman's saga began in the 1970s. That decade's turmoil threatened the survival of his family's cattle-grazing operation, founded in the 1930s and located near the town of Saguache in south-central Colorado. Between the energy crisis, inflation, and declining demand, they were fighting what Mel described as a "losing battle." The minutes of a company meeting in the summer of 1976 capture the family's woes in terse terms: "Inflation costs and depressed cattle market have made it impossible for the corporation to continue on as we have." Six months later, the family pondered the possibility of refinancing the grazing operation or selling their cows, their pasture acres, or both. All told, they lost nearly a half-million dollars from 1975 to 1978. "We had to do something — and quickly — or we were going to lose everything," Mel said.

That "something" arrived thanks to Mel and wife Polly's daughter-in-law, Nancy Coleman, married to their son Greg. The younger Colemans had recently moved from Saguache to the Boulder area, then as now a bastion of hippie entrepreneurism and counterculture lifestyles (the Naropa Institute and Celestial Seasonings were only two of the town's alternative enterprises). Nancy had been raised on good food and sought it out at local "health food stores," as they were called then, of which there were many in and around Boulder. But she could not find anything like the beef that she'd grown up eating. On a trip back to Saguache, and presumably knowing that the family's cattle operation was in trouble, she suggested that her father-in-law change tactics. Instead of selling his livestock to conventional meatpackers, why didn't he slaughter it himself and sell the beef as a natural, drug-free product? Mel said later that a "tingle ran down [his] spine" when he heard her idea. In 1979, the family incorporated Coleman Natural Meats, a company that the then-fifty-four-year-old Mel ran.

The Coleman family's strategy for survival unfolded against a backdrop of renewed enthusiasm for organic agriculture, which had first gained substantive support in the United States back in the 1930s. During that decade, prolonged drought and soil exhaustion spawned spectacular dust storms; massive clouds of dust spun from topsoil rolled across the plains states, carrying their gritty rain as far as the East Coast. The devastation prompted some in the agricultural establishment to urge farmers to return to more "organic" approaches to working the land. But support for this alternative to factory farming waned under pressure of wartime demand for food, and in the 1950s, alternative agriculture and the establishment parted company thanks to what plant breeder Richard Harwood described as a McCarthyist "mood of intolerance" among the nation's scientists. He remembered that decade as one when human and scientific "arrogance" spawned an "intellectual wasteland." "I was . . . the most arrogant bastard that you want to run across," he said later. He and his colleagues assumed that science would "dominate the universe. And we proceeded as if [it] would," thanks in part, he admitted, to their belief that supplies of "very cheap energy" would never run dry. (Harwood eventually concluded that his arrogance was misplaced. In the 1970s, he began conducting research on sustainable agriculture and by the late 1990s occupied an endowed university chair in the subject.)

But in the wake of the environmental alarms and food famine of the 1960s and 1970s, many Americans questioned the wisdom of an agricultural model that relied more on petroleum products than on nature. At what point, some asked, did the environmental costs of antibiotics, commercial fertilizers, and pesticides outweigh the need for cheap food? If agriculture itself was toxic, would global demand for food eventually lay waste to the planet? Questions like these multiplied, especially after the Environmental Protection Agency (EPA) targeted agriculture in general and livestock operations in particular as major sources of water pollution.

Among those who questioned the status quo was Ken Monfort, and in 1971, he instructed his feedlot employees to isolate a thousand yearlings from the rest of the herd and feed them rations free of antibiotics and DES. In addition, the animals went to slaughter minus the chemical dip used to destroy parasites that otherwise burrowed into their flesh. Monfort sold his E-Colo-Beef to health food stores on the West Coast at a price about 40 percent higher than that of his conventional meat. (The brand name is not as unfortunate as it now sounds to our ears: *E. coli* bacteria had not yet achieved celebrity status.) The project didn't last long. The cattle needed 10 to 15 percent longer than conventional stock to reach market weight, which meant that Monfort spent 10 percent more on feed. Once slaughtered, the carcasses yielded less meat because three-quarters of the livers were diseased and parasite-infected flesh had to be cut away. "When you start trimming away $2 a pound meat to get rid of grubs it starts getting expensive," admitted a Monfort executive. (A company vice president later described the short-lived project as "a colossal blunder . . . that [would not] happen again.")

But Monfort's failure did not alter his view that Americans needed to rethink their appetite for meat. "Food is a scarce item," he argued. "It will be scarcer." He openly supported "small planet" advocates who urged Americans to feed the world by eating less meat. The idea gained credence in part because of the food famine, but also because of the work of Frances Moore Lappé, a California social worker. Her 1971 book *Diet for a Small Planet* popularized the idea that meat production was both inefficient and wasteful because farmers planted millions of acres to raise food for livestock rather than humans and polluted air and water in the process. Ken Monfort agreed. "It's obvious humans should come first," he said, and livestock "last on the list" of those getting grain. He argued that cattle producers could conserve grain by keeping herds on grass until they were at least two years old instead of sending them to feedlots at twelve or fourteen months. In 1976 he predicted that beef consumption would drop by 15 to 20 percent as Americans cut back on meat in order to provide food for hungry nations. (As we've seen, he was right about the decline, but wrong about the reason.)

Other pockets of support for alternative agriculture flourished here and there. In 1971, alt-farmers in New England organized the National Organic Farmers Association (later the Northeast Organic Farming Association), and an organic farming group in Maine had five hundred members by the mid-seventies. Stewart Brand's *Whole Earth Catalog,* first published in 1968, provided fringe farmers with information and inspired the creation of dozens of "alternative technology centers" in North America, many of which included a gardening or farming component and more than a few of which were attached to universities and colleges. The agricultural outliers proved to be a mixed bag. When reporters for the *New York Times* went looking for alternative farmers in the 1970s and early 1980s, they found college professors, an anthropologist, a scientist, and a former official of the Federal Trade Commission, hardly the long-haired dope smokers of the stereotype. At the center of this early national nexus stood J. I. Rodale (born Jerome Irving Cohen) and his son Robert of Pennsylvania. For decades, the Rodales had published magazines and books devoted to organic gardening and farming but otherwise worked in relative isolation, scorned by most (the "Don Quixote of the compost heap," wrote one reporter in 1966). During the sixties and seventies, however, their reputations and profits soared as a new generation of farmers embraced hoe and compost.

More important, however, advocates of alternative farming elbowed their way back into the scientific and academic mainstream, most notably at Washington University in St. Louis, Missouri, where Barry Commoner established the Center for the Biology of Natural Systems. Commoner, a scientist who picked up the environmental standard after Rachel Carson's death in 1964, urged Americans to regard agriculture as part of a larger whole, although for quite different reasons from those John Davis elaborated when he'd developed the concept of agribusiness. An "ecosystem," Commoner said, "cannot be divided into manageable parts," and agriculture was but a piece of a "larger, over-all system of life which occupies a thin layer on the surface of the earth — the biosphere." Commoner warned that Americans courted disaster because they ignored the damage inflicted by industrial agriculture's "massive intervention into nature." Commoner's uncommon viewpoint and his scientific credentials attracted others who questioned the tenets of mainstream science and agriculture. Among them was physicist William Lockeretz. During the sixties, he, like many of his colleagues, was dismayed by the role that the scientific establishment played in the Vietnam War and by extension his attachment to that establishment. In 1971, he took a job at Commoner's center to investigate the science of alternative agriculture. Lockeretz shied away from the mysticism espoused by some alternative enthusiasts; indeed, he avoided using the word *organic* because of its hippie connotation. "As far as our methods and our ideology we are very solidly within mainstream academic research," he said. "The only thing that is unconventional is the particular system that we are studying."

Lockeretz's wariness was justified. At the time, and regardless of their credentials, supporters of alternative agriculture faced not just scorn but outright hostility. Some of it was perhaps warranted: many advocates linked alt-agriculture to mysticism, and others painted farming as a pastoral utopia. Farmers, wrote one essayist, must be allowed to seek "voluntary simplicity" and "must derive happiness and humane satisfaction from a life" free of the "consumerism, leisure, and delirious pursuit of novelty that characterizes [sic] our society." Why farmers alone should do so was not clear, and that perspective ignored the history of American agriculture, which was a tale of farm families demanding access to "consumerism" and a standard of living on par with that of urban Americans. Still, at a moment when global food shortages captured headlines, it's not surprising that many in the agricultural establishment scoffed at the idea of returning to old-fashioned techniques of crop and livestock production. Chief among them was Earl Butz, who shouldered the role of head cheerleader for conventional agriculture and made no effort to conceal his disdain for those who rejected it. That was obvious when he and Wendell Berry butted heads during a 1978 debate. Berry, a Kentucky college professor who owned a small farm where he cultivated his land using horses rather than machinery ("I like horses," he explained; using them allowed him to remain independent of "the oil companies"), had emerged as the poet laureate, as it were, of alternative agriculture. In 1977, he published *The Unsettling of America*, a critique of, among other things, Butz's view of agriculture. Berry believed that "independent" farmers embodied the "traditional values" necessary to a good society: "thrift, stewardship, private property, [and] political liberties." But those values had been eroded by ones rooted in the "urban industrial" worldview. Butz dismissed Berry and his ilk as muddle-headed idealists, able to spin agricultural fantasies only because "modern, scientific, technological agriculture" had freed them from the drudgery of producing their own food. Agriculture was not a romantic retreat for poets and professors but a "machine" designed to make food and fiber. "We can go back to organic agriculture in this country if we must," said Butz, but "someone must decide which 50 million of our people will starve!"

Faced with such derision, it's unlikely that alt-agriculturalists would have made much progress moving into the mainstream on their own. But they benefited from the support of three other groups. First were environmentalists, at the time the most well organized and well funded of the public interest advocate-activists. Emboldened by the EPA's linkage of agriculture and pollution, eco-warriors argued that factory farming relied too heavily on nonrenewable resources; that too many farms had been carved from fragile, unsuitable terrain; and that livestock confinement systems, pesticides, fertilizers, and the like were poisoning land, air, and water. Nor were these head-in-the-cloud dreamers. They were well trained in Naderist watchdog/attack-dog tactics, including litigation, which had become an effective tool for negotiating social change; the Environmental Defense Fund and the Natural Resources Defense Council, for example, mounted court challenges to the use of hormones in livestock production. They also knew how to work the halls of Congress, where rule one was: Compromise and negotiate or go home.

The rural activists fighting corporate farming also supported alternative agriculture, in part for a practical reason: there were so few farmers and rural residents that those working to improve their plight could gain influence only by forging alliances with other advocacy groups. But the goals of the anticorporate crusaders dovetailed with those of alternative agriculturalists. As the cofounder of a rural advocacy organization put it, struggling small farmers needed "practical alternatives" to factory farming. By the mid-1970s, his group, the Center for Rural Affairs (CRA), one of the earliest and longest-standing rural interest groups, was sponsoring research into "appropriate farm technology and organic methods" with the goal of helping farmers wean themselves from expensive, energy-inefficient inputs. This was no hippie-feelgood, Garden-of-Eden project. CRA's leaders grabbed science-based information as fast as the staff at Commoner's laboratories generated it.

Scholars and university faculty, especially rural sociologists, most of whom worked at land grant institutions, also supported and enriched the alternative agriculture ethos. Like so many scholarly fields, sociology was transformed by the activist idealism of the 1960s and 1970s and by the Hightower critique of land grant research agendas. As important, by that time, many sociologists had concluded that the Green Revolution — the global project to transplant modern agriculture to impoverished countries — was harming rather than helping communities, farmers, and the environment; they communicated their findings and their dismay in scholarly journals and at conferences. All of it inspired sociologists to ponder the negative social and economic consequences of industrial agriculture. Although Americans prided themselves on feeding the world, these academic critics argued that everyone paid a high price for that accomplishment, whether as family farmers run off the land, rural main streets lined with empty shops, or environmental damage. Like alt-agriculturalists and environmentalists, many sociologists framed their work around a holistic perspective: farmer and field could not be isolated from the "natural" environment or from communities near, dependent on, and catering to agriculture.

Numbers and diversity gave the nascent alt-agriculture alliance the clout needed to gain traction with the establishment. They pressured the EPA to maintain its scrutiny of agriculture as a source of pollution, and the 1976 farm bill contained legislation aimed at creating more markets for small farmers: "farm-to-consumer" projects, or as they're called now, farmers' markets. In 1979, the USDA sponsored a study of organic agriculture in the United States and Europe. "Energy shortages, food safety, and environmental concerns have all contributed to the demand for more comprehensive information on organic farming technology," wrote Secretary of Agriculture Bob Bergland. The final report "strongly" recommended that the USDA support research and education that would "address the needs and problems of organic farmers." The 1981 farm bill authorized "multidisciplinary organic farming research projects" aimed at implementing the report's ideas and recommendations. Garth Youngberg, a political scientist who chaired the organic study team, was hired by the USDA to coordinate those programs.

• • •

It's not clear how much Mel Coleman knew about these activities in the early eighties, but this much we do know: he already boasted a healthy environmental perspective because experience had taught him and his family to avoid using chemicals and drugs on their ranch. Back in the 1930s, a mining company had dumped residue into a creek near Coleman land, killing the water's fish, an event that stayed in Mel's memory for the rest of his life. "It will permanently warp you to have to deal with something like that," he said. In the late 1940s, the family had dusted cattle with the insecticide DDT. The experience left a bad taste in Mel's mouth and bad air in his lungs: the chemical would soak his coat so thoroughly that he had trouble breathing, even out in the open air of the Colorado range. As for that farmers' darling of the 1950s, DES, he wanted none of it. The first time he encountered cattle dosed with the hormone, the animals' strange behavior "made [his] . . . lip curl." He was equally skeptical about antibiotics, which the family used briefly in the 1960s to protect calves from pneumonia. But in the mid-1970s during an outbreak of "scours," a form of dysentery, Coleman and his veterinarian dosed calves with antibiotics to no avail. Fifteen percent of the animals died. "I believed that the harmful bacteria had developed a resistance to antibiotics, and that scared me," he said. "Right there, we stopped using [them]." Make no mistake: in 1979, Coleman wasn't running a 100 percent "natural" operation. He inoculated newborns and fed his cattle hay grown with manufactured fertilizers as well as protein supplements that contained synthetic materials.

But the family's operation was more "natural" than most, and so the decision to incorporate Coleman Natural Beef made sense both ethically and financially. Mel was assigned the task of turning idea into dollars. The owner of a small local feedlot agreed to finish the Colemans' cattle on a drug-free diet, and a nearby meat locker contracted to slaughter the stock and process the carcasses. Persuading retailers to carry the beef was much harder. The obvious outlets were natural food stores, but many catered to vegetarians and weren't interested in selling meat, natural or otherwise. Other would-be dealers didn't understand the product. "If you don't have to buy antibiotics and hormones," one asked Coleman, "shouldn't natural beef cost less?" "If I stock your beef and call it 'natural,' what does that say about the rest of my beef?" queried another. "That it's bad because it's full of chemicals?" By 1982, Mel had landed just two accounts — one natural food store and a Denver hospital — but he'd also exhausted the possibilities in Colorado. His son persuaded him to try California, arguing that when it came to fads, culinary or otherwise, Californians led rather than followed. Off Coleman went, renting a car (which also served as his hotel) and driving from one retailer to another.

The break finally came when he visited the headquarters of Mrs. Gooch's Ranch Markets, a small chain of Southern California health food stores ("just a bunch of hippies sellin' food," according to Coleman). The owners wanted to carry natural meats but had not been able to find a decent product. One look at Mel Coleman, however, who was dressed in his usual Colorado-ranch attire of cowboy hat and jeans, and a company executive knew that he'd found the real deal. The Gooch family signed a contract and spread the word to owners of other health food stores around the country. Two years later, an executive with Grand Union, a major East Coast grocery chain, visited the Coleman booth at a natural foods trade show. That encounter led to a contract to deliver five hundred cattle a week, a quantity that the Colemans could not supply as quickly as Grand Union wanted meat in its refrigerators. But other Colorado ranchers were hanging on by a financial thread, and the family obtained a letter of credit from Grand Union that allowed them to contract with others to raise cattle on their behalf.

Grand Union spared no expense in promoting the meat to its customers, touting beef that hailed from a place where "the mountain air is clear, the water pure, and soil uncontaminated." Polly and Mel Coleman flew east to help introduce the product, grilling steaks in store parking lots and handing out samples. Not everyone was impressed. One customer accused Mel of wearing a cowboy hat and boots in order to "look like a real rancher." On another occasion, a man who identified himself as a college professor accused Coleman of lying; it was impossible to raise cattle without the use of drugs. "How do you think we did it in the 1930s?" Mel retorted. But Mel and Polly converted shoppers taste sample by taste sample — one five-hundred-count box of toothpicks a day. Grand Union opened other doors; more orders trickled in. Health food retailers asked for lamb, veal, pork, and rabbit, which the Colemans were able to access from other ranchers. The family built a fabricating plant in Denver (they shipped their product as boxed beef) and moved headquarters from a spare room at the family ranch to a rented room at a nearby motel to a building in downtown Saguache. But the town still relied on an old-fashioned party-line phone system, and express delivery service arrived only twice a week. Practicality trumped sentiment, and the family moved the office to Denver, too.

While Mel Coleman pursued customers one toothpick at a time, alt-agriculturalists battled the establishment and scored wins of their own. In 1985, the same year that Grand Union approached the Colemans, Congress approved a farm bill that authorized the creation of an "agricultural productivity research" program. That bland wording concealed a major victory for sustainable agriculture: a mandate that required the USDA to sponsor and support research into and development of "Low-Input Sustainable Agriculture" (LISA). As is typical of farm bill legislation, the measure itself provided no funding; it was up to the USDA to request money. The department, by then a decidedly Reaganesque body, declined to do so. But in 1986 and 1987, the coalition returned to Capitol Hill and persuaded Congress to part with nearly $4 million to get LISA up and running. Between that date and 1992, Congress handed over more than $26 million for the support of alternative agriculture. Add in matching grants and funds from nonprofits, universities, and agribusiness, and all told, LISA's 183 projects had received $39 million by the early 1990s.

The congressional generosity is all the more startling given the Reagan administration's hostility to alternative agriculture.

Garth Youngberg, the man hired by the USDA after the department released its 1980 report on organic agriculture, was one
of the first out the door after Reagan defeated Jimmy Carter in
the 1980 election. "The word came down," Youngberg said, that
the USDA was not interested in promoting "organic." Moreover,
the arrival of LISA inspired an extraordinary display of public
mockery from many in the agricultural mainstream. A writer for
a farm magazine scoffed that the program represented a foolish desire to "replac[e] the mechanical and scientific advance-
ments of the past 50 years with sweat and a lower standard of
living." A ConAgra executive suggested an alternative name for
the alternative package: "I'd call it FIDO, fewer inputs, declining
outputs. A real dog." Another agribusiness insider was even less
kind. "Our worthless opponents are not constrained [by] hon-
esty." Otherwise, "they wouldn't call it LISA, they would call it
LILO — Low Input, Low Output." So the creation of and funding
for LISA raise some obvious questions: What happened? How
did activists manage to score such an impressive win? Part of the
explanation is that by the late 1980s, Naderites had made significant inroads into the USDA and other federal agencies; many
had gone from being jeans-wearing outsiders to suit-jacketed insiders, and when reformers lobbied for what became LISA, they
were coached by sympathetic USDA employees. But another factor that led to LISA can be understood by examining the legislative machinations that produce the "farm bill." During the 1970s,
that process had been upended, and the ensuing turmoil created
an opening that turned the tide for alternative agriculture and
won it a permanent seat at the USDA table.

Congressional legislation, whether for agriculture, education, or
defense, typically begins life in a committee made up of senators
or representatives. Those committee members rely on others —
interns and staff, outside experts, and lobbyists — to serve as conduits to the facts, research, and science on which legislation rests.
The more informed, reliable, and reputable those conduits are,
the more likely it is that senators and representatives will take

their advice. The corollaries are two: The more input that groups of experts or lobbyists provide, the more likely it is that the resulting legislation will meet their needs. The more useful and reliable their input, the more likely that a senator or representative will rely on them again in the future. As a result, subsequent bills echo earlier ones, and the information in–legislation out cycle repeats itself.

That's been particularly true for what are known as the "farm bills." As we saw in chapter 4, in 1933 Congress passed legislation that provided direct subsidies to farmers. Approximately every five years since, that body has hammered out a new farm bill rich with programs to support agriculture. Critics have long complained that these legislative packages are skewed toward big farmers at the expense of small ones, and crop monoculture at the expense of diversified agriculture. It's true that from the 1930s to the 1960s, farm bill legislation primarily targeted major commodities such as hogs and cotton because those were crucial to the logic of that first farm bill: in the 1930s, commodities were among the nation's most important agricultural products and Congress intended to pay for those first subsidies by taxing processors who converted commodities into food and fiber. Those initial farm bills were also structured to encourage farmers to practice factory farming. Indeed, in the 1940s and 1950s, lawmakers, the USDA, and other government departments and agencies actively tried to move marginal farmers into other lines of work, not because agribusiness kept lawmakers and bureaucrats on a leash, but because economic policymakers believed that big farms could provide food and fiber to an urban population more cheaply than small ones. This focus on commodities and factory farming led congressional committee members to rely on experts who could provide reliable information about both. That included USDA analysts who studied crop yields, consumer behavior, and export markets, as well as lobbyists for commodity producers and farmers' organizations. Among the latter was the American Farm Bureau Federation; the bureau, born in the early twentieth century, had been founded by farmers and manufacturers who supported businesslike farm management and industrial-style agriculture. For some thirty years, this "iron triangle"— the House and Senate agriculture committees, relevant outside experts, and the USDA— promoted, protected, and reinforced legislation aimed at supporting the industrial model of agriculture.

By the 1980s, however, a series of events had shattered the iron triangle. As we saw earlier, during the 1970s many government officials believed that agriculture had become "too important" to leave to agriculturalists. But factory farming itself contributed to the collapse of the iron triangle. The industrial model of farming is predicated on specialization, and as the model became more entrenched, so did special-interest groups — corn growers, broiler makers, cattle grazers, cattle feeders — each of them demanding its share of the farm bill. Factory farming also fostered geographic specialization. Texas cattle feeders had few commonalities with in/out Corn Belt feeders, and Iowa chicken farmers none at all with Georgia broiler growers. Those regional interests prodded their own representatives and senators to make demands on their behalf with the House and Senate agriculture committees. The secretary of agriculture became less important to the bill-making process than the heads of specialized bureaus and agencies who, in their turn, attracted lobbyists' attention. Congressional committees fractured into multiple subcommittees whose chairs gained their own clout. Negotiations became increasingly contentious as myriad demands by multiple interests spawned farm bills of mind-numbing complexity and detail. As the number of farmers dwindled, the political clout of politicians from agricultural states diminished, and they were forced to garner support for increasingly expensive agricultural legislation by making deals with lawmakers from urban areas. By the 1970s, the "farm" bill had morphed into a "farm and food" bill that included, for example, food stamp programs that primarily served urban populations.

The disarray fractured relations among the triangle's traditional power players, leaving fissures through which poured con-

sumer advocates, environmentalists, anti-hunger activists, nutritionists, and, of course, alternative agriculturalists, all of them
demanding their own share of the farm bill. As Don Paarlberg, a
well-known agricultural economist who spent years working at
the USDA, put it, the "agricultural establishment had lost control of the farm policy agenda." The onslaught infuriated many in
the old guard. One economist pronounced it "unthinkable" that
farm policy had "tilted towards consumers' interests" and other
groups "so completely alien to farmers' thinking and tradition."
He grudgingly conceded the need for cooperation, but only because he feared that resisting the invaders would lead to "unrest
in society." He didn't have much choice. Many of those storming
the gates were skilled Naderist negotiators who had no intention
of being denied a role in shaping such an expensive piece of legislation.

But the farm crisis that began in the late 1970s inadvertently
eased the invaders' way. As we saw in the previous chapter, many
farmers who had heeded the call to feed the world's starving had
ended up in debt or foreclosure. The ensuing crisis inspired the
creation of the American Agriculture Movement (AAM), a loose-
knit but militant, neopopulist group of farmers who blamed government for their woes. In early 1979, the AAM captured national
attention when its "tractorcade" descended upon Washington,
DC, with demands that Capitol Hill repair what it had ruined. As
far as the protesters were concerned, rage mattered more than
diplomacy, and AAM leaders proved mostly unwilling to compromise with legislators accustomed to civility and negotiation.
For all its missteps, however, the movement grabbed media attention. Talk show hosts, broadcast news anchors, and big-city
reporters descended on the Midwest. Three actresses who had
portrayed farm wives in films testified before a congressional task
force. (The spotlight proved a mixed blessing. A staff member of
one rural advocacy group groused that journalists were often less
interested in facts than in finding "a farmer who [would] cry on
camera.") Given the ongoing tragedy — the number of suicides
was sobering — and the attention it received, the senators and

representatives charged with putting together the 1985 farm bill found it impossible to be against family farms or programs aimed at helping them.

The alt-agriculture coalition seized the opportunity, and thus LISA was born. The activists' strategy reveals how adept they had become at navigating the belly of the beast. They framed their proposal as support for "low-input sustainable agriculture" because they knew that "low-input" would appeal to Republican budget slashers. When they returned to Capitol Hill two years later to lobby for money for LISA, the coalition deliberately excluded people and groups that openly promoted "organic" farming. (That included an otherwise enthusiastic supporter, the Center for Science in the Public Interest; presumably the sight of Michael Jacobson would only remind the establishment of his antics on *The Mike Douglas Show* a few years earlier.) "We warned everybody that you don't even use the word organic," explained one of the participants. "If you're asked, you can answer the question, but you don't even mention it when you're up there [on the Hill lobbying]." Instead, the alt-agriculturalists employed more powerful rhetoric: their party of persuaders included two of the nation's most successful alternative farmers, Dick Thompson of Iowa and Fred Kirschenmann of North Dakota.

Mel Coleman knew about the funding victory, but at the time, the task of building the family business occupied all his energy. Coleman Natural Beef was selling $20 million in meat products a year, and Mel had cobbled together a vertically integrated operation of the kind that characterized the broiler industry: he contracted with thirty ranchers scattered over two states to raise cattle according to his detailed specifications, and he briefly owned his own slaughterhouse (the family was forced to sell it when operating expenses threatened to devour their still-narrow profit margins). He marketed his meats directly to retailers rather than handing them off to a wholesaler or jobber, and by the end of the decade, Coleman meats could be found in more than 1,500 retail outlets. Although he hired a professional marketing manager after landing the Grand Union account, Mel remained the company's best sales pitch. His strategy was simple: find the buyer, preferably by handing him or her a sample of the product in a grocery store. "There's a particular person out there's who's interested in our meat, just the same way I buy Diet Coke." He'd also introduced a "starter" meat: Rocky Mountain Pure, beef made from cattle finished on additive-free feed but not necessarily raised on organic grasses or hay. Mel was convinced that once customers tried Rocky Mountain Pure, they would "upgrade" to his 100 percent organic beef, which continued to sell for 25 percent more than conventional meats.

There's no doubt that Mel Coleman's perseverance contributed to the company's early success, but in the 1980s, the family also benefited from a surprisingly lively "natural" food niche. Granola, the mainstay of hippie co-ops in the 1970s, had gone mainstream by the eighties as major food manufacturers discovered the (profitable) virtues of "countercuisine." Finding whole-wheat natural cookies on grocery store shelves eased shoppers' decisions to add Coleman meats to their carts. But the Colemans also reaped the rewards offered by another, related food niche: demand for culinary exotica, a niche that played out primarily in restaurants. Mainstream chains like Red Lobster aimed for a mass audience; they could not satisfy consumers interested in, and willing to pay for, a more rarefied dining experience. Restaurants that catered to exotica enthusiasts distinguished themselves from the herd not just by price — high-end dining was nothing new — but by the food, which ranged from the esoteric to the weird and often included a backstory. The clientele at Alice Waters's Chez Panisse restaurant in Berkeley, California, for example, were told that the meat on their plates came from animals that had lived a "wholesome" life or had been raised "biodynamically," concepts presumably lost on the hoi polloi at Red Lobster. At Nora's in Washington, DC, menus identified the precise origins of the meats served, including the name of the West Virginia pond that provided its trout. The chef at Quilted Giraffe in Manhattan offered his diners grilled free-range chicken. The price? A mere $75 (that's a staggering $196 today). "Before they became available," the chef admitted, "we never deigned to serve chicken." Only the "cachet" of organic-natural had given him "the nerve to sell chicken at that price," he explained. Not everyone could afford such gastronomic thrills, but that was the point. In a country where food cost so little, one way to differentiate the haves from the have-nots was with the unusual, the rare, the precious. Thus Grand Union's enthusiasm for Coleman Natural. "We tell retailers that our product will bring in . . . people who buy dollar-fifty chicken and Häagen-Dazs ice cream," explained the Colemans' marketing consultant. (Hooey, scoffed the meat buyer for a major Southern California grocery chain, who pronounced Coleman's meat "overpriced and overbilled" and natural beef a "fad.")

As aficionados of upscale ice cream and pricey poultry multiplied, so did Coleman's competitors, especially because cattlemen were desperate to stanch the bleeding in beef consumption. Given that Coleman beef sold for a 25 percent premium over conventional stuff, who wouldn't want a piece of the action? During the 1980s, others entered the arena. An alliance of Wyoming ranchers began marketing branded grass-fed beef, and a Mennonite cooperative in Kansas launched a beef line marketed as (mostly) free of hormones and other additives. In Northern California, Bill Niman and Orville Schell, who'd started a cattle ranch in the 1970s, supplied natural beef primarily to local restaurants. At the time, Schell's name carried the weight because he had published first a series of articles and then a book about the livestock and meat industries' addiction to pharmaceuticals. "I hope I don't radiate any aura of holier-than-thou," Schell told a reporter in 1986. He and Niman could "charge more" for their product, he explained, because "[f]ood consciousness" in the San Francisco Bay Area had "reached a state of evolution that [was] almost off the charts." (That prompted an eye-rolling retort from Mel Coleman: "We sold to Los Angeles, Austin, Houston and Boston before Marin and Boulder came around. The Bay Area is really slow in doing this.")

Unfortunately for Coleman and other honest purveyors of alternative meats, the USDA had opened the gates and thrown away the key. In 1984, the department diluted the value of Coleman's labels when it issued new rules that allowed any meat to be labeled "natural" as long as it contained no artificial ingredients and the carcass had been "minimally processed," a vague stipulation that could include anything and everything. Fly-by-nights weaseled into the niche. A grocery chain in Coleman's home state of Colorado stopped carrying natural meats because its buyer couldn't distinguish good guys like Coleman from the less-than-honest. "I've got ranchers coming in here every week asking me to buy their natural beef," he said, and he was "skeptical" about their credentials. Nor was the free-for-all limited to beef. Consider "Rocky the Range" chicken, which landed on the market in the mid-1980s. The company's owners marketed their birds as "free-range" and "stress-free," presumably because those descriptions resonated with their intended audience: laid-back Californians. But Rocky, which cost twice as much as conventional broilers, had less to do with pure and organic than with inventive salesmanship. It was the brainchild of food marketers, not farmers, and the chickens were raised by a conventional grower in Petaluma, the West Coast chicken capital. The farm's owner cut doors in the sides of some of his coops so birds could roam freely — more or less: the coops were fenced. Chickens destined for Rockyhood were fed and watered exactly like the rest of the grower's flock; no foraging allowed. A curious reporter persuaded two Los Angeles chefs, including Wolfgang Puck, one of the first to surf the food fetish–celebrity chef wave, to conduct a blind taste test of Rocky and a plain old broiler. Rocky failed, and Puck was annoyed that his own taste buds couldn't tell the difference. "I definitely think we should find out why they charge so much money," he announced. USDA officials were even less impressed. In 1990, the department told the company's owners to cease and desist with its terminology. "We don't have a working definition for range," explained a USDA spokesman. "What is 'range' in the regulatory sense? . . . A horse rounding up chickens on the range?" The department also nixed the "stress-free" claim. "We can't be wasting the government's time with words we can't enforce," he said. "I guess a chicken could be stress free, but how could you tell?" Who could blame the department? The burgeoning natural foods industry was a morass of misinformation, wacky claims, and blatant lies. Who knew if biodynamically raised beef or pork was superior to conventional meat in taste or nutrition? What advertising leeway should be allowed to the rabbit grower who claimed that caging his animals in wooden pens maximized the impact of "beneficial magnetic forces"?

Mel Coleman was prepared to stand his ground against frauds, but then came a blow that infuriated him. In 1989, the USDA announced that it would no longer certify beef as hormone-free; a department spokeswoman explained that it lacked the "wherewithal" and expertise to make such a judgment. (To be fair, bovines, like humans, have hormones and no meat is hormone-free.) Mel Coleman denounced the decision as a "great injustice." First he'd lost "natural"; now he was being forced to give up "hormone-free," the last card in his hand. He was no fan of excessive government, but in this case, he said, "[a]s bad as our government is, it still does have a little bit of credibility for consumers." Federal labeling was his main defense against the fakes and "essential" to the success of his venture, he argued. "It's all we are."

That explains why he joined other crusaders during the 1990 round of negotiations for a new farm bill: he and they wanted Congress to establish federal standards for organic produce and meat. Coleman, by then an old hand when it came to schmoozing bureaucrats and power players, worked with Senator Patrick Leahy, a Vermont Democrat, longtime supporter of alternative agriculture, and at the time chair of the Senate's agriculture committee, to write a bill that would give him and others legal access to the term *organic*. In June 1990, Coleman and others testified at a hearing over the matter hosted by two subcommittees of the House agriculture committee.

Coleman quickly discovered he'd overestimated the overlords' enthusiasm for change. A congressman from Missouri opened the hearing by complaining that the term *organic farming* implied that organic crops and meat were "better than food produced by other farming methods." "I don't, personally, believe that to be the case," he said. "We have a safe, reliable, and affordable food supply with ample choices for all consumers," he argued, and neither organic foods nor a standard for them was necessary. "I'm still trying to figure out how you can have an organic cow," he added. The chair of the House agriculture committee, Texan Eligio "Kika" de la Garza, was even more skeptical. He told the assembled that during some preliminary on-the-scene investigating, he'd talked to an organic farmer. The congressman asked her where she obtained the fertilizer for her four-acre urban farm. "I assume you use manure," he'd told her. "No, no, no," she replied. "I use commercial fertilizer." The congressman quizzed her further and discovered that she defined hers as an organic farm because she didn't use synthetic pesticides. "Goodness knows," de la Garza told the audience, "sheep, goat, poultry, cattle — it's all too complicated. If someone uses manure, you have to go back to see that the manure didn't come from cattle that had chemical therapeutic treatment."

The two USDA representatives who attended the hearing were even less enthusiastic. "[T]here is not much about this bill that we like," said the head of the Agricultural Marketing Service, adding that the department opposed the establishment of federal organic standards for beef, pork, and poultry. The "greatest" threat to the nation's food supply, he argued, was posed by "microbial contaminations" like salmonella rather than the "pesticides, animal drugs, or other chemicals" cited as problematic in the proposed legislation. Banning the latter did nothing to address the dangers of the former. The other USDA spokesman was even more dismissive. Livestock was "constantly exposed to parasites, bacteria, and viruses," and in his opinion it was "impossible" to produce cattle, hogs, and chickens without using "synthetic drugs" and "therapeutic doses of antibiotics." If only we could travel back in time and watch Mel Coleman's reaction. If he wasn't banging his head against the nearest wall, he probably wanted to do so. Making organic meat wasn't impossible; he'd been doing it for years.

Eventually a bill made its way out of committee and into the House and Senate, but the debates in both chambers proved to be unexpectedly contentious, and few lawmakers were willing to commit to "organic." (If the content of the discussion is any indication, it's also clear that most of them were confused about what the word meant.) Worse, during farm bill negotiations, Senator Charles Grassley, an Iowa Republican with seniority and clout, tried to eliminate much of LISA. In the end, the two bodies compromised by establishing a National Organic Standards Board (NOSB) and charging it with writing a set of standards (knowing, presumably, that in Washington, the best way to avoid conflicts and decision was by studying something to death). LISA survived but got a new name, one that reflected the alternative agriculturalists' ability to use language that appealed rather than threatened: Sustainable Agriculture Research and Education (SARE), "sustainable" having by that time become code for environmentally sound but not too far out (it was also punchier than "low-input").

Mel Coleman wasn't willing to wait for the NOSB to hammer out the details. In 1991, he launched a new marketing campaign based on a slogan that avoided what he called the "o" word but adhered to the law: "What would beef be without hormones, steroids or antibiotics: It would be Coleman." Coleman's livestock and meat-making peers decided they'd had enough of him (although perhaps they'd had their fill of alternative agriculturalists and a public that turned up its nose at beef). Leaders of the Colorado Cattlemen's Association and the National Cattlemen's Association protested what they described as Coleman's "negative advertising." When he touted his meats as organic and natural, they complained, he cast "doubt on the safety and wholesomeness of the generic beef supply." "Our problem with this campaign is that it clearly implies that Coleman beef is safer to eat than other beef and the scientific facts simply do not support that," they explained. "Isn't there some way to promote your product without kicking undue 'mud' in the face of the rest of the beef industry?" (It was surely no coincidence that Monfort/ConAgra, which processed Coleman's cattle, picked that moment to raise its per-head slaughter fee by $5.) Coleman refused to back down. "I've paid a lot of dues in this industry and I'm not going to apologize just because we do things differently," he said. "All the ads do is say our animals don't get [chemical additives] and if you're interested in that kind of a product, we've got it."

The uproar over organic standards and the near-loss of LISA/ SARE persuaded alt-agriculturalists that they had to forge new alliances in order to strengthen their numbers. They sensed that more supporters were out there. The agricultural crisis of the 1980s and the encroachment of corporate hog farms had convinced many farmers that if they wanted to survive, they had to rethink their strategy. Sustainable agriculture proponents were eager to tap into that frustration. But they also recognized that they were in danger of losing control of their agenda because the idea of "sustainable agriculture" had been coopted by outsiders. As three longtime advocates put it, the phrase had "been embraced by virtually every constituency with an interest in agriculture," from consumers to food processors to the input manufacturers at the heart of agribusiness. Whatever alternative agriculture had meant back in the sixties and seventies, by the 1990s it meant everything and thus nothing. Activists had to figure out how to differentiate their agenda. In 1991 and 1992, a consortium of sustainable agriculture groups organized a road show of seminars, panels, and round tables — a "national dialogue," they called it — aimed at uncovering hidden pockets of support and determining where to go next and how to get there.

Those gatherings pointed toward an inescapable conclusion: sustainable agriculturalists had to diversify their primarily rural agenda and link it to a broader community. In 1994, they launched the National Campaign for Sustainable Agriculture, a loose-knit collection of reformers whose interests ranged from immigrant farm workers to minority farmers to consumer protection. But two years later, the movement took a great leap forward when it formally allied itself with activists engaged in building urban food systems. The new Community Food Security Coalition (CFSC) linked farm to city and city to farm. Over the next fifteen years, the CFSC would inspire the "eat local" campaign; turn farmers' markets into a minor industry; and force the NOSB to establish organic standards, especially for beef, poultry, and pork.

The urban activists who partnered with the sustainable agriculture advocates came out of the "food security" movement. The working definition of *food security* can be summed briefly: every person, every community, every nation is secure when food supplies are available, accessible, and adequate. The idea was a by-product of World War II. As the war came to an end, world leaders organized the FAO (now housed at the United Nations) to monitor global food supplies and address a tragic paradox: people in some parts of the world suffered malnutrition and starvation even as farmers in other regions collapsed into bankruptcy thanks to overproduction of foodstuffs. The FAO wanted to organize the distribution and sale of surpluses in a way that would guarantee food security for everyone. During the 1970s, food security provided the conceptual framework for managing the global food crisis that scarred that decade. The FAO, which hosted a conference to address the famine and coordinate the response to it, urged global leaders to construct a "systematic world food security policy."

The food security of the United States loomed large in that effort because so much of the world's population depended on American agriculture. Scholars, politicians, and activists pondered the nation's food security at conferences and congressional hearings, and most arrived at a surprising conclusion: despite an abundance of cheap food and a hyperefficient production and distribution system, the United States was food insecure. Most people lived in cities and relied on food supplies trucked in from other parts of the country, and an average supermarket held only about two days' worth of food for the people it regularly served.

A powerful storm, a railroad strike, or a military-related event could wipe shelves clean. Environmentalists argued that, in addition, U.S. food insecurity was systemic because farmers relied on petroleum-based inputs; agriculture as practiced was unsustainable and therefore food supplies were anything but secure. Others contended that Americans would enjoy food security only when they replaced big food manufacturers with what the Naderist Exploratory Project for Economic Alternatives called "a decentralized, safe, and ecologically sound food production and marketing system." According to this view, Americans needed fewer factory farms and giant food processors, and more "localized, small-scale production of fruits and vegetables."

The desire for a more food-secure America inspired grass-roots projects as well as federal legislation that linked farmers directly to local consumers. In 1976, Congress passed the Farmer-to-Consumer Direct Marketing Act, which authorized $1.5 million for projects that would forge connections "between the urban consumer and the small farmer." To name one example, New Yorkers used some of the money to establish greenmarkets where area farmers could (and still do) sell their produce to city residents who otherwise relied on foods grown and manufactured elsewhere. The most influential and long-lived of these 1970s projects unfolded in Hartford, Connecticut. That city was as food insecure as most, dependent as it was on supplies transported long distances. But Hartford's poorest neighborhoods were particularly insecure. As was true in other big cities, grocery chains had deserted Hartford's inner city, forcing impoverished urbanites to pay higher-than-average prices for whatever food they could find at convenience stores. Using federal funds, Hartford officials commissioned the Public Resource Center, another Naderist nonprofit, to develop a food security strategy based on urban gardens, food clubs, cooperatives, and farmers' markets stocked with locally grown produce. Hartford was not alone, and in 1979, the Conference on Alternative State and Local Policies published a nearly three-hundred-page compendium that described dozens of food security projects and organizations around the country.

Although some, like the Hartford endeavor, focused on low-income neighborhoods, what linked all the ventures was their emphasis on fostering community self-reliance. No one expected towns and cities to become 100 percent food self-sufficient; that was both impossible and unnecessary. But they could become more self-reliant so that in case of an extended emergency, they need not wait for trains or trucks to bring food.

Once the crisis-riddled seventies ended, enthusiasm for self-reliant communities and local food production might have gone the way of lower thermostat settings, but food security advocates got an unexpected boost in the 1980s thanks to the election of Ronald Reagan as president. As part of the Reagan agenda to reduce government, Congress slashed $12 billion from federal food stamp and child nutrition programs; almost overnight, demands for food overwhelmed taxpayer-funded and private relief organizations. In 1982, for example, the number of Cleveland residents seeking food assistance rose more than 100 percent. In Denver, food distribution to the needy doubled during that year, and over a hundred food banks scrambled to keep pace. A national network of emergency operations — two hundred food banks, twenty-three thousand food pantries, more than three thousand soup kitchens — struggled to keep up with demand, and Detroit mayor Coleman A. Young pronounced hunger the "most prevalent and most insidious" problem in American cities.

That long moment of anguish taught a valuable lesson to food activists, nutritionists, and policymakers: managing hunger on an emergency-to-emergency basis was exhausting, often futile, and at best a bandage rather than a cure. By the end of the decade, anti-hunger activists had reframed the problem of urban hunger as one of community food insecurity. The distinction was more than semantic. As two analysts with the Urban Institute explained, individuals suffered hunger, but communities experienced food insecurity. Rather than treat hunger as a short-term, person-by-person emergency, it made more sense to reframe it as a community problem. That shift in focus necessitated a change in strategy: rather than race from one food emergency to the next, activists turned their energy to building long-term, stable food supplies with projects like the one in Hartford with its mixture of gardens, food clubs, and farmers' markets.

Thus was born the coalition forged by alt-agriculturalists and food security advocates. Each had something the other wanted: small, independent farmers needed outlets for their crops; food security activists needed stable sources of local food. Merging their agendas wasn't easy. Over the years, significant "tension" had developed between the alt-agriculturalists and anti-hunger activists, one observer said, a situation she blamed on agribusiness-generated "myths" that sustainable foods were priced out of reach of the urban poor. That tension had "prevented a dialogue between" the two groups, and when both trooped to Capitol Hill in 1990 to engage in negotiations over that year's farm bill, they were, in the words of one participant, "like two trains passing in the night." By the mid-1990s, however, the trains were on the same track and had added more passengers by wooing another group that initially rejected pleas to join the new alliance: environmentalists had long supported sustainable agriculture but couldn't see how food security benefited their eco-agenda. CFSC members reminded them of a point food security proponents had raised back in the 1970s: the distance that foodstuffs traveled from farm to plate, some 1,400 miles on average. Food systems based on local products, usually grown by ecologically minded farmers, were more sustainable and thus more environmentally sound.

But there was more to the new alliance's agenda than supporting farmers and feeding the urban poor. These activists adhered to a grand American tradition: like crusaders for other causes in earlier generations — think Prohibition and Abolition as well as the religious awakenings of the early nineteenth century — those engaged in building an alternative food system hoped to reform and renew the nation's soul. In their minds, food was a lens through which Americans would learn to view town and country as parts of a whole and themselves as citizens of a unified

environmental, economic, and social community. Three scholars — and university faculty played key roles in building the new
coalition — outlined this mission in a 1996 essay. Because Americans relied on food that came "from a global everywhere" and
thus from "nowhere . . . in particular," they wrote, most had no
idea "how and by whom what they consume is produced, processed, and transported." Americans were disconnected "from
each other and from the land" and consequently "less responsible
to each other and to the land." "Where do we go from here? How
can we come home again?" The way home, they contended, lay
in "withdrawing from" the global and national food economy and
building an alternative food system rooted in regional and local
food sheds that linked town and country, city dweller and farmer.
Only then would Americans "reassemble" their "fragmented
identities, reestablish community, and become native not only to
a place but to each other." All of that sounds hopelessly utopian.
But that was precisely the point of placing food at the center of
this project. Food linked everyone, regardless of class, geography,
race, or income. Making food production and delivery more visible — whether through urban gardens, family farms, or farmers'
markets — would encourage Americans to shoulder greater responsibility for their air, water, soil, and neighbors. Legislation
could go only so far in addressing environmental degradation
and economic injustice, but both could be alleviated, and spiritual awakening nurtured, one farmer, one garden, one market,
and one meal at a time.

This utopian project reaped real-world rewards. In 1995
and 1996, the alliance persuaded the House and Senate to add
a "Community Food Projects" agenda to the farm bill, a victory
that expanded the USDA resources committed to alternative
food and farming. New Internet-based technology and the World
Wide Web fertilized the food security crusade by enabling orga-
nizers to communicate quickly and to attract new adherents. A
public demonstration of the alliance's clout came in 1997 when
the NOSB finally proposed a set of organic standards and the
USDA prepared to accept them. By that time, many people in-

volved in agriculture had become enamored of biotechnology, and the proposed standards would have allowed organic food-stuffs to include or be raised with genetically modified organisms and permitted the use of irradiation and fertilizers manufactured from sewage sludge. The food security alliance urged supporters to submit comments, the method by which the USDA gathered input from the public. Well over a quarter-million people and or-ganizations did just that, bombarding the department with ob-jections to what opponents dubbed the "Big Three" (presumably because they believed those three items were the brainchildren of Big Ag and Big Food). The USDA backed down, dumped the pro-posed standards, and told the NOSB to try again.

The food security coalition transformed the nation's culi-nary landscape. From 1990 on, sales of organic foods rose about 20 percent a year, and by the early twenty-first century, Ameri-cans were spending $8 billion a year on "alternative" foods, buy-ing about half of it in conventional retail outlets such as health food stores and chain supermarkets; 73 percent of all of the lat-ter carried organic foods of some kind, even if only frozen pizza. The translation of utopian ideal into practical reality inadver-tently obscured the alliance's original missions of fostering so-cial justice and food security. Two sociologists who studied the movement (and participated in it as well) reported that farmers' markets, community-supported agriculture projects, and coun-try food stands had proliferated "like robins in spring"; farm-ers' markets increased by more than 60 percent in the late 1990s alone. Customers for them, alas, had not. Alternative food sys-tems, it appeared, required as much marketing and public rela-tions as Mel Coleman's natural beef. Thus began the "buy local" campaign that captured the attention of the middle class. That tactic originated in 1999 when a Massachusetts group, Commu-nity Involved in Sustaining Agriculture, launched a sophisticated public relations drive aimed at wooing shoppers. Stickers, pam-phlets, and advertisements urged area residents to be "Local He-roes" and buy food from local farmers. Other communities and organizations quickly latched on to the idea. (Presumably no one anticipated the heated debate over "local miles" that erupted several years later.)

A cycle developed: the more chic that alternative foods became — and the role that status and cachet played in fueling the growth of this niche cannot be denied — the higher the premiums those foods commanded (and not always because demand outstripped supplies), the more likely farmers were to switch to organic production in order to nab those premiums, and the less interested they were in serving the needs of poor urbanites. The fetishization of alternative foods — celebrity chefs and farmers, menus detailing the ecologically correct origins of every ingredient in a dish, farmers' market as hipster carnival — lured more consumers eager to spend food dollars in order to experience the niche. Surely no one was surprised when in 2006, Wal-Mart announced plans to expand its offerings of organic foods.

Alternative livestock and meat production, however, lagged behind that of alt-staples like arugula and organic boxed macaroni and cheese; in 2000, meats constituted just 3 percent of the organic sector. Part of the problem was logistical: every year more farmers shifted more land into organic production, but most of that was devoted to raising vegetables and fruits. Relatively few people were interested in growing organic corn for livestock feed or in devoting acres to grazing rather than crop production, especially because meats made up such a small piece of the organic pie. The smaller the sector, of course, the less inclined farmers were to raise feed. That was the first Catch-22. Another was that so few farmers, and especially livestock producers, controlled their agricultural destinies. Broiler growers, to name the obvious example, were contractors. But by the turn of the century, the number of independent cattle feeders had dwindled, and contract hog farming had gained traction among small farmers struggling to make ends meet. Put another way, there weren't that many livestock producers left to go organic. That explains why, statistically, a large proportion of the people producing organic meats came to the industry with no prior farming experience.

But many otherwise interested farmers held back, waiting for the USDA to establish standards for organic livestock and meat production. The rules that the USDA finally issued in 2002 were straightforward (or as much so as possible when bureaucrats, lawyers, and lobbyists are involved). Farmers and retailers could market beef, pork, and poultry as organic if the meats came from animals raised without growth-inducing hormones or antibiotics and fed diets of organically grown, all-vegetable feedstuffs manufactured in an organic-certified mill. Farmers were required to provide livestock with access to the outdoors, although confinement was allowed under limited conditions and only for brief periods. (One of those conditions, however, constituted a significant loophole: producers could confine their livestock if they believed that leaving them on pasture posed "a risk to soil or water quality.") Finally, the livestock had to be slaughtered and processed in an organic-certified facility.

Those seemingly simple guidelines were littered with bureaucratic land mines. Consider the case of Peaceful Pastures in Tennessee, whose owners raised and marketed organic poultry. Tennessee law mandated that all poultry slaughter take place in a USDA-inspected facility. There were plenty of such operations around, but they were set up to handle conventional poultry. The couple couldn't find a USDA-supervised slaughterhouse that would provide "custom-kill" services and adhere to organic standards. The pair considered building a small processing facility on their farm — until they read the fine print in the rules. "I'd have to build an office for the inspector," said Peaceful Pastures owner Jenny Drake, complete with a separate phone line. The couple would have to pave their parking lot and install handicapped-accessible bathrooms. "We have to meet the same physical standards as a Tyson's, and we just can't do it," she sighed. "[I'm] so right-wing I make Rush Limbaugh look like a liberal," she added, but as far as she was concerned, big business and what she termed the "rich agribusiness lobby" were making her life miserable. Virginia farmer Joel Salatin agreed. He raised organic hogs, chickens, and cattle, and he, too, tried to build an on-farm slaughter facility. USDA officials directed him to the guidelines, a detailed list of necessities that infuriated Salatin, who saw no need to build employee bathrooms. "I told them we were 50 feet away from two houses with bathrooms, and besides, we're a family operation: We don't have employees. It didn't matter to them," he complained. "Then they said we had to have twelve changing-lockers for employees — even if we didn't have employees." Salatin denounced the obstacles as "bureaucracy in action," a bureaucracy with but one purpose: to "protect big agribusiness from rural independent competition." USDA employees were sympathetic, to a point. The official who dealt with the Tennessee couple understood that these rules would likely prevent someone who wanted to slaughter and sell a few hundred chickens a year from earning any profit. But, he asked, "do we want to let people slaughter meat in the backyard and sell it on the sidewalk?" Doing so, he feared, could introduce tainted meats into the nation's food supply. That argument carried zero weight with those trying to change the nation's hearts, minds, and diets. One only needed to consult a daily newspaper to know that whatever else they might be, conventional foodstuffs, and especially meat, were hardly safe.

Given these obstacles, it's a miracle anyone bothered to produce and market organic meats, and many people decided not to do so. A Massachusetts man who'd built up a clientele for his meat at a local farmers' market wanted the organic designation, but to get it, he complained, he'd have to "hire someone to do the paperwork, pay twice the price for organic feed, and find a certified slaughterhouse that would take a small amount of animals." His customers were already paying up to $5 a pound for his ground beef. The cost of obtaining and maintaining organic certification would "price [him] out of the ball game." He decided that because he dealt with his clientele face-to-face, it made more sense simply to explain to buyers that his products were organic.

But as the previous example indicates, and as the Coleman family had known for years, many shoppers were prepared to pay top dollar for alternative meats. Those shoppers' ranks increased in the early twenty-first century thanks to widely broadcast recalls of tainted meats, outbreaks of bovine spongiform encephalopathy, and new concerns about antibiotic resistance. So red tape notwithstanding, organic meat production attracted conventional cattle and hog farmers looking for something, anything, to boost the still-sagging sales of beef and pork. That was particularly true of cattle growers, many of whom pinned their hopes on the high end of the market. After all, exotica enthusiasts had snapped up certified Angus steaks, or highly marbled, flavorful cuts from Wagyu or Kobe cattle, or pricey "lite" beef from livestock bred for lean rather than fat.

In the early years of the new century, the winner of the carnivorous exotica contest was grass-fed beef. The idea was not new; since the 1940s, the trade journal *Stockman Grass Farmer* had catered to the interests of a small but dedicated group of ranchers who specialized in finishing cattle on grass. Grass-fed beef had enjoyed a brief moment of glory in the 1970s as some feeders, including Ken Monfort, bought range cattle and sent them directly to slaughter rather than finish them on high-priced grain. The beef went to grocery stores labeled as "grass-fed" and carrying a lower price tag than grain-fed beef. But in the late 1990s and early 2000s, some ranchers and farmers reversed that equation and promoted grass-fed as a premium product, one that was (allegedly) healthier than grain-fed beef. Conventional cattle ranchers Wendy and Jon Taggert, Texans who'd long sold their livestock to commercial cattle feeders, began keeping back part of their herd, finishing it on grass, and marketing it directly to consumers under the name New Image Grass Beef. Jon explained that they wanted "a little bit bigger piece of the pie" to stay on their own plates. Beef "is a very healthy product," Wendy Taggert told a reporter by way of elaboration. "We're just making it healthier."

The popularity of grass-fed beef reflected how far the alternative food movement had traveled, but it also laid bare the fracture lines emerging among alternative food producers. In early 2002, some Northern California ranchers banded together to sell grass-fed beef to high-end area restaurants. A reporter who covered the story noted that the group found plenty of takers for their product — which cost about twice as much as conventional beef — because of grass-fed's "political and culinary appeal" to upscale buyers. But demand for grass-fed escalated markedly that year after a writer named Michael Pollan published a *New York Times Magazine* article in which he argued that conventional beef production was bad for both cattle and people. Marshaling the same argument that sustainable agriculture advocates had been making for nearly thirty years, Pollan told readers that there was nothing cheap or healthy about meat, not if one "add[ed] in the invisible costs: of antibiotic resistance, environmental degradation, heart disease, E. coli poisoning, corn subsidies, imported oil and so on."

Pollan's essay was enough to convince Alice Waters, by then a "foodie" celebrity, to serve grass-fed beef in her restaurant rather than the grain-finished meat she'd been buying from Niman Ranch. Bill Niman, that company's cofounder, was aghast. He'd been raising organic cattle for years, finishing them on (organic) grains before slaughter, and he resented the notion that his beef was unhealthy or ecologically incorrect. Niman dispatched an e-mail to Pollan. "As you know," he told the writer, "the story is very complicated and the lay public considers all feedlot cattle the same. This is absolutely not true." The belief that grass-fed beef or other free-range meats could replace conventional stuff was also unrealistic, Niman told a reporter. "People want to imagine a beautiful vision of a chicken out there eating earwigs and cows roaming free around the pasture," he said. But that vision could not "feed millions of people every day." That was particularly true of grass-fed beef, he explained, which was as seasonal as "a peach or a tomato. Eat it in May or June 'cause that is when it is peaking."

Niman's arguments carried little weight with those eager to claim a share of the exotica niche or to change the world. Inspired by Pollan's article, the Chefs Collaborative, a collection of what one reporter described as "prominent" chefs, restaurateurs, and food activists, launched a campaign to persuade restaurant owners to switch to grass-fed beef. The project raised a few eyebrows. An executive with a small chain of upscale steakhouses found it "ironic" that the collaborative claimed to have been inspired by the "standard of excellence" found in European meats, and yet every day Europeans poured into his restaurants searching for quality beef of a sort they could not find at home. A founder of the Center for Consumer Freedom, a watchdog group opposed to what it described as "nanny culture," denounced the collaborative as "a haughty organization with an elitist point of view" and a "let them eat cake" attitude. "We are an elitist organization," said collaborative member Eric Schlosser, "but change has to start someplace, and people who have better access to information and spending power can be the start of all sorts of changes." Schlosser, who had recently published *Fast Food Nation*, a *Jungle*-like exposé of the fast-food industry in general and fast-food meat in particular, argued that many historically significant movements, including Abolition and women's suffrage, had been "led by educated, middle- and upper-income people," and he believed that the crusade for a more sustainable food system was another such movement.

Change was on the way, although perhaps not the kind Schlosser intended. Several months later, two alt-meat pioneers, Coleman and Niman Ranch, were snapped up by investment groups. Niman Ranch lost its independence first. In the thirty-odd years since Bill Niman and Orville Schell had founded their venture, the company had never earned a profit. That had not stopped Niman from pursuing a strategy of aggressive growth after Schell left in the late 1990s. ("I consciously deferred profitability [in order] to expand the brand," he explained.) He added organic pork to his array of products, a move that required him to contract with a small army of hog producers, and expanded his market from Northern California to the entire United States. His ambitions outstripped his funds, and in late summer 2002, Chicago-based Natural Food Holdings committed two of its executives and a fistful of cash to the task of saving Niman; in exchange, Natural commandeered four of the seven seats on the Niman board of directors. The new investors sold the original feedlot, choosing instead to send cattle to conventional feeders for finishing and shipping the livestock long distances to slaughter. Those decisions generated profits but infuriated Bill Niman. When the investors acquired the company outright in 2009, Niman resigned, publicly berating the new owners for betraying his mission.

The Coleman family also cashed out in 2002. Mel Coleman Jr., company president since the death of his father earlier in the year, sold to Petaluma Holdings, an investment consortium that owned Petaluma Poultry, one of the country's largest processors of organic poultry, as well as Swift & Company. (Swift was the new name of what had been ConAgra Beef, the Greeley outfit that once belonged to the Monforts.) The new owners planned to position their portfolio of natural and organic meats in chain stores like Costco and Safeway. Over the next few years, they merged with what had been Natural Food Holdings and then with a third investment firm, KDSB Holdings. In 2006, this new entity incorporated Coleman Natural Foods as the parent company for its many alternative meat brands and companies, which by then included Rocky the Range Chicken, Rocky Jr., and Rosie the Organic Chicken.

These moves were not surprising — at least not to those with a nose for business. The organic food sector made up just 4 percent of all American food sales, but it was growing at the rate of about 20 percent a year. Sales of organic meats, however, were ratcheting upward at a rate of 50 percent a year. While that number needs to be seen in perspective — the $600 million that consumers spent on organic meat was a mere jot of the $158 billion that Americans spent on all beef, pork, and poultry — signs pointed toward continued growth. Tyson and other mainstream meat makers were launching lines of natural meats (presumably banking on the fact that few consumers understood the difference between natural and organic labels). Retail behemoth Wal-Mart had announced plans to expand its organic food offerings, a decision that translated into pressure on packers and food processors to come up with the goods. Then there was the 2006 publication of Michael Pollan's *Omnivore's Dilemma*, which became an immediate bestseller and remained one for several years. The book's centerpiece and most indelible image was Pollan's portrayal of conventional livestock production: thousands of cattle crammed into feedlots and standing shin-deep in manure, their bodies riddled with bacteria and damaged by a diet of corn. From an investor's point of view, that grim scenario translated into the hottest ticket to profit since the microwave oven: organic alternatives to conventional beef, pork, and poultry. It's not surprising that investment groups like Natural Holdings and Petaluma Poultry were on the prowl for sources of alternative meat.

Not that "alternative" meats were all that alternative. By the time Pollan's book appeared, half of all organic food purchases were made in conventional grocery stores, including Costco and other big-box retailers, and every major grocery chain boasted its own private-label brands of organic goods, including meat. Of the other 50 percent of organic food sales, most were made at natural food stores, primarily Whole Foods and similar chains. The demand from those grocery outlets spawned a new industry of middlemen: organic "handlers," as they were called, scoured the countryside grabbing up, and often contracting in advance for, organic carrots, apples, and chickens, anything alternative that could be processed and packaged for sale to giant retailers. In the race to supply the new alt-powerhouses — Safeway, Kroger, and Costco — farmers' markets and other local farmer-to-consumer outlets ran a distant third. Shoppers still flocked to the Saturday-morning farmer-food carnivals, but the prices they paid there inched up because farmers who once struggled to find outlets for their carrots and broilers held the upper hand. Why bother with a farmers' market when organic handlers crowded the farmhouse door, begging for supplies that were scarce relative to demand? Eyed from the retail end, the new food utopia, it appeared, looked much like the old mainstream. Was alternative the new normal?

• • •

Down on the farm, the distinction between sustainable and conventional livestock production was becoming equally blurry. In
2002, several animal rights activist groups, including the Humane Society of the United States (HSUS), launched a campaign
to end the use of gestation stalls, the narrow metal pens that hog
farmers used to confine sows during and after pregnancy. Farmers had long isolated sows in order to protect them from harm
(hogs, especially females, are both territorial and hierarchical;
weak ones, especially females, don't last long in a group); the
stalls were only the latest version of that practice. Activists argued that the pens' small size constituted cruelty to animals: the
sows had little room to move and could not turn around while in
them. The anti-stall crusade began innocuously enough with a
letter-writing campaign: "The Easter holiday celebrates the res-
urrection of the Prince of Peace," read the text of the form letter
that supporters sent to their local newspapers in the spring of
2002. "Yet some of us still observe this special occasion by serving
ham, produced by abusing and killing a sentient, innocent, gentle
creature, as the centerpiece of their holiday dinner."

Those letters marked the opening foray of a sophisticated crusade. Over the next few years, animal rights activists released un-
dercover videos shot at hog farms, marshaled scientific research
that indicated that the stalls cost rather than saved money, and
launched ballot initiatives aimed at banning the stalls. Livestock
producers fought back, brandishing science that proved stalls
protected sows, arguing that the expense of switching from stalls
to large pens or pasture would bankrupt small farmers and leave
more of the business in the hands of Big Ag, and painting their
opponents as meddlers who didn't understand animal psychol-
ogy. "Nothing [is] more heartbreaking than watching a timid
sow cower in the corner, afraid to approach the feed and water
until the dominant sow [leaves] the area," one farmer wrote in a
newspaper opinion piece. (The anti-stall coalition shrugged off
such concerns and urged the livestock industry to breed less aggressive animals.)

The reformers had the upper hand. Over the next few years,

voters in several states endorsed stall bans; major hog producers, including Smithfield (by then the world's largest), agreed to phase out the stalls; and many of the nation's largest food makers and retailers, from Costco and Safeway to Cheesecake Factory, Burger King, and McDonald's, agreed to stop buying pork made from hogs raised by stall-using producers. Emboldened by these successes, the campaigners expanded their aim. In 2008, Californians approved an HSUS initiative that banned not just gestation stalls but conventional poultry cages (a typical cage has a footprint about the size of a sheet of notebook paper) and the single-animal pens used to confine sheep. Nor was this the only crusade that changed the meat Americans ate. In 2003, McDonald's announced that it would no longer buy meat made from animals fed antibiotics also used by humans. The fast-food titan arrived at that decision after working with an anti-antibiotic coalition, but it's likely that McDonald's executives were also inspired by the success of one of its major investments. In 1999, McDonald's had bought majority shares in Chipotle, a small fast-food chain dedicated to serving "food with integrity," including organic and natural meats, and then watched integrity translate into success: 578 Chipotle outlets by 2006 and double-digit growth each year. (McDonald's sold the last of its Chipotle stock in 2006.)

It's not hard to understand why these crusades were so successful. As we've seen, by the early twenty-first century a substantial food reform infrastructure was in place, even at the USDA. But food reformers had also figured out how to exploit a fundamental fact about most Americans: they don't live on farms and have never met a farmer. Where livestock producers saw an ignorant urban population, food reformers saw a populace that believed farms ought to be Elysian idylls like the one operated by Joel Salatin. That farms like Salatin's could not begin to feed the nation, and that farms like his had been all but extinct for well over a half-century, was irrelevant. That disconnect between Americans and their food, between ideal and reality, had become the reformers' most powerful weapon, one that allowed them to imagine a new future for meat in America.

CONCLUSION

I F MEAT'S AMERICAN history tells us anything, it is that we Americans generally get what we want. Meat three times a day? No problem. Meat precut, deboned, and ready to cook? There it is. Meat precooked, mixed with pasta, and ready to zap? We've got it. Organic, grass-fed, local pork and beef? All yours, as long as you don't mind paying the price or taking the time to find it (a chain store will sell you organic, grass-fed meat, but if it's local you're after, you're on your own).

But we Americans also possess an infinite sense of possibility. We believe that social and personal perfection are within our grasp, a conviction that has inspired a host of reform movements in our history. That sense of infinite possibility has changed, and will continue to change, the way we make meat.

It won't be easy. We're a complicated group, we Americans, and we struggle to reconcile our conflicting desires and passions. On one hand, many of us want meat, lots of it, and we don't care how it's made as long as it doesn't cost much. On the other, some of us are determined to break the chains that bind livestock production and meatpacking to assembly-line processes. How to accomplish both — produce immense quantities of meat at an affordable price while relying on (relatively) inefficient methods of producing it — is not clear. Of course critics argue that "efficiency" is in the eye of the beholder, and that given the environmental costs of conventional livestock production, there's nothing "efficient" about it. But others will argue that our ability to make affordable meat not just for ourselves but for the rest of the world is worth the price.

Therein lies our American dilemma: whose version of efficiency best serves the needs and wants of the majority? Are we prepared to turn our backs on the practicalities of conventional agriculture in order to make organic the new normal? And is it practical, if by "practical" we mean an agriculture model that allows most of us the luxury of pondering these issues rather than spending our days tending crops and livestock? Can we have the best of both worlds: a majority urban population and small-scale agriculture, too?

The debate over meat in America won't end anytime soon, if only because as a nation, we have a hard time answering tough questions like these. Consider the "pink slime" uproar of 2012, which encapsulated the perplexities and conundrums of our desire to have it all. Early in that year, newshounds learned that the USDA was supplying school lunch programs with hamburger laced with Lean Finely Textured Beef — pink slime to its critics — a product that even many fast-food burger chains refused to use. A Texas food activist launched an online petition to demand that the department get pink slime out of school kitchens. The USDA agreed to let school districts make their own decisions about its use, and by early summer nearly every state education department had said no to LFTB. (The holdouts were Iowa, Nebraska, and North Dakota.)

The need that inspired the invention of LFTB — to utilize every last bit of a carcass — was not new; the dressed-beef men of the 1880s built their empires by extracting profit from carcasses. During the 1970s when inflation, rising fuel costs, and declining demand cut into meatpackers' profits, they adopted LFTB's predecessor: "mechanical deboning," a technology that utilized bladed devices to scrape bits of meat from bone. Prodded by consumer advocates, the USDA banned that process because of fears that bone slivers would end up in the beef. In the early 1980s, entrepreneur Eldon Roth invented an alternative: he exchanged blades for centrifuges that freed scraps of fat and gristle and yielded mushy but bone-free, lean beef. Roth compacted these beef bits into blocks and sold those to meatpackers and food processors, most of whom mixed it with fattier beef to make the lean ground beef that consumers preferred. During the 1990s, and inspired by the 1993 Jack in the Box episode, Roth refined his process by subjecting the scraps to a brief blast of ammonia (a natural component of beef) that destroyed *E. coli*. Bottom line, LFTB helped meatpackers do what they'd always done: earn a profit while giving Americans meat at the price they would pay. Eldon Roth and his company, Beef Products Inc., were (and are) highly regarded in the meat industry, not just for Roth's considerable inventive prowess and his product, but also for his rigorous attention to sanitation and food safety. Indeed, BPI's stock-in-trade was a commitment to providing packers with a clean product, and Roth's facilities were touted as among the most sanitary in the country.

There wasn't, and isn't, anything dangerous about LFTB — it's beef. Nor, as some critics claimed, was LFTB "dog food." Meatpackers had long sold meat scraps to pet food manufacturers, not because the scraps were unfit for human consumption, but because packers had no USDA- or FDA-approved way to salvage those otherwise edible bits. As soon as federal authorities gave the green light to Roth's innovation, edible beef scraps that once went into pet food could be used for other purposes.

Eldon Roth's process was simply a high-tech version of what frugal cooks have done since humans stood upright: it allowed processors to utilize every available morsel of protein and calories. Only a food-rich society like ours enjoys the luxury of dispensing with frugality. In the end, the view that Americans need not bother with cheap filler trumped the view that LFTB made meat affordable to consumers at every income level. Within weeks, Roth had shut down three of his four plants.

The din drowned out voices that asked important questions: Were taxpayers prepared to spend more on school lunch programs in order to cover the cost of more expensive meat products? Were parents prepared to give up their evenings so that they could attend school board meetings and demand that Big Food be evicted from school cafeterias? Were teachers and parents prepared to reduce classroom time devoted to math and reading so that kids could gain an appreciation of good food, preferably by planting and weeding schoolyard gardens? Were those who wanted an end to LFTB, and cattle feedlots, and antibiotics — and they tended to be one and the same — willing to turn off their laptops and iPads, move to the country, and put in the long days that "natural" farming demands? In short, and like so many other moments detailed in this book, the LFTB episode embodied the messy complexity that is not just meat in America, but Americans themselves.

Whatever we think of Wendell "Boss Hog" Murphy or Eldon Roth on one hand, and Michael Jacobson and Michael Pollan on the other, we are all responsible for what we have wrought. Decade upon decade, we've insisted on having it all — cheap food *and* odor-free air *and* quality meat *and* disposable incomes that enable us to buy cell phones. If the devastation wrought in the rains of North Carolina or the debacle over pink slime teaches us anything, it is that we won't transform our meat culture by taming Big Food or replacing Big Ag with a locavore-centered, alternative food system, but by examining our sense of entitlement and the way it contributes to the high cost of cheap living.

Not long after Roth turned out the lights in his plants, another event took place, one that went largely unnoticed: in August 2012, the Community Food Security Coalition announced that it would shut down its operations at the end of the year. CFSC directors explained that the organization had sown its seeds so successfully that there was no longer enough grant money to go around for all the related, connected, and spinoff groups that wanted it. The

CFSC would hand off the food-reform baton to others who had been inspired by its work. That's a "clean out your desk" moment we can applaud. Organic foods are supermarket staples; alternative is the new normal; the premium we pay for grass-fed beef and organic pork is our act of commitment to a better world. We Americans, the masters of having it all, have had our desires — for convenience, for cachet, for doing good — satisfied once again.

As I wrote in the introduction to this book, I'm not buying it. I don't believe we can have it all.

I leave you with a final point to consider: we reaped the benefits of the CFSC, and yes, LFTB, because factory farming freed so many of our parents, grandparents, and great-grandparents, and thus us, from the need to grow and process food; freed them, and us, to instead dream big, think deep, and yes, launch crusades. Pollan, Schlosser, and I can write books in large part because we don't have to spend time planting seeds and pulling weeds. Factory farming's biggest crop is intellectual capital. So, thanks, Big Ag — and the USDA and family and corporate farmers — for giving us the cheap food that has nourished an extraordinary abundance of creative energy. Now let's do something with it. Let's decide what kind of society we want — not what kind of farming, not what kind of meat, but what kind of society.

In the United States, deep change happens slowly. Our political machinery is less well oiled than it is unwieldy and cantankerous, but, like an old Farmall tractor, it will get the job done. Two things, however, are certain: We won't move forward until we can talk to rather than at each other about the high price of cheap food. And we won't starve while we try to decide how, if at all, to reinvent the American way of meat.

ACKNOWLEDGMENTS

I'd planned to keep these thoughts brief — until I was so close to the end that its breath tickled my ear and I thought: Seven years is a serious chunk of life. The hell with brief. I want to honor the people who got me here.

On this book and my previous one, I worked with Andrea Schulz, editor-in-chief at Houghton Mifflin Harcourt. She is this book's true hero, its head cheerleader, its guide, its brains, not least because she coached me so skillfully through the beer book that I had the confidence to attempt this project. If this work has any merit, it is because of her efforts. For its flaws, blame me.

I thank her and everyone at Houghton Mifflin Harcourt for their patience; seven years is a long time to wait for a payoff. I admire, too, their good cheer and resolve during 2008 and 2009, a grim moment in American publishing. I am grateful, and so should all of us be, that HMH and other publishers support complex projects like this one. The publishing industry, under so much attack these days from so many writers, is a major patron and subsidizer of intellectual work, especially for projects that require years rather than weeks to complete.

Agents facilitate that patronage. I am grateful to Jay Mandel at William Morris Endeavor Entertainment: for his patience and forbearance, for his dry humor (so much the opposite of mine), and above all for his mild eye rolls that motion me toward even keel amid my random, off-keel enthusiasms.

Once again, I thank the staff at Parks Library at Iowa State University. (If only we could convince the state legislature of its importance.) I also visited and received help from the staffs at the University of Iowa library and its special collections department, the Milwaukee Public Library, and the New-York Historical Society. For assistance at the Society for the Prevention of Cruelty to Animals, I thank Marcy Altman, Valerie K. Angeli, Layna DeLaurentis, and Steve Zawistowski. I am particularly grateful to Layna for her hospitality, and to Steve for taking time to share with me his knowledge of the Buffet transcriptions of Henry Bergh's letters. Sibella Kraus supplied me with a copy of a document she'd written. I thank Nancy Hallock and Keith Arbour for their friendship and scholarly solidarity. When I needed some last-minute help, they dispatched it immediately. Onward, comrades!

I thank the small army of physicians, surgeons, nurses, physical therapists, and massage therapists who gave me back my right arm. For a long moment, I was not sure I would be able to finish this book or any other. They pulled me out of the dark and into full health. There are no words to express my gratitude.

My thanks to Twitter, Facebook, and WordPress, to the people who created these marvels of media, and to all those who've chosen to participate in and shape the New Community. In my mind, the finest aspect of "social" media is the way it allows different generations to talk to and work with each other. During the years I devoted to this book, I learned so much from, and was constantly inspired by, people half my age. I thank all of them.

When the beer book came out in 2006, I landed smack in the middle of the craft beer industry, home to an extraordinary collection of creative, lively, engaging, ambitious, determined people, from those who make the beer, to those who sell it, to those who drink it. Most of all, I appreciate the camaraderie of those who write about craft beer. Every day I read their work and ponder their ideas, and my life is richer for that. Their passion, dedication to critical thinking and good writing, generosity, and friendship inspire me to reach higher and dig deeper. Folks: the next round's on me.

Where I would be without my friends, I do not know. They know who they are, but I especially thank Carrie and Mark Kabak for the love, laughter, and food; and Anat Baron for her inspiring eye, mind, and will. The Spalings showed up late in the game and almost single-handedly (groupedly?) got me through the last year of this project, and for that, and much more, I am grateful.

As for my family—no one is more fortunate than I. In descending order by age: Bill Robinson, Kay Arvidson, Alys Sterling, Bernard van Maarseveen, Jen Robinson, Trevor Barnes, and the newest member of our tiny tribe, Willem Robinson van Maarseveen.

Of that tribe, my beloved Bill is the center, the heart, the soul. I pray that his noble spirit will be my companion for many more years. Certainly it graces each page of this book.

Finally, the book's acknowledgment honors Bernard and Jen, who have shared, and with such loving generosity, the greatest of gifts.

NOTES

Although most of these notes simply document the sources of quotations, a number of them elaborate on points made in the text. Some digital sources do not contain page numbers; in those cases, I've noted that the document was accessed online.

INTRODUCTION
page

ix "Truly we may be called": "Consumption of Meat," *American Farmer and Spirit of the Agricultural Journals of the Day* 3, no. 2 (June 2, 1841): 9.

xi I respect the critics: Readers should note that my general argument in this book is a rejection, overt or otherwise, of the Marxists' critique of "capital." I am aware of that argument, and its complexities. I don't agree with it and find it singularly useless for making substantive change.

1. CARNIVORE AMERICA

2 "[ran] over the grass": Quoted in Virginia DeJohn Anderson, "King Philip's Herds: Indians, Colonists, and the Problem of Livestock in Early New England," *William and Mary Quarterly* 3d series, 51 (October 1994): 604.

"savage people": Quoted in ibid., 604.

"advantageously . . . scituated": Quoted in James S. Magg, "Cattle

Raising in Colonial South Carolina" (master's thesis, University of Kansas, 1964), 26.

"Hogs swarm like Vermine": Quoted in Lewis Cecil Gray, *History of Agriculture in the Southern United States to 1860* (Carnegie Institution of Washington, 1933), 206.

In Maryland in the late 1600s: The example is from Henry Michael Miller, "Colonization and Subsistence Change on the 17th Century Chesapeake Frontier" (Ph.D. dissertation, Michigan State University, 1984), 378.

3 "live stock": Quoted in Virginia DeJohn Anderson, *Creatures of Empire: How Domestic Animals Transformed Early America* (Oxford University Press, 2004), 143.

When we bite: The discussion of the biology, chemistry, and nutrition of meat is based primarily on two sources, both of which are marvels of accessible prose: First, the two editions of Harold Mc-Gee's masterwork *On Food and Cooking: The Science and Lore of the Kitchen.* The original edition appeared in 1984 (Collier Books). The revised and updated version — for which McGee rewrote nearly every page — was published in 2004 (Scribner). Second, Alan Davidson's *Oxford Companion to Food,* 2d ed. (Oxford University Press, 2006). One of the best general sources for information about meat in early human history is Kenneth F. Kiple and Kriemhild Coneè Ornelas, eds., *The Cambridge World History of Food* (Cambridge University Press, 2000).

The average white colonial American: Colonial and preindustrial statistics represent the best estimates compiled by many scholars. I relied on information in Edwin J. Perkins, "Socio-Economic Development of the Colonies," in *A Companion to the American Revolution,* ed. Jack P. Greene and J. R. Pole (Blackwell Publishers, 2000); and Carole Shammas, *The Pre-Industrial Consumer in England and America* (Clarendon Press, 1990).

4 "[E]ven in the humblest": Gottlieb Mittelberger, *Journey to Pennsylvania,* ed. and trans. Oscar Handlin and John Clive (Belknap Press of Harvard University Press, 1960), 49.

"because he thought": Quoted in James E. McWilliams, *A Revolution in Eating: How the Quest for Food Shaped America* (Columbia University Press, 2005), 185.

"Custom of ye Country": All quotes from "A Mutiny of the Servants," *William and Mary Quarterly* 11 (July 1902): 34–37.

"The Cattle of *Carolina*": Quoted in Magg, "Cattle Raising," 28.

5 "there was no longer any holding": William Bradford, *Of Plymouth Plantation, 1620–1647*, ed. Samuel Eliot Morison (Alfred A. Knopf, 1959), 253, 254.

"deer and skins": Quoted in Anderson, *Creatures of Empire*, 207.

6 "Your hogs & Cattle": Quoted in ibid., 221.

"Violent Intrusions": Quoted in ibid., 240.

"[W]hat will Cattell": Quoted in ibid., 236.

7 One of the most important: For a good description of the cattle-corn-hog complex by one of its practitioners, see William Renick, *Memoirs, Correspondence and Reminiscences* (Union-Herald Book and Job Printing, 1880), 11, 12. Renick originally wrote the essay for the 1860 United States Census. The best surveys of this phase of American agriculture are in John C. Hudson, *Making the Corn Belt: A Geographical History of Middle-Western Agriculture* (Indiana University Press, 1994); and Paul C. Henlein, *Cattle Kingdom in the Ohio Valley, 1783–1860* (University of Kentucky Press, 1959).

8 "long moving lines": Rev. I. F. King, "The Coming and Going of Ohio Droving," *Ohio Archaeological and Historical Society Publications* 17 (1908): 249.

9 "up the river": Quoted in James Westfall Thompson, *A History of Livestock Raising in the United States, 1607–1860* (1942; reprint, Scholarly Resources, 1973), 95. The book was initially published as the U.S. Department of Agriculture's Agricultural History Series no. 5, November 1942.

10 "I alwase": Harris's life is recounted in Mrs. Mary Vose Harris, ed., "The Autobiography of Benjamin Franklin Harris," *Transactions of the Illinois State Historical Society for the Year 1923* 30 (1923): 72–101.

11 "There are few things": "Consumption of Meat," 9.

12 One popular cookery book: For this example see "General Operations of Cookery," *American Farmer* 7, no. 35 (November 18, 1825): 278.

"nicely": A Farmer's Wife, "Household Affairs," *Cultivator* 1 (April 1834): 31.

"free negroes": Quoted in "Cobbett on the Expenses of House-Keeping in America," *The American Farmer* 6, no. 16 (July 9, 1824): 123.

13 "highly-seasoned flesh-meat": Quoted in Stephen Nissenbaum, *Sex, Diet, and Debility in Jacksonian America: Sylvester Graham and Health Reform* (Greenwood Press, 1980), 34.

"overload[ed] the stomach": *Cincinnati Mirror,* November 26, 1831, p. 35.

"beyond all question": Jno. Stainback Wilson, "Health Department," *Godey's Lady's Book and Magazine* 60 (February 1860): 178.

14 "excessive use of fat": Jno. Stainback Wilson, "Health Department," *Godey's Lady's Book and Magazine* 57 (November 1858): 372.

15 "Eastern demand": "Meats, Milk, and Fruits," *New York Times,* May 25, 1852, p. 2.

16 *"great law of the movement"*: Silas L. Loomis, "Distribution and Movement of Neat Cattle in the United States," *Report of the Commissioner of Agriculture for the Year 1863* (Government Printing Office, 1863), 259; emphasis in original. Also published as HR Ex. Doc. no. 91, 38th Cong., 1st sess.

"western": Charles W. Taylor, "Importance of Raising and Feeding More Cattle and Sheep," *Report of the Commissioner of Agriculture for the Year 1864* (Government Printing Office, 1865), 255. Also published as HR Ex. Doc. no. 68, 38th Cong., 2d sess.

"as literally to blacken": Quoted in William Cronon, *Nature's Metropolis: Chicago and the Great West* (W. W. Norton & Company, 1991), 215.

17 "Why": Quoted in Scott Michael Kleeb, "The Atlantic West: Cowboys, Capitalists and the Making of an American Myth" (Ph.D. dissertation, Yale University, 2006), 88.

"long-legged": "New-York Cattle Market," *New York Tribune,* July 4, 1854, p. 8.

18 "Stampeded last night": "Driving Cattle from Texas to Iowa, 1866," *Annals of Iowa* 14, no. 4 (April 1924): 252, 253.

"contented to live quietly": Joseph G. McCoy, "Historic and Biographic Sketch," *Kansas Magazine* 1 (December 1909): 49. For a marvelous appreciation of McCoy, see Don D. Walker, "History Through a Cow's Horn: Joseph G. McCoy and His Historical Sketches of the Cattle Trade," in *Clio's Cowboys: Studies in the Historiography of the Cattle Trade* (University of Nebraska Press, 1981), 1–24.

"establish a market": Joseph G. McCoy, *Historical Sketches of the Cattle Trade of the West and Southwest,* ed. Ralph P. Bieber (1874; reprint, Arthur H. Clark Company, 1940), 112.

19 "a man of hasty temper": C. F. Gross to J. B. Edwards, May 4, 1925, J. B. Edwards Collection, microfilm version, Kansas State Historical Society.

"log huts": Quoted in Ralph P. Bieber, "Introduction," in Joseph G.

McCoy, *Historical Sketches of the Cattle Trade of the West and Southwest* (1874; reprint, Arthur H. Clark Company, 1940), 58.

"Texas fever": In the 1860s, theories abounded about the cause of Texas fever, but another quarter-century passed before veterinarians discovered the source of the disease: microscopic organisms that attacked the animals' blood cells. Ticks spread the disease from one animal to another.

20 "to stop the drover": McCoy, *Historical Sketches*, 96.

21 "only the one place": Thomas Dove Foster to John Morrell, March 9, 1875; Box 1, Morrell Meat Packing Company Collection, University of Iowa Libraries, Iowa City, Iowa.

23 "great facilities": Quoted in Percy Wells Bidwell and John I. Falconer, *History of Agriculture in the Northern United States, 1620–1860* (1925; reprint, Carnegie Institution of Washington, 1941), 399.

"The number of swine": Quoted in ibid., 439.

The numbers were stark: Statistics are in William P. McDermott, "Rushing the Milk Train: The Harlem Valley in Transition, 1845–1875," *Hudson Valley Regional Review* 18, no. 1 (March 2001): 36.

24 "was a business that moved itself": New York State Legislature, Special Committee on Railroads, *Proceedings of the Special Committee on Railroads* (Evening Post Steam Presses, 1879–1880), vol. 4, p. 3317. The report is often referred to as the Hepburn Report, after committee chair A. B. Hepburn.

"this butcher and that": Ibid., vol. 4, p. 3318.

"The more you can concentrate": Ibid., vol. 2, p. 1727.

2. "WE ARE HERE TO MAKE MONEY"

27 "abominable nuisances": "Dressed Beef," *New York Times*, November 15, 1882, p. 4. The description of the facility is in "A Huge Meat Refrigerator," *New York Times*, October 10, 1882, p. 8.

"trying to force their beef": Quoted in "Dressed Beef and Live Cattle," *New York Times*, November 15, 1882, p. 5.

"sharks": Quoted in "Western Dressed Beef," *Boston Globe*, November 23, 1882, p. 1.

28 "gigantic fortunes": Quoted in "The Fresh-Beef War," *Boston Herald*, November 14, 1882, p. 11. Swift made the comments about his early days as a cattle dealer at a moment when the railroads threatened to retaliate. Swift is not identified by name in this article, but it's clear from details in it that the reporter was interviewing Swift and a partner, presumably his brother Edwin.

29 "simply enormous": Ibid.

"right over the fence": U.S. Senate, Senate Select Committee on Interstate Commerce, *Report of the Senate Select Committee on Interstate Commerce*, 49th Cong., 1st sess., 1886, p. 661.

31 "There is perhaps nothing": "The Hog and Cow Question," *Milwaukee Sentinel*, December 4, 1863, p. 1.

32 "not very elegant language": *Sanitary Condition of the City: Report of the Council of Hygiene and Public Health of the Citizens' Association of New York*, 2d ed. (1866; reprint, Arno Press, 1970), 168.

"snorted and pranced": "A Fumigation," *Milwaukee Sentinel*, October 17, 1866, p. 1.

"often lost a meal": "Board of Health," *New York Times*, August 29, 1866, p. 5.

33 "old-fashioned, clumsy and wasteful": All quotes from "Report on Slaughtering for Boston Market," *First Annual Report of the State Board of Health of Massachusetts* (Wright & Potter, 1870), 20, 21, 22.

"cramped [slaughterhouses]": "Facilities for Slaughter-houses," *San Francisco Bulletin*, January 2, 1868, p. 2.

34 "great central slaughter-house[s]": Quoted in City of Boston, *Report on the Sale of Bad Meat in Boston* ([1871]), 56.

"sticker": All the quotes and the description are from "Opening of the New Abbattoirs [*sic*] — Great Celebration at Communipaw," *New York Times*, October 18, 1866, p. 2.

35 "arbitrary, tyrannical and unjust": Quoted in "Local Intelligence," *New York Times*, June 20, 1866, p. 8.

"Long Island": Quoted in ibid.

36 "oppressive, and create[d]": "The City of Chicago *v.* Louis Rumpff. Same *v.* James Turner," 45 Ill. 90 (1862), 97, 99.

"skimming the scum": Quoted in "The State of Louisiana, ex re., S. Belden, Attorney General, *v.* Wm Fagan, et al.," 22 La. Ann. 545 (1870), 552.

"the personal rights": Quoted in Ronald M. Labbé and Jonathan Lurie, *The Slaughterhouse Cases: Regulation, Reconstruction, and the Fourteenth Amendment* (University Press of Kansas, 2003), 106.

37 "general police power": "State of Louisiana, ex re.," 555.

"Liberty": Quoted in Labbé and Lurie, *Slaughterhouse Cases*, 133.

"compelled": Quoted in ibid., 187, 208.

38 "outrage": "The Slaughter-House Nuisance," *New York Times*, May 3, 1875, p. 4.

"dangerous": "The Fifty-ninth-Street Abattoir," *New York Times,* April 10, 1875, p. 2.

"comparatively poor": "The Abattoir Nuisance," *New York Times,* April 14, 1875, p. 12.

39 "fear and apprehension": "The Market Systems of the Country, Their Usages and Abuses," *Report of the Commissioner on Agriculture for the Year 1870* (Government Printing Office, 1871), 251. I also tracked public dissatisfaction with the use of railroad transport by reading annual reports issued by the American Society for the Prevention of Cruelty to Animals, founded by Henry Bergh, as well as a transcript collection of his letters held by the society. Bergh hired "detectives" to investigate the condition of livestock in Chicago, at watering stops, and at abattoirs like Communipaw.

"chemical decomposition": "Bringing Cattle to Market," *New York Evangelist,* September 3, 1868, p. 7.

"endanger[ed] the health": Quoted in City of Boston, *Report on the Sale of Bad Meat,* 11, 12.

"deep red blotches": E. H. Dixon, "The Beef Market," *New-York Tribune,* August 22, 1868, p. 2.

40 "right off the grass": "Frozen Meat," *Prairie Farmer* 42 (July 22, 1871): 228.

"excellent condition": "Cheaper Beef for the East," *New York Times,* December 8, 1873, p. 2.

41 "be regarded with": Quoted in J. C. Hoadley, "On the Transportation of Live-Stock," *Sixth Annual Report of the State Board of Health of Massachusetts* (Wright & Potter, 1875), 93, 94.

44 "vision": Louis F. Swift and Arthur Van Vlissingen Jr., *The Yankee of the Yards: The Biography of Gustavus Franklin Swift* (A. W. Shaw Company, 1927), 24, 29–30, 201, 208.

45 "New England Fresh Meat Express": "Boston Enterprise," *Boston Journal,* July 26, 1879, p. 3.

"coolers": "The Western Refrigerator Beef," *Trenton State Gazette,* October 23, 1882, p. 3.

46 "era of cheap beef": "Cheaper Beef," *Harper's Weekly* 26 (October 21, 1882): 663.

"Everything with us": Quoted in "The Western Refrigerator Beef," p. 3.

"has ceased to be": Ibid.

"panicky feeling": See the dispatch from the *Chicago Tribune* published as "Chicago Dressed Beef" in *New York Times*, October 15, 1882, p. 3.

"[I]f you showed me": U.S. Senate, Select Committee on Transportation and Sale of Meat Products, *Investigation of Transportation and Sale of Meat Products with Testimony*, S. Rpt. 829, 51st Cong., 1st sess., 432; hereafter *Investigation of Transportation and Sale*. The document is often referred to as the Vest Report after committee chair George G. Vest. As is true of Swift, there are no substantive biographies of Armour. The best way to understand the man is by reading the newspaper coverage of his exploits as well as the many obituaries published at the time of his death in January 1901 (although as with any of the "robber barons," those must be approached with care). A marvelously fictional biography is *Armour and His Times*, by Harper Leech and John Charles Carroll (D. Appleton-Century Company, 1938). Also see Cora Lillian Davenport, "The Rise of the Armours, an American Industrial Family" (master's thesis, University of Chicago, 1930), as well as a string of biographical essays prompted by the early-twentieth-century "trust-busting" movement. I pieced together Armour's early career primarily from Milwaukee newspapers. Like most things economic, cogent explanations of futures trading, corners, and the like are hard to come by. An excellent description and analysis written for the non-economist can be found in Cronon, *Nature's Metropolis*.

48 "did not understand": U.S. Senate, *Investigation of Transportation and Sale*, 432.

"refrigerator": "The Pressed Beef Business," *Springfield (MA) Republican*, February 16, 1883, p. 2; reprinted from the *Philadelphia Press*.

"no waste at all": Quoted in ibid.

"There can be only": "Dressed Beef," *Chicago Tribune*, October 24, 1882, p. 5.

"only stupid and sluggish minds": "The Dressed Beef Innovation," *Wheeling Register*, March 27, 1883, p. 2.

"fat and comfortable": "Dressed Beef," *New York Times*, November 15, 1882, p. 4.

49 "[A]ll of this is nothing more": "Steady Growth of the Dressed Beef Trade," *American Farmer* 9th ser. 1, no. 21 (November 1, 1882): 305; this article first appeared in *Drovers' Journal*. The shipment numbers are in Norman J. Colman, "Dressed-Meat Traffic," *Third Annual Report of the Bureau of Animal Industry for the Year 1886* (Govern-

ment Printing Office, 1887), 278. A lower estimate was made in Treasury Department, *Report on the Internal Commerce of the United States,* H. Rpt. 7, 48th Cong., 2d sess., 264; that document is typically referred to as the Nimmo Report for its author, Joseph Nimmo Jr.

"bright and sweet": "City Article," *Boston Journal,* September 8, 1883, p. 3.

Families satisfied: The butcher's comments are in "Bulging Beef," *Oshkosh Daily Northwestern,* May 16, 1882, unpaginated.

50 "Even a laborer": U.S. Senate, *Investigation of Transportation and Sale,* 407.

"Do you suppose": Quoted in W. O. Atwater, "Pecuniary Economy of Food: The Chemistry of Foods and Nutrition V.," *Century* 35, no. 3 (January 1888): 443.

In 1894: The prediction is in Warren Belasco, *Meals to Come: A History of the Future of Food* (University of California Press, 2006), 27. It's impossible to read nineteenth-century magazines and newspapers without encountering discussions of the relationships among nation-building, national power, and food. Two good surveys are in Belasco, *Meals to Come;* and Mark R. Finlay, "Early Marketing of the Theory of Nutrition: The Science and Culture of Liebig's Extract of Meat," in *The Science and Culture of Nutrition, 1840–1940,* ed. Harmke Kamminga and Andrew Cunningham (Rodopi, 1995), 48–74. Finlay's essay is especially good for the European view.

"rice-eating": "The Non-Beef-Eating Nations," *Saturday Evening Post,* November 13, 1869, p. 8.

The cultural and nutritional significance: On this point, see especially Vincent J. Knapp, "The Democratization of Meat and Protein in Late Eighteenth- and Nineteenth-Century Europe," *The Historian* 59, no. 3 (March 1997): 541–51.

51 "makes an enormous return": Quoted in Kleeb, "The Atlantic West," 57.

"good business management": James S. Brisbin, *The Beef Bonanza; or, How to Get Rich on the Plains* (1881; reprint, University of Oklahoma Press, 1959), 36.

"riding through plains": Quoted in Richard Graham, "The Investment Boom in British-Texan Cattle Companies, 1880–1885," *Business History Review* 34, no. 4 (Winter 1960): 423, 424.

"The cost of both": Brisbin, *Beef Bonanza,* 74.

"a young Wall Street": Quoted in Ernest Staples Osgood, *The Day of the Cattleman* (1929; reprint, University of Chicago Press, 1966), 96.

"clever bait": Quoted in ibid., 103.

52 "ranch to table": "A Marquis under Arrest," *New York Times*, May 20, 1887, p. 1. For more on the marquis, see Donald Dresden, *The Marquis de Morès: Emperor of the Bad Lands* (University of Oklahoma Press, 1970); and D. Jerome Tweton, *The Marquis de Morès: Dakota Capitalist, French Nationalist* (North Dakota Institute for Regional Studies, 1972).

"We propose": Quoted in D. Jerome Tweton, "The Marquis De Mores [*sic*] and His Dakota Venture: A Study in Failure," *Journal of the West* 6, no. 4 (October 1967): 529.

"distinguished scholar, gentleman": "De Mores [*sic*]," *Brooklyn Eagle*, October 5, 1885, p. 2.

"an agreeable cross": "In the Bad Lands," *Bismarck Tribune*, January 20, 1885, p. 6.

53 "I have tried everybody": Quoted in Kleeb, "The Atlantic West," 189, 190.

"contain the enormous car-loads": Quoted in ibid., 220.

"men who did not know": U.S. Senate, *Investigation of Transportation and Sale*, 4.

"I do not think": Ibid., 5.

54 "monopoly": Quoted in "Opposed to the Chicago Men," *New York Times*, February 28, 1886, p. 2.

"dressed beef syndicate": Quoted in "Views of a Ranchman," *New York Times*, November 26, 1886, p. 6.

55 "I want part": U.S. Senate, *Investigation of Transportation and Sale*, 360–61.

57 "at the mercy": "Butchers to Protect Themselves," *New York Times*, March 9, 1886, p. 3.

"an age of organizations": Quoted in ibid.

58 Most of them unloaded: The Iowan's comments are in U.S. Senate, *Investigation of Transportation and Sale*, 255.

"entirely unfamiliar": Quoted in ibid., 82, 83.

59 Phil Armour begged: All of Armour's comments and statistics are in ibid., 425, 472, 480.

61 "artificial and abnormal": Ibid., 33.

3. THE (HIGH) PRICE OF SUCCESS

63 "BEEF TRUST SQUEEZES": "Beef Trust Squeezes Poor for $100,000,000," *New York Herald*, March 28, 1902, p. 3. The "Beef

Trust" label stuck despite the fact that packers sold as much pork as beef; nor did the packers ever organize a formal, legal trust.

"secretly": "Beef Trust Now Seeks Corner in Egg Supply," *New York Herald*, April 18, 1902, p. 3.

"grip": Ibid.

64 "Cattle and meat": "Prosperity Causes High Meat Prices," *Duluth News Tribune*, March 30, 1902, p. 5.

"Corn is the corner-stone": George Buchanan Fife, "The So-Called Beef Trust," *Century* 65 (November 1902): 150.

65 "wholly unfit": "Unwholesome Meats," *Worcester (MA) Daily Spy*, April 30, 1884, p. 6.

"It is made to look": Quoted in James Harvey Young, "'This Greasy Counterfeit': Butter Versus Oleomargarine in the United States Congress, 1886," *Bulletin of the History of Medicine* 53, no. 3 (Fall 1979): 398.

"oleomargarine sacred?": Quoted in James Harvey Young, *Pure Food: Securing the Federal Food and Drugs Act of 1906* (Princeton University Press, 1989), 89.

66 "how long will it be": From debate during the 57th Congress, quoted in Young, *Pure Food*, 161–62.

"a pestilential lot": Quoted in ibid., 162.

"We are no longer": Mary Hinman Abel, "Safe Foods and How to Get Them," *Delineator* 66 (September 1905): 394, 396.

68 "for the purpose": Fife, "The So-Called Beef Trust," 155, 156.

69 "If we have done anything": Quoted in Michael McGerr, *A Fierce Discontent: The Rise and Fall of the Progressive Movement in America, 1870–1920* (Oxford University Press, 2003), 156, 157.

70 "the wheels of modern progress": Quoted in Hans B. Thorelli, *The Federal Antitrust Policy: Origination of an American Tradition* (The Johns Hopkins University Press, 1955), 414. More than a half-century after publication, Thorelli's study remains one of the most useful histories, and certainly the most thorough one, of antitrust policy in the late nineteenth and early twentieth centuries.

71 "combination": Quoted in Mary Yeager, *Competition and Regulation: The Development of Oligopoly in the Meat Packing Industry* (JAI Press, 1981), 184.

"simply a dead multi-millionaire": "Object to Half-Mast Flag," *New York Times*, April 1, 1903, p. 2.

72 "Daylight": Quoted in Thorelli, *Federal Antitrust Policy*, 430.

"the great corporations": Quoted in Arthur M. Johnson, "Theodore Roosevelt and the Bureau of Corporations," *Mississippi Valley Historical Review* 45, no. 4 (March 1959): 578.

"young ladies": "The Public and the Beef Business," *New York Sun*, April 29, 1905, p. 6.

73   "exceptionally poor": *Report of the Commissioner of Corporations on the Beef Industry*, H. Doc. 382, 58th Cong., 3d sess., xxvii.

"tedious and voluminous reports": "The Public and the Beef Business," 6.

"popular demands": Quoted in Gabriel Kolko, *The Triumph of Conservatism: A Reinterpretation of American History, 1900–1916* (The Free Press of Glencoe, 1963), 81.

"the greatest trust in the world": Charles Edward Russell, *The Greatest Trust in the World* (Ridgway-Thayer Co., 1905), 89. Russell's work originally appeared in *Everybody's Magazine* from February to September 1905. For background and a biography, see Robert Miraldi, *The Pen Is Mightier: The Muckraking Life of Charles Edward Russell* (Palgrave Macmillan, 2003).

"The experiences": Elting E. Morison, ed., *The Letters of Theodore Roosevelt*, vol. V, *The Big Stick, 1905–1907* (Harvard University Press, 1952), 176.

76   "One feels": Quoted in Suk Bong Suh, *Upton Sinclair and "The Jungle": A Study of American Literature, Society, and Culture* (Seoul National University, 1997), 89.

"I am going to do my share": Quoted in ibid., 74. A useful recent biography of Sinclair is Anthony Arthur, *Radical Innocent: Upton Sinclair* (Random House, 2006).

"blood and guts": Quoted in Suh, *Upton Sinclair*, 87.

77   "seriously embarrassed": Arthur, *Radical Innocent*, 70. According to Arthur, Sinclair's book got a boost when, a few weeks after publication, an attorney for Armour descended upon the Doubleday offices and invited Frank Doubleday to lunch, ostensibly to discuss the possibility of buying advertising in *World's Work*. The rule about free lunches never proved so true. In exchange for advertising dollars, the attorney explained, Armour wanted Doubleday and Page to curb their support and publicity for the novel. Frank Doubleday was infuriated by the "unbounded cheek" of the suggestion. "Of all the moral degenerates that I ever saw, he was the worst," fumed the publisher. Doubleday had not been particularly interested in *The Jungle* and certainly not in Upton Sinclair (a "wild man," according to Double-

day), but the bribery offer turned indifference into a desire to fight Armour. See Arthur, *Radical Innocent*, 71.

"I have such awful times": Morison, ed., *Letters of Theodore Roosevelt*, vol. V, 140.

"Personally": Ibid., 179.

"charitable view": Ibid., 190.

78 "merely perfunctory investigation": Ibid., 176. Roosevelt wrote the letter after he'd requested Wilson to investigate; the investigators arrived in Chicago on March 10.

"My dear Mr. Sinclair": Ibid., 208, 209.

79 "the apostles of sensationalism": Quoted in Young, *Pure Food*, 239.

80 "not if Little Willie": Quoted in John Braeman, "The Square Deal in Action: A Case Study in the Growth of the 'National Police Power,'" in *Change and Continuity in Twentieth-Century America*, ed. John Braeman, Robert H. Bremner, and Everett Walters (Ohio State University Press, 1964), 61.

In 1908, Americans consumed: Statistics are in U.S. Department of Commerce, Bureau of the Census, *Historical Statistics of the United States, Colonial Times to 1970* (Government Printing Office, 1975), 1:329–30. Also published as H. Doc. 93–78-pt.1, 93d Cong., 1st sess.

81 "We make great outcry": Emerson Hough, "Owners of America VIII: The Swifts," *Cosmopolitan* 46 (March 1909): 406–7.

"a hundred and one million": Quoted in "Armour Official's Statement Before House Committee," *Fort Worth Star-Telegram*, July 9, 1916, p. 11.

"We shall have": Quoted in David B. Danbom, *The Resisted Revolution: Urban America and the Industrialization of Agriculture, 1900–1930* (Iowa State University Press, 1979), 102.

83 "sedition and criminal anarchy": Quoted in Linda J. Bradley and Barbara D. Merino, "Stuart Chase: A Radical CPA and the Meat Packing Investigation, 1917–1918," *Business and Economic History* 23, no. 1 (Fall 1994): 197. For the socialist leanings of FTC staff members, see the memorandum reprinted as Appendix II in David Gordon, "The Beef Trust: Antitrust Policy and the Meat Packing Industry, 1902–1922" (Ph.D. dissertation, Claremont Graduate School, 1983), 339–40.

84 Armour's post-decree fortunes: The best summary of Armour & Company's post-founder history is in N.S.B. Gras and Henrietta M. Larson, *Casebook in American Business History* (F. S. Crofts & Co., 1939), 623–44.

Consider the breakfast cereal: For the cereal examples, see E.H.S. Bailey, "When Does a Food Become a Luxury?" *Popular Science* 77 (December 1910): 592.

85 "It is not so much": "Breakfast Foods," *The Independent* 61 (December 27, 1906): 1577, 1578.

86 "herald[ed] the collapse": "Explosion of a Fundamental Fallacy in Diet," *Current Literature* 43 (September 1907): 327–28.

"proteid (meat) poisoning": Stoddard Goodhue, "Adding Years to Your Life," *Cosmopolitan* 55 (September 1913): 434, 438.

"gout, rheumatism": Mary Davies Swartz, "How Much Meat?" *Good Housekeeping* 50, no. 1 (January 1910): 108.

"not essential": C. F. Langworthy, "Cheese and Other Substitutes for Meat in the Diet," in U.S. Department of Agriculture, *Yearbook of the Department of Agriculture 1910*, 359, 369. Langworthy's report appeared as part of the USDA's annual *Yearbook*, a volume watched closely by home economists, nutritionists, and teachers, who carried its messages into classrooms around the country.

"We have a great surplus": Herbert Hoover, "Food and the War," in U.S. Department of Agriculture, United States Food Administration Women's Committee, Council of National Defense, *The Day's Food in War and Peace* (United States Food Administration, [1918]), 11. The document was intended for use as a "textbook" that the government issued in hopes of teaching Americans how to restrict their diets without losing flavor or nutritive value.

87 "incontrovertible evidence": Quoted in Michael Ackerman, "Interpreting the Newer Knowledge of Nutrition: Science, Interests, and Values in the Making of Dietary Advice in the United States, 1915–1965" (Ph.D. dissertation, University of Virginia, 2005), 59–60.

"Feed your body vitamines": W. A. Freehoff, "Feed Your Body Vitamines," *Illustrated World* 31 (June 1919): 499.

"carefully balanced": Ellwood Hendrick, "Vitamines: New Light on the Mysteries of Nutrition," *Harper's Magazine* 142 (March 1921): 495.

88 "unsuited": Quoted in "Advocate's Fight for Frankfurter Progressing," *Butchers' Advocate and Market Journal* 82, no. 10 (December 15, 1926): 9.

"This is an open attack": "New York School Board Attacks Frankfurters," *Butchers' Advocate and Market Journal* 82, no. 9 (December 8, 1926): 11.

"puts us back ten years": Quoted in "Advocate's Fight for Frankfurter Progressing," 9.

"wholesome, appetizing": B. F. McCarthy, "Frankfurters as Wholesome Food," *Butchers' Advocate and Market Journal* 82, no. 16 (January 26, 1927): 9.

89 "shabby mane and beard": "How 'Meat for Health Week' Was Put Over," *National Provisioner* 69, no. 2 (July 14, 1923): 23.

"the nation's best brains": "Experiment Station to Aid in Research Work on Meat," *Meat and Live Stock Digest* 5, no. 9 (April 1925): 2.

4. FACTORIES, FARMERS, AND CHICKENS

90 "shot": Quoted in "An Interview with Jesse Jewell," *Broiler Industry* 22, no. 3 (March 1959): 8. The only substantive account of Jewell's early years is in Gordon Sawyer, *The Agribusiness Poultry Industry: A History of Its Development* (Exposition Press, 1971), 86–89; but I also relied on interviews with Jewell in poultry and farming trade magazines. I pieced together early interest in broiler making in Georgia and the South from newspapers and government documents, but a dissertation that focuses on Georgia is Monica Richmond Gisifoli, "From Cotton Farmers to Poultry Growers: The Rise of Industrial Agriculture in Upcountry Georgia, 1914–1960" (Ph.D. dissertation, Columbia University, 2007). Another valuable source is chapter 4 of Lu Ann Jones, "Re-visioning the Countryside: Southern Women, Rural Reform, and the Farm Economy in the Twentieth Century" (Ph.D. dissertation, University of North Carolina, 1996).

93 "sucked the food": Quoted in James H. Shideler, *Farm Crisis, 1919–1923* (University of California Press, 1957), 20.

95 "a cheap and abundant food-supply": W. O. Atwater, "The Food-Supply of the Future," *Century* 43, no. 1 (November 1891): 111.

96 "last great nest of chaos": Deborah Fitzgerald, *Every Farm a Factory: The Industrial Ideal in American Agriculture* (Yale University Press, 2003), 28.

"When a nation depends": Ernest Hamlin Abbott, "Editorial Correspondence from Washington," *The Outlook,* February 8, 1922, p. 211.

"The wars of the future": Quoted in Danbom, *Resisted Revolution,* 42.

"industrial agriculture": Frank App, "The Industrialization of Agriculture," *Annals of the American Academy of Political and Social Science* 142, no. 231 (March 1929): 232.

100 "green-strucks": U.S. Department of Agriculture, "Marketing Poultry," *Farmers' Bulletin,* no. 1377 (1924), p. 24. There are no substantive histories of the chicken as part of the American diet, or of the early efforts to raise chickens for meat. My account is based on extensive reading in poultry trade journals.

101 "Under the machine system": Franklin Morton, "Feeding Poultry by Machinery," *Technical World* 7, no. 6 (February 1907): 643. This magazine was published by the Armour Institute of Technology, founded by the Armour family. Philip Armour had a long history of encouraging education in general and technical education in particular. A short but useful summary of other meatpackers' failed forays into poultry is "Chicken Meat in the Diet," *National Provisioner* 30, no. 26 (June 25, 1904): 22.

"it remain[ed] with others": "Kosher Killing Poultry," *New York Produce and American Creamery* 62, no. 25 (October 20, 1926): 1024.

"Of all the toothsome": The Philly quotes are from [M. K. Boyer], "'Philadelphia' Poultry," *New York Poultry Review and American Creamery* 18 (February 19, 1913): 796; and P. T. Woods, "Producing High Quality Chicken Meat," *Reliable Poultry Journal* 7, no. 10 (December 1910): 1046.

102 "swell spreads": John H. Robinson, *Broilers and Roasters: The Specialties of the Market Poultrymen* (Farm-Poultry Publishing Co., 1905), 6. Robinson was a knowledgeable observer of and prolific writer about the early-twentieth-century commercial poultry industry.

"Hotel men and restaurant keepers": "New York's Poultry Needs," *New York Produce Review and American Creamery* 69, no. 9 (January 1, 1930): 430.

But size mattered, too: This observation is based on comments in John H. Robinson, "Laying the Foundations of a Great Broiler Industry," *Reliable Poultry Journal* 34, no. 9 (November 1927): 534.

"juicy, milk-fed": M. E. Pennington, "The Handling of Dressed Poultry a Thousand Miles from the Market," in U.S. Department of Agriculture, *Yearbook of the Department of Agriculture 1912,* 286.

103 "A Chicken in Every Pot": Advertisement, "A Chicken in Every Pot," *New York Times,* October 30, 1928, p. 23.

Bankers encouraged these projects: There is a great deal of information about the gravy trains in regional newspapers, but also see pp. 134–35 of Jones, "Re-visioning the Countryside."

"scrubs": "Poultry Raising Rapidly Growing," *Augusta (GA) Chronicle*, March 6, 1924, p. A7.

104 Other subsidized research: For the role of chickens in research, I am indebted to William Boyd, "Making Meat: Science, Technology, and American Poultry Production," *Technology and Culture* 42, no. 4 (October 2001): 631–64. Also see, for example, F. B. Hutt, "Research with a Hen," *Science* n.s. 78, no. 2029 (November 17, 1933): 449–52.

105 "phenomenal": D. C. Kennard, "The Trend Toward Confinement in Poultry Management," *Poultry Science* 8 (October–November 1928): 23.

"commercialized production": [Oscar B. Hornbeck], "Poultry Standardization," *New York Produce Review and American Creamery* 62, no. 24 (October 13, 1926): 962.

107 "and have a few dollars left": M. M. Daugherty, "Short History of the Broiler Industry," in *Agricultural Extension Service Pamphlet*, no. 15 (University of Delaware, 1944), unpaginated.

When Jewell signed contracts: For the wartime stipulations, see Gisifoli, "From Cotton Farmers to Poultry Growers," 112–14.

108 "arranged to help": Quoted in ibid., 114.

109 "serious bottleneck": From the unpaginated foreword to H. H. Mitchell, "Is Animal Protein an Essential Constituent of Swine and Poultry Rations?" *Ninth Report of the Committee on Animal Nutrition of the NRC, May 1943* (National Research Council, 1943). Also published as NRC's Circular 117.

"to repeat feeding trials": Noble Clark, "The Responsibility of Research Workers in Livestock Production in the War Program," *Journal of Animal Science* 2 (1943): 85.

110 "The ultimate objective": Quoted in Nicolas Rasmussen, "Plant Hormones in War and Peace: Science, Industry, and Government in the Development of Herbicides in 1940s America," *Isis* 92, no. 2 (June 2001): 295.

"evolutionary changes": "Some Results of Colchicine Injections," *Science* 92 (July 26, 1940): 80. Also see William L. Laurence, "Finds Twin Stars Change in Circling," *New York Times*, December 31, 1940, p. 17; and "Drug Speeds Chicken's Growth," *Science Digest* 12, no. 1 (July 1942): 72.

In the late 1940s: For the anemia research, see Edward L. Rickes et al., "Crystalline Vitamin B_{12}," *Science* 107 (April 16, 1948): 396; and "New Vitamin from Liver," *Science News Letter* 53, no. 17 (April 24, 1948): 259.

111 "the lid clear off": "They've Doubled Gains with New Drugs," *Successful Farming* 48, no. 6 (June 1950): 45.

"[n]ever again": "Antibiotics Now Proved in Hog and Poultry Ratios, They're the Biggest Feeding News in 40 Years!" *Successful Farming* 49, no. 3 (March 1951): 33. Other useful accounts are in "Drug Promotes Growth," *Science News Letter* 57 (April 22, 1950): 243; and "New Vitamin from Liver." The B_{12} news overshadowed another announcement made almost simultaneously. A scientist working at a corporate laboratory in Indiana had isolated what he believed to be APF. The man's employer manufactured animal feed that contained soybean plants and dried brewery wastes. When hens ate the stuff, they laid healthier eggs, and their chicks flourished and "grew rapidly." The scientist speculated that the brewery waste contained a microorganism that facilitated growth. See the reports in William L. Laurence, "New Vitamin Aids Battle on Anemia," *New York Times*, August 26, 1948, p. 23; William L. Laurence, "Discoveries Concerning Vitamin B-12 Open New Fields in the Science of Nutrition," *New York Times*, December 5, 1948, p. E9; and Waldemar Kaempffert, "Clinical Advances That Aid Medicine Are Brought to Light by the Chemists," *New York Times*, September 25, 1949, p. E9.

112 "pave the way": Quoted in Nick Cullather, "The Foreign Policy of the Calorie," *American Historical Review* 112, no. 2 (April 2007): 363. For a superb assessment of the long march toward food-based diplomacy, see chapters 1 and 2 of Cullather's *The Hungry World: America's Cold War Battle Against Poverty in Asia* (Harvard University Press, 2010).

"moving forward": Lauren Soth, "America's No. 1 Farm Problem," *Successful Farming* 49, no. 3 (March 1951): 47, 63.

113 One USDA analyst: See "Beef Production in U.S. Undergoes Marked Changes," *Meat and Live Stock Digest* 3, no. 5 (December 1922): 4. Also see the analysis in W. C. Davis, "Methods and Practices of Retailing Meat," in U.S. Department of Agriculture, *Department Bulletin*, no. 1441, 1926.

"[t]ime-saving, convenience": U.S. House of Representatives, Joint Commission of Agricultural Inquiry, *The Agricultural Crisis and Its Causes*, H. Rep. 408, 67th Cong., part IV, pp. 3, 4.

"one head or 1/7,680 of a car": "Distribution of Perishable Commodities in the Chicago Metropolitan Area," *University Journal of Business* 4, no. 2 (April 1926): 163. For the study of and typical comments about inexperienced grocers, see A. H. Fenske, "'Too Many Retailers,'" *National Provisioner* 69, no. 18 (November 2, 1923): 52; also see Day Monroe and Lenore Monroe Stratton, *Food Buying and Our Markets* (1925; reprint, M. Barrows & Company, 1929).

114 These inefficiencies: On the history of the chain stores, see especially Tracey Deutsch, *Building a Housewife's Paradise: Gender, Politics, and American Grocery Stores in the Twentieth Century* (University of North Carolina Press, 2010); and Richard S. Tedlow, *New and Improved: The Story of Mass Marketing in America* (Basic Books, 1990). But also see Susan Strasser, *Satisfaction Guaranteed: The Making of the American Mass Market* (Pantheon Books, 1989); and Gene Arlin German, "The Dynamics of Food Retailing, 1900–1975" (Ph.D. dissertation, Cornell University, 1978). For A&P in particular, see Marc Levinson, *The Great A&P and the Struggle for Small Business in America* (Hill and Wang, 2011); and William I. Walsh, *The Rise and Decline of the Great Atlantic and Pacific Tea Company* (Lyle Stuart, 1986).

115 "[c]hain store merchandising": "Merchandizing [*sic*] Packaged Meats Without Freezing," *National Provisioner* 82, no. 16 (April 19, 1930): 21.

"It is now possible": Howard C. Pierce, "Looking Forward in Marketing Poultry and Eggs," *United States Egg and Poultry Magazine* 37, no. 3 (March 1931): 67. Pierce made his remarks to a gathering of poultry producers, but his point applied to the chain's policy for all meats.

"The packaging of coffee": Gove Hambidge, "Meats in Packages," *Ladies' Home Journal* 46 (December 1929): 89.

"should be of no significance": Quoted in [John H. Cover], *Consumer Attitude Toward Packaging of Meats* (National Provisioner, 1930), 43.

116 "we've got to sell": Claude W. Gifford, "Are 'Chains' Dictating Your Prices?" *Farm Journal* 83 (June 1959): 33.

"This starts the price-cutting": Quoted in Howard H. Fogel, "What Retailers Say About Broilers," *Broiler Industry* 27, no. 1 (January 1964): 19, 20.

"See that batch": Quoted in Frederick G. Brownell, "Super Cows and Chickens," *American Magazine* 141 (June 1946): 110. For the USDA calculation, see "Improvement in Meat Chicken Astonishes Even the Experts," *American Egg and Poultry Review* 12 (April 1951): 36.

117 "Integration has made chicken": Quoted in Grant Cannon, "Vertical Integration," *Farm Quarterly* 12, no. 4 (Winter 1958): 90.

"cost-conscious": Quoted in Bernard F. Tobin and Henry B. Arthur, *Dynamics of Adjustment in the Broiler Industry* (Division of Research, Graduate School of Business Administration, Harvard University, 1964), 77.

118 "As a whole": Quoted in "Contract Farming: Brings Higher Income, Lower Prices," *Time*, February 3, 1958; accessed online.

"revolutionize the production": Quoted in Cannon, "Vertical Integration," 96.

120 "agriculture as an industry": All quotes are from John H. Davis and Ray A. Goldberg, *A Concept of Agribusiness* (Harvard University, 1957), 1, 22. Davis and Goldberg spread the blame for this shortsightedness, but they were particularly critical of organizations like the American Farm Bureau, whose leaders, the two argued, insisted on treating agriculture as an independent economic sector rather than as part of a larger whole.

5. "HOW CAN WE GO WRONG?"

123 "touch of the Old West": William M. Blair, "Broad Changes Sweep the Cattle Industry," *New York Times*, April 30, 1966, p. 12. For a detailed description of the feedlot operation, see "Feeding Cattle on a Grand Scale," *National Provisioner* 154, no. 8 (February 18, 1966): 20–21.

125 They also noted: For the experiment station research, see, for example, H. B. Osland, E. J. Maynard, and George E. Morton, *Colorado Fattening Rations for Cattle*, Bulletin 422, Colorado Experiment Station, Colorado State College, February 1936.

"During the 20s": Quoted in Walt Barnhart, *Kenny's Shoes: A Walk Through the Storied Life of the Remarkable Kenneth W. Monfort* (Infinity Publishing, 2008), 18. Barnhart relied in part on information from an unpublished 1971 document written by William Hartman. I was not able to obtain a copy of it.

126 "aggressive": Quoted in Bruce Wilkinson, "Warren and Ken Monfort Commercial Feeders of the Year," *Feedlot Management* 16, no. 2 (February 1974): 16.

By the end: For useful information about the early years of the feedlot, see Lynn Heinze, "Monfort Sees Cattle as World Food Buffer — Although Less Beef Consumption Likely, Cattle Have Future," *Greeley Tribune*, March 9, 1976, p. B-23.

127 "a slightly lower grade": Quoted in ibid. For meat consumption from

the fifties on, I used figures from Susan B. Carter, ed., *Historical Statistics of the United States: Earliest Times to the Present*, millennial ed. (Cambridge University Press, 2006), Table A212, pp. 160–61; the data is calculated in terms of retail weight.

"Our products are like cake mixes": Quoted in John A. McWethy, "Canned Meat: Steak, Pigs' Feet and Corned Beef Hash Rush in Tins to the Table," *Wall Street Journal*, April 13, 1953, p. 8.

129   "meat, vegetables and gravy": Ibid.

But in postwar America: Statistics are from "The Franchise Restaurant Boom . . . Big New Market for Beef," *Farm Journal* 93 (October 1969): B10–B11, B13. For McDonald's, see J. Anthony Lukas, "As American as a McDonald's Hamburger on the Fourth of July," *New York Times Magazine*, July 4, 1971, p. 22. The Mr. Steak example is from "Franchise Restaurant Boom."

130   But consider these numbers: For the fed-beef statistics, see Table 43, p. 88, in U.S. Department of Agriculture, Economic Research Service, *Cattle Feeding in the United States*, by Ronald A. Gustafson and Roy N. Van Arsdall, Economic Report no. 186, October 1970; and Table 1, p. 2, including the note for that table, in U.S. Department of Agriculture, Economic Research Service, *Cattle Feeding, 1962–89*, by Kenneth R. Krause, Agricultural Economic Report no. 642, April 1991. Many sources document the transformation from range to feedlot, but the most useful summaries are in the two reports mentioned as well as U.S. Department of Agriculture, Economics and Statistics Service, *Structural Change in Agriculture: The Experience for Broilers, Fed Cattle, and Processing Vegetables*, by Donn A. Reimund, J. Rod Martin, and Charles V. Moore, Technical Bulletin no. 1648, April 1981, pp. 15–29; and U.S. Department of Agriculture, Economics, Statistics, and Cooperatives Service, J. Rod Martin, "Beef," in *Another Revolution in U.S. Farming?* by Lyle P. Schertz et al., Agricultural Economic Report no. 441, December 1979, pp. 85–118.

"Just to raise the calves": Quoted in "Falling Market Hits Colorado's Steak Raisers," *Springfield (MA) Union*, April 15, 1952, p. 20.

Nor did Monfort: Information about the decline of the range is scattered among federal documents, but two good summaries of changing range use are U.S. Department of Agriculture, Agricultural Research Service, *Major Uses of Land in the United States: Summary for 1954*, Agriculture Information Bulletin no. 168, January 1957;

and U.S. Department of Agriculture, *Federal and State Rural Lands, 1950, with Special Reference to Grazing,* by R. D. Davidson, Circular 909, May 1952.

131 "lust": Bernard DeVoto, "Sacred Cows and Public Lands," *Harper's Magazine* 197 (July 1948): 55. The conflict of the 1940s is typically portrayed as one where ranchers sought to continue a longtime practice of engaging in land grabs, but the conflict was far more complicated. See Karen R. Merrill, *Public Lands and Political Meaning: Ranchers, the Government, and the Property Between Them* (University of California Press, 2002), especially 178–204.

132 "More of the growing period": Quoted in "Falling Market Hits Colorado's Steak Raisers," 20.
"across the mountains": William M. Blair, "Packers Battle Chain Stores in Marketing 'Revolution,'" *New York Times,* March 24, 1958, p. 42.

133 Consider the McDougal: For the McDougal operation, see "Look What's Happening to Cattle Feeding!" *Farm Journal* 79 (October 1955): 39. For Tovrea, see Charles R. Koch, "Super-Sized Feed Lot," *Farm Quarterly* 12, no. 1 (Spring 1957): 60–63, 136–43.

134 "beef factory": "Big Beef Factory Turns Out the Best Steaks," *Lowell (MA) Sun,* December 10, 1950, p. 17.
He was an imposing: The description of Ken Monfort is based on information in Barnhart, *Kenny's Shoes.*

135 "a heck of an asset to the industry": Quoted in "Neighborhood Bully?" *Feedlot Management* 16, no. 2 (February 1974): 27.
"I can walk into that town": Quoted in Orville Howard, "Feeder Cattle Eat Way to $250-Million Industry," *Amarillo Globe-Times,* November 28, 1962, p. 2.
"We used to have to ship": Quoted in "Look What's Happening," 221.
The manager: The Amarillo Club example is in Jack Hanicke, "Range Change: Ranchers Fatten More Cattle at Home, Using Cheap Grain Sorghums," *Wall Street Journal,* February 13, 1959, p. 1.

136 "Our feature": Ibid.
"impossible": The packer is quoted in U.S. House of Representatives, Committee on Agriculture, *Prohibit Feeding of Livestock by Certain Packers: Hearings Before the Subcommittee on Livestock and Feed Grains of the Committee on Agriculture,* 89th Cong., 2d sess., 233.

137 "I'm getting out": All quoted in Victor J. Hillery, "Steak vs. Controls: Midwest Cattlemen Cut Meat Output to Grow Corn — for Storage Bins," *Wall Street Journal,* April 16, 1953, p. 1.

"No question": Quoted in "Look What's Happening," 221.

"the small, one-or-two": Quoted in Hanicke, "Range Change," 1.

"only one aim": Quoted in Committee on Agriculture, *Prohibit Feeding of Livestock*, 232.

138 "As in most any business": Quoted in "Look What's Happening," 38.

"beef feeding on a factory basis": Ibid.

"less nourishing": "Why Pork Is Losing Popularity," *Farm Journal* 80 (December 1956): 123.

"more of a gamble": Quoted in Albert R. Karr, "Gains from a Glut: Federal Grain Storage Payments Lead Farmers to Cut Other Activities," *Wall Street Journal*, September 22, 1958, p. 1.

139 "Inherent in all this": "Standardization Comes to the Farm," *Business Week*, March 21, 1959, p. 167.

"This is the beginning": Quoted in "Contract Farming: Brings Higher Income, Lower Prices," *Time*, February 3, 1958; accessed online.

"If you don't want": Quoted in William M. Blair, "Hog Raisers Eye a Contract Plan," *New York Times*, March 2, 1958, pp. 1, 69. For typical coverage of contract hog farming see "Contract Farming: Brings Higher Income, Lower Prices"; "Is the Hog Business Headed for a Shake-up?" *Farm Journal* 81 (April 1957): 30–31, 186, 190; and "Hog Contracts: How Near Your Door?" *Farm Journal* 82 (February 1958): 35, 132.

140 "happy": Fred Knoop, "No Privacy in the Rumen," *Farm Quarterly* 3, no. 4 (Winter 1948): 40, 42. Over the next few years, bovine nutritionists exchanged flank holes for artificial rumens.

Burroughs's work with corncobs: Garst's experiments were reported in a number of farm journals. For an example see Knoop, "No Privacy," 43, 124. The notion of "dynamic" feed rations as a way to maximize growth is explored in Alan I Marcus, "The Newest Knowledge of Nutrition: Wise Burroughs, DES, and Modern Meat," *Agricultural History* 67, no. 3 (Summer 1993): 66–85. The details of Burroughs's research are in Marcus, "Newest Knowledge," especially 71–72.

142 "female feathers": "Chemists in Convention," *Time*, September 20, 1943; accessed online.

143 "poisoned": Quoted in "Effemination," *Time*, April 16, 1951; accessed online. A New Jersey court ruled that the man, John Stepnowski, was eligible for workers' compensation, but for no other damages. A summary of that ruling and a related appeal by Stepnowski is in Stepnowski *v.* Specific Pharmaceuticals, Inc., 18 N.J. Super. 495 (1952).

"devirilizing effect": Quoted in Nancy Langston, "The Retreat from

Precaution: Regulating Diethylstilbestrol (DES), Endocrine Disruptors, and Environmental Health," *Environmental History* 13 (January 2008): 50. The company in question was Arapahoe Chemicals, Inc., of Colorado. The owner wrote to the FDA to express his
fears about the drug. An FDA official responded by saying, in effect, that the agency knew nothing and could do nothing and suggested that the owner contact the United States Public Health Service. It's not clear how the situation ended. The exchange of letters is
detailed in Langston, "Retreat from Precaution," note 45, pp. 63 and
64.

"cut out a carcass": Quoted in "Stilbestrol-Fed Cattle: How They're
Selling Now," *Farm Journal* 79 (August 1955): 16.

"My family": Quoted in Chester Charles, "Stilbestrol," *Farm Quarterly* 10, no. 1 (Spring 1955): 49.

"fortify": Ibid., 48.

"become the bright hope": Ibid.

144 "sweater girls": Ibid., 49.

"Amazing?": John A. Rohlf, "Two Million Head on Stilbestrol!" *Farm
Journal* 79 (March 1955): 38.

"complete loss": Cameron Hervey, "Barnyards Without Mud," *Farm
Journal* 73 (March 1949): 20.

145 "You can't *afford*": Ibid. Studies like this one explain why researchers
in the 1940s equated confinement with keeping livestock on a paved
"drylot." Also see "Mechanical Pastures," *Farm Quarterly* 10, no. 2
(Summer 1955): 104; and Dick Braun, "Pasture or Drylot: Which Is
Cheaper?" *Farm Journal* 79 (June 1955): 32, 118. As this book was
being written, I learned that historian James McWilliams was working on a project that would place confinement's roots in the nineteenth century. I was not able to read his manuscript.

Two Indiana brothers: See "Cost-Conscious Feedlot," *Farm Quarterly* 15, no. 3 (Autumn 1960): 62–63, 128–29, 130.

"He's got what I call": All quoted in George A. Montgomery, "Weather
Can't Hurt This Feeder," *Farm Journal* 84 (October 1960): 38, 40.

146 "We were getting killed": Quoted in Iowa Development Commission,
Agricultural Division, *Beef Confinement Can Pay in Iowa*, 1974, p. 18.

"I can't afford": Quoted in Braun, "Pasture or Drylot," 33.

"I analyzed my work schedule": Quoted in "Automation of a Hog
Farm," *Farm Quarterly* 14, no. 4 (Winter 1960): 79.

147 An Iowa farmer: The dysentery example is from J. L. Anderson, *In-*

dustrializing the Corn Belt: Agriculture, Technology, and Environment, 1945-1972 (Northern Illinois University Press, 2009), 94.

Confinement also enhanced: I found these and many other examples in midcentury agricultural and farm magazines.

148 "technical assistance": Blair, "Hog Raisers Eye a Contract Plan," 69. For the rental agreement, see Ovid Bay, "Now They're Leasing Hog Breeding Herds," *Farm Journal* 82 (March 1958): 39, 72. For other examples see "Pig Hatcheries," *Farm Quarterly* 6, no. 2 (Summer 1951): 28–29, 94, 96, 98; Dayle Wahlert, "'I'll Raise the Hogs'—'I'll Raise the Corn,'" *Successful Farming* 56, no. 4 (April 1958): 50–51, 110–12; Dick Seim, "One Way for Family Farms to Stay in Hogs," *Farm Journal* 85 (November 1961): 34–35, 67–68; and John F. Hughes, "Does Multiple Farrowing Pay?" *Farm Quarterly* 12, no. 1 (Spring 1957): 44–45, 99–102.

"You don't have to go": Quoted in "Half the Work Twice the Hogs," *Farm Journal* 87 (June 1963): 50F. The connection between his sons' plans and the switch is implied in the text.

"more power, more interest": Quoted in John Harvey, "What Farmers Like and Don't Like About Confinement Hog Setups," *Successful Farming* 64 (July 1966): 41.

"It boils down to": Quoted in Iowa Development Commission, *Beef Confinement Can Pay*, 5.

149 "You need some kind": Quoted in Dick Braun, "Clean Hog Lots with a Pump," *Farm Journal* 82 (December 1958): 34.

"float[ed]": Ibid.

"hardly a whiff": Ray Dankenbring and Ovid Bay, "Lagoons — Everybody's Building 'Em!" *Farm Journal* 84 (November 1960): 38.

"County health officials": Quoted in Ovid Bay, "How to Build and Use a Lagoon," *Farm Journal* 86 (May 1962): 60F.

"just pull[ed] the plug": Quoted in ibid.

"How stupid": See the letter from B. E. Burger in *Farm Journal* 85 (March 1961): 20.

150 "You can call it a lagoon": Quoted in "Lagoons Aren't Magic but They Can Save You Work," *Farm Quarterly* 18, no. 3 (Fall 1963): 48.

"faced all the problems": Ibid. The calculations are from "The Big Fuss Over Lagoons," *Farm Journal* 88 (April 1964): 57.

"You've got a stick": All quoted in John Russell, "Manure Odors Can Land You in Court!" *Farm Journal* 89 (August 1965): 19.

"caught in the middle": Ralph Sanders, "Animal Wastes — Pollution — Your Problem, Too," *Successful Farming* 68, no. 11 (October 1970): 34.

151 "If you were [an employer]": All quoted in Marc Newton, "Feed Lot Park Proposed," *Greeley Tribune*, May 10, 1969, p. 1.

"no question": Quoted in Ralph E. Winter, "Antipollution Laws Force Livestock Men to Devise Ways to Collect, Use Manure," *Wall Street Journal*, March 5, 1974, p. 38. For a useful look at how the Clean Water Act affected livestock operations, see John H. Martin Jr., "The Clean Water Act and Animal Agriculture," *Journal of Environmental Quality* 26 (1997): 1198–1203.

6. THE VACUUM AT THE TOP

153 "at the mercy": Quoted in U.S. House of Representatives, Committee on Agriculture, *Prohibit Feeding of Livestock by Certain Packers: Hearings Before the Subcommittee on Livestock and Feed Grains of the Committee on Agriculture*, 89th Cong., 2d sess., 229.

154 "Most of the big packers": Quoted in Heinze, "Monfort Sees Cattle as World Food Buffer," B-23.

"legal hassles": Quoted in ibid.

The slaughterhouse that opened: For the plant, see "Light Is Built into Colorado On-Line Beef Plant," *National Provisioner* 143, no. 1 (July 2, 1960): 17, 19.

155 "When we opened": Quoted in Jim Hitch, "Monfort Pack, Union Reach Agreement," *Greeley Tribune*, February 23, 1965, p. 18.

The second factor: For the loss of byproducts, see John A. McWethy, "Meat & Synthetics: The Rise of Man-Made Materials Hurts Packers' By-Products Business," *Wall Street Journal*, January 3, 1953, pp. 1, 3.

156 "was something less": Quoted in U.S. House, *Prohibit Feeding of Livestock*, 229.

157 Every step drove up the final retail price: For the study, see A. T. Kearney & Company, *The Search for a Thousand Million Dollars: Cost Reduction Opportunities in the Transportation and Distribution of Grocery Products* (National Association of Food Chains, 1966). A summary of the meat-related contents is in "Food Distribution Survey Proposes Cutback in Beef Handling Steps," *National Provisioner* 155, no. 19 (November 5, 1966): 18–20.

In Chicago: In the early 1960s, the Jewel grocery chain sued the meat cutters' union, arguing that the rule constituted restraint of trade. The case wound from district court to appeals and finally to the Supreme Court; in 1965, that court determined that the six o'clock clause was a work rule and did not violate the Sherman Antitrust Act. In 1977, the union agreed to abandon the rule and allow Chicagoans to buy fresh meat after six.

158 "vehicle for selling services": Quoted in "Packing Industry Lags Behind Other Foods in Many of Its Market Concepts," *National Provisioner* 151, no. 15 (October 10, 1964): 56.

"automated electronic beef": "Cattle Feeding, Slaughtering Makes Future Bright," *Greeley Tribune*, April 3, 1970, p. 32.

"the only way": "Where Packing Takes On a New Dimension," *National Provisioner* 156, no. 5 (February 4, 1967): 16–17.

159 "LBJ hat": Peter H. Prugh, "Beefing Up Profit," *Wall Street Journal*, May 4, 1966, p. 1.

"Andy's a genius": Quoted in ibid., 22.

"DENISON, IOWA": Advertisement in *Wall Street Journal*, April 9, 1956, p. 9.

160 "A farmer a day": "Good Investment," *Denison (IA) Bulletin*, March 25, 1960, p. 2B. The history of Anderson's first Denison venture demonstrates his resistance to unions. As at the Monfort plant, the men employed at CCPC were local and unskilled. But during the plant's first year of operation, a field representative with the United Packinghouse Workers of America persuaded the men that they could and should earn the same high wages paid at big-city packing plants like those owned by Armour and Swift. By a one-vote margin, the Denison men agreed to allow the UPWA to represent them. When the employees' original contract came up for renewal in the summer of 1959, negotiations turned ugly. The union demanded that employees be paid according to union job classifications, whether they possessed the skills attached to those classifications or not. Anderson pointed out that most of CCPC's workers were unskilled and inexperienced; the union representative offered to bring in skilled union butchers from Omaha or Sioux City — if management would agree to pay higher wages. Anderson was adamant: he wanted to employ local people and Crawford County Packing Company, still a new venture, could not pay such wages. He explained that he'd worked for packers in the 1930s for less than 40 cents an hour to "help put them in the position" that eventually enabled them to pay hefty union-scale wages. He also noted that men who had started at the plant for a dollar an hour were making as much as $2.30 an hour and enjoyed a guaranteed thirty-six-hour workweek plus paid vacations and insurance. Anderson pleaded for understanding. "I

must have this training and organizing period to develop not only production but buying and processing, and everything that makes such an industry successful." The union, he argued, would "strangle" the company's future. All quotes from "No Agreement on Contract Reached by Union, CCPC," *Denison [IA] Bulletin*, September 4, 1959, p. 1.

The negotiations soon collapsed (aided by what was presumably an intentional bit of business on Anderson's part: he left town on a two-week vacation). The union negotiator announced plans for a strike, retracted that statement, then issued another call for a strike. Given the uncertainty, CCPC's staff had no choice but to stop buying hogs: there was no guarantee that the company's line crews would show up to slaughter and process the animals. In early October, employees announced that they wanted to sever ties with the UPWA, organize their own union, and negotiate directly with management. The UPWA lobbed one legal obstacle after another at the locals in an effort to prevent decertification. In January 1960, the Denison workforce was finally permitted to decertify and soon after filed papers for their own union. A few days later, Andy Anderson resigned and began laying the groundwork for IBP.

161 "We don't believe": Quoted in Prugh, "Beefing Up Profit," 1.

"Think Money": Information here from ibid.; Margaret D. Pacey, "Everything but the Moo," *Barron's National Business and Financial Weekly* 40 (July 22, 1968): 3; and Kenneth C. Crowe and Michael Under, "Iowa Beef's Money Motto Out; but Message Remains," *Des Moines Register*, April 22, 1973, p. 6B. The latter article originally appeared in *Newsday*.

By the end of the first year: For announcements of these efforts and company progress, see "Over 200 Stockholders Hear of IBP Progress Monday," *Denison (IA) Bulletin*, December 22, 1961, p. 1; "IBP Killing 120 per Hour," *Denison (IA) Bulletin*, September 1, 1961, p. 1; and Ed Heins, "Big Union Gaining at Meat Plants," *Des Moines Register*, August 10, 1964, p. 3.

162 "chains of history": Quoted in Arlo Jacobson, "IBP Tells Grocers: Beef Carcasses 'Old-Fashioned,'" *Des Moines Sunday Register*, December 5, 1971, p. 1F.

"We're trying to revolutionize": Quoted in Seth S. King, "Union Unrest Splits Plains Town," *New York Times*, December 17, 1969, p. 45.

"business as we pursue it": Quoted in Jonathan Kwitny, "Troubled

Packer: Iowa Beef's History of Shady Characters Far Outruns '74 Case," *Wall Street Journal,* December 17, 1976, p. 1. Currier Holman has come to personify IBP's evils, but he is frustratingly difficult to wrestle into the company's history. In the late 1960s and early 1970s, he identified himself as an IBP cofounder, but in the mid- to late 1970s, he described himself as its founder. He claimed that he designed the company's plants. He claimed he'd played for Knute Rockne at Notre Dame. He claimed, as it turned out, many things that, as near as can be ascertained, are false. He attended but did not graduate from Notre Dame. He tried out for the school's football team but apparently never played in a game. There is ample evidence that Andy Anderson, not Holman, designed IBP's plants. As to Holman's claim that he cofounded the company: Holman is not mentioned in any of the local news coverage of IBP's early days in Denison. Not during the fundraising stage, when Andy Anderson raced from meeting to meeting, persuading bankers, farmers, and veterans to support the venture. Not during the construction phase, when architects, engineers, and equipment suppliers routinely described Anderson as the brains behind the plant designs. Not as the company neared its first day of operation, when extensive local press coverage mentioned and identified foremen, managers, and executive officers — but not Currier Holman. The first indication of Holman's involvement dates to December 1961, when a local paper described him as a member of the board of directors; by that time he was also managing the plant, apparently a step up from his first job at the company: head cattle buyer.

Here is what I learned about Holman (other than the fact that he played loose with facts): He grew up in Sioux City, where he worked for a time in a Swift packing plant, first on the floor hauling sheep guts, and then in the office. But most of his pre-IBP meat career was spent as a cattle buyer. According to Jonathan Kwitny, a *Wall Street Journal* reporter who covered the IBP conspiracy and Mafia scandal, and who wrote the 1979 *Vicious Circles: The Mafia in the Marketplace,* Anderson and Holman met each other in Sioux City sometime before Anderson moved to Denison. By that time (the late 1950s), Holman was operating a cattle-buying business. Holman told Kwitny that the two men often discussed the idea of building a revolutionary new meatpacking plant. But Holman relayed these events nearly twenty years after the fact, and as near as I can tell, Kwitny did not verify that information with Anderson. Kwitny interviewed Holman's friends and family from the Sioux City area, and according to them, Holman was annoyed by the way union recalcitrance drained the profits out of meatpacking and determined to build a modern, and presumably nonunion, plant. That may be the case, and presumably it's true that Holman and Anderson knew each other before Anderson moved to Denison. But I found evidence that in May 1960, when Anderson was laying plans and raising money for his new company, Holman was still living in Sioux City and, according to family and friends, working seven days a week as a cattle buyer. In other words, I found nothing to indicate that he cofounded IBP (except in the sense that he was hired before the doors opened). (I did not, I should add, attempt to persuade what is now IBP to let me look at early company records. If those still exist, they may tell a different story.)

163 "I never bribed anybody": Quoted in "Rough Riders," *Forbes* 113 (June 1974): 66.

"victim of the extortionate practices": Quoted in "Iowa Beef and Its Cochairman Convicted for Plotting to Bribe Union and Retailers," *Wall Street Journal,* October 8, 1974, p. 4. Holman's saga, at times tragic, at others comical, was detailed in newspaper and meat industry trade journals and in Jonathan Kwitny, *Vicious Circles: The Mafia in the Marketplace* (W. W. Norton & Company, 1979).

Holman avoided jail: According to Jonathan Kwitny, the *Wall Street Journal* reporter who tracked the IBP case and wrote about the Mafia's involvement in the food industry, after the ruling, IBP continued to make payments to union officials on the East Coast, payments that the company made no attempt to conceal.

"ancient and obsolete plants": Quoted in U.S. House, *Prohibit Feeding of Livestock,* 229. For the Armour operation, see Jerrold Lanes, "Meat-Packing Progress," *Barron's National Business and Financial Weekly* 42, no. 7 (February 12, 1962): 18.

164 "people would stand waiting": Quoted in Kwitny, *Vicious Circles,* 282.

"Turbo-chill": Dana L. Thomas, "More Meat on the Bones: The Lean Years May Be Over for the Nation's Packers," *Barron's National Business and Financial Weekly* 39, no. 30 (July 27, 1959): 15.

"We're going to spend": Quoted in Richard F. Janssen, "Packers on the Move: Meat Concerns Step Up Outlays on New Plants. Aim to Fatten Profits," *Wall Street Journal,* July 5, 1961, p. 1. Useful information about this situation is in [Arval L. Erikson], "Change Has Been

Key Word in Industry Except for Consistently Low Earnings," *National Provisioner* 147, no. 14 (October 6, 1962): 52–54.

"moved from very big": Quoted in Harold B. Meyers, "For the Old Meatpackers, Things Are Tough All Over," *Fortune* 79 (February 1969): 92.

165 "Suppose the moonshot fails": Quoted in Paul Ingrassia, "Repackaged Packer: As Fresh-Meat Business Grows Leaner, Swift Samples Other Fare," *Wall Street Journal,* August 10, 1978, p. 29.

166 "half a cent": Quoted in Richard Elliott Jr., "Sow's Ear or Silk Purse?" *Barron's National Business and Financial Weekly* 47, no. 15 (April 10, 1967): 14.

"What meat packing assets": Quoted in ibid.

"After World War II": Quoted in "Meatpackers Beef It Up," *Business Week,* August 30, 1969, pp. 83, 84.

168 "A year ago": Quoted in "Doubts Voiced in Bigger Cattle Push," *Aberdeen (SD) American News,* July 17, 1973, p. 6.

169 "We've taken beatings": Quoted in Bill Hosokawa, "In Colorado, Bad Days for a Cattleman," *New York Times,* May 31, 1974, p. 33.

"It seemed like a good idea": Quoted in "Taking a Bath in Beef," *Forbes* 113, no. 9 (May 1, 1974): 18.

"I'll boycott": Quoted in "Rising Clamor for Tough Price Controls," *Time,* April 16, 1973; accessed online.

"two men with good appetites": Quoted in "The Great Meat Furor," *Newsweek,* April 9, 1973, p. 19.

"Don't Eat Beef!": See the ad in John Russell, "What the Producers Should Learn from . . . the Meat Price Uproar," *Farm Journal* 97 (May 1973): 15.

"appalled by how little": Quoted in Marian Burros, "A Maverick's Views," *Washington Post,* January 8, 1976, p. D8.

170 "We've got a worldwide food panic": Quoted in Norman H. Fischer and John A. Prestbo, "Cost of Eating: Soaring Grain Prices Seen Braking Output of Meat, Milk, Bread," *Wall Street Journal,* June 11, 1973, p. 1.

"Let's just say": Quoted in Mitchell C. Lynch, "Land of Plenty: For the Government, the Farm Boom Means Worry and Confusion," *Wall Street Journal,* October 31, 1973, p. 21.

171 "had become far too important": Quoted in ibid. For the economists' claims, see, for example, Norman H. Fischer, "Land of Plenty: Growing Enough Food for the Future May Tax U.S. Farms' Capacity," *Wall Street Journal,* November 19, 1973, p. 1.

"We're on the threshold": Quoted in John A. Prestbo, "Land of Plenty: The Quick Turnaround in Agriculture Picture Brought Joys, Woes," *Wall Street Journal,* October 9, 1973, p. 41.

"farm belt": Quoted in Joseph Winski, "Land of Plenty: For Agribusiness Firms, the Farm Boom Means a Return to Riches," *Wall Street Journal,* October 15, 1973, p. 1.

172   "foreign dignitaries": "Pigs in the Sky," *National Provisioner* 169, no. 25 (December 22, 1973): 23.

"I don't think": Quoted in "Work Expected to Begin in March on Large Hog Plant," *Joplin (MO) Globe,* February 17, 1974, p. 3D. McQuoid's adventure was covered by trade journals and Missouri newspapers, but the most accessible accounts, and ones that ponder the implications of large-scale farming for rural America, are Calvin Trillin, "U.S. Journal: Kahoka, Missouri," *New Yorker,* May 6, 1974, pp. 88, 90, 92–94, 96–97; and Gene A. Meyer, "If Proposed Corporate Hog Farm Succeeds, Future of Small Producer May Be in Doubt," *Wall Street Journal,* February 19, 1974, p. 34.

"glimmering row": Quote is from a photo caption on p. 29 of Dean Houghton, "An Exclusive Look at Tyson, the Nation's Largest Hog Farm," *Successful Farming* 77 (August 1979).

173   "It's got all the advantages": Quoted in ibid., 30.

"ought to scare the hell": Dick Hanson, "Across the Editor's Desk," *Successful Farming* 77 (August 1979): 3.

"a very ambitious man": Quoted in Brent E. Riffel, "The Feathered Kingdom: Tyson Foods and the Transformation of American Land, Labor, and Law" (Ph.D. dissertation, University of Arkansas, 2008), 148.

"gregarious, voluble fellow": Paul Duke Jr. and Rick Christie, "Don Tyson Marshals His Flock to Fight," *Wall Street Journal,* October 13, 1988; accessed online; and Kim Clark and Melanie Warner, "Tough Times for the Chicken King," *Fortune* 134, no. 8 (October 28, 1996); accessed online.

"If it makes money": Quoted in Clark and Warner, "Tough Times."

174   "The business of politics": Quoted in Riffel, "Feathered Kingdom," 231.

"[T]here is": Quoted in ibid., 201.

"He's one of those": Quoted in Clark and Warner, "Tough Times."

"Don Tyson": Quoted in ibid.

In the spring of 1962: The example is from Riffel, "Feathered Kingdom," 121.

"expand or expire": Quoted in Marvin Schwartz, *Tyson from Farm to Market* (University of Arkansas Press, 1991), 12.

175 "We're not committed": Quoted in "Tyson's Foods Looks at Future," *Broiler Industry* 27, no. 3 (March 1964): 12, 14.

"I've had two turkey plants": Quoted in Riffel, "Feathered Kingdom," note 20, p. 156.

176 "easy to grow pigs": Quoted in "Don Tyson Suggests a Better 'Game Plan,'" *Broiler Industry* 37, no. 6 (June 1974): 34.

"on an integrated basis": Quoted in ibid.

"It's a question": Quoted in Robert B. Cullen, "McLean Stakes $60 Million on Giant Farming Venture," *The (Lamberton, NC) Robesonian,* November 10, 1974, p. 4C.

"the same relation": Ibid.

"the food crisis": Quoted in Nash Henderson, "N.C. Corporate Farming — I: Companies Escaping Ecology Laws Requirements," *High Point (NC) Enterprise,* October 30, 1974, p. 13A. This series on the environmental and political impact of corporate farms first appeared in the *Winston-Salem Sentinel* and was reprinted by the Associated Press.

177 NF was owned by: On the Bass family holdings, see Ann Crittendon, "Even for Texans, the Basses Are Rich," *New York Times,* December 13, 1981, pp. F1, F17.

"a God-given mission": Quoted in Robert Dorr, "Center-Pivot Irrigation Boom Slows to Trickle," *Omaha World-Herald,* December 16, 1984; accessed online.

"leading edge": Quoted in "Here Comes the Corporate Sow," *Farm Journal* 108 (October 1984): 15; and "The $50 Million Hog Farm," *Farm Journal* 108 (October 1984): 13. Haw did not mention another factor that surely informed his decision: thanks to a 1981 change in the federal tax code, the company's investment in the necessary buildings would earn tax credits and qualify National for accelerated depreciation, both of which would enhance the project's profitability.

"We think the basic": Quoted in "Conagra [*sic*] Positioning for Future," *New York Times,* January 31, 1981, p. 31.

"booming voice": Quoted in Sue Shellenbarger, "ConAgra Grows Rapidly Despite Missteps by Shrewdly Acquiring and Reviving Firms," *Wall Street Journal,* December 7, 1982, p. 35.

178 "awful, awful disaster": Quoted in Joseph Winski, "The Grand and Daring Strategy of ConAgra," *Chicago Tribune,* October 18, 1978, p. C10.

"The guy buys things": Quoted in Bill Saporito, "ConAgra's Performance," *Fortune* 114, no. 9 (October 27, 1986): 70.

"They were thinking of Skylab": Quoted in David P. Garino, "New Owner Rejuvenates Banquet Foods," *Wall Street Journal*, February 8, 1982, p. 29.

179 "We should have moved": Quoted in "A Meatpacker Discovers Consumer Marketing," *Business Week*, May 28, 1979, p. 164.

180 "like a bunch of piranhas": Quoted in Betsy Morris and Roy J. Harris Jr., "ConAgra to Buy Greyhound Unit for $166 Million," *Wall Street Journal*, June 30, 1983, p. 8.

"Armour's dead": Quoted in Alexander Stuart, "Meatpackers in Stampede," *Fortune* 103 (June 29, 1981): 71. The rest of this analysis is from "The Old-Line Meatpackers Struggle to Survive," *Business Week*, November 13, 1978, pp. 78, 80.

"Monfort wants to return": Quoted in Barnhart, *Kenny's Shoes*, 208.

"the 'big friend'": Quoted in "How ConAgra Grew Big—and Now, Beefy," *Business Week*, May 18, 1987, p. 87.

181 "Pork has been there": Quoted in "Iowa Beef: Moving In for a Kill by Automating Pork Processing," *Business Week*, July 14, 1980, p. 100. Retailer pressure is mentioned in Judy Daubenmier, "Super Packing Plants Seen by End of Decade," *Cedar Rapids Gazette*, December 11, 1980, p. 13A.

"increase world food production": Quoted in Bill Sing, "Hammer Makes Point with IBP Acquisition," *Cedar Rapids Gazette*, June 7, 1981, p. 10C. Sing's article first appeared in the *Los Angeles Times*.

"We think food": Quoted in "Occidental to Acquire Iowa Beef," *New York Times*, June 2, 1981, p. D1. For IBP's plans and a description of the plant, see Bill Fleming, "From Packages to Plant—IBP Set to Enter Pork Business," *National Hog Farmer* 27, no. 10 (October 15, 1982): 31–32, 37.

182 "I just don't see": Quoted in Francis C. Brown III, "Wilson Foods Corp. Is Facing Bleak Outlook," *Wall Street Journal*, September 6, 1985, p. 6.

"We are confident": Quoted in Rick Christie, "Tyson Foods Proposes to Buy Holly Farms," *Wall Street Journal*, October 12, 1988, p. A5. For the sour relations between the two men, see Duke Jr. and Christie, "Don Tyson Marshals His Flock," B12.

"battle helmet": Ibid.

183 "This is a very tasty morsel": Quoted in Karen Blumenthal and Rob-

ert L. Rose, "Tyson Foods Wins Holly Farms Fight, Gains Brand, Debt," *Wall Street Journal*, June 26, 1989, p. A3.

"[I]nternational customers": Quoted in Jim Stafford, "Cattle Industry in Oklahoma Faces Challenging Future," *Daily Oklahoman*, April 25, 1993; accessed online.

184 "fuzzy": For the discussion of signals, see Alan Barkema and Michael L. Cook, "The Changing U.S. Pork Industry: A Dilemma for Public Policy," *Economic Review* 78, no. 2 (Second Quarter 1993): 49–65. On quality control as a transaction cost, see V. James Rhodes, "The Industrialization of Hog Production," *Review of Agricultural Economics* 17, no. 2 (May 1995): 112–13. Rhodes's work is crucial for understanding late-twentieth-century changes in hog farming. He conducted much of his research in agricultural economics at the University of Missouri–Columbia in partnership with Glenn Grimes. For decades, they analyzed hog production, and their work provides the most complete set of statistical analyses of changes in the industry.

"I can do well": Quoted in Bill Fleming, "Opinion Page," *National Hog Farmer* 38, no. 5 (May 15, 1993): 13.

"product development": Barkema and Cook, "Changing U.S. Pork Industry," 55.

185 "We want everything": Quoted in Chris Mayda, "Passion on the Plains: Pigs on the Panhandle" (Ph.D. dissertation, University of Southern California, 1998), 157.

"entrepreneurial organization": Quoted in ibid., 162.

"technical . . . assistance": "Clause in 1991 Bill Opened Gates for Corporate Hog Farms," *Daily Oklahoman*, May 18, 1997; accessed online. For the Tyson operations, see Michael McNutt, "Swing Operation Prompts Watchdog Group — Strict Regulations Sought to Guard Environment," *Daily Oklahoman*, March 2, 1994; accessed online. Also see Jim Stafford, "Cattle Industry in Oklahoma Faces Challenging Future," *Daily Oklahoman*, April 25, 1993; accessed online.

186 "Now why do the poor people": Both quoted in Mayda, "Passion on the Plains," 176. On the area's economic woes, see Ann DeFrange, "Rural Revival — State Towns Taking Charge of Their Economic Future," *Daily Oklahoman*, October 2, 1994; accessed online; and Michael McNutt, "Guymon's Economy Booming," *Daily Oklahoman*, December 11, 1994; accessed online.

"The trouble is": Quoted in Mayda, "Passion on the Plains," 212.

"pigs came": Quoted in ibid.

"you control": Quoted in ibid., 195.

"I'm an advocate": Quoted in ibid., 213.

"a group like the Sierra Club": Quoted in ibid., 318.

7. THE DOUBTERS' CRUSADE

188 "innuendo, implication": "NPPC to Answer Network Jibes," *National Hog Farmer* 26, no. 5 (May 15, 1981): 25.

189 "100%": The Nixon quotes are from "The Administration: Looking After the Hotdog," *Time*, June 27, 1969; accessed online; and "Mrs. Knauer Says Nixon Opposes Fat Hot Dogs," *New York Times*, July 13, 1969, p. 22.

190 "citizen consumers": The phrase is from Lizabeth Cohen's superb *A Consumers' Republic: The Politics of Mass Consumption in Postwar America* (Vintage Books, 2003). Two other essential works are Gary Cross, *An All-Consuming Century: Why Commercialism Won in Modern America* (Columbia University Press, 2000); and Meg Jacobs, *Pocketbook Politics: Economic Citizenship in Twentieth-Century America* (Princeton University Press, 2005).

191 "private governments": Quoted in Patrick Anderson, "Ralph Nader, Crusader; or, The Rise of a Self-Appointed Lobbyist," *New York Times*, October 29, 1967, p. SM103.

192 "into the air": "Environment v. Man," *Time*, September 26, 1960; accessed online.

"a major national problem": Quoted in Richard D. Lyons, "Salmonella Rise Disturbs Experts," *New York Times*, April 9, 1967, p. 47.

"infection that [could] spread": Quoted in ibid.

193 "The Consumer Revolt": See "The U.S.'s Toughest Customer," *Time*, December 12, 1969; accessed online.

"Evidently there's a dearth": Quoted in Lucia Mouat, "Will the Real Bargain Stand Up?" *Christian Science Monitor*, February 2, 1970, p. 9.

"Other issues such as Vietnam": Quoted in Lucia Mouat, "The Consumer Fights Back," *Christian Science Monitor*, January 26, 1970, p. 9.

194 Keys's ideas: My take on the history of the heart disease epidemic and Keys's role in it is informed by Gary Taubes, *Good Calories, Bad Calories: Challenging the Conventional Wisdom on Diet, Weight Control, and Disease* (Alfred A. Knopf, 2007); and Todd Michael Olszewski, "Cholesterol: A Scientific, Medical and Social History, 1908–1962" (Ph.D. dissertation, Yale University, 2008). During World War

II, Keys helped develop the K-rations fed to troops and conducted an important study of the impact of starvation on human physiology.

196 "Once upon a time": "Frankfurters," *Consumer Reports* 37, no. 2 (February 1972): 73.

197 "pig swill": The consumer comments are quoted in "P.S. on Pig Snouts," *National Provisioner* 168, no. 5 (February 3, 1973): 30, 32, 34.

"wiener is being clobbered": Joseph M. Winski, "Makers of Hog Dogs, Speaking Frankly, Say Sales Aren't So Hot," *Wall Street Journal,* May 29, 1973, p. 1.

"personal affronts": Quoted in ibid.

198 "I have an answer": "'Egghead' Proposals Make Reader Sizzle," *National Provisioner* 166, no. 11 (March 11, 1972): 19.

"aesthetics": "Aesthetics No Basis for Byproducts Ban," *National Provisioner* 168, no. 2 (January 13, 1973): 15–16. A summary of the new rules is in "U.S. Sets New Rules for Processed Meat," *New York Times,* June 2, 1973, p. 16.

"Most of us": Quoted in John S. Lang, "Cancer-Inciting Hormone Found in U.S. Beef Supply," *Des Moines Register,* June 24, 1970, p. 1. Lang's report was carried by the AP and appeared in newspapers nationwide. There are only two general sources of information about the history of the DES-in-beef controversy: Harrison Wellford, *Sowing the Wind: A Report from Ralph Nader's Center for the Study of Responsive Law on Food Safety and the Chemical Harvest* (Grossman Publishers, 1972); and Alan I. Marcus, *Cancer from Beef: DES, Federal Food Regulation, and Consumer Confidence* (The Johns Hopkins University Press, 1994). Of the two, Marcus's is the more complete account, although he is less interested in the history of DES regulation than in the way that the DES battle exemplified the fracturing of scientific authority at midcentury. Wellford was one of Ralph Nader's colleagues, and his account is oriented toward the politics of the regulatory mechanisms. His take on DES also appeared as Harrison Wellford, "Behind the Meat Counter: The Fight Over DES," *Atlantic* 230 (October 1972): 86–90. For a useful look at the politics of DES regulation (and to a lesser extent antibiotics), also see U.S. House of Representatives, *Regulation of Diethylstilbestrol (DES) and Other Drugs Used in Food Producing Animals,* HR 93–708, 93d Cong., 1st sess.

200 "intellectually fascinating": Quoted in Walter Sullivan, "Bacteria Passing On Resistance to Drugs," *New York Times,* August 9, 1966,

pp. 1, 31. The editorial appeared in the *New England Journal of Medicine* on August 4, 1966. For scientists' and veterinarians' take on the state of knowledge in the mid-1960s, see the essays in *Use of Drugs in Animal Feeds: Proceedings of a Symposium,* Publication 1679 (National Academy of Sciences, 1969). The British were not as reticent. In 1969, the authors of a Parliament-sponsored investigation announced that they did "not accept the statement that 20 years of experience goes to show that there are no serious ill-effects from giving antibiotics to animals." They argued that Parliament should ban human-use antibiotics in animal feeds. "In the long term," the committee wrote, "we believe it will be more rewarding to study and improve the methods of animal husbandry than to feed diets containing antibiotics." Quoted in Alvin Shuster, "Britain to Curb Antibiotic Feed," *New York Times,* November 21, 1969, p. 17.

"potential health hazard": Quoted in Harold M. Schmeck Jr., "Limitation on Antibiotics in Feed for Livestock Urged by F.D.A.," *New York Times,* February 1, 1972, p. 19.

"bad news": Neal Black, "FDA Antibiotic Order Not as Bad as Feared," *National Hog Farmer* 18, no. 7 (July 19, 1973): 4.

201   "better research": Quoted in George Getschow, "Meat Producers Fear FDA Will Curb Use of Antibiotics, Thus Reducing Supplies," *Wall Street Journal,* January 6, 1975, p. 18.

"grossly inadequate": Quoted in Rex Wilmore, "They Want to Ban Antibiotics from Feed," *Farm Journal* 96 (March 1972): 23.

202   "the furthest from being": "Why United Packers Has Closed Its Doors," *National Provisioner* 167, no. 26 (December 23, 1972): 18.

203   The critique of agribusiness: My take on the impact of the Hightower critique is an educated guess pieced together as I worked on this book. This is yet another example of the lack of historical research on topics relevant to contemporary America. To date, historians have ignored the turmoil in late-twentieth-century agriculture, particularly the spread of corporate hog farming and the rural activism that accompanied it. As of this writing — 2013 — for example, there are no comprehensive histories of the emergence of rural activism in the 1960s and 1970s, nor have historians studied the links between, say, programs in rural sociology and rural activism, to say nothing of the history of confinement, lagoons, or much else connected with agriculture since the 1950s.

204   "relatively free": "Bill Would Ban Large Corporate Farms," *Omaha World-Herald,* January 6, 1972, p. 6.

"Do you get the feeling": See the letter to the editor from Larry G. Hauer, "Small Producers Being Forced Out," *National Hog Farmer* 28, no. 10 (October 1983): 29.

"If the people of Nebraska": Quoted in C. David Kotok, "Stock Feeder: Initiative 300 Could Cripple the Industry," *Omaha World-Herald*, June 22, 1983, p. 2.

205 burg of Doland: See Russ Keen, "Hog-Farm Opinions Split Doland Folk," *Aberdeen (SD) American News*, February 21, 1988, p. 1B.

206 "They can get [it] cheaper": Quoted in Kent Warneke, "Local Farmers, Businesses Supportive — Atkinson Farm Corporation Not Seen as Villain," *Omaha World-Herald*, December 30, 1984; accessed online.

"stoop to anything": Quoted in "Missouri Gains Hog Farm That Iowa Turned Away," *St. Louis Post-Dispatch*, May 7, 1989, p. 8E.

"It's going to be a big help": Quoted in ibid.

207 "We don't need": Quoted in ibid. For the Morrell example, see Charles Siler, "Where Did All the Pigs Go?" *Forbes* 145, no. 6 (March 19, 1990); accessed online.

"rest[ed] largely with": U.S. Department of Agriculture, Economic Research Service, "Economies of Size in Hog Production," by Roy Van Arsdall and Kenneth E. Nelson, Technical Bulletin no. 1712, December 1985, pp. 39, 41.

208 "large corporate hog farms": See Bill Fleming, "Opinion Page," *National Hog Farmer* 32, no. 11 (November 15, 1987): 9.

"within 10 years": Quoted in Bill Fleming, "Opinion Page," *National Hog Farmer* 31, no. 5 (May 15, 1986): 10.

There's no better place: For discussions of these changes, see Walter Kiechel III, "The Food Giants Struggle to Stay in Step with Consumers," *Fortune* 98, no. 5 (September 11, 1978): 50–56; Walter Kiechel III, "Two-Income Families Will Reshape the Consumer Markets," *Fortune* 101, no. 5 (March 10, 1980): 110–14, 117, 119–20; Jean Kinsey, "Changes in Food Consumption from Mass Market to Niche Markets," in Lyle P. Schertz and Lynn M. Daft, *Food and Agricultural Markets: The Quiet Revolution*, NPA Report no. 270 (National Planning Association, 1994), 19–43; Jean Kinsey and Ben Senauer, "Consumer Trends and Changing Food Retailing Formats," *American Journal of Agricultural Economics* 78, no. 5, Proceedings Issue (December 1996): 1187–91; and Alan Barkema, Mark Drabenstott, and Kelly Welch, "The Quiet Revolution in the U.S. Food Market," *Economic Review* 76, no. 3 (May/June 1991): 25–41. The late-twentieth-century shift in eating and cooking habits is often attributed to the increase in numbers of women working outside the home. But, as noted in the text, that cliché obscures another transformation: more households were headed by adults, male and female, who worked outside the home. As the divorce rate soared, for example, more households were the domain of single men or part-time dads who had no interest in cooking. Some analysts argue that while women were more "liberated" and educated, they also worked because they had no choice: their families were being squeezed by declining wages and rising economic inequality. But again, that easy explanation does not go far enough to explain the complexities of the change. Consider an obvious if uncomfortable alternative view: Postwar Americans grew up in an era of extraordinary affluence. They assumed that their homes would contain more than one change of clothes, a television or two, and gizmos and gadgets designed to make life easier (electric can openers and toothbrushes). Americans who suffered declining incomes in the 1970s could have adjusted their way of life accordingly. Some did but more did not, even if it meant carrying credit card debt to do so.

211 "young and leisure-oriented shoppers": W. G. Vander Ploeg, "Packers Are Still Facing Effects of 'Deli Revolution,'" *National Provisioner* 171, no. 19 (November 9, 1974): 174.

"The supermarkets are crying": Quoted in "Tyson Foods: Putting Its Brand on High-Margin Poultry Products," *Business Week*, August 20, 1979, p. 48.

"I think my mother": Quoted in "Don Tyson Tells How He Hopes to Earn 20% Net," *Broiler Industry* 40, no. 2 (February 1977): 27.

212 "We really were": Quoted in Taubes, *Good Calories, Bad Calories*, 45. For the report, see U.S. Senate, Select Committee on Nutrition and Human Needs, *Dietary Goals for the United States*, 95th Cong., 1st sess.

"hell broke loose": Quoted in Taubes, *Good Calories, Bad Calories*, 47. The example of the egg industry consultant is in ibid., 51. The Hegsted/Frito-Lay connection is in ibid., 53.

213 "antimicrobial-resistant organisms": Quoted in "Poisoning Linked to Cattle Germs," *New York Times*, September 6, 1984, p. A20. A fascinating profile of the investigation is in Marjorie Sun, "In Search of Salmonella's Smoking Gun," *Science* 226, no. 4670 (October 5, 1984): 30–32.

"health reasons": Bill Fleming, "Survey Confirms: Pork Still Has Image Problem!" *National Hog Farmer* 28, no. 12 (December 15, 1983): 6. On the McRib, see, for example, Dean Houghton, "Pork's Fast-Food Foothold," *Successful Farming* 79 (September 1981): H6, H8; and Debra Switzky, "McRib's Future Uncertain," *National Hog Farmer* 28, no. 9 (September 15, 1983): 48.

214 "A story about": Quoted in Terri Minsky, "Bleak Pastures: Cattlemen Lose Money as Prices Fail to Rise with Production Costs," *Wall Street Journal,* May 8, 1981, p. 1.

"Nobody eats beef anymore": Quoted in ibid., 17.

"the Mercedes of Meat": Terri Minsky, "Beef Industry Turning to Ads to Change Meat's Reputation," *Wall Street Journal,* April 1, 1982, p. 29.

"We thought everybody": Quoted in Robert Reinhold, "Beef Industry Reduces Use of Disputed Drugs in Feed," *New York Times,* February 16, 1985, p. 8.

215 "inference": Quoted in ibid.

"By dropping antibiotics": Quoted in ibid.

"the harsh reality": Quoted in Marj Charlier, "State of the Steak: Beef's Drop in Appeal Pushes Some Packers to Try New Products," *Wall Street Journal,* August 28, 1985, p. 1.

"It's the younger": Quoted in Bill Eftink, "Chickens Are Stampeding Our Beef Customers," *Successful Farming* 79 (May 1981): 23.

216 "delicious chunks": "Just What Is a Chicken McNugget," *Wall Street Journal,* October 3, 1985, p. 33. Consumption statistics are in U.S. Department of Agriculture, Economic Research Service, *Economics of the U.S. Meat Industry,* by Richard J. Crom, Agriculture Information Bulletin no. 545, November 1988, Table 4, p. 7; and U.S. Department of Agriculture, Economic Research Service, *Food Consumption, Prices, and Expenditures, 1970–97,* by Judith Jones Putnam and Jane E. Allshouse, Statistical Bulletin no. 965, April 1999, Table 4.

Indeed, researchers theorized: For speculation about the role of vaccinations see Tom Paulson, "Risky Food — Why Now? — 10 Years After First Appearance, Tiny Bug Is Still Baffling Experts," *Seattle Post-Intelligencer,* February 22, 1993; accessed online.

217 "so infected": Paul Shukovsky, "Roadblocks to Reform — Why Agency Didn't Act," *Seattle Post-Intelligencer,* February 23, 1993; accessed online.

"They don't know": Quoted in Carole Sugarman, "U.S. Meat Inspections Come Under Scrutiny," *Washington Post*, February 9, 1993; accessed online.

"not against technology": Ibid. The inspection example is from Mike McGraw and Mike Hendricks, "Consumers Can't Depend on USDA for Meat Safety; Inspectors Seldom Test for Pathogens That Must Be Killed in Cooking," *Kansas City Star*, January 31, 1993; accessed online.

218   In the wake of: The reporter's point about the two agencies is in Christopher Hanson, "Roadblocks to Reform—U.S. Inspectors Know Trouble but Action Slow," *Seattle Post-Intelligencer*, February 23, 1993; accessed online.

219   "we wanted to find out": Quoted in Bettie Fennell, "Success Keeps Murphy Farms High on the Hog," *Wilmington (NC) Star-News*, January 18, 1987, p. 1E.

Deliverance arrived: For brief histories of Smithfield, see Mitchell Gordon, "High on the Hog," *Barron's National Business and Financial Weekly* 65, no. 47 (November 25, 1985); accessed online; and Sharon Reier, "High on the Hog," *Financial World* 157, no. 14 (June 28, 1988); accessed online.

"We are not against": Quoted in Stuart Leavenworth, "250 Debate Animal-Waste Issue at Public Hearing," *Raleigh News & Observer*, June 24, 1992; accessed online.

220   "wildly cheering": Quoted in Martha Quillin, "Bladen Divided Over Plant—Slaughterhouse's Jobs Wanted, Not Its Waste," *Raleigh News & Observer*, March 7, 1991; accessed online.

"All of a sudden": Quoted in Greg Barnes, "Factory Farms Take Hold," *Fayetteville (NC) Observer*, December 16, 2003; accessed online.

"Didn't nobody mean": Quoted in Joby Warrick, "Hog-Waste Spill Fouls Land, River in Onslow," *Raleigh News & Observer*, June 23, 1995; accessed online. A solid account of the North Carolina spills as well as other conflicts over industrial farms in the 1990s is in David Kirby, *Animal Factory: The Looming Threat of Industrial Pig, Dairy, and Poultry Farms to Humans and the Environment* (St. Martin's Press, 2010).

221   "environmental Alamo": Joby Warrick, "Hog Spills Change Lawmakers' Views," *Raleigh News & Observer*, August 6, 1995; accessed online.

"AIDS look like": Quoted in Sam Howe Verhovek, "Talk of the Town: Burgers v. Oprah," *New York Times*, January 21, 1998, p. A10.

8. UTOPIAN VISIONS, RED TAPE REALITY

223 "I don't have papers": The exchanges between Coleman and the inspectors are recounted in Stephen M. Voynick, *Riding the Higher Range: The Story of Colorado's Coleman Ranch and Coleman Natural Beef* (Glenn Melvin Coleman, 1998), 156.

224 "losing battle": Quoted in ibid., 139.
"Inflation costs": Ibid., 145.
"We had to do something": Ibid., 149.

225 "tingle ran down": Quoted in ibid., 152.
"mood of intolerance": Quoted in Mary Elizabeth Barham, "Sustainable Agriculture in the United States and France: A Polanyian Perspective" (Ph.D. dissertation, Cornell University, 1999), 153, 154.

226 But in the wake: For a useful discussion of changes in attitude, see Randal S. Beeman and James A. Pritchard, *A Green and Permanent Land: Ecology and Agriculture in the Twentieth Century* (University Press of Kansas, 2001), especially 89ff.
"When you start trimming": Quoted in Jessica Frazier, "Monfort of Colorado Markets Organic Beef," *Greeley Tribune*, December 26, 1971, p. 18.
"a colossal blunder": Quoted in George Getschow, "Meat Producers Fear FDA Will Curb Use of Antibiotics, Thus Reducing Supplies," *Wall Street Journal*, January 6, 1975, p. 18. University economists confirmed the gap between idea and profit. One study predicted that putting beef cattle back on pasture would result in a short-term 50 percent drop in beef, and that livestock producers would earn higher profits. But they concluded that over the long haul, eliminating antibiotics and hormones would drive up farmers' production costs and lead to higher meat prices for consumers who would likely respond by reducing their consumption. (Economists did not calculate an important intangible — how consumers would respond to the taste of grass-fed beef — nor did they factor in rising land prices.) As for hogs, analysts predicted that returning to pasture and natural breeding schedules would prevent meatpackers from running their plants at capacity year-round, so they'd charge more for their products. A good summary of the "what if" studies is in *Antibiotics in Animal Feeds: A Report Prepared by the Committee on Animal Health and the Committee on Animal Nutrition [and] Board on Agriculture and Renewable Resources* (National Academy of Sciences, 1979); but also see Henry C. Gilliam et al., *Economic Consequences of Banning the*

Use of Antibiotics at Subtherapeutic Levels in Livestock Production,
Departmental Technical Report no. 73–2 (Department of Agricultural Economics and Sociology and Texas Agricultural Experiment
Station, 1973); and Henry C. Gilliam Jr. and J. Rod Martin, "Economic Importance of Antibiotics in Feeds to Producers and Consumers of Pork, Beef and Veal," *Journal of Animal Science* 40, no. 6
(1975): 1241–55.

"Food is a scarce item": Quoted in Marian Burros, "A Maverick's
Views," *Washington Post*, January 8, 1976; accessed online.

227   "It's obvious": Quoted in Lynn Heinze, "Although Less Beef Consumption Likely, Cattle Have Future," *Greeley Tribune*, March 9,
1976, p. B-23.

At the center of: The elder Rodale died in 1971. The most substantive
study of the Rodale empire is Andrew N. Case, "Looking for Organic
America: J. I. Rodale, the Rodale Press, and the Popular Culture of
Environmentalism in the Postwar United States" (Ph.D. dissertation,
University of Wisconsin–Madison, 2012).

228   "Don Quixote": Quoted in Suzanne Peters, "The Land in Trust: A Social History of the Organic Farming Movement" (Ph.D. dissertation,
McGill University, 1979), 221.

"ecosystem": Quoted in Beeman and Pritchard, *Green and Permanent Land,* 93, 94. For Commoner, see Michael Egan, "Barry Commoner and the Science of Survival" (Ph.D. dissertation, Washington
State University, 2004).

"massive intervention into nature": Quoted in Beeman and Pritchard,
Green and Permanent Land, 93.

"As far as our methods": Quoted in Peters, "Land in Trust," 279.

229   "voluntary simplicity": Quoted in Curtis E. Beus and Riley E. Dunlap, "Conventional Versus Alternative Agriculture: The Paradigmatic Roots of the Debate," *Rural Sociology* 55, no. 4 (Winter 1990):
608–9.

"I like horses": Quoted in "Earl Butz Versus Wendell Berry," *CoEvolu-
tion Quarterly* 17 (Spring 1978): 57.

"independent": Quoted in ibid., 55.

"modern, scientific": Quoted in ibid., 51.

"machine": Quoted in Beus and Dunlap, "Conventional Versus Alternative," 606.

"We can go back": Quoted in ibid., 609.

230   "practical alternatives": Quoted in Peters, "Land in Trust," 283.

"appropriate farm technology": Quoted in ibid., 287.

231 "Energy shortages": U.S. Department of Agriculture, Study Team on
Organic Farming, *Report and Recommendations on Organic Farming*, July 1980, p. iii.
"strongly": Ibid., xiv.

232 "It will permanently warp you": Quoted in Lynn Bronikowski, "Mel
Coleman: A Trailblazer Naturally," *Rocky Mountain News*, April 22,
1990; accessed online.
"made [his] ... lip curl": Quoted in Voynick, *Riding the Higher
Range*, 119.
"I believed": Quoted in ibid., 143.

233 "If you don't have to buy": Quoted in ibid., 166.
"If I stock your beef": Quoted in ibid.
"just a bunch of hippies": Quoted in Clay Evans, "Rancher Becomes
'Natural Beef' Guru," *Juneau Empire*, June 21, 1998; accessed online.
The article originally appeared in the *Boulder Daily Camera*.
"the mountain air is clear": Quoted in Voynick, *Riding the Higher
Range*, 179.
"look like a real rancher": Quoted in ibid., 179–80.

234 "Low-Input Sustainable Agriculture": There are no substantive histories of the late-century effort to insert sustainable agriculture into
the establishment, but a useful recounting of events by a participant
is J. Patrick Madden, *The Early Years: The LISA, SARE, and ACE Programs* (Western SARE, n.d.); accessed online. Also see U.S. General
Accounting Office, Report to Congressional Requesters, *Sustainable
Agriculture: Program Management, Accomplishments, and Opportunities*, GAO/RCED-92-233, September 1992. There is also useful
information from participants in Barham, "Sustainable Agriculture";
and Andrew Marshall, "Sustaining Sustainable Agriculture: The Rise
and Fall of the Fund for Rural America," *Agriculture and Human
Values* 17, no. 3 (September 2000): 267–77.

235 "The word came down": Quoted in Barham, "Sustainable Agriculture," 176.
"replac[e] the mechanical": Quoted in Beus and Dunlap, "Conventional Versus Alternative Agriculture," 610.
"I'd call it FIDO": Quoted in ibid.
"Our worthless opponents": Quoted in ibid.

237 "iron triangle": My understanding of the agricultural legislative proc-
ess and how it changed is informed by James T. Bonnen, William P.
Browne, and David B. Schweikhardt, "Further Observations on the
Changing Nature of National Agricultural Policy Decision Processes,

1946–1995," *Agricultural History* 70, no. 2 (Spring 1996): 130–52; William P. Browne, *Private Interests, Public Policy, and American Agriculture* (University Press of Kansas, 1988); William P. Browne, *Cultivating Congress: Constituents, Issues, and Interests in Agricultural Policymaking* (University Press of Kansas, 1995); Harold D. Guither, *The Food Lobbyists: Behind the Scenes of Food and Agri-Politics* (D. C. Heath and Company, 1980); Don F. Hadwiger and William P. Browne, eds., *The New Politics of Food* (D. C. Heath and Company, 1978); Don F. Hadwiger, *The Politics of Agricultural Research* (University of Nebraska Press, 1982); and Don Paarlberg, *Farm and Food Policy: Issues of the 1980s* (University of Nebraska Press, 1980). One consequence of the disarray is obvious: the more, and the more diverse, players involved, the more difficult it was to accomplish anything beyond the basics, in this case support for commodities. None of the players had any interest in, and thus no focus on, "agriculture" as a whole or its relation to the totality of American society. All any could hope was that he/she/it would manage to forge an alliance with other players in an effort to insert his/her/its agenda into the bill. As a result, fundamental agricultural "reform," argued a trio of political scientists who had watched this process unfold over the years, "fails not because agricultural policy making is closed to" everyone but "agribusiness," a "bit of conventional wisdom [that] is badly out of date," but because "there are too many players, each seeking something from decision processes" (Bonnen, Browne, and Schweikhardt, "Further Observations," 151).

238 "agricultural establishment": Don Paarlberg, "Agriculture Loses Its Uniqueness," *American Journal of Agricultural Economics* 60, no. 5 (December 1978): 772. Paarlberg served on the faculty at Purdue University, helped launch the Food for Peace program in the 1950s, and worked in high positions at the USDA under three secretaries. This 1978 publication is based on a speech he gave in 1975 at the National Public Policy Conference. For that, see Garth Youngberg, "Alternative Agriculturalists: Ideology, Politics, and Prospects," in *New Politics of Food*, ed. Hadwiger and Browne, 242–43. For one of Paarlberg's more blunt assessments see Paarlberg, "The Farm Policy Agenda," *Increasing Understanding of Public Problems and Policies, 1975* (Farm Foundation, 1975), 95–102. Paarlberg elaborated on the implications of this shift in his *Farm and Food Policy: Issues of the 1980s* (University of Nebraska Press, 1980).

"unthinkable": Luther Tweeten, "Domestic Food and Farm Policy Issues and Alternatives," *Increasing Understanding of Public Problems and Policies, 1975* (Farm Foundation, 1975), 103, 104, 111.

"a farmer who [would] cry": Browne, *Private Interests, Public Policy,* 88.

239 "We warned everybody": Quoted in Barham, "Sustainable Agriculture," 161.

240 "There's a particular person": Quoted in Martin Everett, "How Coleman Sells the Sizzle," *Sales & Marketing Management* 139 (August 1, 1987); accessed online.

"upgrade": Quoted in Michelle M. Mahoney, "Coleman Launches a Branded Beef Line," *Adweek's Marketing Week,* November 6, 1989; accessed online.

"countercuisine": The delightful term is from Warren Belasco, *Appetite for Change: How the Counterculture Took On the Food Industry,* 2d ed. (Cornell University Press, 2007).

"wholesome": Jane Mayer, "Now You Can Dine Knowing the Entree Lived a Happy Life," *Wall Street Journal,* April 6, 1989, p. 1; and Sonia L. Nazario, "Are Organic Foods Spiritual Enough? Not for Everyone," *Wall Street Journal,* July 21, 1989, p. A1.

241 "Before they became available": Quoted in Kathleen A. Hughes, "If Fitness Matters, Shouldn't a Chicken Do a Workout Too?" *Wall Street Journal,* July 16, 1986, p. 1.

"We tell retailers": Quoted in Everett, "How Coleman Sells the Sizzle"; accessed online.

"overpriced and overbilled": Ibid.

An alliance: For the Wyoming and Kansas examples, see Steve Painter, "Producers of 'Natural' Meat Claim Growing Market Share," *Lexington (KY) Herald-Leader,* May 4, 1986; accessed online.

"I hope I don't radiate": Quoted in Katy Butler, "'Natural' Beef Is Big Business," *San Francisco Chronicle,* February 19, 1986; accessed online. In the late 1990s, Schell took a position at the University of California–Berkeley as dean of the School of Journalism and sold his share of the ranch to Niman. Several years later, Schell helped recruit a new faculty member: Michael Pollan, a journalist who had published, among other things, a series of articles about the food industry. The influence of the older man on the younger can be seen by reading Schell's *Modern Meat* and Pollan's *Omnivore's Dilemma.*

"We sold to Los Angeles": Ibid.

242 "I've got ranchers": Quoted in Keith Schneider, "The Profitable Road to Natural Beef," *New York Times,* September 5, 1986, p. A10.

"I definitely think": Quoted in Hughes, "If Fitness Matters," 17.

"We don't have a working definition": Quoted in Carrie Dolan, "Federal Agents Lay Down the Law to Some Chicken-Livered Rangers," *Wall Street Journal,* January 29, 1990, p. B1.

243 "beneficial magnetic forces": Nazario, "Are Organic Foods Spiritual Enough?" A1.

"wherewithal": Quoted in Judith Blake, "'Hormone-Free' Label Raises Questions," *Seattle Times,* March 1, 1989; accessed online. The story was a bit more complicated than that. The European Community had recently voted to ban imports of U.S. beef from cattle raised on synthetic hormones. That prompted a trade war, and one way to end the dispute was by eliminating any chance that some beef was hormone-free and some wasn't.

"great injustice": Quoted in Judith Blake, "Federal 'Natural Beef' Program's Future Concerns Participants," *Seattle Times,* March 8, 1989; accessed online.

"essential": Quoted in Marj Charlier, "Raisers of 'Natural' Cattle Fear Losing Market Niche," *Wall Street Journal,* May 17, 1989; accessed online.

244 "better than food produced": Quoted in U.S. House of Representatives, Committee on Agriculture, *Proposed Organic Certification Program,* 101st Cong., 2d sess., June 19, 1990, p. 11.

"I'm still trying": Quoted in ibid., 49.

"I assume": Quoted in ibid., 22.

"[T]here is not": Quoted in ibid., 18.

"constantly exposed": Quoted in ibid., 26.

245 "negative advertising": Quoted in Michelle Mahoney, "Discouraging Words Heard over Ads for Natural Beef," *Denver Post,* March 29, 1991; accessed online.

246 "I've paid a lot of dues": Quoted in ibid.

"been embraced": Garth Youngberg, Neill Schaller, and Kathleen Merrigan, "The Sustainable Agriculture Policy in the United States: Politics and Prospects," in *Food for the Future: Conditions and Contradictions of Sustainability,* ed. Patricia Allen (John Wiley & Sons, 1993), 295.

247 "systematic world": Howard R. Cottam, "Toward a World Food System," in U.S. Senate, Committee on Agriculture and Forestry, Subcommittee on Agricultural Production, Marketing, and Stabilization of Prices, *U.S. and World Food Security,* 93d Cong., 2d sess., March 15, 1974, p. 71. For a brief but useful summary of the politics of post-

war hunger, see A. H. Boerma, "The Thirty Years War Against World Hunger," *Proceedings of the Nutrition Society* 34, no. 3 (1975): 146–57.

248 "a decentralized, safe": Joe Belden and Gregg Forte, *Toward a National Food Policy* (Exploratory Project for Economic Alternatives, 1976), 34.

"localized, small-scale production": Ibid., 121.

"between the urban consumer": Quoted in ibid., 34.

To name one example: The federal marketing act lost its funding in 1980 over the strenuous objection of the General Accounting Office, which argued that such projects represented a way to reduce the nation's energy costs and urban reliance on "out-of-region food sources." See U.S. General Accounting Office, *Direct Farmer-to-Consumer Marketing Program Should Be Continued and Improved*, CED-80–65, July 9, 1980, p. 1; accessed online. There are no substantive histories of these early self-reliance, food security projects, but useful information is in Joe Belden et al., *New Directions in Farm, Land and Food Policies: A Time for State and Local Action* (Conference on Alternative State and Local Policies, Agriculture Project, [1979]; Belden and Forte, *Toward a National Food Policy;* and Kate Clancy, Janet Hammer, and Debra Lippoldt, "Food Policy Councils: Past, Present, and Future," in *Remaking the North American Food System: Strategies for Sustainability,* ed. C. Clare Hinrichs and Thomas A. Lyson (University of Nebraska Press, 2007), 121–43.

The most influential and long-lived: For the Hartford plan, see City of Hartford, *A Discussion Draft for Community Review: A Strategy to Reduce the Cost of Food for Hartford Residents,* by Catherine Lerza (Hartford, 1978). A summary of the plan is in Belden et al., *New Directions,* 276–77; but also see Mark Winne, *Closing the Food Gap: Resetting the Table in the Land of Plenty* (Beacon Press, 2008). Winne was hired to run the original program and worked there for several decades. An important compendium of ideas is in Catherine Lerza and Michael Jacobson, eds., *Food for People, Not for Profit: A Sourcebook on the Food Crisis* (Ballantine Books, 1975). This book was issued in conjunction with Food Day.

249 "most prevalent and most insidious": Howard Kurtz, "Mayors Say Hunger in Cities Is Growing Faster Than Aid," *Washington Post,* June 13, 1983; accessed online. An excellent recounting of the hunger crisis of the 1980s is in Janet Poppendieck, *Sweet Charity? Emergency Food and the End of Entitlement* (Viking, 1998). Another use-

ful assessment is Katherine L. Clancy, "Sustainable Agriculture and Domestic Hunger: Rethinking a Link Between Production and Consumption," *Food for the Future*, ed. Allen, 251–93.

As two analysts: See Barbara E. Cohen and Martha R. Burt, *Eliminating Hunger: Food Security Policy for the 1990s* (The Urban Institute, 1989).

250 "tension": Quoted in Barbara Ruben, "Common Ground," *Environmental Action* 27, no. 2 (Summer 1995); accessed online.

"like two trains": Winne, *Closing the Food Gap*, 134. For a general description of the tensions and conflicts in those early years, written by a participant, see Robert Gottlieb, *Environmentalism Unbound: Exploring New Pathways for Change* (The MIT Press, 2001), 226ff. For the food miles calculation, which came from Mark Winne, see Ruben, "Common Ground." Food miles were much discussed by participants in the 1990s.

251 "from a global everywhere": Jack Kloppenburg Jr., John Hendrickson, and G. W. Stevenson, "Coming in to the Foodshed," *Agriculture and Human Values* 13, no. 3 (Summer 1996): 34, 36, 38. For a good summary of the community food security idea and the problems of putting it into practice, see Molly D. Anderson and John T. Cook, "Community Food Security: Practice in Need of Theory?" *Agriculture and Human Values* 16, no. 2 (June 1999): 141–50. The merger of sustainable agriculture and food security activists energized both communities, but so did their shared interest in another movement that took shape in the 1990s: resistance to globalization. During that decade, world leaders replaced the General Agreement on Tariffs and Trade (GATT), which dated to the 1940s, with the World Trade Organization (WTO), a move that amounted to more than a change in name: WTO replaced long-standing policies that defined food as a right with ones that dumped food into the same general category, trade-wise, as "spark plugs and refrigerators." Negotiations over GATT and WTO, as well as the North American Free Trade Agreement (NAFTA), galvanized activists who argued that global corporations had taken over the planet's food supplies and were wreaking havoc on the environment as well as the lives and health of billions of people. In the United States, resistance to globalization translated into enthusiasm for building local, sustainable food systems that could be controlled by those who participated in them. The food security agenda also rested on and benefited from the institutional infrastructure that had been cobbled together over the years. By centu-

ry's end, land grant schools, once scorned by critics, housed dozens of programs and centers devoted to the study of sustainable agriculture, food security, urban gardening, and the like. Professors who specialized in sustainability and food security research taught cadres of students who went to work in community programs or at the USDA or as professors who taught more students. In many respects, the new food activism echoed the civil, gender, and sexuality rights projects of the 1960s and 1970s, when colleges and universities responded to social change by introducing programs and majors in African American, Native American, women's, and "queer" studies. Once in place, those programs perpetuated themselves thanks to successive generations of students and scholars. So it was with alternative food studies.

252 "Big Three": A useful account of the battle for standards is in Samuel Fromartz, *Organic, Inc.: Natural Foods and How They Grew* (Harcourt, 2006), chapter 6.

"like robins": C. Clare Hinrichs and Patricia Allen, "Selective Patronage and Social Justice: Local Food Consumer Campaigns in Historical Context," *Journal of Agricultural and Environmental Ethics* 21 (2008): 330. Their essay details the background of the campaign.

253 Alternative livestock and meat production: On the complications of making meat, see Chelsea Bardot Lewis and Christian J. Peters, "A Capacity Assessment of New England's Large Animal Slaughter Facilities as Relative to Meat Production for the Regional Food System," *Renewable Agriculture and Food Systems* 27, no. 3 (September 2012): 192–99; Lauren Elizabeth Gwin, "New Pastures, New Food: Building Viable Alternatives to Conventional Beef" (Ph.D. dissertation, University of California–Berkeley, 2006); and Lauren Gwin, "Scaling-up Sustainable Livestock Production: Innovation and Challenges for Grass-Fed Beef in the U.S.," *Journal of Sustainable Agriculture* 33 (2009): 189–209. The point about lack of livestock farmers is made in C. Clare Hinrichs and Rick Welsh, "The Effects of the Industrialization of US Livestock Agriculture on Promoting Sustainable Production Practices," *Agriculture and Human Values* 20, no. 2 (Summer 2003): 125–41.

254 The rules that the USDA: For a summary of the rules, see U.S. Department of Agriculture, Economic Research Service, Market and Trade Economics Division and Resource Economics Division, *Recent Growth Patterns in the U.S. Organic Foods Market,* by Carolyn Dimitri and Catherine Greene, Information Bulletin no. 777, September 2002, p. 19.

"custom-kill": Quoted in Rod Dreher, "USDA-Disapproved: Small Farmers and Big Government," *National Review* 27 (January 2003); accessed online. Dreher interviewed Jenny Drake, who, at this writing, still owns Peaceful Pastures. She eventually found USDA-sanctioned slaughtering facilities.

"I'd have to build": Quoted in ibid.

255   "I told them": Quoted in ibid.

"do we want to let people": Quoted in ibid.

"hire someone": The Massachusetts man's problem is detailed in Molly Colin, "Elite Meat: Shoppers Sold on Organic Produce Find Its Main-Course Counterpart — Certified Beef, Poultry, and Pork — to Be Elusive," *Christian Science Monitor,* July 14, 2003; accessed online.

256   "a little bit bigger piece": Quoted in Worth Wren Jr., "Beefing Up Bottom Line — Cattle Industry Using Range of Marketing Initiatives," *Fort Worth Star-Telegram,* May 7, 2000; accessed online. A useful survey of the state of grass-fed beef just after the turn of the century is John Lozier, Edward Rayburn, and Jane Shaw, "Growing and Selling Pasture-Finished Beef: Results of a Nationwide Survey," *Journal of Sustainable Agriculture* 25, no. 2 (2004): 93–112.

257   "political and culinary appeal": Kim Severson, "Grass Roots Revolution — Will New Beef Put Corn-Raised Cattle out to Pasture?" *San Francisco Chronicle,* June 19, 2002; accessed online.

"add[ed] in the invisible costs": Michael Pollan, "Power Steer," *New York Times Magazine,* March 31, 2002; accessed online.

"As you know": Quoted in Kim Severson, "High Stakes — Bay Area at the Forefront of the Big-Bucks Battle Between Proponents of Grass-Fed Beef and Traditional Cattlemen," *San Francisco Chronicle,* June 19, 2002; accessed online.

"People want to imagine": Quoted in ibid.

"prominent": Milford Prewitt, "Chefs Challenge Peers to Serve Grass-Fed Beef," *Nation's Restaurant News,* May 20, 2002, p. 3.

258   "ironic": Quoted in ibid., 235.

"nanny culture": Ibid.

"a haughty organization": Quoted in ibid.

"We are an elitist": Quoted in ibid.

"I consciously deferred": Quoted in Stacy Finz, "Founder Says New Owners Changing Product Protocol," *San Francisco Chronicle,* February 22, 2009; accessed online.

260   Then there was: It's clear that *The Omnivore's Dilemma,* like *The*

Jungle and *Silent Spring,* was less launching pad than tipping point. It resonated with a public accustomed to asserting its consumer rights and to the allure of alternative foods, whether meat or arugula. But there's no doubt that it also energized a new generation of food activists and converted millions of otherwise indifferent consumers into organic aficionados.

261   "The Easter holiday": See "Letters," *Lancaster (PA) Intelligencer Journal,* March 28, 2002. I found many examples of these form letters, including ones sent on the occasion of World Farm Animals Day, October 2, also the birthday of Mahatma Gandhi.

"Nothing [is] more heartbreaking": Steve Moest, "Why Pork Producers Do What They Do," *Freeport (IL) Journal-Standard,* May 6, 2012; accessed online.

BIBLIOGRAPHY

Five minutes into this project, I realized that its potential bibliography was approximately the size of the known universe and that I could spend the next decade doing nothing but wading through primary sources — newspapers and magazines, meatpacking and agricultural trade journals, congressional hearings, USDA reports, various other federal, state, and city government documents, and the like. And that didn't include an equally stupefying quantity of secondary sources: what other historians as well as sociologists, geographers, anthropologists, and random writers had written about cattle, hogs, chickens, slaughterhouses, ranching and ranchers, feedlots, food retailing, veterinary medicine, vegetarianism, and a nerve-shattering collection of other topics more or less related to meat.

Conclusion: Trying to read every relevant source was a fool's game. Nor, I soon realized, could I include everything that I read in this bibliography; a full list would run to hundreds of pages and my editors would hate me. What follows, then, is the rational middle ground: a bibliography of primary and secondary sources that I found to be the most useful. (Many additional sources, however, are cited in the notes.)

As a historian, I focus on primary documents; I want to find out for myself "what happened," rather than another historian's interpretation of what happened. That meant that I read thousands of primary documents. Rather than detail each one (another fool's errand), I've instead identified the databases and catalogs from which I drew sources, as well as the titles of the most important newspapers on which I relied and serials that are not in-dexed in the databases.

Note: Most of the databases listed are attached to digital *indexes,* but the magazines, journals, and documents to which those indexes refer are not necessarily digitized. This project involved hours of communing with mi-crofilm and microfiche machines.

DATABASES AND CATALOGS

19th Century Historical United States Newspapers
19th Century Masterfile
ABI/INFORM Global
Access World News
Accessible Archives
Agricola
Alt-Press Watch
American Historical Imprints
American Periodical Series (digital and microfilm)
Archive Finder
Catalog of U.S. Government Publications
Core Historical Literature of Agriculture (CORE)
Early American Imprints
Early American Newspapers
Early American Periodicals
EBSCOhost
genealogybank.com
HarpWeek
Hathi Trust Digital Library
Home Economics Archive:
    Research, Tradition, History (HEARTH)
Index to USDA Agricultural Economic Reports
Index to USDA Agriculture Information Bulletins
Making of America
National Agricultural Library
newspaperarchive.com
ProQuest Congressional
ProQuest Dissertations & Theses
Readers' Guide Retrospective
WorldCat

PERIODICALS AND NEWSPAPERS

Alternative Agriculture News
American Egg and Poultry Review
American Poultry Advocate
American Poultry Journal
Boston Globe
Chicago Tribune
Des Moines Register
Farm Journal
Farm Quarterly
Feedstuffs
Godey's Lady's Book
Meat and Live Stock Digest
Milwaukee Sentinel
National Hog Farmer
National Provisioner
New York Produce Review and American Creamery
New York Times
Poultry Science
Reliable Poultry Journal
Successful Farming
Wallaces Farmer
Wall Street Journal
Washington Post

OTHER PRIMARY AND SECONDARY SOURCES

Ackerman, Michael. "Interpreting the Newer Knowledge of Nutrition: Science, Interests, and Values in the Making of Dietary Advice in the United States, 1915–1965." Ph.D. dissertation, University of Virginia, 2005.

Aduddell, Robert, and Louis Cain. "The Consent Decree in the Meatpacking Industry, 1920–1956." *Business History Review* 55, no. 3 (Autumn 1981): 359–78.

———. "Location and Collusion in the Meat Packing Industry." In *Business Enterprise and Economic Change: Essays in Honor of Harold F. Williamson,* edited by Louis P. Cain and Paul J. Uselding, 85–117. The Kent State University Press, 1973.

———. "Public Policy Toward 'The Greatest Trust in the World.'" *Business History Review* 55, no. 2 (Summer 1981): 217–42.

Allen, Patricia. "Reweaving the Food Security Safety Net: Mediating Entitlement and Entrepreneurship." *Agriculture and Human Values* 16, no. 2 (June 1999): 117–29.

———. "Sustainability and Sustenance: The Politics of Sustainable Agriculture and Community Food Security." Ph.D. dissertation, University of California–Santa Cruz, 1998.

———. *Together at the Table: Sustainability and Sustenance in the American Agrifood System*. The Pennsylvania State University Press, 2004.

Allen, Patricia, ed. *Food for the Future: Conditions and Contradictions of Sustainability*. John Wiley & Sons, 1993.

Amstutz, David Lee. "Nebraska's Live Stock Sanitary Commission and the Rise of American Progressivism." *Great Plains Quarterly* 28, no. 4 (Fall 2008): 259–75.

Anderson, E. N. *Everyone Eats: Understanding Food and Culture*. New York University Press, 2005.

Anderson, Jay Allan. "'A Solid Sufficiency': An Ethnography of Yeoman Foodways in Stuart England." Ph.D. dissertation, University of Pennsylvania, 1971.

———. *Industrializing the Corn Belt: Agriculture, Technology, and Environment, 1945–1972*. Northern Illinois University Press, 2009.

———. "Lard to Lean: Making the Meat-Type Hog in Post–World War II America." In *Food Chains: From Farmyard to Shopping Cart*, edited by Warren Belasco and Roger Horowitz, 29–46. University of Pennsylvania Press, 2009.

Anderson, Molly D., and John T. Cook. "Community Food Security: Practice in Need of Theory?" *Agriculture and Human Values* 16, no. 2 (June 1999): 141–50.

Anderson, Virginia DeJohn. *Creatures of Empire: How Domestic Animals Transformed Early America*. Oxford University Press, 2004.

Apple, Rima D. *Vitamania: Vitamins in American Culture*. Rutgers University Press, 1996.

Appleby, Joyce. "Commercial Farming and the 'Agrarian Myth' in the Early Republic." *Journal of American History* 68 (March 1982): 833–49.

Arnould, Richard J. "Changing Patterns of Concentration in American Meat Packing, 1880–1963." *Business History Review* 45, no. 1 (Spring 1971): 18–34.

Aronson, Naomi. "Nutrition as a Social Problem: A Case Study of Entrepreneurial Strategy in Science." *Social Problems* 29, no. 5 (June 1982): 474–87.

———. "Social Definitions of Entitlement: Food Needs, 1885–1920." *Media, Culture and Society* 4 (1982): 51–61.

Arthur, Anthony. *Radical Innocent: Upton Sinclair.* Random House, 2006.

Atkinson, Eva Lash. "Kansas City's Livestock Trade and Packing Industry, 1870–1914: A Study in Regional Growth." Ph.D. dissertation, University of Kansas, 1971.

Backer, Kellen. "World War II and the Triumph of Industrialized Food." Ph.D. dissertation, University of Wisconsin–Madison, 2012.

Baker, Andrew H., and Holly V. Izard. "New England Farmers and the Marketplace, 1780–1865: A Case Study." *Agricultural History* 65 (Summer 1991): 29–52.

Baker, Andrew H., and Holly Izard Paterson. "Farmers' Adaptations to Market in Early-Nineteenth-Century Massachusetts." In *The Farm; The Dublin Seminar for New England Folklife: Annual Proceedings 1986,* edited by Peter Benes, Jane Montague Benes, and Ross W. Beales. Boston University, 1988.

Barham, Mary Elizabeth. "Sustainable Agriculture in the United States and France: A Polanyian Perspective." Ph.D. dissertation, Cornell University, 1999.

Barkema, Alan, and Michael L. Cook. "The Changing U.S. Pork Industry: A Dilemma for Public Policy." *Economic Review* 78, no. 2 (Second Quarter 1993): 49–65.

Barnett, L. Margaret. "'Every Man His Own Physician': Dietetic Fads, 1890–1914." In *The Science and Culture of Nutrition, 1840–1940,* edited by Harmke Kamminga and Andrew Cunningham, 155–78. Rodopi, 1995.

Barnhart, Walt. *Kenny's Shoes: A Walk Through the Storied Life of the Remarkable Kenneth W. Monfort.* Infinity Publishing, 2008.

Beal, Thomas David. "Selling Gotham: The Retail Trade in New York City from the Public Market to Alexander T. Stewart's Marble Palace, 1625–1860." Ph.D. dissertation, State University of New York–Stony Brook, 1998.

Beeman, Randall S., and James A. Pritchard. *A Green and Permanent Land: Ecology and Agriculture in the Twentieth Century.* University Press of Kansas, 2001.

Beers, Diane L. *For the Prevention of Cruelty: The History and Legacy of Animal Rights Activism in the United States.* Swallow Press/Ohio University Press, 2006.

Belasco, Warren J. *Appetite for Change: How the Counterculture Took On the Food Industry.* 2d ed. Cornell University Press, 2007.

———. *Meals to Come: A History of the Future of Food.* University of California Press, 2006.

Belasco, Warren, and Roger Horowitz, eds. *Food Chains: From Farmyard to Shopping Cart.* University of Pennsylvania Press, 2009.

Belden, Joe, Gibby Edwards, Cynthia Guyer, and Lee Webb. *New Directions in Farm, Land and Food Policies: A Time for State and Local Action.* Conference on Alternative State and Local Policies, Agriculture Project, [1979].

Belden, Joe, and Gregg Forte. *Toward a National Food Policy.* Exploratory Project for Economic Alternatives, 1976.

Bellows, Anne C., and Michael W. Hamm. "U.S.-Based Community Food Security: Influences, Practice, Debate." *Journal for the Study of Food and Society* 6, no. 1 (Winter 2002): 31–44.

Benjamin, Gary L. "Industrialization in Hog Production: Implications for Midwest Agriculture." *Economic Perspectives* 21, no. 1 (January/February 1997): 2–13.

Berry, Jeffrey M. "Consumers and the Hunger Lobby." *Proceedings of the Academy of Political Science* 34, no. 3 (1982): 68–78.

———. *Lobbying for the People: The Political Behavior of Public Interest Groups.* Princeton University Press, 1977.

Beus, Curtis E., and Riley E. Dunlap. "Conventional Versus Alternative Agriculture: The Paradigmatic Roots of the Debate." *Rural Sociology* 55, no. 4 (Winter 1990): 590–616.

Bidwell, Percy Wells, and John I. Falconer. *History of Agriculture in the Northern United States, 1620-1860.* 1925. Reprint, Carnegie Institution of Washington, 1941.

Bieber, Ralph P. "Introduction." In Joseph G. McCoy, *Historic Sketches of the Cattle Trade of the West and Southwest,* edited by Ralph P. Bieber, 17–68. 1874. Reprint, Arthur H. Clark Company, 1940.

Blum, Joseph A. "South San Francisco: The Making of an Industrial City." *California History* 63 (Spring 1984): 114–34.

Bonanno, Alessandro, and Douglas H. Constance. "Corporations and the State in the Global Era: The Case of Seaboard Farms and Texas." *Rural Sociology* 71, no. 1 (2006): 59–84.

———. "Mega Hog Farms in the Texas Panhandle Region: Corporate Actions and Local Resistance." *Research in Social Movements, Conflicts and Change* 22 (2000): 83–110.

Bonnen, James T., William P. Browne, and David B. Schweikhardt. "Further Observations on the Changing Nature of National Agricultural Policy Decision Processes, 1946-1995." *Agricultural History* 70, no. 2 (Spring 1996): 130–52.

Bosso, Christopher J. *Pesticides and Politics: The Life Cycle of a Public Issue.* University of Pittsburgh Press, 1987.

Boston, Massachusetts. City Document no. 74. *Report on the Sale of Bad Meat in Boston.* N.p., [1871].

Bovee, David. "The Church and the Land: The National Catholic Rural Life Conference and American Society, 1923–1985." Ph.D. dissertation, University of Chicago, 1986.

Bowen, Joanne. "A Comparative Analysis of the New England and Chesapeake Herding Systems." In *Historical Archaeology of the Chesapeake,* edited by Paul A. Shackel and Barbara J. Little, 155–67. Smithsonian Institution Press, 1994.

———. "A Study of Seasonality and Subsistence: Eighteenth-Century Suffield, Connecticut." Ph.D. dissertation, Brown University, 1990.

Boyd, William. "Making Meat: Science, Technology, and American Poultry Production." *Technology and Culture* 42, no. 4 (October 2001): 631–64.

Boyd, William, and Michael Watts. "Agro-Industrial Just-in-Time: The Chicken Industry and Postwar American Capitalism." In *Globalising Food: Agrarian Questions and Global Restructuring,* edited by David Goodman and Michael Watts, 192–225. Routledge, 1997.

[Bradley, Cyrus P.] "Journal of Cyrus P. Bradley." *Ohio Archaeological and Historical Publications* 15 (1906): 207–70.

Bradley, Karen J. "Agrarian Ideology and Agricultural Policy: California Grangers and the Post-World War II Farm Policy Debate." *Agricultural History* 69, no. 2 (Spring 1995): 240–56.

Bradley, Linda J., and Barbara D. Merino. "Stuart Chase: A Radical CPA and the Meat Packing Investigation, 1917–1918." *Business and Economic History* 23, no. 1 (Fall 1994): 190–200.

Braeman, John. "The Square Deal in Action: A Case Study in the Growth of the 'National Police Power.'" In *Change and Continuity in Twentieth-Century America,* edited by John Braeman, Robert H. Bremner, and Everett Walters, 35–80. Ohio State University Press, 1964.

Brantz, Dorothee. "Slaughter in the City: The Establishment of Public Abattoirs in Paris and Berlin, 1780–1914." Ph.D. dissertation, University of Chicago, 2003.

Breitbach, Carrie. "Changing Landscapes of Social Reproduction in South Dakota: Restructuring the Cattle Beef Industry." Ph.D. dissertation, Syracuse University, 2006.

Brinkley, Douglas. *The Wilderness Warrior: Theodore Roosevelt and the Crusade for America.* HarperCollins, 2009.

Broadway, Michael J., and Donald D. Stull. "'I'll Do Whatever You Want, but It Hurts': Worker Safety and Community Health in Modern Meatpacking." *Labor: Studies in Working-Class History of the Americas* 5, no. 2 (2008): 27–37.

———. "The Wages of Food Factories." *Food & Foodways* 18, no. 1/2 (2010): 43–65.

Brody, David. *The Butcher Workmen: A Study of Unionization.* Harvard University Press, 1964.

Brooks, Richard David. "Cattle Ranching in Colonial South Carolina: A Case Study in History and Archaeology of the Lazarus/Catherina Brown Cowpen." Master's thesis, University of South Carolina, 1988.

Brown, Ralph H. *Historical Geography of the United States.* Harcourt, Brace and Company, 1948.

Browne, William P. "Challenging Industrialization: The Rekindling of Agrarian Protest in a Modern Agriculture, 1977–1987." *Studies in American Political Development* 7 (Spring 1993): 1–34.

———. *Cultivating Congress: Constituents, Issues, and Interests in Agricultural Policymaking.* University Press of Kansas, 1995.

———. *Private Interests, Public Policy, and American Agriculture.* University Press of Kansas, 1988.

Bugos, Glenn E. "Intellectual Property Protection in the American Chicken-Breeding Industry." *Business History Review* 66, no. 1 (Spring 1992): 127–68.

Buhr, Brian Lee. "Economic Impacts of Growth Promotants in the Beef, Pork, and Poultry Industries." Ph.D. dissertation, Iowa State University, 1992.

Burnett, Edmund Cody. "Hog Raising and Hog Driving in the Region of the French Broad River." *Agricultural History* 20 (April 1946): 86–103.

Burnett, Paul. "The Visible Land: Agricultural Economics, US Export Agriculture, and International Development, 1918–65." Ph.D. dissertation, University of Pennsylvania, 2008.

Busch, Lawrence, and William B. Lacy, eds. *Food Security in the United States.* Westview Press, 1984.

Butler, Jon. *Becoming American: The Revolution Before 1776.* Harvard University Press, 2000.

Buttel, Frederick H. "Ever Since Hightower: The Politics of Agricultural Research Activism in the Molecular Age." *Agriculture and Human Values* 22 (2005): 275–83.

———. "The Sociology of Agricultural Sustainability: Some Observations on the Future of Sustainable Agriculture." *Agriculture, Ecosystems and Environment* 46 (1993): 175–86.

Butz, Dale E., and George L. Baker. *The Changing Structure of the Meat Economy*. Harvard University, Graduate School of Business Administration, Division of Research, 1960.

Calabria, Mark Anthony. "On the Origins of Federal Food and Drug Regulation." Ph.D. dissertation, George Mason University, 1995.

Caldwell, Dorothy J. "David Rankin: 'Cattle King' of Missouri." *Missouri Historical Review* 66 (April 1972): 377–94.

Carolan, Michael. *The Real Cost of Cheap Food*. Earthscan, 2011.

Carpenter, Clifford D. "The Early Cattle Industry in Missouri." *Missouri Historical Review* 47 (April 1953): 201–15.

Carr, Lois Green, Russell R. Menard, and Lorena S. Walsh. *Robert Cole's World: Agriculture and Society in Early Maryland*. University of North Carolina Press, 1991.

Case, Andrew N. "Looking for Organic America: J. I. Rodale, the Rodale Press, and the Popular Culture of Environmentalism in the Postwar United States." Ph.D. dissertation, University of Wisconsin–Madison, 2012.

Cassedy, James H. "Applied Microscopy and American Pork Diplomacy: Charles Wardell Stiles in Germany, 1898–1899." *Isis* 62, no. 1 (Spring 1971): 5–20.

Center for Rural Affairs. *Who Will Sit Up with the Corporate Sow?* Walthill, NE, [1974].

Clancy, Katherine L. "Sustainable Agriculture and Domestic Hunger: Rethinking a Link Between Production and Consumption." In *Food for the Future: Conditions and Contradictions of Sustainability*, edited by Patricia Allen, 251–93. John Wiley & Sons, 1993.

Clark, Lisa F. "Organic Limited: The Corporate Rise and Spectacular Change in the Canadian and American Organic Food Sectors." Ph.D. dissertation, Simon Fraser University, 2007.

Clarke, Sally H. *Regulation and the Revolution in United States Farm Productivity*. Cambridge University Press, 1994.

Clawson, Marion. *The Western Range Livestock Industry*. McGraw-Hill Book Company, 1950.

Clemen, Rudolf Alexander. *The American Livestock and Meat Industry*. The Ronald Press, 1923.

Clements, Roger V. "British Investment and American Legislative Restrictions in the Trans-Mississippi West, 1880–1890." *Mississippi Valley Historical Review* 42, no. 2 (September 1955): 207–28.

Cobb, James C. *The Selling of the South: The Southern Crusade for Industrial Development, 1936–1990*. 2d ed. University of Illinois Press, 1993.

Cochran, Thomas C. *Railroad Leaders, 1845–1890: The Business Mind in Action.* Harvard University Press, 1953.

Cochrane, Willard W. *The Curse of American Agricultural Abundance: A Sustainable Solution.* University of Nebraska Press, 2003.

——. *The Development of American Agriculture: A Historical Analysis.* 2d ed. University of Minnesota Press, 1993.

Cohen, Barbara E., and Martha R. Burt. *Eliminating Hunger: Food Security Policy for the 1990s.* The Urban Institute, 1989.

Cohen, Lizabeth. *A Consumers' Republic: The Politics of Mass Consumption in Postwar America.* Vintage Books, 2003.

Collingham, Lizzie. *The Taste of War: World War Two and the Battle for Food.* Allen Lane, Penguin Group, 2011.

Conkin, Paul K. *A Revolution down on the Farm: The Transformation of American Agriculture Since 1929.* University Press of Kentucky, 2008.

Connor, John M., and William A. Schiek. *Food Processing: An Industrial Powerhouse in Transition.* 2d ed. John Wiley & Sons, 1997.

Cooke, Kathy J. "From Science to Practice, or Practice to Science? Chickens and Eggs in Raymond Pearl's Agricultural Breeding Research, 1907–1916." *Isis* 88, no. 1 (March 1997): 62–86.

Coppin, Dawn Michelle. "Capitalist Pigs: Large-Scale Swine Facilities and the Mutual Construction of Nature and Society." Ph.D. dissertation, University of Illinois–Urbana-Champaign, 2002.

Craig, Lee A., Barry Goodwin, and Thomas Grennes. "The Effect of Mechanical Refrigeration on Nutrition in the United States." *Social Science History* 28, no. 2 (Summer 2004): 325–36.

Cronon, William. *Nature's Metropolis: Chicago and the Great West.* W. W. Norton & Company, 1991.

Crouse, Janet Kay Willhousen. "The Decline of German-American Friendship: Beef, Pork, and Politics, 1890–1906." Ph.D. dissertation, University of Delaware, 1980.

Cuff, Robert. "The Dilemmas of Voluntarism: Hoover and the Pork-Packing Agreement of 1917–1919." *Agricultural History* 53, no. 4 (October 1979): 727–47.

Cullather, Nick. "The Foreign Policy of the Calorie." *American Historical Review* 112, no. 2 (April 2007): 337–64.

——. *The Hungry World: America's Cold War Battle Against Poverty in Asia.* Harvard University Press, 2010.

Dahlberg, Kenneth A. "Regenerative Food Systems: Broadening the Scope and Agenda of Sustainability." In *Food for the Future: Conditions and*

Contradictions of Sustainability, edited by Patricia Allen, 75–102. John Wiley & Sons, 1993.

Dale, Edward Everett. *The Range Cattle Industry: Ranching on the Great Plains from 1865 to 1925*. 1930. Reprint, University of Oklahoma Press, 1960.

Danbom, David B. *Born in the Country: A History of Rural America*, 2d ed. The Johns Hopkins University Press, 2006.

———. *The Resisted Revolution: Urban America and the Industrialization of Agriculture, 1900–1930*. Iowa State University Press, 1979.

Davidson, Alan. *The Oxford Companion to Food*. 2d ed. Edited by Tom Jaine. Oxford University Press, 2006.

Davis, John H., and Ray A. Goldberg. *A Concept of Agribusiness*. Harvard University, 1957.

Dean, Virgil W. *An Opportunity Lost: The Truman Administration and the Farm Policy Debate*. University of Missouri Press, 2006.

Deutsch, Tracey. *Building a Housewife's Paradise: Gender, Politics, and American Grocery Stores in the Twentieth Century*. University of North Carolina Press, 2010.

———. "From 'Wild Animal Stores' to Women's Sphere: Supermarkets and the Politics of Mass Consumption, 1930–1950." *Business and Economic History* 28, no. 2 (Fall 1999): 143–53.

Devereaux, Charan. "Food Fight: The US, Europe, and Trade in Hormone-Treated Beef." Case N14–02–1677.0. Kennedy School of Government, Case Program, Harvard University, 2002.

Dilorenzo, Thomas J. "The Origins of Antitrust: An Interest-Group Perspective." *International Review of Law and Economics* 5 (1985): 73–90.

Doyle, William Michael. "The Evolution of Financial Practices and Financial Structures Among American Manufacturers, 1875–1905: Case Studies of the Sugar Refining and Meat Packing Industries." Ph.D. dissertation, University of Tennessee, 1991.

Drabenstott, Mark. "Industrialization: Steady Current or Tidal Wave?" *Choices: The Magazine of Food, Farm & Resource Issues* 9, no. 4 (4th Quarter 1994). Accessed online.

———. "This Little Piggy Went to Market: Will the New Pork Industry Call the Heartland Home?" *Economic Review* (Federal Reserve Bank of Kansas City) 83, no. 3 (1998): 79–97.

Dudley, Kathryn Marie. "The Entrepreneurial Self: Identity and Morality in a Midwestern Farming Community." In Jane Adams, *Fighting for the Farm: Rural America Transformed*, 175–91, 282–83. University of Pennsylvania Press, 2003.

Duffy, John. *The Sanitarians: A History of American Public Health.* University of Illinois Press, 1990.

Dunbar, Gary S. "Colonial Carolina Cowpens." *Agricultural History* 35 (July 1961): 125–30.

Dunlap, Thomas R. *DDT: Scientists, Citizens, and Public Policy.* Princeton University Press, 1981.

Dupree, A. Hunter. *Science in the Federal Government: A History of Policies and Activities to 1940.* Belknap Press of Harvard University Press, 1957.

Durning, Alan B., and Holly B. Brough. *Taking Stock: Animal Farming and the Environment.* Worldwatch Paper 103. July 1991.

Dykstra, Robert R. *The Cattle Towns.* Alfred A. Knopf, 1968.

Egan, Michael. "Barry Commoner and the Science of Survival." Ph.D. dissertation, Washington State University, 2004.

Emerson, William D. *History and Incidents of Indian Corn, and Its Culture.* Wrightson & Co., 1878.

Enfield, Edward. *Indian Corn: Its Value, Culture, and Uses.* D. Appleton and Company, 1866.

Fausold, Martin L. "James W. Wadsworth Sr. and the Meat Inspection Act of 1906." *New York History* 51, no. 1 (January 1970): 43–61.

Feenstra, Gail W. "Local Food Systems and Sustainable Communities." *American Journal of Alternative Agriculture* 12, no. 1 (1997): 28–36.

Ferleger, Louis, and William Lazonick. "The Managerial Revolution and the Developmental States: The Case of U.S. Agriculture." *Business and Economic History* 22, no. 2 (Winter 1993): 67–98.

Fiddes, Nick. *Meat: A Natural Symbol.* Routledge, 1991.

[Fink, Albert]. *Report upon the Relative Cost of Transporting Live Stock and Dressed Beef.* Russell Brothers, 1883.

Finlay, Mark R. "Early Marketing of the Theory of Nutrition: The Science and Culture of Liebig's Extract of Meat." In *The Science and Culture of Nutrition, 1840–1940,* edited by Harmke Kamminga and Andrew Cunningham, 48–74. Rodopi, 1995.

———. "Hogs, Antibiotics, and the Industrial Environments of Postwar Agriculture." In *Industrializing Organisms: Introducing Evolutionary History,* edited by Susan R. Schrepfer and Philip Scranton, 237–60. Routledge, 2004.

Fisher, Andrew, and Robert Gottlieb. "Community Food Security: Policies for a More Sustainable Food System in the Context of the 1995 Farm Bill and Beyond." The Ralph and Goldy Lewis Center for Regional Policy Studies, School of Public Policy and Social Research, University of California–Los Angeles. Working Paper no. 13. March 1995.

Fite, Gilbert C. *American Farmers: The New Minority*. Indiana University Press, 1981.

Fitzgerald, Deborah. *Every Farm a Factory: The Industrial Ideal in American Agriculture*. Yale University Press, 2003.

Frazier, William C., and Dennis C. Westhoff. *Food Microbiology*. 4th ed. McGraw-Hill Book Company, 1988.

Freidberg, Susanne. *Fresh: A Perishable History*. Belknap Press of Harvard University Press, 2009.

Freyer, Tony A. "The Federal Courts, Localism, and the National Economy, 1865–1900." *Business History Review* 53, no. 3 (Autumn 1979): 343–63.

Friedman, Karen J. "Victualling Colonial Boston." *Agricultural History* 47 (July 1973): 189–205.

Friedmann, Harriet. "After Midas's Feast: Alternative Food Regimes for the Future." In *Food for the Future: Conditions and Contradictions of Sustainability,* edited by Patricia Allen, 213–33. John Wiley & Sons, 1993.

———. "Distance and Durability: Shaky Foundations of the World Food Economy." *Third World Quarterly* 13, no. 2 (1992): 371–83.

———. "The Political Economy of Food: The Rise and Fall of the Postwar International Food Order." *American Journal of Sociology* 88, Supplement (1982): S248–S286.

Frink, Maurice, W. Turrentine Jackson, and Agnes Wright Spring. *When Grass Was King*. University of Colorado Press, 1956.

Fromartz, Samuel. *Organic, Inc.: Natural Foods and How They Grew*. Harcourt, 2006.

Furuseth, Owen J. "Restructuring of Hog Farming in North Carolina: Explosion and Implosion." *Professional Geographer* 49, no. 4 (1997): 391–403.

Fusonie, Alan E. "John H. Davis: Architect of the Agribusiness Concept Revisited." *Agricultural History* 69, no. 2 (Spring 1995): 326–48.

Gardner, Bruce L. *American Agriculture in the Twentieth Century: How It Flourished and What It Cost*. Harvard University Press, 2002.

Garrison, J. Ritchie. "Farm Dynamics and Regional Exchange: The Connecticut Valley Beef Trade, 1670–1850." *Agricultural History* 61 (Summer 1987): 1–17.

Gates, Paul Wallace. "Cattle Kings in the Prairies." *Mississippi Valley Historical Review* 35 (December 1948): 379–412.

———. "Frontier Landlords and Pioneer Tenants." *Journal of the Illinois State Historical Society* 38 (June 1945): 143–206.

———. "Hoosier Cattle Kings." *Indiana Magazine of History* 44 (March 1948): 1–24.

Geib, Paul E. "'Everything but the Squeal': The Milwaukee Stockyards and

Meat-Packing Industry, 1840–1930." *Wisconsin Magazine of History* 78, no. 1 (Autumn 1994): 3–23.

German, Gene Arlin. "The Dynamics of Food Retailing, 1900–1975." Ph.D. dissertation, Cornell University, 1978.

Gignilliat, John L. "Pigs, Politics, and Protection: The European Boycott of American Pork, 1879–1891." *Agricultural History* 35, no. 1 (January 1961): 3–12.

Gilliam, Henry C., J. Rod Martin, William G. Bursch, and Richard B. Smith. "Economic Consequences of Banning the Use of Antibiotics at Subtherapeutic Levels in Livestock Production." *Departmental Technical Report Number 73-2*. Department of Agricultural Economics and Sociology, Texas Agricultural Experiment Station, 1973.

Gisolfi, Monica Richmond. "From Cotton Farmers to Poultry Growers: The Rise of Industrial Agriculture in Upcountry Georgia, 1914–1960." Ph.D. dissertation, Columbia University, 2007.

Glaeser, Edward L., and Andrei Shleifer. "The Rise of the Regulatory State." *Journal of Economic Literature* 41, no. 2 (June 2003): 401–25.

Glickman, Lawrence B. *Buying Power: A History of Consumer Activism in America*. University of Chicago Press, 2009.

Goodwin, Lorine Swainston. *The Pure Food, Drink, and Drug Crusaders, 1879–1914*. McFarland & Company, 1999.

Gordon, David. "The Beef Trust: Antitrust Policy and the Meat Packing Industry, 1902–1922." Ph.D. dissertation, Claremont Graduate School, 1983.

Gordon, Sanford D. "Attitudes Toward the Trusts Before the Sherman Act." *Southern Economic Journal* 30, no. 2 (October 1963): 156–67.

Gordon, Stephen Canning. "The City as 'Porkopolis': Some Factors in the Rise of the Meat Packing Industry in Cincinnati, 1825–1861." Master's thesis, Miami University, 1981.

———. "From Slaughterhouse to Soap-Boiler: Cincinnati's Meat Packing Industry, Changing Technologies, and the Rise of Mass Production, 1825–1870." *IA* 16 (1990): 55–67.

Gottlieb, Robert. *Environmentalism Unbound: Exploring New Pathways for Change*. The MIT Press, 2001.

Gottlieb, Robert, and Andrew Fisher. "Community Food Security and Environmental Justice: Searching for a Common Discourse." *Agriculture and Human Values* 3, no. 3 (Summer 1996): 23–32.

———. "'First Feed the Face': Environmental Justice and Community Food Security." *Antipode* 28, no. 2 (1996): 193–203.

Gottlieb, Robert, and Anupama Joshi. *Food Justice*. The MIT Press, 2010.

Graves, Russell. "Garden City: The Development of an Agricultural Community on the Great Plains." Ph.D. dissertation, University of Wisconsin–Madison, 2004.

Gressley, Gene M. *Bankers and Cattlemen*. Alfred A. Knopf, 1966.

Grey, Mark A. "Those Bastards Can Go to Hell! Small-Farmer Resistance to Vertical Integration and Concentration in the Pork Industry." *Human Organization* 59, no. 2 (Summer 2000). Accessed online.

Grier, Katherine C. "'The Eden of Home': Changing Understandings of Cruelty and Kindness to Animals in Middle-Class American Households, 1820–1900." In *Animals in Human Histories: The Mirror of Nature and Culture*, edited by Mary J. Henninger-Voss, 316–62. University of Rochester Press, 2002.

Grob, Gerald N. *The Deadly Truth: A History of Disease in America*. Harvard University Press, 2002.

Guither, Harold D. *The Food Lobbyists: Behind the Scenes of Food and Agri-Politics*. D. C. Heath and Company, 1980.

Guthman, Julie. *Agrarian Dreams: The Paradox of Organic Farming in California*. University of California Press, 2004.

———. *Weighing In: Obesity, Food Justice, and the Limits of Capitalism*. University of California Press, 2011.

Guthman, Julie, Amy W. Morris, and Patricia Allen. "Squaring Farm Security and Food Security in Two Types of Alternative Food Institutions." *Rural Sociology* 71, no. 4 (2006): 662–84.

Gwin, Lauren Elizabeth. "New Pastures, New Food: Building Viable Alternatives to Conventional Beef." Ph.D. dissertation, University of California–Berkeley, 2006.

———. "Scaling-Up Sustainable Livestock Production: Innovation and Challenges for Grass-Fed Beef in the U.S." *Journal of Sustainable Agriculture* 33 (2009): 189–209.

Hadwiger, Don F., and William P. Browne. *The New Politics of Food*. D. C. Heath and Company, 1978.

Hall, Tom G. "Wilson and the Food Crisis: Agricultural Price Control During World War I." *Agricultural History* 47, no. 1 (January 1973): 25–46.

Halweil, Brian. *Home Grown: The Case for Local Food in a Global Market*. Worldwatch Paper 163. November 2002.

Hamilton, Shane. "Analyzing Commodity Chains: Linkages or Restraints?" In *Food Chains: From Farmyard to Shopping Cart*, edited by Warren Belasco and Roger Horowitz, 16–25. University of Pennsylvania Press, 2009.

———. "The Economies and Conveniences of Modern-Day Living: Frozen

Foods and Mass Marketing, 1945–1965." *Business History Review* 77, no.
1 (Spring 2003): 33–60.

———. *Trucking Country: The Road to America's Wal-Mart Economy*. Princeton University Press, 2008.

Hamlin, Christopher, and John T. McGreevy. "The Greening of America, Catholic Style, 1930–1950." *Environmental History* 11 (July 2006): 464–99.

Hansen, John Mark. *Gaining Access: Congress and the Farm Lobby, 1919–1981*. University of Chicago Press, 1991.

Harding, T. Swann. *Two Blades of Grass: A History of Scientific Development in the U.S. Department of Agriculture*. University of Oklahoma Press, 1947.

Harley, C. Knick. "Steers Afloat: The North Atlantic Meat Trade, Liner Predominance, and Freight Rates, 1870–1913." *Journal of Economic History* 68, no. 4 (December 2008): 1028–58.

Hart, John Fraser. *The Changing Scale of American Agriculture*. University of Virginia Press, 2003.

Hays, Samuel P. *Conservation and the Gospel of Efficiency: The Progressive Conservation Movement, 1890–1920*. Harvard University Press, 1959.

Hazlett, O. James. "Chaos and Conspiracy: The Kansas City Livestock Trade, 1886–1892." *Kansas History* 15, no. 2 (Summer 1992): 126–44.

Henlein, Paul C. *Cattle Kingdom in the Ohio Valley, 1783–1860*. University of Kentucky Press, 1959.

———, ed. "Journal of F. and W. Renick on an Exploring Tour of the Mississippi and Missouri Rivers in the Year 1819." *Agricultural History* 30 (October 1956): 174–86.

Hilliard, Sam Bowers. *Hog Meat and Hoecake: Food Supply in the Old South, 1840–1860*. Southern Illinois University Press, 1972.

Himmelberg, Robert F., ed. *The Rise of Big Business and the Beginnings of Antitrust and Railroad Regulation, 1870–1900*. Garland Publishing, 1994.

Hinrichs, C. Clare, and Patricia Allen. "Selective Patronage and Social Justice: Local Food Consumer Campaigns in Historical Context." *Journal of Agricultural and Environmental Ethics* 21 (2008): 329–52.

Hinrichs, C. Clare, and Thomas A. Lyson, eds. *Remaking the North American Food System: Strategies for Sustainability*. University of Nebraska Press, 2007.

Hinrichs, C. Clare, and Rick Welsh. "The Effects of the Industrialization of US Livestock Agriculture on Promoting Sustainable Production Practices." *Agriculture and Human Values* 20, no. 2 (Summer 2003): 125–41.

Hofstader, Richard. "What Happened to the Antitrust Movement? Notes on the Evolution of an American Creed." In *Antitrust and Business Regulation in the Post War Era, 1946–1964*, edited by Robert F. Himmelberg, 71–151. 1964. Reprint, Garland Publishing, 1994.

Hoganson, Kristin L. *Consumers' Imperium: The Global Production of American Domesticity, 1865–1920*. University of North Carolina Press, 2007.

Homenuck, Henry Peter Michael. "Historical Geography of the Cincinnati Pork Industry: 1810–1883." Master's thesis, University of Cincinnati, 1965.

Hopkins, John A. *Economic History of the Production of Beef Cattle in Iowa*. State Historical Society of Iowa, 1928.

Horowitz, Roger. "'Be Loyal to Your Industry': J. Frank Gordy, Jr., the Cooperative Extension Service, and the Making of a Business Community in the Delmarva Poultry Industry, 1945–1970." *Delaware History* 27, no. 1/2 (Spring 1996): 3–18.

———. *Putting Meat on the American Table: Taste, Technology, Transformation*. The Johns Hopkins University Press, 2006.

Horowitz, Roger, Jeffrey M. Pilcher, and Sydney Watts. "Meat for the Multitudes: Market Culture in Paris, New York City, and Mexico City over the Long Nineteenth Century." *American Historical Review* 109, no. 4 (October 2004): 1054–83.

Hoy, Suellen, and Walter Nugent. "Public Health or Protectionism? The German-American Pork War, 1880–1891." *Bulletin of the History of Medicine* 63 (1989): 198–244.

Hudson, John C. *Making the Corn Belt: A Geographical History of Middle-Western Agriculture*. Indiana University Press, 1994.

Hudson, Michael A., Bruce J. Sherrick, and Michael A. Mazzocco. "A Changing Food and Agribusiness Sector: Its Impacts on Farm Structure." In *Size, Structure, and the Changing Face of American Agriculture*, edited by Arne Hallam, 412–43. Westview Press, 1993.

Hurt, R. Douglas. "Pork and Porkopolis." *Cincinnati Historical Society Bulletin* 40 (1982): 191–215.

———. *Problems of Plenty: The American Farmer in the Twentieth Century*. Ivan R. Dee, 2002.

Igler, David. *Industrial Cowboys: Miller & Lux and the Transformation of the Far West, 1850–1920*. University of California Press, 2001.

Isenberg, Andrew C. *The Destruction of the Bison: An Environmental History, 1750–1920*. Cambridge University Press, 2000.

Jacobs, Meg. "'How About Some Meat?': The Office of Price Administration, Consumption Politics, and State Building from the Bottom Up, 1941–1946." *Journal of American History* 84, no. 3 (December 1997): 910–41.

——. *Pocketbook Politics: Economic Citizenship in Twentieth-Century America*. Princeton University Press, 2005.

Janzen, Mark Ryan. "The Cranberry Scare of 1959: The Beginning of the End of the Delaney Clause." Ph.D. dissertation, Texas A&M University, 2010.

Johnsen, Carolyn. *Raising a Stink: The Struggle Over Factory Farms in Nebraska*. University of Nebraska Press, 2003.

Johnson, Arthur M. "Theodore Roosevelt and the Bureau of Corporations." *Mississippi Valley Historical Review* 45, no. 4 (March 1959): 571–90.

Johnson, H. Thomas. *Agricultural Depression in the 1920s: Economic Fact or Statistical Artifact?* Garland Publishing, 1985.

Johnson, Lindgren. "To 'Admit All Cattle Without Distinction': Reconstructing Slaughter in the *Slaughterhouse Cases* and the New Orleans Crescent City Slaughterhouse." In *Meat, Modernity, and the Rise of the Slaughterhouse*, edited by Paula Young Lee, 198–215. University of New Hampshire Press, 2008.

Jones, Elizabeth Ann. "The EC Hormone Ban of U.S. Meat: The U.S. Response." Master's thesis, University of Texas at Austin, 1990.

Jones, Lu Ann. "Re-visioning the Countryside: Southern Women, Rural Reform, and the Farm Economy in the Twentieth Century." Ph.D. dissertation, University of North Carolina, 1996.

Jones, Robert Leslie. "The Beef Cattle Industry in Ohio Prior to the Civil War." *Ohio Historical Quarterly* 64, no. 2 (April 1955): 168–94.

Jordan, Terry G. *North American Cattle-Ranching Frontiers: Origins, Diffusion, and Differentiation*. University of New Mexico Press, 1993.

Kamminga, Harmke, and Andrew Cunningham. "Introduction: The Science and Culture of Nutrition, 1840–1890." In *The Science and Culture of Nutrition, 1840–1940*, edited by Harmke Kamminga and Andrew Cunningham, 1–14. Rodopi, 1995.

Kane, R. James. "Populism, Progressivism, and Pure Food." *Agricultural History* 38, no. 3 (July 1964): 161–66.

Kastner, Justin, Douglas Powell, Jason Ackelson, Terry Crowley, and Karen Huff. "Lessons from Long Island: Public Health Science and Agricultural Trade." *Long Island Historical Journal* 17, no. 1 (May 2004): 151–67.

Keller, Morton. *Regulating a New Economy: Public Policy and Economic Change in America, 1900–1933*. Harvard University Press, 1990.

Keuchel, Edward F. "Chemicals and Meat: The Embalmed Beef Scandal of the Spanish-American War." *Bulletin of the History of Medicine* 48 (1974): 249–64.

Kiple, Kenneth F., and Kriemhild Coneè Ornelas, eds. *The Cambridge World History of Food*. Cambridge University Press, 2000.

Kirby, David. *Animal Factory: The Looming Threat of Industrial Pig, Dairy, and Poultry Farms to Humans and the Environment.* St. Martin's Griffin, 2010.

Kirk, Andrew G. *Counterculture Green: The Whole Earth Catalog and American Environmentalism.* University Press of Kansas, 2007.

Kleeb, Scott Michael. "The Atlantic West: Cowboys, Capitalists and the Making of an American Myth." Ph.D. dissertation, Yale University, 2006.

Klonsky, Karen. "Forces Impacting the Production of Organic Foods." *Agriculture and Human Values* 17, no. 3 (September 2000): 233–43.

Kloppenburg, Jack Ralph, Jr. *First the Seed: The Political Economy of Plant Biotechnology,* 2d ed. University of Wisconsin Press, 2004.

Kloppenburg, Jack, Jr., John Hendrickson, and G. W. Stevenson. "Coming In to the Foodshed." *Agriculture and Human Values* 13, no. 3 (Summer 1996): 33–42.

Knapp, Joseph G. "A Review of Chicago Stock Yards History." *The University Journal of Business* 2 (June 1924): 331–46.

Knapp, Vincent J. "The Democratization of Meat and Protein in Late Eighteenth- and Nineteenth-Century Europe." *The Historian* 59, no. 3 (March 1997): 541–51.

Krause, Kenneth R., and Leonard R. Kyle. "Economic Factors Underlying the Incidence of Large Farming Units: The Current Situation and Probable Trends." *American Journal of Agricultural Economics* 52, no. 5 (December 1970): 748–61.

Kulikoff, Allan. *From British Peasants to Colonial American Farmers.* University of North Carolina Press, 2000.

Kwitny, Jonathan. *Vicious Circles: The Mafia in the Marketplace.* W. W. Norton & Company, 1979.

Labbé, Ronald M., and Jonathan Lurie. *The Slaughterhouse Cases: Regulation, Reconstruction, and the Fourteenth Amendment.* University Press of Kansas, 2003.

Laing, Wesley Newton. "Cattle in Early Virginia." Ph.D. dissertation, University of Virginia, 1952.

Lamoreaux, Naomi R. *The Great Merger Movement in American Business, 1894–1904.* Cambridge University Press, 1985.

Landon, David B. "Feeding Colonial Boston: A Zooarchaeological Study." *Historical Archaeology* 30, no. 1 (1996): 1–153.

Langston, Nancy. "The Retreat from Precaution: Regulating Diethylstilbestrol (DES), Endocrine Disruptors, and Environmental Health." *Environmental History* 13 (January 2008): 41–65.

Lauck, Jon. *American Agriculture and the Problem of Monopoly: The Politi-*

cal Economy of Grain Belt Farming, 1953–1980. University of Nebraska Press, 2000.

Law, Marc T. "The Origins of State Pure Food Regulation." *The Journal of Economic History* 63, no. 4 (December 2003): 1103–30.

Leavitt, Charles Townsend. "The Meat and Dairy Livestock Industry, 1819–1860." Ph.D. dissertation, University of Chicago, 1931.

———. "Some Aspects of the Western Meatpacking Industry." *The Journal of Business of the University of Chicago* 4 (January 1931): 68–90.

Lee, Elizabeth Oliver. "'Potomac's Valley Shall Become a Domain We Create': Commercialism and the South Branch Valley, 1750–1800." Ph.D. dissertation, West Virginia University, 2008.

Lee, Paula Young, ed. *Meat, Modernity, and the Rise of the Slaughterhouse*. University of New Hampshire Press, 2008.

Leech, Harper, and John Charles Carroll. *Armour and His Times*. D. Appleton-Century, 1938.

Lemmer, George F. "The Spread of Improved Cattle Through the Eastern United States to 1850." *Agricultural History* 21 (April 1947): 79–93.

Lemon, James T. "Household Consumption in Eighteenth-Century America and Its Relationship to Production and Trade: The Situation Among Farmers in Southeastern Pennsylvania." *Agricultural History* 41 (January 1967): 59–70.

Lerza, Catherine, and Michael Jacobson, eds. *Food for People, Not for Profit: A Sourcebook on the Food Crisis*. Ballantine Books, 1975.

Levenstein, Harvey. *Paradox of Plenty: A Social History of Eating in Modern America*. Rev. ed. University of California Press, 2003.

———. *Revolution at the Table: The Transformation of the American Diet*. 1988. Reprint, University of California Press, 2003.

Levinson, Marc. *The Great A&P and the Struggle for Small Business in America*. Hill and Wang, 2011.

Libecap, Gary D. "The Rise of the Chicago Packers and the Origins of Meat Inspection and Antitrust." *Economic Inquiry* 30 (April 1992): 242–62.

Lockeretz, William. "Sustaining Agriculture Near Cities: An Introduction." In *Sustaining Agriculture Near Cities*, edited by William Lockeretz, xv–xxii. Soil and Water Conservation Society, 1987.

Lyson, Thomas A., G. W. Stevenson, and Rick Welsh, eds. *Food and the Mid-Level Farm: Renewing an Agriculture of the Middle*. The MIT Press, 2008.

Maag, James S. "Cattle Raising in Colonial South Carolina." Master's thesis, University of Kansas, 1964.

MacDonald, James. *Food from the Far West; or, American Agriculture with Special Reference to the Beef Production and Importation of Dead Meat from America to Great Britain.* William P. Nimmo, 1878.

Macleod, David I. "Food Prices, Politics, and Policy in the Progressive Era." *Journal of the Gilded Age and Progressive Era* 8, no. 3 (July 2009): 365–406.

MacMaster, Richard K. "The Cattle Trade in Western Virginia, 1760–1830." In *Appalachian Frontiers: Settlement, Society, & Development in the Pre-industrial Era,* edited by Robert D. Mitchell, 127–49, 314–18. University Press of Kentucky, 1991.

Mallin, Michael A. "Impacts of Industrial Animal Production on Rivers and Estuaries." *American Scientist* 88, no. 1 (January–February 2000): 26–37.

Marcello, Patricia Cronin. *Ralph Nader: A Biography.* Greenwood Press, 2004.

Marcus, Alan I. *Cancer from Beef: DES, Federal Food Regulation, and Consumer Confidence.* The Johns Hopkins University Press, 1994.

———. "The Newest Knowledge of Nutrition: Wise Burroughs, DES, and Modern Meat." *Agricultural History* 67, no. 3 (Summer 1993): 66–85.

Marlett, Jeffrey. *Saving the Heartland: Catholic Missionaries in Rural America, 1920–1960.* Northern Illinois University Press, 2002.

Marousek, Gerald E. "The Western Cattle Feeding Industry: Structural and Marketing Changes, 1952–1962." *Idaho Agricultural Experiment Station Bulletin* 481, July 1967.

Marshall, Andrew. "Sustaining Sustainable Agriculture: The Rise and Fall of the Fund for Rural America." *Agriculture and Human Values* 17, no. 3 (September 2000): 267–77.

Martin, Albro. *Railroads Triumphant: The Growth, Rejection, and Rebirth of a Vital American Force.* Oxford University Press, 1992.

———. "The Troubled Subject of Railroad Regulation in the Gilded Age — a Reappraisal." *Journal of American History* 61, no. 2 (September 1974): 339–71.

Martin, Edgar R. *The Standard of Living in 1860: American Consumption Levels on the Eve of the Civil War.* University of Chicago Press, 1942.

Martin, John H., Jr. "The Clean Water Act and Animal Agriculture." *Journal of Environmental Quality* 26, no. 5 (September–October 1997): 1198–1203.

Matusow, Allen J. *Farm Policies and Politics in the Truman Years.* Harvard University Press, 1967.

Maxwell, Simon. "Food Security: A Post-Modern Perspective." *Food Policy* 21, no. 2 (1996): 155–70.

Mayda, Chris. "Passion on the Plains: Pigs on the Panhandle." Ph.D. dissertation, University of Southern California, 1998.

McCarry, Charles. *Citizen Nader.* Saturday Review Press, 1972.

McCarty, H. H., and C. W. Thompson. *Meat Packing in Iowa.* Iowa Studies in Business, no. 12. State University of Iowa, 1933.

McCorkle, Chester O., Jr., ed. *Economics of Food Processing in the United States.* Academic Press, 1988.

McCoy, Joseph G. *Historic Sketches of the Cattle Trade of the West and Southwest,* edited by Ralph P. Bieber. 1874. Reprint, Arthur H. Clark Company, 1940.

McCurdy, Charles. "American Law and the Marketing Structure of the Large Corporation, 1875–1890." *Journal of Economic History* 38, no. 3 (September 1978): 631–49.

McFarlane, Larry A. "Nativism or Not? Perceptions of British Investment in Kansas, 1881–1901." *Great Plains Quarterly* 7, no. 4 (1987): 232–43.

——. "Opposition to British Agricultural Investment in the Northern Plains States, 1884–1900." *Nebraska History* 67, no. 2 (1986): 115–33.

McGee, Harold. *The Curious Cook: More Kitchen Science and Lore.* Northpoint Press, 1990.

——. *On Food and Cooking: The Science and Lore of the Kitchen.* Collier Books, 1984.

——. *On Food and Cooking: The Science and Lore of the Kitchen.* Rev. ed. Scribner, 2004.

McGerr, Michael. *A Fierce Discontent: The Rise and Fall of the Progressive Movement in America.* Oxford University Press, 2003.

McGinity, Richard Charles. "Technological Change and Agribusiness Structure: The Beef System." Ph.D. dissertation, Harvard University, 1980.

McGlade, Jacqueline. "More a Plowshare Than a Sword: The Legacy of US Cold War Agricultural Diplomacy." *Agricultural History* 83, no. 1 (Winter 2009): 79–102.

McGrath, Maria. "Food for Dissent: A History of Natural Foods and Dietary Health Politics Since the 1960s." Ph.D. dissertation, Lehigh University, 2005.

McMahon, Sarah F. "A Comfortable Subsistence: The Changing Composition of Diet in Rural New England, 1620–1840." *William and Mary Quarterly* 42 (January 1985): 26–65.

——. "'A Comfortable Subsistence': A History of Diet in New England, 1630–1850." Ph.D. dissertation, Brandeis University, 1981.

McNall, Neil Adams. *An Agricultural History of the Genesee Valley, 1790–1860.* University of Pennsylvania Press, 1952.

McNamee, Thomas. *Alice Waters and Chez Panisse: The Romantic, Impracti-cal, Often Eccentric, Ultimately Brilliant Making of a Food Revolution.* Penguin Press, 2007.

McNeur, Catherine. "The 'Swinish Multitude': Controversies Over Hogs in Antebellum New York City." *Journal of Urban History* 37, no. 5 (2011): 639–60.

McWilliams, James. *Just Food: Where Locavores Get It Wrong and How We Can Truly Eat Responsibly.* Little, Brown and Company, 2009.

———. *A Revolution in Eating: How the Quest for Food Shaped America.* Co-lumbia University Press, 2005.

Meisner, Joseph Charles. "Investor Capital, Taxes and the Structure of Cattle Feeding." Ph.D. dissertation, University of Missouri–Columbia, 1974.

Meisner, Joseph C., and V. James Rhodes. *The Changing Structure of U.S. Cattle Feeding.* Special Report 167. Agricultural Economics. University of Missouri–Columbia. November 1974.

Merrigan, Kathleen. "National Policy Options and Strategies to Encourage Sustainable Agriculture: Lessons from the 1990 Farm Bill." *American Journal of Alternative Agriculture* 8, no. 4 (1973): 158–60.

Merrill, Karen R. *Public Lands and Political Meaning: Ranchers, the Govern-ment, and the Property Between Them.* University of California Press, 2002.

Miller, Henry M. "An Archaeological Perspective on the Evolution of Diet in the Colonial Chesapeake, 1620–1745." In *Colonial Chesapeake Society,* edited by Lois Green Carr, Philip D. Morgan, and Jean B. Russo, 176–99. University of North Carolina Press, 1988.

———. "Colonization and Subsistence Change on the 17th Century Chesapeake Frontier." Ph.D. dissertation, Michigan State University, 1984.

Milner, Clyde A., II, Carol A. O'Connor, and Martha A. Sandweiss, eds. *The Oxford History of the American West.* Oxford University Press, 1994.

Morton, Alan Q. "Packaging History: The Emergence of the Uniform Product Code (UPC) in the United States, 1970–75." *History and Technology* 11, no. 1 (1991): 101–11.

Mudry, Jessica. "Quantifying an American Eater." *Food, Culture & Society* 9, no. 1 (2006): 44–67.

Mueller, Willard F. "The Food Conglomerates." *Proceedings of the Academy of Political Science* 34, no. 3 (1982): 54–67.

National Research Council. *Use of Drugs in Animal Feeds: Proceedings of a Symposium.* Publication 1679. National Academy of Sciences, 1969.

———. Board on Agriculture. Committee on the Role of Alternative Farm-

ing Methods in Modern Agriculture. *Alternative Agriculture.* National
Academy Press, 1989.

———. Board on Agriculture. Committee on Technological Options to Improve
the Nutritional Attributes of Animal Products. *Designing Foods: Animal
Product Options in the Marketplace.* National Academy Press, 1988.

———. Committee on Animal Health. *Antibiotics in Animal Feeds: A Report
Prepared by the Committee on Animal Health and the Committee on
Animal Nutrition [and] Board on Agriculture and Renewable Resources,
National Research Council.* National Academy of Sciences, 1979.

Nestle, Marion. *Food Politics: How the Food Industry Influences Health and
Nutrition.* University of California Press, 2002.

New York State Legislature. Special Committee on Railroads. *Proceedings of
the Special Committee on Railroads,* 6 vols. Evening Post Steam Presses,
1879–1880.

Nierenberg, Danielle. *Happier Meals: Rethinking the Global Meat Industry.*
Worldwatch Institute. Worldwatch Paper 171. September 2005.

Nissenbaum, Stephen. *Sex, Diet, and Debility in Jacksonian America: Sylvester Graham and Health Reform.* Greenwood Press, 1980.

Nordin, Dennis S., and Roy V. Scott. *From Prairie Farmer to Entrepreneur:
The Transformation of Midwestern Agriculture.* Indiana University
Press, 2005.

Norwood, F. Bailey, and Jayson Lusk. *Compassion, by the Pound: The Economics of Farm Animal Welfare.* Oxford University Press, 2011.

Novak, William J. *The People's Welfare: Law and Regulation in Nineteenth-
Century America.* University of North Carolina Press, 1996.

Okun, Mitchell. *Fair Play in the Marketplace: The First Battle for Pure Food
and Drugs.* Northern Illinois University Press, 1986.

Olmstead, Alan L., and Paul W. Rhode. *Creating Abundance: Biological Innovation and American Agricultural Development.* Cambridge University
Press, 2008.

Olszewski, Todd Michael. "Cholesterol: A Scientific, Medical, and Social History, 1908–1962." Ph.D. dissertation, Yale University, 2008.

Omo-Osagie, Solomon Iyobosa, II. "Commercial Poultry Production on Maryland's Lower Eastern Shore and the Involvement of African Americans,
1930s to 1990s." Ph.D. dissertation, Morgan State University, 2007.

Orland, Barbara. "Turbo-Cows: Producing a Competitive Animal in the Nine-
teenth and Early Twentieth Centuries." In *Industrializing Organisms:
Introducing Evolutionary History,* edited by Susan R. Schrepfer and
Philip Scranton, 167–89. Routledge, 2004.

Osgood, Ernest Staples. *The Day of the Cattleman*. 1929. Reprint, University of Chicago Press, 1957.

Otto, John Solomon. "Livestock-Raising in Early South Carolina, 1670–1700: Prelude to the Rice Plantation Economy." *Agricultural History* 61 (Fall 1987): 13–24.

Paarlberg, Don. *Farm and Food Policy: Issues of the 1980s*. University of Nebraska Press, 1980.

Paarlberg, Robert. *Food Politics: What Everyone Needs to Know*. Oxford University Press, 2010.

Paarlberg, Robert, and Don Paarlberg. "Agricultural Policy in the Twentieth Century." *Agricultural History* 74, no. 2 (Spring 2000): 136–61.

Parmet, Wendy E. "From Slaughter-House to Lochner: The Rise and Fall of the Constitutionalization of Public Health." *American Journal of Legal History* 40 (1996): 476–505.

Pelto, Gretel H., and Pertti J. Pelto. "Diet and Delocalization: Dietary Changes Since 1750." *Journal of Interdisciplinary History* 14, no. 2 (Autumn 1983): 507–28.

Percy, David O. "Of Fast Horses, Black Cattle, Woods Hogs, and Rat-Tailed Sheep: Animal Husbandry Along the Colonial Potomac." The National Colonial Farm Research Report no. 4, 1979.

Perkins, John H. "Insects, Food, and Hunger: The Paradox of Plenty for U.S. Entomology, 1920–1970." *Environmental Review* 7, no. 1 (Spring 1983): 71–96.

———. *Geopolitics and the Green Revolution: Wheat, Genes, and the Cold War*. Oxford University Press, 1997.

———. "Reshaping Technology in Wartime: The Effect of Military Goals on Entomological Research and Insect-Control Practices." *Technology and Culture* 19, no. 2 (April 1978): 169–86.

Perren, Richard. *The Meat Trade in Britain*. Routledge & Kegan Paul, 1978.

———. "The North American Beef and Cattle Trade with Great Britain, 1870–1914." *Economic History Review* n.s. 24, no. 3 (August 1971): 430–44.

———. *Taste, Trade and Technology: The Development of the International Meat Industry Since 1840*. Ashgate, 2006.

Peters, Suzanne. "The Land in Trust: A Social History of the Organic Farming Movement." Ph.D. dissertation, McGill University, 1979.

Peterson, Everett B., Paul V. Preckel, Thomas W. Hertel, and Anya M. McGuirk. "Impacts of Stimulants in the Domestic Livestock Sector." *Agribusiness* 8, no. 4 (July 1992): 287–307.

Petrick, Gabriella M. "The Arbiters of Taste: Producers, Consumers and the

Industrialization of Taste in America, 1900–1960." Ph.D. dissertation, University of Delaware, 2006.

———. "Feeding the Masses: H. J. Heinz and the Creation of Industrial Food." *Endeavour* 33, no. 1 (2008): 29–34.

Pierce, Bessie Louise. *A History of Chicago,* vols. I and II. Alfred A. Knopf, 1940, 1957.

Piott, Steven L. "Missouri and the Beef Trust: Consumer Action and Investigation, 1902." *Missouri Historical Review* 76, no. 1 (October 1981): 31–52.

Pollan, Michael. *The Omnivore's Dilemma: A Natural History of Four Meals.* Penguin Press, 2006.

Poppendieck, Janet. *Sweet Charity? Emergency Food and the End of Entitlement.* Viking, 1998.

Porter, Glenn, and Harold C. Livesay. *Merchants and Manufacturers: Studies in the Changing Structure of Nineteenth-Century Marketing.* The Johns Hopkins University Press, 1971.

Rasmussen, Nicolas. "The Forgotten Promise of Thiamin: Merck, Caltech Biologists, and Plant Hormones in a 1930s Biotechnology Project." *Journal of the History of Biology* 32, no. 2 (Autumn 1999): 245–61.

———. "Plant Hormones in War and Peace: Science, Industry, and Government in the Development of Herbicides in 1940s America." *Isis* 92, no. 2 (June 2001): 291–316.

———. "Steroids in Arms: Science, Government, Industry, and the Hormones of the Adrenal Cortex in the United States, 1930–1950." *Medical History* 46 (2002): 299–324.

Rauchway, Eric. "The High Cost of Living in the Progressives' Economy." *Journal of American History* 88, no. 3 (December 2001): 898–924.

Raup, Philip M. "Corporate Farming in the United States." *Journal of Economic History* 33, no. 1 (March 1973): 274–90.

Renner, G. K. "The Kansas City Meat Packing Industry Before 1900." *Missouri Historical Review* 55 (October 1960): 18–29.

Rhodes, V. James. "The Industrialization of Hog Production." *Review of Agricultural Economics* 17, no. 2 (May 1995): 107–18.

Rhodes, V. James, Robert M. Finley, and Glenn Grimes. *A 1974 Survey of Large-Scale Hog Production in the U.S.* Special Report no. 165. Extension Division. University of Missouri–Columbia. September 1974.

Rice, Otis K. "Importations of Cattle into Kentucky, 1785–1860." *Register of the Kentucky Historical Society* 49 (1951): 35–47.

Richardson, Jennifer Jeanne. "Cowboys and Celebrities: Reading Rhetorics at the *Texas Beef v. Oprah Winfrey* Trial." Ph.D. dissertation, Washington State University, 2003.

Riffel, Brent E. "The Feathered Kingdom: Tyson Foods and the Transformation of American Land, Labor, and Law." Ph.D. dissertation, University of Arkansas, 2008.

——. "The *Nuevo* South: Tyson Foods and the Transformation of American Labor." *Southern Historian* 29 (Spring 2008): 21–35.

Rome, Adam. *The Bulldozer in the Countryside: Suburban Sprawl and the Rise of American Environmentalism.* Cambridge University Press, 2001.

Rosen, Christine Meisner. "Businessmen Against Pollution in Late Nineteenth Century Chicago." *Business History Review* 69 (Autumn 1995): 351–97.

——. "Costs and Benefits of Pollution Control in Pennsylvania, New York, and New Jersey, 1840–1906." *Geographical Review* 88, no. 2 (April 1998): 219–40.

——. "Differing Perceptions of the Value of Pollution Abatement Across Time and Place: Balancing Doctrine in Pollution Nuisance Law, 1840–1906." *Law and History Review* 11, no. 2 (Fall 1993): 303–81.

——. "'Knowing' Industrial Pollution: Nuisance Law and the Power of Tradition in a Time of Rapid Economic Change, 1840–1864." *Environmental History* 8 (October 2003): 563–95.

——. "Noisome, Noxious, and Offensive Vapors: Fumes and Stenches in American Towns and Cities, 1840–1865." *Historical Geography* 25 (1997): 49–82.

——. "The Role of Pollution Regulation and Litigation in the Development of the U.S. Meatpacking Industry, 1865–1880." *Enterprise & Society* 8 (June 2007): 297–347.

Rosenberg, Charles E. *The Cholera Years: The United States in 1832, 1849, and 1866.* 1962. Reprint, University of Chicago Press, 1987.

Ross, Drew Eliot. "Topography of Taste: Globalization, Cultural Politics, and the Making of California Cuisine." Ph.D. dissertation, University of Wisconsin–Madison, 1999.

Ross, Michael A. "Justice Miller's Reconstruction: The *Slaughter-Houses Cases,* Health Codes, and Civil Rights in New Orleans, 1861–1873." *Journal of Southern History* 64, no. 4 (November 1998): 649–76.

Rothman, Hal K. *The Greening of a Nation? Environmentalism in the United States Since 1945.* Harcourt Brace College Publishers, 1998.

——. *Saving the Planet: The American Response to the Environment in the Twentieth Century.* Ivan R. Dee, 2000.

Rothstein, Morton. "The Big Farm: Abundance and Scale in American Agriculture." *Agricultural History* 49, no. 4 (October 1975): 583–97.

Ruben, Barbara. "Common Ground." *Environmental Action* 27, no. 2 (Summer 1995). Accessed online.

Saloutos, Theodore, and John D. Hicks. *Agricultural Discontent in the Middle West, 1900–1939*. University of Wisconsin Press, 1951.

Sanders, Elizabeth. *Roots of Reform: Farmers, Workers, and the American State, 1877–1917*. University of Chicago Press, 1999.

Sawyer, Gordon. *The Agribusiness Poultry Industry: A History of Its Development*. Exposition Press, 1971.

Schell, Orville. *Modern Meat: Antibiotics, Hormones, and the Pharmaceutical Farm*. Random House, 1984.

Schertz, Lyle P., and Lynn M. Daft. *Food and Agricultural Markets: The Quiet Revolution*. NPA Report no. 270. National Planning Association, 1994.

Schlebecker, John T. *Cattle Raising on the Plains, 1900–1961*. University of Nebraska Press, 1963.

Schlosser, Eric. *Fast Food Nation: The Dark Side of the All-American Meal*. Houghton Mifflin, 2001.

Schneidau, Robert E., and Lawrence A. Duwer. *Symposium: Vertical Coordination in the Pork Industry*. The AVI Publishing Company for the Purdue Research Foundation, 1972.

Schnell, Steven N. "Food with a Farmer's Face: Community-Supported Agriculture in the United States." *Geographical Review* 97, no. 4 (October 2007): 550–64.

Scott, James C. *Seeing Like a State: How Certain Conditions to Improve the Human Condition Have Failed*. Yale University Press, 1998.

Sebold, Kimberly R. "The Delmarva Broiler Industry and World War II: A Case in Wartime Economy." *Delaware History* 25, no. 3 (Spring/Summer 1993): 200–214.

Seftel, Howard. "Government Regulation and the Rise of the California Fruit Industry: The Entrepreneurial Attack on Fruit Pests, 1880–1929." *Business History Review* 59, no. 3 (Autumn 1985): 369–402.

Senauer, Ben, Elaine Asp, and Jean Kinsey. *Food Trends and the Changing Consumer*. Eagan Press, 1991.

Shammas, Carole. *The Pre-Industrial Consumer in England and America*. Clarendon Press, 1990.

Shapiro, Laura. *Perfection Salad: Women and Cooking at the Turn of the Century*. Henry Holt and Company, 1986.

Shephard, Sue. *Pickled, Potted, and Canned: How the Art and Science of Food Preserving Changed the World*. Simon & Schuster, 2000.

Shideler, James H. *Farm Crisis, 1919–1923*. University of California Press, 1957.

Shintani, Kiyoshi. "Cooking Up Modernity: Culinary Reformers and the Making of Consumer Culture, 1876–1916." Ph.D. dissertation, University of Oregon, 2008.

Shover, John L. *First Majority — Last Minority: The Transforming of Rural Life in America*. Northern Illinois University Press, 1976.

Skaggs, Jimmy M. *The Cattle-Trailing Industry: Between Supply and Demand, 1866–1890*. 1973. Reprint, University of Oklahoma Press, 1991.

———. *Prime Cut: Livestock Raising and Meatpacking in the United States, 1607–1983*. Texas A&M University Press, 1986.

Smith, Arthur H., and William E. Martin. "Socioeconomic Behavior of Cattle Ranchers, with Implications for Rural Community Development in the West." *Journal of Agricultural Economics* 54, no. 2 (May 1972): 217–25.

Smith-Howard, Kendra. "Antibiotics and Agricultural Change: Purifying Milk and Protecting Health in the Postwar Era." *Agricultural History* 84, no. 3 (Summer 2010): 327–51.

Soule, George. *Vertical Integration in the Broiler Industry on the Delmarva Peninsula and Its Effect on Small Business*. N.p., 1960.

Stanley, Kathleen. "Industrial and Labor Market Transformation in the U.S. Meatpacking Industry." In *The Global Restructuring of Agro-food Systems*, edited by Philip McMichael, 129–44. Cornell University Press, 1994.

Stapleford, Thomas A. *The Cost of Living in America: A Political History of Economic Statistics, 1880–2000*. Cambridge University Press, 2009.

State of New York. *Proceedings of the Special Committee on Railroads Appointed under a Resolution of the Assembly to Investigate Alleged Abuses in the Management of Railroads Chartered by the State of New York*, vols. 1–6. Evening Post Steam Presses, 1879.

Steele, Zulma. *Angel in Top Hat*. Harper & Brothers, 1942.

Stewart, Mart A. "'Whether Wast, Deodand, or Stray': Cattle, Culture, and the Environment in Early Georgia." *Agricultural History* 65, no. 3 (Summer 1991): 1–28.

Stockwell, Ryan. "The Family Farm in the Post–World War II Era: Industrialization, the Cold War and Political Symbol." Ph.D. dissertation, University of Missouri–Columbia, 2008.

Stoll, Steven. *The Fruits of Natural Advantage: Making the Industrial Countryside in California*. University of California Press, 1998.

Stover, John F. *American Railroads*. 2d ed. University of Chicago Press, 1997.

Stoykovich, Eric Carlos. "In the National Interest: Improving Domestic Animals and the Making of the United States, 1815–1870." Ph.D. dissertation, University of Virginia, 2009.

Strasser, Susan. *Satisfaction Guaranteed: The Making of the American Mass Market.* Pantheon Books, 1989.

Strausberg, Stephen F. *From Hills and Hollers: Rise of the Poultry Industry in Arkansas.* Arkansas Agricultural Experiment Station, [1995].

Striffler, Steve. *Chicken: The Dangerous Transformation of America's Favorite Food.* Yale University Press, 2005.

Stull, Donald D., and Michael J. Broadway. *Slaughterhouse Blues: The Meat and Poultry Industry in North America.* Thomson/Wadsworth, 2004.

Suh, Suk Bong. *Upton Sinclair and "The Jungle": A Study of American Literature, Society, and Culture.* Seoul National University, 1997.

Summons, Terry G. "Animal Feed Additives, 1940–1966." *Agricultural History* 42, no. 4 (October 1968): 305–13.

Tangires, Helen. *Public Markets and Civic Culture in Nineteenth-Century America.* The Johns Hopkins University Press, 2003.

Taubes, Gary. *Good Calories, Bad Calories: Challenging the Conventional Wisdom on Diet, Weight Control, and Disease.* Alfred A. Knopf, 2007.

Tedlow, Richard S. *New and Improved: The Story of Mass Marketing in America.* Basic Books, 1990.

Thiboumery, Arion Jean. "Small Meat Processors Working Group: Managing Knowledge in a New Era of Agriculture." Ph.D. dissertation, Iowa State University, 2009.

Thompson, James Westfall. *A History of Livestock Raising in the United States, 1607–1860.* 1942. Reprint, Scholarly Resources, 1973. Also published as U.S. Department of Agriculture, Agricultural History Series no. 5, November 1942.

Thompson, Michael D. "High on the Hog: Swine as Culture and Commodity in Eastern North Carolina." Ph.D. dissertation, Miami University, 2000.

Thorelli, Hans B. *The Federal Antitrust Policy: Origination of an American Tradition.* The Johns Hopkins University Press, 1955.

Thu, Kendall M., and E. Paul Durrenberger, eds. *Pigs, Profits, and Rural Communities.* State University of New York Press, 1998.

Tobin, Bernard F., and Henry B. Arthur. *Dynamics of Adjustment in the Broiler Industry.* Harvard University, 1964.

Tolbert, Lisa C. "The Aristocracy of the Market Basket: Self-Service Food Shopping in the New South." In *Food Chains: From Farmyard to Shopping Cart,* edited by Warren Belasco and Roger Horowitz, 179–95. University of Pennsylvania Press, 2009.

Troutman, Richard Laverne. "Stock Raising in the Antebellum Bluegrass." *Register of the Kentucky Historical Society* 55 (January 1957): 15–28.

Turner, James. *Reckoning With the Beast: Animals, Pain, and Humanity in the Victorian Mind*. The Johns Hopkins University Press, 1980.

Turner, Katherine Leonard. "Good Food for Little Money: Food and Cooking Among Urban Working-Class Americans, 1875–1930." Ph.D. dissertation, University of Delaware, 2008.

——. "Tools and Spaces: Food and Cooking in Working-Class Neighborhoods, 1880–1930." In *Food Chains: From Farmyard to Shopping Cart*, edited by Warren Belasco and Roger Horowitz, 217–32. University of Pennsylvania Press, 2009.

Ufkes-Daniels, Frances M. "Agrarian Ideology, Market Structure and the Reproduction of Consent: Producer-Packer Relations in an Era of U.S. Meat Industry Restructuring." Ph.D. dissertation, University of Iowa, 1995.

U.S. Congress, Joint Economic Committee. *Policy for Commercial Agriculture: Its Relation to Economic Growth and Stability*. 85th Cong., 1st sess., 1958.

U.S. Department of Agriculture. *Federal and State Rural Lands with Special Reference to Grazing*, by R. D. Davidson. Circular 909. May 1952.

——. "The Food Value of Maize," by H. W. Wiley. In *Report on the Use of Maize (Indian Corn) in Europe and on the Possibilities of Its Extension*, 17–21. Government Printing Office, 1891.

——. "The Indian Corn Industry in the United States," by B. W. Dodge. In *Report on the Use of Maize (Indian Corn) in Europe and on the Possibilities of Its Extension*, 23–36. Government Printing Office, 1891.

——. "Report on the Introduction of Maize into Europe," by Charles J. Murphy. In *Report on the Use of Maize (Indian Corn) in Europe and on the Possibilities of Its Extension*, 5–16. Government Printing Office, 1891.

——. *Report and Recommendations on Organic Farming*, by USDA Study Team on Organic Farming. July 1980.

U.S. Department of Agriculture, Bureau of Agricultural Economics. *Changing Technology and Employment in Agriculture*, by John A. Hopkins. May 1941. Also published as Works Projects Administration. *National Research Project on Reemployment Opportunities and Recent Changes in Industrial Techniques*.

U.S. Department of Agriculture, Economic Research Service. *The Beef Cow-Calf Industry, 1964–87*, by Kenneth R. Krause. Agricultural Economic Report no. 659. June 1992.

——. *Cattle Feeding, 1962–89*, by Kenneth R. Krause. Agricultural Economic Report no. 642. April 1991.

———. *Cattle Feeding in the United States,* by Ronald A. Gustafson and Roy N. Van Arsdall. Agricultural Economic Report no. 186. October 1970.

———. *Cattle Raising in the United States,* by Roy N. Van Arsdall and Melvin D. Skold. Agricultural Economic Report no. 235. January 1973.

———. *Economies of Size in Hog Production,* by Roy N. Van Arsdall and Kenneth E. Nelson. Technical Bulletin no. 1712. December 1985.

———. *Economics of the U.S. Meat Industry,* by Richard J. Crom. Agriculture Information Bulletin no. 545. November 1988.

———. *Food Availability (Per Capita) Data System.* Accessed online.

———. *Rearranging the Economic Landscape: The Food Marketing Revolution, 1950–91,* by Alden C. Manchester. Agricultural Economic Report no. 660. September 1992.

U.S. Department of Agriculture, Economic Research Service, Food and Rural Economics Division. *America's Eating Habits: Changes and Consequences,* by Elizabeth Frazão. Agriculture Information Bulletin no. 750. April 1999.

U.S. Department of Agriculture, Economics, Statistics, and Cooperatives Service. *Another Revolution in U.S. Farming?* by Lyle P. Schertz et al. Agricultural Economic Report no. 441. December 1979.

———. "Beef," by Rod J. Martin. In *Another Revolution in U.S. Farming?* by Lyle P. Schertz et al., 85–118. Agricultural Economic Report no. 441. December 1979.

———. "Poultry and Eggs," by George B. Rogers. In *Another Revolution in U.S. Farming?* by Lyle P. Schertz et al., 148–89. Agricultural Economic Report no. 441. December 1979.

U.S. Department of Agriculture, Economics and Statistics Service. *Structural Change in Agriculture: The Experience for Broilers, Fed Cattle, and Processing Vegetables,* by Donn A. Reimund, J. Rod Martin, and Charles V. Moore. Technical Bulletin no. 1648. April 1981.

U.S. Department of Agriculture, Packer and Stockyards Division. Consumer and Marketing Service. *Packer Feeding of Cattle: Its Volume and Significance.* Marketing Research Report no. 776. November 1966.

U.S. Federal Trade Commission. *Report of the Federal Trade Commission on the Meat-Packing Industry.* Government Printing Office, 1918–1919.

U.S. General Accounting Office. *Animal Agriculture: Information on Waste Management and Water Quality Issues.* GAO/RCED-95-200BR. June 1995.

———. *Direct Farmer-to-Consumer Marketing Program Should Be Continued and Improved.* CED-80-65. July 9, 1980.

——. *Sustainable Agriculture: Program Management, Accomplishments, and Opportunities.* GAO/RCED-92–233. September 1992.

U.S. House of Representatives, Committee on Government Operations. *Consumer Problems of the Poor: Supermarket Operations in Low-Income Areas and the Federal Response.* H. Rpt. 1851. 90th Cong., 2d sess., 1968.

——. *Regulation of Diethylstilbestrol (DES) and Other Drugs Used in Food Producing Animals.* H. Rpt. 93–708. 93 Cong., 1st sess., 1973.

U.S. House of Representatives, Committee on Government Regulations. *Regulation of Food Additives — Nitrites and Nitrates.* H. Rpt. 92–1338. 92d Cong., 2d sess., 1972.

U.S. Office of Technology Assessment. *Drugs in Livestock Feed.* Government Printing Office, June 1979.

——. *Impacts of Antibiotic-Resistant Bacteria.* OTA-H-629. Government Printing Office, September 1995.

U.S. Senate, Committee on Agriculture, Nutrition, and Forestry. "The Changing Structure of the Hog Industry," by V. James Rhodes and Glenn Grimes. In *Farm Structure: A Historical Perspective on Changes in the Number and Size of Farms,* 185–195. 96th Cong., 2d sess., April 1980.

——. *Farm Structure: A Historical Perspective on Changes in the Number and Size of Farms.* 96th Cong., 2d sess, April 1980.

U.S. Senate, Select Committee. *Investigation of Transportation and Sale of Meat Products with Testimony.* S. Rpt. 829. 51st Cong., 1st sess., 1888.

U.S. Temporary National Economic Committee. Investigation of Concentration of Economic Power. Monograph no. 35. *Large-Scale Organization in the Food Industries.* Government Printing Office, 1940.

Vileisis, Ann. *Kitchen Literacy: How We Lost Knowledge of Where Food Comes From and Why We Need to Get It Back.* Island Press, 2008.

Vogeler, Ingolf. *The Myth of the Family Farm: Agribusiness Dominance of U.S. Agriculture.* Westview Press, 1981.

Voynick, Stephen M. *Riding the Higher Range: The Story of Colorado's Coleman Ranch and Coleman Natural Beef.* Glenn Melvin Coleman, 1998.

Wade, Louise Carroll. *Chicago's Pride: The Stockyards, Packingtown, and Environs in the Nineteenth Century.* University of Illinois Press, 1987.

Walker, Don D. *Clio's Cowboys: Studies in the Historiography of the Cattle Trade.* University of Nebraska Press, 1981.

Walsh, Lorena S. "Consumer Behavior, Diet, and the Standard of Living in Late Colonial and Early Antebellum America, 1770–1840." In *American Economic Growth and Standard of Living Before the Civil War,* edited by Robert E. Gallman and John Joseph Wallis, 217–61. University of Chicago Press, 1992.

Walsh, William I. *The Rise and Decline of the Great Atlantic and Pacific Tea Company.* Lyle Stuart, 1986.

Wellford, Harrison. *Sowing the Wind: A Report from Ralph Nader's Center for the Study of Responsive Law on Food Safety and the Chemical Harvest.* Grossman Publishers, 1972.

Whitaker, James. *Feedlot Empire: Beef Cattle Feeding in Illinois and Iowa, 1840–1900.* Iowa State University Press, 1975.

White, John H. *The American Railroad Freight Car: From the Wood-Car Era to the Coming of Steel.* The Johns Hopkins University Press, 1993.

———. *The Great Yellow Fleet: A History of American Railroad Refrigerator Cars.* Golden West Books, 1986.

White, Richard. "Animals and Enterprise." In *The Oxford History of the American West,* edited by Clyde A. Milner II, Carol A. O'Connor, and Martha A. Sandweiss, 237–73. Oxford University Press, 1994.

———. *"It's Your Misfortune and None of Mine": A New History of the American West.* University of Oklahoma Press, 1991.

Wilde, Mark William. "Industrialization of Food Processing in the United States, 1860–1960." Ph.D. dissertation, University of Delaware, 1988.

Wilder, Julia R. "An Upbeat Look at Government Policies and Proposals Involving Cattle and Sustainable Agriculture." *Journal of Sustainable Agriculture* 4, no. 2 (1993): 81–98.

Wilson, Warren J. *Tied to the Great Packing Machine: The Midwest and Meatpacking.* University of Iowa Press, 2007.

Wimberley, Ronald C., Craig K. Harris, Joseph J. Molnar, and Terry J. Tomazic, eds. *The Social Risks of Agriculture: Americans Speak Out on Food, Farming, and the Environment.* Praeger Publishers, 2002.

Winders, Bill. *The Politics of Food Supply: U.S. Agricultural Policy in the World Economy.* Yale University Press, 2009; paperback edition 2012.

Winne, Mark. *Closing the Food Gap: Resetting the Table in the Land of Plenty.* Beacon Press, 2008.

Wood, Charles L. *The Kansas Beef Industry.* The Regents Press of Kansas, 1980.

Wood, Donna J. "The Strategic Use of Public Policy: Business Support for the 1906 Food and Drug Act." *Business History Review* 59 (Autumn 1985): 403–32.

———. *Strategic Uses of Public Policy: Business and Government in the Progressive Era.* Pitman Publishing, 1986.

Worster, Donald. *Dust Bowl: The Southern Plains in the 1930s.* Oxford University Press, 1979.

Wrenn, Lynette Boney. *Cinderella of the New South: A History of the Cotton-seed Industry, 1855–1955*. University of Tennessee Press, 1995.

Wright, David E. "Alcohol Wrecks a Marriage: The Farm Chemurgic Movement and the USDA in the Alcohol Fuels Campaign in the Spring of 1933." *Agricultural History* 67, no. 1 (Winter 1993): 36–66.

Yeager, Mary. *Competition and Regulation: The Development of Oligopoly in the Meat Packing Industry*. JAI Press, 1981.

Young, James Harvey. *Pure Food: Securing the Federal Food and Drugs Act of 1906*. Princeton University Press, 1989.

Youngberg, Garth. "Alternative Agriculturalists: Ideology, Politics, and Prospects." In *The New Politics of Food*, edited by Don F. Hadwiger and William P. Browne, 227–46. D. C. Heath and Company, 1978.

Youngberg, Garth, Neill Schaller, and Kathleen Merrigan. "The Sustainable Agricultural Policy Agenda in the United States: Politics and Prospects." In *Food for the Future: Conditions and Contradictions of Sustainability*, edited by Patricia Allen, 295–318. John Wiley & Sons, 1993.

INDEX